More Advance Praise for
America's Great Game

"*America's Great Game* is an epic story of how the American search for adventure and idealism contributed to coups and counter-revolutions in the Middle East. Drawing on extensive research, Wilford explains the rise of the CIA, the tortured American relationship with Arabs and Jews, and Washington's Cold War complicity with British imperial interests. What makes this book most enthralling is that the author builds the story around the grandsons of Theodore Roosevelt. This is a valuable history and a fascinating read—a true page-turner."

—Jeremi Suri, Mack Brown Distinguished Chair for Leadership in Global Affairs, University of Texas at Austin, and author of *Liberty's Surest Guardian: American Nation-Building from the Founders to Obama*

"This is a great book: well written with compelling details, good stories, and impressive use of primary evidence. It is tied together by a first-rate thesis that will make people think again about the Middle East."

—Rhodri Jeffreys-Jones, author of *In Spies We Trust: The Story of Western Intelligence*

AMERICA'S
GREAT GAME

AMERICA'S GREAT GAME

The CIA'S SECRET ARABISTS *and the*
SHAPING *of the* MODERN MIDDLE EAST

Hugh Wilford

BASIC BOOKS
A Member of the Perseus Books Group
New York

Published by Basic Books,

A Member of the Perseus Books Group

Books published by Basic Books are available at special discounts for bulk purchases in the United States by corporations, institutions, and other organizations. For more information, please contact the Special Markets Department at the Perseus Books Group, 2300 Chestnut Street, Suite 200, Philadelphia, PA 19103, or call (800) 810-4145, ext. 5000, or e-mail special .markets@perseusbooks.com.

Designed by Pauline Brown
Typeset in 11 point Stempel Garamond LT Std by the Perseus Books Group

Library of Congress Cataloging-in-Publication Data

Wilford, Hugh, 1965–
    America's Greatest Game: the CIA's Secret Arabists and the Shaping of the Modern Middle East / Hugh Wilford.
        pages cm
    Includes bibliographical references and index.
    ISBN 978-0-465-01965-6 (hardcover)—ISBN 978-0-465-06982-8 (ebook) 1. Middle East—Relations—United States—History. 2. United States—Relations—Middle East—History. 3. Arab countries—Relations—United States—History. 4. United States—Relations—Arab countries—History. 5. United States. Central Intelligence Agency I. Title.
DS63.2.U5W49 2013
327.73056—dc23
                                            2013029982

10 9 8 7 6 5 4 3 2 1

For
JONATHAN

I meant to make a new nation, to restore a lost influence, to give twenty millions of Semites the foundations on which to build an inspired dream-palace of their national thoughts.

—T. E. Lawrence, *Seven Pillars of Wisdom* (1922)

I had formed a beautiful and gracious image and I saw it melting before my eyes. Before every noble outline had been obliterated, I preferred to go; in spite of my love for the Arab nation and my sense of responsibility for its future, I did not think I could bear to see the evaporation of the dream which had guided me.

—Gertrude Bell to King Faisal of Iraq (1922)

Contents

Abbreviations

ACJ	American Council for Judaism
AFME	American Friends of the Middle East
AIOC	Anglo-Iranian Oil Company
AIPAC	American Israel Public Affairs Committee
AMCOMLIB	American Committee for Liberation
ARAMCO	Arabian American Oil Company
AUB	American University of Beirut
AYC	American Youth Congress
BA&H	Booz, Allen & Hamilton
BP	British Petroleum
CBS	Columbia Broadcasting System
CCMCC	Continuing Committee on Muslim-Christian Cooperation
CIA	Central Intelligence Agency
CIC	Counter Intelligence Corps
CIG	Central Intelligence Group
CJP	Committee for Justice and Peace in the Holy Land
COI	Coordinator of Information
FBI	Federal Bureau of Investigation
FOIA	Freedom of Information Act
GID	General Investigations Directorate
MP	Member of Parliament
NEA	Near East/Africa Division
NSC	National Security Council
OCB	Operations Coordinating Board
OPC	Office of Policy Coordination
OSO	Office of Special Operations
OSS	Office of Strategic Services
OWI	Office of War Information
PWB	Psychological Warfare Branch
RAF	Royal Air Force
RCC	Revolutionary Command Council

SIS	Secret Intelligence Service (also known as MI6)
TAPLINE	Trans-Arabian Pipeline
UAR	United Arab Republic
UN	United Nations
VOA	Voice of America

Dramatis Personae
THE PLAYERS

The CIA Arabists

KERMIT "KIM" ROOSEVELT JR.: Chief of CIA covert operations in the Middle East. Grandson of Theodore Roosevelt (TR), son of the businessman and explorer Kermit Roosevelt Sr. and Belle Willard Roosevelt, and husband of Mary "Polly" Gaddis.

ARCHIBALD B. ROOSEVELT JR.: Another grandson of TR and CIA officer; expert on the Middle East but beaten out to the role of covert operations chief by his cousin Kim. Married first to Katherine Winthrop "KW" Tweed, then Selwa "Lucky" Showker.

MILES A. COPELAND JR.: Alabaman friend of the Roosevelt cousins, Kim's lieutenant in CIA, and later author of controversial books about intelligence. Married Lorraine Adie.

Their Predecessors, the OSS Arabists

WILLIAM A. EDDY: Lebanon-born Arabist, marine, scholar, intelligence officer, and American minister to Saudi Arabia, he blazed the CIA's trail in the Arab world.

HAROLD B. HOSKINS: Eddy's cousin; a businessman and diplomat who also pioneered American intelligence in the Middle East during World War II.

STEPHEN B. L. PENROSE JR.: Educator and chief of the OSS station in Cairo.

Other Americans

OSS/CIA

WILLIAM J. DONOVAN: Head of the OSS and Roosevelt family friend.

ALLEN DULLES: Donovan's European deputy in the OSS; later deputy director of the CIA and then director between 1953 and 1961; a keen advocate of covert operations.

WALTER BEDELL SMITH: Dulles's irascible predecessor as CIA director.

FRANK G. WISNER: OSS chief in southeastern Europe and first head of CIA covert operations.

DONALD N. WILBER: Scholarly expert on Iran who was stationed there as an OSS officer during World War II; later helped plan the Iranian coup operation of 1953.

MICHAEL G. MITCHELL: First head of the CIA's Middle East section, he recommended Kim over Archie Roosevelt as covert operations chief for the region.

STEPHEN J. MEADE: Tough army officer periodically loaned to the OSS and CIA to perform special missions.

MATHER GREENLEAF ELIOT: Young CIA case officer for the American Friends of the Middle East (AFME).

LORRAINE NYE NORTON: Eliot's successor as AFME case officer (they later married).

JAMES M. EICHELBERGER: Wartime Counter Intelligence Corps colleague of Miles Copeland; later advertising executive and CIA station chief in Cairo.

JAMES BURNHAM: Ex-Trotskyist intellectual and CIA consultant whose writings influenced Agency operations in Nasser's Egypt.

EDWARD G. LANSDALE: Kim Roosevelt's "nation-building" colleague in the Far East; often identified as the model for Graham Greene's *The Quiet American.*

JAMES JESUS ANGLETON: Legendary head of CIA counterintelligence, he also ran the Agency's "Israeli account."

HOWARD "ROCKY" STONE: Young member of the CIA team in Iran in 1953. He attempted unsuccessfully to mount a similar operation in Syria in 1957.

WILBUR CRANE EVELAND: Army officer and Middle East adventurer loaned to Allen Dulles from 1956 to plot regime change in Syria.

State Department

DEAN ACHESON: Director of the Lend-Lease program during World War II, secretary of state from 1949 to 1953, and patron of Kim Roosevelt.

JOHN FOSTER DULLES: Brother of Allen Dulles; Acheson's sternly moralistic successor as secretary of state.

EDWIN M. WRIGHT: Middle East specialist in army intelligence during World War II and State Department afterward.

LOY W. HENDERSON: Veteran foreign service officer and Soviet expert; assistant secretary of state for Near Eastern affairs in the run-up to the creation of Israel; ambassador to Iran at the time of 1953 coup.

JAMES HUGH KEELEY JR.: Arabist diplomat serving as ambassador to Syria at the time of the 1949 coup there.

JEFFERSON CAFFERY: Veteran diplomat serving as US ambassador to Egypt at the time of the 1952 Egyptian Revolution.

HENRY A. BYROADE: Young ex-soldier and assistant secretary for Near Eastern affairs; selected as Caffery's successor in Egypt to cultivate Nasser but undermined by CIA "crypto-diplomacy."

Kim Roosevelt's Arabist, Anti-Zionist Citizen Network

GEORGE L. LEVISON: Prominent anti-Zionist American Jew; close friend of Kim Roosevelt.

ELMER BERGER: Anti-Zionist rabbi and another intimate of Kim Roosevelt's; executive director of the American Council for Judaism.

JAMES TERRY DUCE: Influential ARAMCO vice president based in Washington.

VIRGINIA C. GILDERSLEEVE: Distinguished educator and high-profile anti-Zionist.

GARLAND EVANS HOPKINS: Minister and editor; executive officer of successive Arabist, anti-Zionist organizations, including AFME.

DOROTHY THOMPSON: Celebrity journalist who presided over AFME.

CORNELIUS VAN H. ENGERT: Retired foreign service officer who helped liaise between Allen Dulles and AFME.

EDWARD L. R. ELSON: Presbyterian pastor of both Dwight Eisenhower and John Foster Dulles; a director of AFME.

The Arab Players

Iraq
'ABD AL-ILAH: Regent of Iraq during minority of King Faisal II.

NURI AL-SA'ID: Pro-British prime minister of Iraq; murdered along with the Hashemite royal family during the 1958 coup.

Saudi Arabia
'ABD AL-'AZIZ AL SA'UD: Ibn Saud, the warrior-king and founder of Saudi Arabia; succeeded by his less impressive son SAUD.

Syria

SHUKRI AL-QUWATLI: Syrian president overthrown in the 1949 military coup but returned to power in 1955.

HUSNI AL-ZA'IM: A Kurdish army officer, he became president after leading the 1949 coup but was deposed and executed only months later.

ADIB AL-SHISHAKLI: Tank commander, friend of Miles Copeland, and participant in numerous coup conspiracies, he became president himself in 1953.

MIKHAIL ILYAN: Conservative Syrian politician who plotted regime change with Wilbur Crane Eveland.

'ABD AL-HAMID SARRAJ: Clever chief of Syrian security service who foiled successive CIA plots to overthrow the government.

Egypt

FAROUK: Licentious young king overthrown in the Egyptian Revolution of 1952.

MUHAMMAD NAGUIB: Popular Egyptian general who led the revolutionary government.

GAMAL 'ABDEL NASSER: Brilliant young army officer who usurped Naguib and, with CIA support, emerged as the Arab world's leading nationalist.

MUHAMMAD HAIKAL: Egyptian journalist and confidant of Nasser's.

'ALI SABRI: Air Force intelligence chief and later director of Nasser's Office of the Prime Minister.

HASSAN AL-TUHAMI: Miles Copeland's liaison with Nasser's government.

ZAKARIA MOHIEDDIN: Nasser's interior minister who oversaw the creation of the General Investigations Directorate.

Transjordan/Jordan

'ABDULLAH I: Hashemite emir, then king, he was assassinated in 1951; succeeded a year later by grandson HUSSEIN, who would later receive CIA support.

Lebanon

CAMILLE CHAMOUN: Pro-American, Christian president whose fate became a crucial test of the Eisenhower Doctrine.

The Israelis

TEDDY KOLLEK: World War II Jewish Agency intelligence official, friend of the Roosevelt cousins, and later mayor of Jerusalem.

DAVID BEN-GURION: Founding father of Israel and the country's first prime minister; helped establish the intelligence partnership between the CIA and Mossad.

The Iranians

MOHAMMED REZA PAHLAVI: Young Shah of Iran covertly backed by the CIA.

MOHAMMED MOSADDEQ: Charismatic nationalist prime minister deposed in the 1953 coup.

The British

RUDYARD KIPLING: Bard of the British empire and Roosevelt family friend whose novel *Kim* inspired later generations of intelligence officers, including the CIA Arabists.

T. E. LAWRENCE: "Lawrence of Arabia," the British army officer who liaised with the Arab Revolt of World War I and fired the imaginations of the Roosevelt cousins.

HARRY ST. JOHN "JACK" PHILBY: Renegade British Arabist, adviser to Ibn Saud, and father of the Soviet mole H. A. R. "KIM" PHILBY.

ANTHONY EDEN: Three-time foreign secretary, he succeeded Winston Churchill as prime minister in 1955 before mounting the disastrous Suez operation that led to his resignation in January 1957.

HAROLD MACMILLAN: Foreign secretary under Eden and prime minister after him, he engineered a post-Suez reconciliation with the Americans while working behind the scenes to restore the British position in the Middle East.

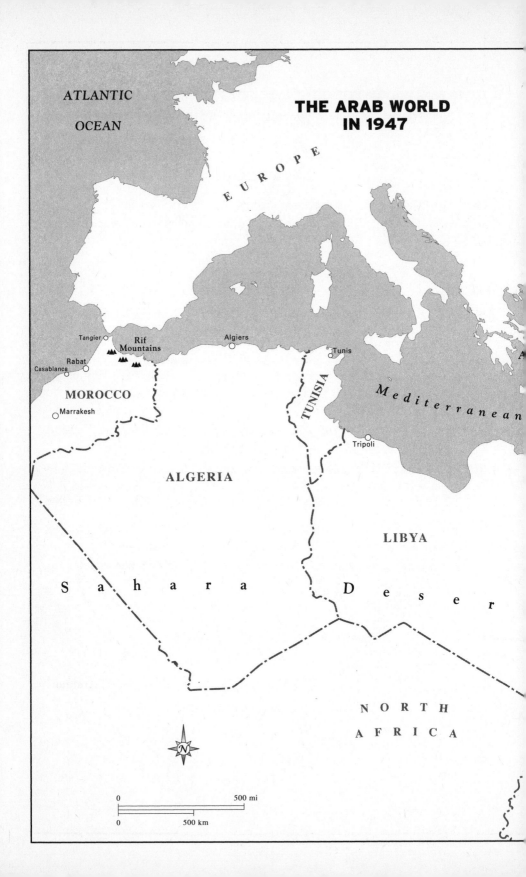

ATLANTIC

OCEAN

**THE ARAB WORLD
IN 1947**

E U R O P E

Tangier

Rif
Mountains

Algiers

Tunis

M e d i t e r r a n e a n

Rabat

Casablanca

MOROCCO

TUNISIA

Tripoli

Marrakesh

ALGERIA

LIBYA

S a h a r a

D e s e r

N O R T H

A F R I C A

0   500 mi

0   500 km

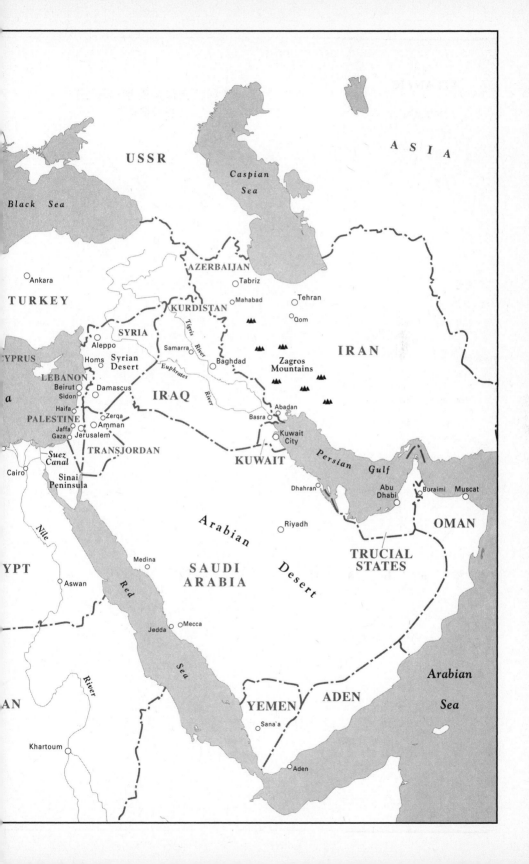

Preface

THIS BOOK BEGAN WITH TWO surprises, the first being that it did not already exist. From the 1953 coup that deposed the nationalist prime minister of Iran, Mohammed Mosaddeq, down to more recent reports of secret prisons, waterboarding, and drone warfare, the Central Intelligence Agency has played a defining role in the troubled relationship between the United States and the Middle East. Yet, apart from several books on the Iran coup and a few scholarly articles, there is no single work specifically devoted to the subject.[1] Not even histories of the Agency itself have much to say about its Middle Eastern operations other than Iran. Quite why this is so I am still not sure. It might have something to do with the inaccessibility of most of the CIA's own records about the subject—although, as I soon found out, other sources were publicly available—or perhaps it is because of the vague air of disreputability that seems to surround such topics in US academic circles. In any case, it struck me that this book was calling out to be written.

The second surprise came as I began delving into the subject. Contrary to what I expected, given the CIA's actions in Iran and diabolical reputation throughout much of the Arab world, the individuals responsible for the first US covert operations in the region were, I discovered, personally very sympathetic toward Arabs and Muslims. Indeed, Kermit "Kim" Roosevelt, the grandson of President Theodore Roosevelt who headed the Agency's Middle East division in its early years and commanded the 1953 operation in Iran, was a friend and supporter of the leading Arab nationalist of the day, Gamal 'Abdel Nasser of Egypt. Even more surprising, Roosevelt arranged secret CIA funding for an effort within the United States to foster American appreciation for Arab society and culture, and to counteract the pro-Israel influence of US Zionists on American foreign policy regarding the Arab-Israeli conflict. In doing so, he was giving expression to a strong "Arabist" impulse in the early history of the CIA that was traceable to its predecessor organization, the World War II Office of Strategic Services (OSS). Particularly influential in this regard was a group of Middle East–born OSS officers who, during the 1940s, had worked secretly to bring the United States and the Arab states closer together and to head off the partition of Palestine. Descended from nineteenth-century American missionaries in the Arab world, these men were anti-Zionist less because of any inherent prejudice against Jews and more because of a fierce—in some cases almost mystical—belief in the overriding importance of American-Arab, and Christian-Muslim, relations. I soon realized that writing a history of the CIA in the Cold War Middle East would involve reconstructing this now lost world of secret American Arabism.

It would also mean having to answer an obvious question: What changed? Why did the CIA go from being sympathetic toward Arabs and Muslims to being seen as their adversary? Certain factors long recognized as affecting US–Middle Eastern relations in general were clearly part of the explanation. There was the influence of the Cold War and the resulting tendency of such US officials as Dwight Eisenhower's secretary of state, John Foster Dulles, to resort to covert operations in order to eliminate nationalist leaders perceived (usually incorrectly) as vulnerable to communist takeover. Washington's determination to preserve Western access to Middle Eastern oil inevitably placed it at odds with local nationalists, who, after more than a century of French and British imperialism in the region, were equally determined to cast off Western influence, including meddling by secret agents. So too, of course, did growing US support for Israel, a phenomenon partly caused by the rise within the United States of the so-called Israel Lobby and the relative decline in power of the Anglo-American elites from whose ranks the CIA Arabists were overwhelmingly drawn. Finally, various third parties—including Arab conservatives who felt threatened by the nationalist movement and officials representing the old European powers in the Arab world, especially the British—proved adept at luring the United States into defending the region's established imperial order, again to the detriment of friendly American relations with nationalists like Nasser.

All of these elements clearly contributed to the eventual eclipse of CIA Arabism and will therefore receive due attention in the narrative that follows. As I researched the subject, however, I became increasingly conscious of another set of pressures acting on Kim Roosevelt and his colleagues that had less to do with grand geopolitical and strategic considerations than with more individual, personal concerns. Like many senior CIA officers of their generation, Kim and his cousin Archie Roo-

sevelt, another chief of the Agency's Middle East division in the early
years of the Cold War, had been raised and educated in an elite environment that conditioned them, long before they ever directly experienced
the region itself, to look upon the Middle East much as the British imperial agents of an earlier generation had: as a place for heroic individual adventure, where a handful of brave and resourceful Western spies
could control the fate of nations. To a certain extent, this legacy of spy
games and kingmaking was offset by the American missionary tradition
conveyed to the early CIA by the OSS, which tended to emphasize instead the moral values of Arab self-determination and mutual cultural
exchange. However, the adventurist tendency was also reinforced by
the presence in the early CIA's Middle East division of another distinct
social type best exemplified by the southerner Miles Copeland: bright,
ambitious young men from nonelite backgrounds who had gotten into
the CIA thanks to the opportunities for social mobility opened up by
World War II (usually via the Counter Intelligence Corps rather than
the more aristocratic OSS) and who, while not possessing the same social origins as the Roosevelt cousins, did share their appetite for game
playing. The story of CIA involvement in the Arab world during the
early years of the Cold War is therefore, in part at least, one of an internal
struggle between two contradictory influences: the British imperial legacy
and the American missionary tradition. If the latter, more moralistic, idealistic impulse shaped the Agency's earlier operations, it was the former—
comparatively pragmatic, realistic, even cynical—that eventually came
to dominate, with the Iran coup acting as a sort of tipping point.

My interest in these personal and sociocultural factors was prompted
by several considerations. The academic field of American diplomatic history has recently followed the example of other historical subdisciplines
by taking a "cultural turn," and even an "emotional turn," exploring the
effect on US foreign policy of a range of issues not usually associated with
the supposedly rational, hardheaded business of diplomacy.[2] Second, I
believe strongly that biography or group biography—foregrounding
individuals and trying to depict their social and emotional lives in all
their complexity—makes for a particularly rich and rewarding kind of
historical writing.[3] Finally, and most important, the evidence seemed to
me to require such an approach. The playing of games, whether it was
an American version of Britain's "Great Game," or the clash of personal
wills that eventually arose between Kim Roosevelt and Gamal Nasser,
or Miles Copeland's abiding interest in game theory, was not merely a

metaphor. It was a crucial historical determinant in the formation and eventual demise of CIA Arabism.

LIKE MOST HISTORIANS WHO WRITE about the history of the CIA, I have largely had to make do without access to the relevant Agency records, the great majority of which either have been destroyed or remain classified (although I was granted sight of the personnel files of Kim and Archie Roosevelt and of Miles Copeland). Fortunately, other official records available to researchers at the US National Archives and presidential libraries, especially those of the State Department, proved surprisingly revealing of US covert operations in the early Cold War era, while British government files in London helped illuminate joint Anglo-American undertakings. Moreover, many of the individuals concerned have left private collections of papers that, while not necessarily disclosing a great deal about their professional lives, provide extensive documentation of their personal attitudes and emotions. One area of CIA operation that *is* well documented in the archives is the program of the domestic Arabist, anti-Zionist citizen network covertly funded by Kim Roosevelt; it is described in detail here for the first time. Then there is the large corpus of published memoirs by CIA Arabists. Admittedly, these accounts present problems as historical sources, and I have been cautious in my use of them, cross-checking factual claims against other records and indicating where any doubts as to their reliability remain. Still, read less as transparent primary sources than as constructed literary texts, they constitute an invaluable, and in my view hitherto underused, body of evidence. Fiction is another important medium for understanding the CIA Arabists, whose perceptions and actions (including, I will argue, some of the major covert operations of the period) were strongly influenced by the adventure stories of a previous generation and who themselves inspired fictional portrayals by other writers. Finally, while the principal intelligence officers portrayed in the pages that follow are sadly all deceased, oral history interviews and personal correspondence with surviving family members, friends, and colleagues provide important insights into their personalities as well as the social and cultural worlds in which they moved.

Specific references to all these sources may be found in the notes at the end of the text.

OVER THE LONG COURSE OF this project, I have incurred a number of debts of gratitude. I wish to thank the following for responding to my inquiries and sharing their memories with me in interviews and in writing: Lennie Copeland, Lorraine Copeland (who was especially helpful, and who passed away just as this book was going into production), Miles Copeland III, Graham Crippin, Lorraine Nye Eliot, Patrice Gaudefroy-Demombynes, Ed Kane, James Noyes, Orin Parker, Jonathan Roosevelt, Kermit Roosevelt III, Selwa "Lucky" Roosevelt, and Anne Eichelberger Tazewell. So many friends and colleagues have provided expert advice, sources, letters of support, or simple encouragement along the way that I am in danger of forgetting names, but here are some I do remember: Richard Aldrich, Robert Amman, Nigel Ashton, Joe Ayella, David Blank, Nathan Citino, Robert Cook, Jerry Davis, Robert Dreyfuss, Mark Gasiorowski, Peter Hahn, Ann Heiss, Ali İğmen, Andy Jenks, Ian Johnson, Matthew Jones, Tim Keirn, Charles Stuart Kennedy, Matthew Kohlstedt, Arlene Lazarowitz, Nelson Lichtenstein, Eileen Luhr, Melani McAlister, Dan Morgenstern, John Palfrey, David Robarge, George Robb, Eugene Rogan, Emily Rosenberg, Dominic Sandbrook, Tony Shaw, R. Harris Smith, Sean Smith, Bill Streifer, Michael Thornhill, Steven Wagner, Jim Wallace, Michael Warner, Patrick White, and Jim Wolf. Amer Ghazal made some excellent translations of Arabic sources, and Houri Berberian gave invaluable advice about the transliteration of Arabic and Persian names. Brandon High, Rhodri Jeffreys-Jones, Scott Lucas, and again Houri Berberian all went above and beyond the call of collegiality and friendship in agreeing to read the manuscript and provide feedback. Roland Popp and Salim Yaqub distinguished themselves with the generosity of their assistance during the research phase of this project and the thoroughness and insightfulness of their commentaries on the manuscript.

Family on both sides of the Atlantic provided hospitality as I trawled the archives: Carol Cleary-Schultz, Jeff Schultz, and their lovely daughters, Kelly and Keira; my mother, Jan Wilford; David and Cath Wilford; and Peter and Gilly Wilford (and my thanks also go to my polymath brother Peter for his comments on earlier drafts). At Groton, Tom Lamont put me up for the night and took time out from his busy day to show me around the school. In Washington, DC, Kim Kluge and Kathryn Vassar were gracious hosts, as were Steve and Anne Scobie in London. Later on in a sometimes grueling writing process, Kitty,

Larry, Meghan, and Allison Adamovic all lent a sympathetic ear and first-class child care. Brian Cleary and Shannon Foss were a constant source of expert and cheerful computing support.

My employer, California State University, Long Beach, granted me several assigned time and mini-grant awards as well as difference-in-pay leave in 2010–2011; I am hugely grateful for this ongoing support, not least as it came at a time of crippling financial crisis in California's public higher education system. I particularly wish to acknowledge the heroic efforts of my outgoing dean, Gerry Riposa, and department chair, Nancy Quam-Wickham, to protect the research agendas of their liberal arts colleagues. The Friends of Princeton University Library awarded me a generous grant to enable me to consult the manuscript collections of the Mudd Library in 2009, and I greatly appreciated the warm welcome offered me there by Andrea Immel, Dan Linke, and Linda Oliveira. Archivists and librarians at a host of other institutions have also given crucial assistance along the way; particular thanks go to my library colleagues at CSULB, who have processed a mountain of my book requests through LinkPlus, an interlibrary lending system whose continued existence is essential to research such as my own.

My literary agents, Felicity Bryan and George Lucas, did a great job of placing my proposal with Basic Books and gave marvelously prompt and wise advice throughout the book's gestation. At Basic, Lara Heimert edited my manuscript with a remarkable combination of skill, energy, and good humor. Her assistant, Katy O'Donnell, was a model of friendly, efficient support. Roger Labrie provided many helpful editorial suggestions later on. Project editor Rachel King and copyeditor Beth Wright of Trio Bookworks expertly shepherded the manuscript through the final stages of production.

My biggest debt, though, is to my wife and fellow historian, Patricia Cleary, who has had to endure several years of my pulling twelve-hour days and six-day weeks, not to mention incessant mealtime talk about the antics of my new imaginary friends, "Miles," "Kim," and "Archie." Despite all this, she had the good grace to read several drafts of the resulting manuscript and provide her customarily invaluable feedback, including translation of unwitting lapses into UK English. She is my intellectual as well as emotional helpmate, and my debt to and love for her go on and on.

This book is dedicated to our baby boy, Jonathan Cleary Owain Wilford, in the hope that one day he might share his parents' love of history. He already likes playing games.

Part One
Pre-Game, 1916–1947

ONE

—

Learning the Game

I've read of the East for years unnumbered,
I've dreamed about it since first I slumbered,
I've learned about it in poems and verses,
I've heard of its comforts, and heard of its curses,
I've talked about it with men who've been there,
I know of the trouble, and dirt, and sin there,
And yet, on putting the facts together,
I still want to go there as much as ever.

—Kim Roosevelt (age fifteen), "The Lure of the East"[1]

WHEN IN JULY 1953 KERMIT "Kim" Roosevelt entered Iran under a false name to carry out perhaps the best-known CIA covert operation of the early Cold War era—the coup that toppled Iranian prime minister Mohammed Mosaddeq—it was not the first time he had pretended to be someone else. About thirty years earlier, when some childhood illness had kept him home from his New England prep school, he had entertained himself by regaling an elderly tutor with, as he recalled later, "story after story" about his "(wholly imaginary) childhood in India." Occasionally, he would apparently forget himself and "throw in a phrase in Hindustani" for effect. One day, though, the old man remarked to the boy's mother, "What a wonderful childhood" young Kermit must have had, "living in Lahore," and his "little ploy was exposed."[2]

— 3 —

The childhood Roosevelt was claiming for himself belonged not to a real person but rather to a fictional character, the eponymous hero of the 1901 novel *Kim*, by British author and poet Rudyard Kipling. Set in British Northwest India in the late nineteenth century, Kipling's book tells the story of Kimball O'Hara, the orphaned son of an Irish soldier and a nursemaid who grows up on the streets of Lahore living on his considerable wits. Hungry for adventure, and capable of passing as a native, Kim attaches himself to a Tibetan lama as he wanders in search of a holy river. While on this quest, the clever but mischievous young hero joins in the "Great Game"—the nineteenth-century contest between the British and Russian empires for strategic control of central Asia—by spying on behalf of an English intelligence officer, Colonel Creighton. The action culminates in the Himalayas, where Kim fights Russian agents and makes off with vital documents for the British. Recovering from his ordeal, he learns that the lama has found his river. Now a man himself, Kim faces a choice between carrying on his own quest for spiritual enlightenment or continuing to play the Great Game.

Young Kermit Roosevelt was by no means alone in his love of *Kim*: the book was immensely popular with audiences in both Britain and America, earning its author the Nobel Prize in 1907. Indeed, it still fascinates readers today, although admiration for Kipling's literary accomplishments, including the vibrant color of the Anglo-Indian characters and locales he evokes, is tempered by acknowledgment of the imperialist assumptions underpinning his story, as well as his sometimes demeaning portrayal of "Orientals." For the critic Edward Said, *Kim* was the supreme literary expression of Orientalism, a Western tradition of perceiving and portraying the "East" based on its colonial subjugation.[3]

There was, though, something unusual about the intensity of Kermit Roosevelt's identification with Kipling's hero. This was apparent not just in the prank he played on his tutor but also in the firmness with which his boyhood nickname of Kim stuck to him, so that as an adult he was still widely known by it. (This book will adopt the same practice, referring to him as Kim Roosevelt, partly in order to help the reader distinguish him from his father, also named Kermit.) The abiding hold of Kipling's story on the imagination of young Kim Roosevelt provides a revealing clue about the distinctive social and cultural background that shaped the future intelligence officer and would later exercise a crucial influence on CIA operations in the Middle East.

BORN IN BUENOS AIRES IN 1916, Kim Roosevelt was the son of the businessman, writer, and adventurer Kermit Roosevelt and Belle Willard, whose family owned numerous properties in and around Washington, DC, including the famously opulent Willard Hotel, near the White House. From his infancy, though, it was the identity of Kim's grandfather, not that of his parents, upon which people first remarked. Theodore Roosevelt, twenty-sixth president of the United States, dominated American culture more than any other member of his generation, and it was therefore hardly surprising that, even after his death in 1919, he should have loomed large in the lives of his grandchildren.

For Archie Roosevelt Jr., Kim's cousin and later colleague in the CIA, TR was "our hero and our playmate." TR's home on Sagamore Hill in Oyster Bay, Long Island, was stuffed with souvenirs of travels in faraway lands, a magical place of childhood adventure. Kim, whose father built his own family home, Mohannes, next door in Oyster Bay, had particularly fond memories of childhood Christmases at Sagamore: "Father carving the roast piglet, . . . the tree in the North Room, . . . [and] spirited, if somewhat murderous, games of field hockey down by the barn." Years later, in 1960, Kim took his two eldest sons to East Africa and reenacted a safari his grandfather and father had undertaken there in 1909. Following the same trails, hunting the same game, even striking the same poses in photographs, Kim developed "an ever growing understanding of, and . . . a sense of intimacy with, TR himself." For generations of Roosevelt men, the ghost of the president and paterfamilias, larger than life even in death, was never far away, a benign presence but also one capable of arousing feelings of inadequacy and loss.[4]

This is not to say that Kim's father, Kermit, was without impressive qualities of his own. Among his male siblings (Theodore Jr., Archibald Sr., and Quentin), Kermit was the most attractive—a slender, handsome young man talented as an athlete and raconteur. The East African safari with TR in 1909 also revealed him to be a brave and resourceful travel companion, a reputation confirmed five years later, when he and his father undertook an even more arduous expedition in Brazil exploring the previously uncharted Rio da Dúvida, or River of Doubt. TR nearly died in the Brazilian jungle, only making it out alive thanks to the grim courage of his son. Kermit described the earlier safari and later trips to the Himalayas and Burma with his brother Ted in published travelogues that met with considerable literary success. Among their admirers was

Rudyard Kipling himself, a family friend and frequent dinner guest of the Roosevelts, who corresponded extensively with Kermit.

It seems that Kim Roosevelt inherited at least some of his love of travel and exploration directly from his father. He was, he recalled later, "brought up" on his father's stories of his "fabulous, adventurous trips." Most relevant of these stories to Kim's future career was Kermit's account of his service in World War I. Urged by their bellicose father, whose charge up Kettle Hill in the 1898 Spanish-American War was his generation's most spectacular act of martial valor, TR's sons vied with one another to prove themselves in the Great War. The eldest, Ted, took an early lead by helping set up an officer-training camp in Plattsburgh, New York, before Woodrow Wilson had officially ended American neutrality, and then embarking for France as soon as war was declared in April 1917. He was soon joined by Archie and Quentin. For the debonair Kermit, however, the western front lacked romance. Instead, it was the "Orient" that beckoned.[5]

In the early twentieth century the United States had almost no political or military presence in the Middle East. The dominant powers in the area were the centuries-old Ottoman Empire, with its capital in Istanbul (still known in the West as Constantinople); the British; and the French. At first, Britain had backed the Ottomans as a way of checking the Russians in the Great Game and safeguarding land routes to India, the "jewel in the crown" of the British Empire. By the time of World War I, however, local nationalist rebellions had badly undermined Istanbul's rule, and the British, who already controlled Egypt and its invaluable strategic asset, the Suez Canal, were muscling in on the oil-rich Persian Gulf. (The French, meanwhile, dominated most of North Africa west of Egypt and were casting covetous glances toward Ottoman possessions in the eastern Mediterranean, or Levant.) After the Ottomans entered the war in alliance with Germany in 1914, Britain and France opened several new overseas fronts, including one in Mesopotamia (modern Iraq). Two years later, the British began furnishing support to an Arab uprising against Ottoman rule, known as the Arab Revolt. The United States, in contrast, never declared war on the Ottoman Empire, even after coming in on the side of the British and French.

"Wouldn't it be wonderful to be at the fall of Constantinople?" Kermit Roosevelt wrote his father in 1917. "The whole thing appeals to me much more than trench warfare." TR sympathized with his son; as a younger man he, too, had been fascinated by the Middle East, regarding it in classic Orientalist fashion as a place of ancient greatness and present-day decadence, an impression apparently confirmed when he had toured the region on horseback in 1872. He also thoroughly approved of Britain's influence in the Arab world, declaring during a return trip to Egypt in 1910 that the British were improving "the seventh century so as to bring it somewhere within touching distance of the twentieth," a "high and honorable" task that "only a great and powerful nation could attempt." Now, eager to see all his sons at war, TR contacted British prime minister David Lloyd George, who gave special permission for Kermit to join up with the Mesopotamian Expeditionary Force, with the rank of captain. Rudyard Kipling, perhaps sensing that the focus of the Great Game was shifting from India to the Middle East, was thrilled by this development. "Hurray!" he wrote Kermit. "We must catch people now where and as we can. . . . Come along!"[6]

Landing in the southern Iraqi city of Basra, Kermit was instantly enthralled by the sights and sounds of the bazaar, which (as he recalled in his 1919 memoir, *War in the Garden of Eden*) seemed to him to possess an "intangible something," an "ever-present exotic." Like many earlier Western visitors to the Middle East, the young American arrived feeling a strong sense of familiarity with the region, thanks to having read about it since his childhood in *The Arabian Nights*. Kermit was therefore gratified to observe a bazaar booth "festooned with lamps and lanterns of every sort, with above it scrawled 'Aladdin-Ibn-Said.'" From Basra it was on to Baghdad, where echoes of the *Arabian Nights* multiplied ("when the setting sun strikes the towers, . . . one is again in the land of Haroun-el-Raschid"), and from there to the ancient Mesopotamian capital of Samarra.[7]

Already an Anglophile, Kermit quickly adapted to British officer culture, hiring an Arab batman and a Sikh groom. He also consorted a great deal with the political officers of the Arab Bureau, a unit of Middle East specialists—scholars, linguists, and explorers—who roamed the region providing the British authorities with crucial strategic intelligence. With their arcane yet profound knowledge and aura of exotic adventure, these British "Arabists" seemed like Kipling characters come to life, and Kermit, who himself rapidly became fluent in Arabic, lost no opportunity to quiz them, especially the brilliant Gertrude Bell, the Bureau's only female officer. As befitted a son of Theodore Roosevelt, he also saw more than his share of actual combat, earning a British Military Cross in August 1918 for capturing an Ottoman platoon outside

Baghdad. His waggish account of stumbling on a Turkish general's "field harem" delighted Kipling, who declared that this action deserved "either a court martial or a V[ictoria].C[ross].," before asking, somewhat pruriently, "How did you explain to the wife?"[8]

From the point of view of his son Kim, Kermit's most exciting encounter of the war likely came after the Ottoman cause had collapsed and he was returning west to join the US Army in France. Passing through Cairo, where the Arab Bureau was headquartered, Kermit met a British colonel, "scarcely more than thirty years of age, with a clean-shaven, boyish face," who recounted his recent experiences organizing Arabian tribes into bands that raided Turkish outposts and blew up railroads. T. E. Lawrence was not yet Lawrence of Arabia, the international celebrity created by American journalist Lowell Thomas during the 1920s, and it is therefore all the more poignant to read Kermit Roosevelt's 1919 word portrait of this "short and slender" British officer: his habit of dressing in "Arab costume," his hatred of "killing the wounded," and his admiration for the Arabs, "their virility—their ferocity—their intellect and their sensitiveness." (There is also the unforeseen irony of Lawrence's reported remark that "he couldn't last much longer, things had broken altogether too well for him, and they could not continue to do so.") Kermit's description of Lawrence, with its Kipling-esque connotations of spying and passing as a native, must surely have fired the imagination of young Kim.[9]

Kermit and Lawrence carried on corresponding after the war, as the latter waged a campaign in the British press for a Middle Eastern settlement favorable to the Arabs. Lawrence's vision did not materialize. Instead, the victorious European powers effectively carved up the Ottomans' Arab possessions between them, the French adding Syria and Lebanon to their colonial possessions in North Africa, the British acquiring control of Palestine, Transjordan, and Iraq. Lawrence retreated into obscurity, enlisting in the Royal Air Force (RAF) under an assumed name. Still, the type of nomadic intelligence officer he had helped model during World War I became crucial to Britain's administration of its new Middle Eastern mandate. During the interwar period, often referred to as "Britain's moment in the Middle East," London created what one historian has described as a "Covert Empire" in the region, reinforced on the ground by a loose network of roving Arabist spies and from the sky by RAF surveillance and occasional bombing. Meanwhile, Lawrence himself never lost his appetite for intelligence work, migrating to the original theater of Kipling's Great Game, India's northwest frontier, in the late 1920s, from where he wrote Kermit Roosevelt, with evident relish, "The pot fairly boils, over Kabul way."[10]

The young Kim Roosevelt no doubt encountered other images of the Orient besides Kipling stories and Lawrence of Arabia. American consumer society of the 1920s was replete with Orientalia, ranging from King Tut to Valentino's Sheik. But Kim was not just any American. While most boys of his generation grew up "with a fantasy of striking out Babe Ruth," so one of his sons observed later, "his childish fantasies had to do with shooting tigers, . . . or exploring the Euphrates." Not only had Kim heard of Tut, but his aunt, Mary Elizabeth Willard, married the nephew of George Herbert, Fifth Earl of Carnarvon, the English aristocrat who financed the excavation of the Egyptian boy king's tomb and died shortly after, reputedly from the "Curse of Tutankhamun." "I've read of the East for years unnumbered," Kim himself explained in a poem published in the May 1931 issue of The American Boy–Youth's Companion, "I've learned about it in poems and verses, . . . I've talked about it with men who've been there." Long before he went to the Middle East in person as a US intelligence officer, Kim Roosevelt had a vivid notion of what the place was like based on stories of British imperial adventure.[11]

IF YOUNG KIM ROOSEVELT WAS not already sufficiently exposed to the culture of the British empire by his family background, then Groton School for Boys assuredly finished the job. Founded in 1884, Groton was the creation of Episcopalian clergyman Endicott Peabody, who was still headmaster when Kim entered the First Form in 1928, at the age of twelve. The scion of an eminent New England family, Peabody had been educated in Britain at an elite public school, Cheltenham College, and at Trinity College, Cambridge, where he thoroughly absorbed the Victorian values of the day: self-discipline, sportsmanship, and Christian "manliness." After returning to the United States and entering a seminary in Cambridge, Massachusetts, Peabody traveled west to the Arizona territory, where he spent the first six months of 1882 as rector of Tombstone's Episcopal Church. At a time when many members of the East Coast aristocracy were worrying about the possible "enervation" of their class by the luxuriousness of modern life, a western ordeal like this was a rite of passage for patrician young men. Theodore Roosevelt himself worked for two years in the 1880s as a cowboy in the Dakota Badlands. It seems that Peabody, with his tall, muscular frame and fierce sense of moral rectitude, acquitted himself very well among Tombstone's frontier roughs. His reputation for virile Victorianism preceded him when he returned east, and it was not long before many of the "best" families in New England and New York were sending their sons to be toughened up at the boarding school he established in the Massachusetts countryside, among them all four of TR's sons.

Modeled after the English public schools, Groton had another purpose, enshrined in its motto, *Cui servire est regnare*, or "For whom to serve is to rule." While some Victorian Americans worried about the softness of their sons, others were beginning to imagine a new role for their country in the world, that of a more vigorous and thrusting successor to the British Empire. For imperialists such as the US senator Henry Cabot Lodge and, of course, President Theodore Roosevelt himself, boarding schools like Groton were training grounds for young Americans destined to govern both at home and, increasingly, abroad. Indeed, after US victory in the 1898 war with Spain, Lodge explicitly encouraged Peabody to create "a class of men precisely like those employed by England in India" to administer America's new island possessions in the Caribbean and Pacific, and the others farther afield that were bound to follow. TR personally saw to it that Groton performed this function, turning up at Sunday chapel to exhort the boys to "use aright the gifts given to them" and "render service to the State," even if doing so meant sacrificing other ambitions. The message clearly sunk in, as an astounding number of Grotties ended up serving in high public office. The first thousand graduates included nine ambassadors, three senators, two governors, two secretaries of state, and one president (the Oyster Bay Roosevelts' Hyde Park cousin, Franklin D. Roosevelt). Kim Roosevelt's generation would produce an astonishingly large number of senior officers in the CIA.[12]

Admission to this elite came at a price: the austere regimen of daily life at the school. Boys slept in bare, six-by-nine-foot dormitory cubicles and were awakened every day by a bell rung at five minutes before seven. Next came a cold shower, breakfast, and then chapel (twice on Sunday). Class, which went from nine to one o'clock, consisted principally of Sacred Studies (taught by Peabody), Classics, and European languages and history, with an emphasis on the rise of Anglo-Saxon civilization. The boys' academic performance was constantly monitored, with the headmaster himself sending parents unsparing monthly reports.

What really mattered, however, was what took place during the afternoon, on the school's playing fields. Peabody was skeptical about the value of learning for learning's sake: "I'm not sure I like boys who think too much," he once pronounced. He believed sports, especially football, which he coached personally, were a truer test of a pupil's character. Indeed, at Groton, as in the English public schools, games served as a metaphor for life in general, so that Peabody, known as "the Rector," disapproved when star quarterback (and future CIA officer) Tracy Barnes showed a rebellious streak, writing his father, "We must work together to impress on Tracy the necessity of 'playing the game' fairly." Sports were also strongly associated with the business of empire building. "The time given to athletic contests . . . and the injuries incurred on the playing field are part of the price the English-speaking world has paid for being world-conquerors," Henry Cabot Lodge stated, lumping together Britons and Americans as one nation. It was no coincidence that the Anglo-Russian imperial rivalry in Central Asia was known as the Great Game.[13]

Kim Roosevelt arrived at Groton only a few years behind Barnes and, unsurprisingly perhaps, seems at first not to have coped well. "It is very dull up here," he wrote his mother, Belle, in October 1928. "I wish I was in Oyster Bay fishing for flounders with Willard" (a reference to his younger brother, who would follow him to Groton two years later). The unfavorable assessment was mutual. In December, after Kim had been ranked 27 out of 28 in his form, Endicott Peabody sent his parents a withering report. "He has ability," noted the Rector. However, "we find him careless and difficult to correct." Things were no better come the winter term. Kim "was not manifesting a spirit of obedience," wrote William E. Mott, secretary of the school's Disciplinary Committee, to Belle. Young Kermit had acquired fifteen disciplinary points or "blackmarks," only five short of the twenty that would require his being sent home. Kim's own letters home had by now acquired a plaintive tone. "When are you coming up here?" he asked his mother. "I was in the infirmary with a slight cold for a day. . . . The snow up here is one foot deep."[14]

By May, however, things had begun to look up for Kim. "I think the spring term is much the nicest, and have been having a great time," he wrote Belle. His grades had improved as well, although he lagged behind in Latin (the Latin master's fault, he assured his parents, not his own). In much the same way that Kipling's fictional character Kim, sent to an English school in Lucknow against his will, eventually thrives in his new environment, so the initially unruly Kim Roosevelt settled down at Groton, learning to play by the rules of the game. It helped that he was naturally interested in sports, his letters home abounding with enthusiastic references to various contests with rival schools, including the annual football game against the dreaded St. Mark's. His own athletic exploits were confined mainly to sprinting and tennis (a game he played throughout his life, with ferocious competitiveness) as opposed to team games. He also began to manifest some genuine academic ability, especially in English and history, regularly contributing poems to the *Grotonian*. These now appear rather tame, conventional efforts, but interesting nonetheless, if only because of what we know about his later career. One, untitled, reads: "The wanderlust has got me / I must follow in the footsteps of Ulysses / Who was the greatest of all vagabonds."[15]

Kim graduated from Groton in 1934, having earned excellent marks in the Harvard entrance exams. "Mother wanted to call the Rector up right away and tell him what she felt with regard to his gloomy forebodings," a proud Kermit Roosevelt wrote his son. Later, Kim would distance himself from the Groton clique at the CIA: "I was not part of that gang," he recalled. Certainly, the adult Kim was not one for the old school tie—he was in fact something of a loner—but it is hard to believe that Endicott Peabody did not leave his stamp on the boy. The two men stayed in touch long after Kim's graduation, corresponding regularly, in intimate, almost familial terms, until Peabody's death in 1944. It is surely telling that, when the time came for him to pick a school to which to send his own sons, Kim chose Groton.[16]

FOR GRADUATES OF CHURCH SCHOOLS like Groton, student life at an Ivy League school during the 1930s offered an undreamed-of degree of personal freedom, and as a Harvard freshman Kim Roosevelt was determined not to miss out on the fun. His grandmother, TR's widow, Edith, loaned him a car, and he used it to drive parties of friends, such as his Groton classmate Benjamin Welles (son of FDR's undersecretary of state, Sumner Welles), out into the New England countryside. There was Radcliffe College and its suitable young ladies, with whom Kim, who had inherited some of his father's good looks, was clearly popular, writing his mother that he hoped "some day life may become less complicated. . . . Two girls don't help at all." And there was the promise of more larks to come: the song-and-dance antics of "the Pudding" (the Hasty Pudding Theatricals society) and serious drinking at the Porcellian or "Pork," the most desirable of "final" clubs for Harvard men. (TR and Kermit Roosevelt had, of course, belonged to both the Pudding and the Pork, and Kim's correspondence with his parents suggests some anxiety about whether he would gain admission to the latter, a good indication of its exclusiveness.) Kim's freshman year was rounded off with a July 1935 hunting expedition in the rainforest of Brazil's Matto Grosso, where, despite a crash landing that wrecked one of his plane's propellers, an incident he reported to his parents with studiedly cool bravado, he succeeded in bagging a good deal of game, including a red wolf. So successful was this trip that he and his father discussed the possibility of undertaking another Roosevelt father-and-son voyage up the River of Doubt the following summer.[17]

During Kim's sophomore year, however, when he was nineteen, things grew more serious. In December 1935, he told his mother he was, "to all intents and purposes," engaged to a Radcliffe student, eighteen-year-old Mary Lowe "Polly" Gaddis of Milton, Massachusetts. Now resolved on graduating as quickly as possible, Kim focused on his schoolwork, abandoning plans for the River of Doubt expedition in order to take summer courses, and opting to join the Signet Society, a club devoted, at least partly, to intellectual and literary endeavors (T. S. Eliot, later Kim's favorite poet, was a member). His professors took note, and by January 1937 they were encouraging him to consider an academic career. Kim graduated that summer, *cum laude*, not bad given that he had gone through in three rather than four years. Shortly afterward he married Polly and began teaching in the Harvard History Department, apparently with some success. "Kim has certainly achieved great things in a very short period," noted Endicott Peabody approvingly in February 1938. "I do hope he will carry on the work for which he has shown so great an aptitude."[18]

Kim himself was not so sure about the academic life. Counteracting his natural scholarly talents and inclinations were a host of other

considerations. His future at Harvard was uncertain, and he soon had a
young family to support: Kermit III arrived in 1938, followed two years
later by Jonathan. It didn't help that his father, Kermit Sr., experienced
a series of business failures during the 1930s that forced him to eat into
Belle's family assets. Indeed, the Oyster Bay, Republican branch of the
Roosevelt family was not doing well generally, suffering from a sense of
collective decline that was only heightened by the spectacular rise of the
Democrat FDR and the Hyde Park Roosevelts. Kermit, always the most
sensitive of TR's progeny, started to go off the rails, drinking heavily and
beginning an affair with a German masseuse that led to long periods when
he was incommunicado with his family. In his absence, Belle tried hard
to conceal the cracks in their marriage, socializing hectically in Washington and ingratiating herself with FDR's White House. Kim and his
brother Willard, who had followed him from Groton to Harvard, were
sufficiently grown up that these events did not cause them any obvious emotional damage; however, their younger siblings, Clochette and
Dirck, never successfully launched themselves into adult life (the troubled Dirck would eventually commit suicide in 1953), and Kim found
himself increasingly involved in their care and support.

Added to all these financial and family worries were Kim's love of
adventure, an appetite unlikely to be satisfied in the cloisters of academe,
and the familial expectation that Roosevelt men sacrifice all in order
to serve their country. After all, his uncles Ted and Archie had both
been wounded in World War I, and the aviator Quentin shot down over
France and killed. With war clouds massing in Europe, this last impulse
was growing stronger than ever.

In the end, Kim found a rather elegant solution to his dilemma. His
doctoral research at Harvard concerned the role of propaganda in the
English civil war, a choice of subject perhaps made with one eye on its
potential relevance to wartime government service. He carried on this
project after moving to Pasadena in 1939 in order to teach history at the
California Institute of Technology. Although he and his young family
enjoyed the perks of life in Southern California, such as horseback riding
in the San Gabriel Mountains, there was a sense of marking time about
this period of Kim's life. The previous year, his father, desperate to re-
deem himself in the eyes of his family, had departed on an espionage
mission for the president, inspecting Japanese installations in the Pacific
while cruising on Vincent Astor's yacht (Kermit and Astor had been
collecting intelligence on an amateur basis since the 1920s as members

of the Room, an informal club of society spies). Then, when war was declared in 1939, Kermit dashed off to join up with the British army again,
this time leading an expeditionary force into Norway. Kim, meanwhile,
wrote letters to his mother back east, asking that if she were "to run into
anyone connected with Intelligence," she "find out whether they want
young men who are well read in, and very critical of, most modern writing on propaganda." With Kermit increasingly out of the picture, the
well-connected Belle seems to have taken on the role of her much-loved
eldest son's career advisor and booster in Washington.[19]

Kim was particularly interested in the possibility of doing work
for Colonel William "Wild Bill" Donovan, the World War I hero, Wall
Street lawyer, and Republican Party stalwart. The Oyster Bay Roosevelts
had been close to Donovan for several years; in 1932, Kermit had lent
prominent support to his unsuccessful bid for the New York governor-
ship. Now, worried that the existing US intelligence apparatus was too
weak and fragmented to respond effectively to the challenge of the war
in Europe, Donovan was campaigning for the creation of a unified, strategic intelligence service. Kim, doubtful of his prospects at Cal Tech, and
hoping for a position in "a Government agency that, although it doesn't
exist yet, will probably be formed soon," bided his time in Pasadena,
lecturing local audiences about the errors of isolationism, planning how
to turn his thesis into "a more or less popular book on propaganda," and
drafting a scholarly article about "the kind of clandestine service organization the U.S. should develop for World War II." In the early summer
of 1941, acting on the advice of reporter Joseph Alsop, his cousin and
fellow Grotonian, Kim showed the article to Donovan, who had just
been appointed coordinator of information (COI) by FDR. Donovan
responded immediately by inviting Kim to come join him in Fairfax,
Virginia, where he was setting up the COI office—in effect, the United
States' first central intelligence agency—on Belle Roosevelt's family estate. Kim did so in August, taking the position of special assistant to the
director of research and analysis. It was still four months before the Japanese attack on Pearl Harbor. Like generations of Roosevelt men before
him, Kim had gotten into the fight early.[20]

KIM ROOSEVELT HAD NEGOTIATED THE difficult business of becoming a Roosevelt man quite skillfully. He had discovered an occupation that reconciled his attraction to both the contemplative and the

active life, while satisfying the Groton ethic that he render service to his country. Moreover, the job of professional spy promised to satisfy his appetite for adventure, for playing the Great Game, which he had developed listening to his father's stories and reading Kipling. By his mid-twenties, Kim Roosevelt already exhibited the qualities that would define his adult personality—coolness, self-confidence, a certain inscrutability—and make him one of the most vaunted CIA officers of his day.

Tragically, his father, for all his considerable talents, never developed the same emotional poise as his son. Discharged from the British army on medical grounds in 1941, he returned to the United States, where his life continued its downward spiral into depression and alcoholism. After an unsuccessful course of treatment in a Connecticut sanatorium, he was posted to a remote military base in Alaska. It was there, in June 1943, that Kermit Roosevelt shot himself to death with his Mesopotamian service revolver. "He gave his life for a great cause with the complete courage which is characteristic of his family," wrote Endicott Peabody to Kermit's widow, Belle, in one of his last letters to the Oyster Bay Roosevelts.[21]

TWO

Beginning the Quest

KIM ROOSEVELT'S CHILDHOOD ENCOUNTER WITH the Middle East—essentially a vicarious one, mediated by the culture of the British Empire—would exercise a powerful influence on the mind-set of the CIA as it first approached the region in the late 1940s. However, Kim's experience was not the only kind of American engagement with the Arab and Muslim worlds prior to the Cold War. Equally if not more important in shaping early CIA attitudes toward the Middle East was a distinctly American tradition of direct, personal contact with the region's inhabitants that likewise dated back to the nineteenth century.

A number of individuals, several of them born and raised in the Middle East itself, would help convey this tradition to the young CIA. One in particular, William Alfred Eddy, came to play a crucial role in bridging the worlds of the official US intelligence community and Middle East–born American Arabists. Yet perhaps the most ardent early advocate of the Arabist viewpoint was not himself from a Middle Eastern background. Rather, he had experienced an almost identical upbringing and education to those of Kim Roosevelt: Kim's cousin Archie.

BORN TWO YEARS AFTER KIM, in 1918, Archibald Bulloch Roosevelt was named for his father, Archibald Sr., the third of TR's sons. After a childhood spent mainly in New York City and Cold Spring Harbor, close to Oyster Bay, Archie Jr. entered Groton in 1930, in the same class as Kim's younger brother Willard. Then it was on to Harvard, where, like Kim, Archie distinguished himself academically despite going through in just three years, graduating in 1939 *magna cum laude* (family lore had it that he would have been *summa* had he not absentmindedly forgotten an examination) and winning a Rhodes Scholarship to Oxford University. He also dutifully found himself a New England wife, Katherine Winthrop Tweed, or "KW"—"I don't believe in getting involved unless one intends to marry the girl," he told his bride-to-be—thereby disqualifying himself from taking up his place at Oxford, as the Rhodes required scholars to be unmarried. Instead, under pressure to earn a livelihood with which to support a young family, he began working as a newspaper "copyboy" and then cub reporter, and ended up in the San Francisco Bay Area.[1]

Nor did the similarities with Kim end there. Like all young Roosevelt males, Archie had been sent west to be toughened up by a spell of frontier life, spending the year before he went to Groton at the Arizona Desert School near Tucson. Indeed, under the influence of Archibald Sr., rather a martinet compared with the romantic Kermit, Archie appears to have been even more exposed to the strenuous life than young Kim. During an especially arduous hunting expedition near Fairbanks, Alaska, he became thoroughly lost and had to camp on his own overnight, surrounded by bear and wolf tracks. As he grew up and it became clearer that his interests and talents mainly lay in intellectual pursuits, Archie drifted away from his father, identifying more with his historian and naturalist grandfather TR, whose hovering presence he sensed throughout his life, simultaneously protecting and judging him. Still, later on, Archie would feel well served by the masculine ordeals of his adolescence. "I had become a man and had found a strength that has never deserted me in time of testing," he recalled of his Alaska experience in his memoirs. Archie had particularly fond memories of his stay in Arizona, an experience that instilled in him "a love for the desert and a nostalgia for it" that was only requited years later when he "attained the deserts on the other side of the world."[2]

This affinity for the "Desert Sublime" was also a characteristic of the English Arabists whom Kermit Roosevelt had befriended during World War I, and it is not surprising to learn that, like Kim's, Archie's childhood was permeated by the culture of the British Empire, particularly texts about the Orient. Archibald Sr. frequently read his son *The Ballad of East and West*, the Kipling poem containing the seminal Orientalist statement "East is East, and West is West, and never the twain shall meet." Sneaking into TR's study at Sagamore, the boy Archie pored over *The Arabian Nights*. Later, at Groton, he ransacked the school library for works on the Arabs, "with Lawrence of Arabia as a starting point." One of Archie's proudest childhood memories was of winning a Groton public-speaking prize for his recitation from *Hassan: A Play in Five Acts* by the English poet James Elroy Flecker. These verses, with their central theme of a spiritual pilgrimage ("Golden Road") to Samarkand, the fabled ancient city on the Silk Road, became a constant refrain in the life of the adult Archie, as he embarked on his own quest in search of an essential yet elusive Orient.[3]

Not all of the Middle Eastern experiences of Archie's childhood were second-hand and British ones. His father's friends included Prince Muhiddin ibn 'Ali al-Haidar, the son of the former emir of Medina and cousin of the Hashemite princes whom T. E. Lawrence and Gertrude Bell had helped install as rulers of Transjordan and Iraq. Later, Archie recalled the excitement of "Prince Mooi's" visits to the family home in Cold Spring Harbor. There was even a brief moment spent in the Arab world itself when, in the course of a tour around the Mediterranean, Archie and his family walked through the Casbah in Algiers. The sixteen-year-old boy was "fascinated by the Moorish scene" that surrounded him: "I was in the land of *Beau Geste*, and wished I could linger."[4]

There were other small but not insignificant differences between the young cousins. Whereas Kim, after the initial shock of life at Groton, settled down and appeared even to enjoy life at the school, Archie never adjusted. A small, toothy boy with extremely bad eyesight, he fared poorly on the playing field and was "usually the last to be chosen for a team." Archie's lack of athleticism was balanced by his performance in the classroom, where he posted consistently excellent grades, especially in history and the classics. Perversely, though, he tended to identify not with past empires and their conquests but rather with "the losers of history": "Carthage against Rome, the Moors of Spain against Castile, and the Byzantines against everybody." And in contrast to the conventionally heroic verses Kim penned for the *Grotonian*, Archie

concocted gloomy Dark Ages sagas, freighted with historical and lin-
guistic allusions.[5]

Small wonder, then, that Archie was not Endicott Peabody's favorite
pupil; indeed, he later suspected that the Rector had toyed with the idea
of moving him to another school. It probably did not help that Archie
had an irrepressible appreciation for the absurd, something he retained
into adult life. The Rector would sprinkle his stern Sunday sermons
with vague yet intriguing references to a bad man—in fact, "the foulest
man [he] ever knew"—who had somehow offended him during his time
in Tombstone, and Archie spent many an hour speculating hilariously
with his classmates about the possible nature of this unfortunate character's transgressions.[6]

Yet, for all his bookishness and irreverence, Archie Roosevelt keenly
felt the Grotonian call to serve the nation. "The values you and Father
gave me as a boy, and the family tradition of public service, have not led
me to attach to money an overwhelming importance," he later wrote
his mother, Grace, after she had chided him for failing to win back the
family fortune. As American entrance into World War II loomed, Archie, possibly taking his lead from cousin Kim, tried to sign up as an
intelligence officer. He had some exceptional qualifications for this role,
not just his innate intellectual abilities but also his language skills: in
addition to the modern and classical languages he had acquired at Groton, he had learned some Russian from an émigré gardener who worked
for his parents, and then at Harvard, as part of his broad field of literature, obtained a special dispensation to study Arabic, supplementing his
schoolwork with private tutoring by a Palestinian friend. The problems
were his extreme nearsightedness and, at age twenty-four, his youth.
Applications to the army's intelligence unit (G-2), the Office of Naval
Intelligence, and Bill Donovan's new outfit all failed, the latter despite
some lobbying on his behalf by Kim.[7]

Eventually, after the intervention of his father (who himself fought
in the Pacific despite having the opposite problem of being too old for
combat service), Archie got into the Army Specialist Corps, a civilian
organization that performed special assignments for the military. After
some intelligence training at Camp Ritchie in Maryland and then boot
camp in Virginia, in October 1942 Archie found himself on a troop-
ship convoy apparently bound for the Senegalese port of Dakar. On
board ship, he learned that his specialist corps was to be abolished and

its members absorbed by the regular army. Then a ship loudspeaker announcement by General George S. Patton informed him that he was in fact on his way to capture a beachhead near Casablanca in Morocco, as part of an operation code-named TORCH.

Like his grandfather charging up Kettle Hill in Cuba, young Archie Roosevelt was about to face his "crowded hour."

THE ARAB WORLD ARCHIE ROOSEVELT was poised to enter in October 1942 was still an exclusively European political and military preserve. There had been the occasional expression of official American interest in the region — TR, for example, had mused about taking over Britain's role in Egypt, reckoning he would soon "have things moving in fine order" — but successive US administrations had by and large been content to defer to the British and French on the so-called Eastern Question. William J. Jardine, the American minister in Cairo during the 1930s (one of only a handful of US government representatives in the Middle East prior to World War II), summed up this attitude: "It appears to me to be quite a sideshow."[8]

This is not to say, however, that there was no American presence at all in the Middle East before the 1940s. Starting in the early 1800s, Protestant missionaries had began journeying from New England to the "Holy Land" to convert the "Mohammedans" dwelling there. Perhaps predictably, these American evangelists failed almost entirely to win Muslim souls for Christ; many suffered terrible hardships in the attempt, and several died. Nonetheless, they did succeed in leaving a lasting impression on the region in the shape of the educational institutions they founded, such as the Syrian Protestant College (later known as the American University of Beirut, or AUB), established in 1866 by the archetypal New England missionary Daniel Bliss. And, surprisingly, they earned quite a lot of goodwill among the Middle Easterners they encountered, if only because their relatively selfless interest in the region compared so favorably with the colonialism of the European powers.[9]

This reputation for "disinterested benevolence," as one Protestant theologian described it, was reinforced by the respect that some, if by no means all, of the missionaries felt for Arab culture, as shown, for example, in Bliss's decision to adopt Arabic as the language of instruction at his university. An unintended consequence of this attitude was that, at the same time they spread modern American ideas and values in the Middle East, institutions such as AUB and its Egyptian counterpart, the American University in Cairo, also began to function as incubators of Arab nationalism. This identification between American influence and Arab independence—logical enough, given the United States' own origins in a war of national liberation—grew stronger still during World War I, when many Arabs noted with approval Woodrow Wilson's support for national self-determination as set out in his famous Fourteen Points.[10]

After the War, Wilson's failure to prevent the revival of European imperialism in the Middle East caused a perceptible falling off in Arab enthusiasm for things American. Meanwhile, US citizens began appearing in the region with less benign intentions than their missionary predecessors: archaeologists wanting to excavate its ancient artifacts and oilmen lured by its fantastic petroleum reserves. (Ironically, the latter's entry into the Middle East was facilitated by an Englishman, the noted Arabist Harry St. John "Jack" Philby, who brokered a concession for Standard Oil of California in Saudi Arabia that signaled the beginning of the end of British domination of the region's oil industry.) Nevertheless, even in the early 1940s, there still existed a large reservoir of admiration for the United States among Arabs and, on the American side, a heritage of positive, personal engagement with the Arab and Muslim worlds that ran counter to the negative imagery of classic Orientalism.[11]

If any one individual personified the several strands of this tradition—missionary work, education, intelligence, and oil—it was William Alfred Eddy. Born in 1896 to Presbyterian missionaries in Lebanon, Bill Eddy grew up speaking colloquial Arabic on the streets of Sidon. His first trip to the United States came when he was sent for his education to Wooster College in Ohio and then to Princeton Theological Seminary—both Presbyterian-founded institutions with ties to the missionary community. During World War I he served with distinction in the Marine Corps, suffering wounds in France that left him carrying his large frame on a lame right leg. Invalided out of active service, he returned to academe and in 1923 took up the chair of the English Department at the recently founded American University in Cairo. Subsequent university appointments in the United States never quite satisfied his yen for military service and foreign adventure, so it was little surprise when he reenlisted in the Marines on the eve of World War II and returned to Cairo in the role of US naval attaché. Shortly after Pearl Harbor, Eddy was moved to Tangier in Morocco, at the special request of Kim Roosevelt's boss, the coordinator of information, Bill Donovan. He was to remain on loan to Donovan, still under the cover of naval attaché, for most of the rest of the war.[12]

Fans of the movie *Casablanca* will have some inkling of the murky, ominous atmosphere of wartime Morocco. Most of the country was still part of France's vast colonial empire in North Africa, yet Nazi Germany pulled the strings of the collaborationist French government in Vichy, and there were fears of a German invasion from either Libya in the east or Spain to the north. Part of Eddy's mission in Tangier was to try to divine German intentions while creating "stay-behind" networks that would sabotage an Axis occupation force. At the same time, he had to prepare for the possibility of the Allies landing an expeditionary force of their own, an eventuality that required him to predict the response of the French—would they welcome Allied troops as liberators or resist them?—and set up beachheads and landing fields. At this stage, in early 1942, it was still far from clear which of these scenarios was the more likely outcome.

Fortunately, Eddy did have some intelligence resources at his disposal. Unlike the British, who had severed relations with Vichy, the United States still had government representation in North Africa, and Eddy was able to use American officials with diplomatic immunity as a ready-made espionage network. Among the Americans already on the ground were several with excellent connections to the majority native population, including a Harvard anthropologist by the name of Carleton S. Coon, who had undertaken several field trips among the Rifi of northern Morocco, a Berber tribe with a history of resistance to European domination. Eddy was also able to draw on his own Arabic and knowledge of Islam, including the ability to recite chapters of the Koran by heart, to befriend local leaders.

Working out of a suite in the spy-infested Minzah Hotel—Tangier's equivalent of *Casablanca*'s Rick's Café—Eddy and his associates ran a dizzying variety of operations. A regional chain of clandestine radio stations reported intelligence ranging from ticket purchases at Casablanca airport to the height of the surf along the Moroccan coastline. Local agents surreptitiously distributed propaganda literature intended to dissuade the French from putting up a fight if and when the Allies landed.

US officials used the diplomatic pouch to smuggle arms to putative resistance groups.

To be sure, there were elements of Kipling-esque game playing about some of these activities. The rambunctious Coon, for example, appeared to be thinking of Lawrence of Arabia when he tried, unsuccessfully, to employ a Rif general with the code name Tassels to raise a tribal revolt. Similarly, various schemes involving Strings, the leader of (in Coon's words) "the most powerful religious brotherhood in Northern Morocco," whose followers would "obey his order to the death," were distinctly reminiscent of the Scottish novelist John Buchan's World War I adventure *Greenmantle*. After the war was over, Coon would delight in telling stories of stay-behind saboteurs mining Moroccan highways with explosives disguised as mule turds.[13]

With his Presbyterian missionary conscience, Bill Eddy did not share Coon's relish for dirty tricks. "It is still an open question whether an operator in OSS or in CIA can ever again become a wholly honorable man," he wrote later, in a surprisingly gloomy unpublished memoir about his wartime experiences. "We deserve to go to hell when we die." Nonetheless, he too arguably exceeded his brief, tending not merely to gather and report intelligence but also actively to try to shape policy. Clearly convinced that the Allies should lose no time in moving on North Africa, Eddy constantly exaggerated both the threat of German invasion and the likelihood of the French welcoming an Allied preemptive strike. "If we sent an expeditionary force to North Africa, there would be only token resistance," he assured a skeptical audience of US top brass in London in July 1942.[14]

Dressed in his marine uniform, Eddy cut an impressive figure—General Patton, on observing the numerous World War I ribbons on his chest, reportedly remarked, "the son of a bitch's been shot at enough, hasn't he?"—and his counsel helped carry the day. After secret meetings in the White House, FDR authorized Operation TORCH, an invasion plan involving over one hundred thousand Allied troops, the great majority of them American (British participation was kept to a minimum because of the possible negative impact on French opinion), under the supreme command of General Dwight D. Eisenhower.[15]

With D-Day set for November 8, 1942, Eddy ramped up his operations, smuggling maritime pilots out of Morocco to join the Allied convoy, supporting Anglo-American measures designed to deceive the Germans about the landing locations, and helping convene secret meetings between Allied and French commanders intended to forestall resistance to the invasion. He even made sure that there were agents on the beaches equipped with flares to guide in the landing craft, and maps to distribute to the disembarking troops. Leaving aside some of the Eddy team's operational mistakes and errors of judgment, it was an impressive intelligence performance, proof of what an American with the right background and approach could achieve in the Arab and Muslim worlds. Bill Eddy, the prototypical Middle East–raised US Arabist, had quite literally prepared the way for the arrival in North Africa of Archie Roosevelt.[16]

IN THE EARLY HOURS OF November 8, 1942, while Bill Eddy and Carleton Coon crouched over a radio set listening for word of TORCH's arrival, Archie sat huddled in a landing craft, speeding through the dark toward red blinkers on a beach near Casablanca. As the bottom of his boat scraped rocks, it became evident that the Eddy team had underestimated French resistance. A fort opened up with its cannon, and the US Navy responded with its big guns, lighting up the sky like a fireworks display. Archie rushed for cover in the brush that lined the shore and then, as morning dawned, began reconnoitering inland. Over the next three days, about 1,400 Americans and 700 French would die in sporadic fighting throughout North Africa. Luckily for Archie, the area around Casablanca was pacified relatively quickly, and the challenge instead became processing the thousands of French and Moroccan soldiers and officers who wanted to surrender. With his outstanding language skills, Archie was soon on call among US commanders, including General Patton himself, as an interpreter. A cease-fire was agreed on during the night of November 11, and the following morning the twenty-four-year-old grandson of TR, dressed in mud-stained fatigues, entered Casablanca, riding through cheering crowds in a jeep alongside a resplendently attired Patton, the whole scene reminiscent of T. E. Lawrence's victorious entry into Damascus at the end of World War I.

A few days later, US headquarters were moved a short way up the Atlantic coast to Morocco's capital, Rabat, and it was then that Archie Roosevelt's love affair with the Arab world began in earnest. Although the ancient walled city, or medina, was off-limits to US troops, he was

able to explore the rose-colored minaret of the Tour Hassan; the Casbah of the Oudaias, with its lovely gardens "perfumed with jasmine and
orange blossoms" (as he wrote later); and the Chellah, burial ground of
past sultans. Accompanying Archie on these explorations was another
GI by the name of Muhammad Siblini, a young Lebanese American
from a prominent Beirut family who had run a fur-importing business
in New York. The two men had met at the Camp Ritchie intelligence
school, where they "established an immediate rapport," and had sailed
together across the Atlantic. In Rabat, Siblini became something of a celebrity with the local Muslim community, and with his support, Archie
Roosevelt gained special permission to enter the medina. There he befriended a number of young Arabs, who entertained him in their homes
and discussed a wide range of issues with him. One in particular sought
him out: Mehdi Ben Barka, a prominent member of the nationalist Is-
tiqlal (Independence) Party, then banned by the French authorities. "He
spent considerable time with me at various places," Archie recalled,
"educating me about French colonialism in Morocco." During the
1960s, Ben Barka would develop a reputation as a major Third World
revolutionary before vanishing, under mysterious circumstances, in
Paris in 1965.[17]

One reason why Ben Barka's history lessons found such a receptive
audience in Archie Roosevelt was that there was a prior history of tension, if not outright conflict, between Americans and French residing in
the Arab world. In the nineteenth-century Levant, Protestant New England missionaries of the sort who founded the American University of
Beirut tended to be at odds with the Catholic Maronites, an indigenous
Christian group heavily identified with the French. This divide deep-
ened after World War I, when the French mandate saw Greater Syria
subdivided and the Maronites elevated to positions of power, while
Arab nationalists were crushed. In World War II North Africa, France's
reputation among American Arabists grew worse still, thanks to the col-
laborationism of Vichy officials, who were allowed to remain in office
even after the Allied invasion.

With his history of interest in the Arab world, and recent exposure
to the influence of Moroccan nationalists, young Archie Roosevelt grew
increasingly troubled by the continuing French presence. Still in Rabat,
but reassigned from his interpreting duties to the task of monitoring Arabic programming on Radio Maroc, he filed a series of reports reflecting,

as he put it later, "the views expressed to me by the nationalists, their aspirations to throw off French rule, and their complaints that the French were taking advantage of the American presence to reinforce their position." Soon, French police began to monitor Archie's movements and harass the young Arab intellectuals with whom he was meeting.[18]

If anything, Archie's sympathy with Arab nationalism only grew stronger with each of his subsequent postings in North Africa. In February 1943, he transferred back to Casablanca and went to work for the Office of War Information (OWI), the wartime US propaganda agency. He was sad to part ways with Muhammad Siblini, who moved to Allied Force Headquarters in Algiers, where he was employed reciting the Koran on Radio Algiers. Nonetheless, Archie soon made new friends who shared his anticolonial views, including Carleton Coon and another American with ties to the rebellious Rifi, reporter and novelist Vincent "Jimmy" Sheean. He also continued to fraternize with Moroccans, enjoying the lavish hospitality of Arab tribal leader Caid el-Ayadi in Marrakesh, a city whose beauty he described lyrically in his memoirs, and discovering a strong attraction to "the appealing femininity [of] many Near Eastern women"—although he resisted any urge to betray his marriage vows to KW. Meanwhile, he carried on criticizing the French, claiming in reports to OWI command that they were trying to turn the local populace against the United States by portraying GIs as "in the habit of having sexual intercourse with donkeys."[19]

Archie also sounded a new theme: with its vast world population of adherents, Islam stood to be "a factor of increasing importance" in the postwar future, and the United States had an unprecedented opportunity in North Africa to establish itself "as the great unselfish friend of the Moslems." With this end in mind, Archie began to advocate two projects intended to demonstrate American benevolence toward the region: the building there of an American university like AUB and the provision of US transport planes to Muslim leaders wishing to make the pilgrimage to Mecca, something they had not been able to do since the beginning of the war. Both these proposals implicitly rebuked the French for their lack of concern about the education and spiritual welfare of the "natives" supposedly under their protection.[20]

In June 1943, with his reputation as an observer of the Muslim and Arab scenes clearly growing, Archie was loaned to the Psychological Warfare Branch (PWB), an Anglo-American team of propaganda specialists who had followed the TORCH invasion force to North Africa. The PWB was a haven for dissidents from the official US line of cooperation with the Vichy French, and its officers were prone to taking vigilante actions against alleged local fascists and to illegally protecting Gaullist resistance fighters; Eisenhower reputedly complained that the PWB gave him "more trouble than all the Germans in Africa." Tasked with reporting on Axis propaganda targeted at the Arabs of North Africa, Archie traveled east to Algiers, meeting with Algerian nationalist leaders, and then on to Tunisia, where his pro-Arab and anticolonial reporting reached a kind of crescendo.[21]

Several experiences in Tunisia appear to have left an especially strong impression on young Archie. One was learning of the pathetic plight of Moncef Bey, the nominal Tunisian sovereign, who had attempted to bring about some moderate nationalist reforms in the country, only for the French to subject him "to great moral and physical pressure" to abdicate (as Archie reported to PWB command). Another was his getting to know the young leaders of the Neo-Destour, the radical wing of the Tunisian nationalist movement, many of whom had only just been released after years of solitary confinement in France. Archie was introduced to the Neo-Destour by the charming Slim Driga, a performing arts impresario who also treated him and another American Arabist, Consul General Hooker Doolittle, to a memorable driving tour of the beautiful Tunisian heartland. Back in Tunis, Archie visited the Neo-Destour president, Habib Bourguiba, in his cramped, side-street apartment. With his "expressive hands and piercing blue eyes," Bourguiba struck Archie "as a visionary, a modern prophet, . . . destined for greatness" (the prediction proved accurate: in 1957 Bourguiba became the first president of the independent Republic of Tunisia). Archie invited each of his new nationalist friends to send him a report on their recent history, which he planned to synthesize into a presentation to the US authorities. Then, on July 4, 1943, while he was at work on this final report, an incident occurred that completed Archie's disillusionment with the official American policy of collaborating with the French. An altercation between Senegalese and Algerian soldiers in Tunis escalated into a riot in which twenty Arab civilians were massacred as French officers either stood by or, according to some reports, joined in the killing. Horrified, Archie delivered to his superiors a blistering denunciation of French colonial rule and US complicity in it.[22]

This was Archie Roosevelt's last official act in Tunisia. A few weeks later, he learned that, along with Hooker Doolittle, he was being recalled to the United States, presumably at the request of the French. In a hastily penned "Report on My Activities," he defended himself against various unnamed detractors, but this attempt "to set the record straight" was to no avail, and his recall went ahead. The night before he was due to leave, Archie was invited by Slim Driga to a farewell party in a villa on the Mediterranean shore. "All the Neo-Destour leaders were there," he remembered later, "and after a sumptuous banquet, a Bedouin girl danced for us, with great poise . . . yet with a wildness in the flash of her black eyes." For the budding young American Arabist, this "magic evening by the sea, lit by the crescent moon," was the perfect climax for his romance with the Arabs of North Africa.[23]

GIVEN ARCHIE'S UPBRINGING AND EDUCATION, it was inevitable that there would be traces of old-fashioned Orientalism in his wartime approach to North Africa. There was, for example, the afternoon he and Hooker Doolittle shared sipping tea on the Tunisian shoreline. "[We] felt like Connecticut Yankees, transferred to an earlier, more tranquil century," Archie wrote later, conjuring up Orientalist notions of the East as a place of premodern simplicity, a romantic refuge from the ravages of Western progress (and, in the case of the Oyster Bay Roosevelts, the loss of family status that had occurred since TR's day). There was also Archie's infatuation with the "exotic" femininity of Near Eastern women, another classic Orientalist theme.[24]

By and large, though, Archie Roosevelt's commentary on his North African experiences suggests a perspective based not so much on European Orientalism, with its relentless "othering" of the colonial subject, as on a distinctively American tradition of more humane, interactive engagement with Arabs and Muslims. This was reflected in the extraordinary access to high-level Arab leaders that Archie enjoyed during his tour of duty, unimaginable for later generations of American intelligence officers operating in the Middle East. In turn, these contacts strengthened his own growing attraction toward Arab nationalism as he developed enduring friendships with a whole generation of North African independence leaders. Combined with his unusual intellectual gifts and openness to new experiences, these influences caused Archie Roosevelt to imagine an American future in the Arab and Muslim worlds that would be very different from the European past.[25]

With Europe's colonial power in the Middle East waning as World War II drew to a close, the question was, Would this vision become a reality? Unbeknownst to Archie, the first serious test of American Arabism was in fact already taking place, down the North African coast in Cairo, where his cousin Kim was to play a leading part in the United States' earliest effort to establish a regional spy network.

THREE

OSS/Cairo

WHEN HE RETURNED TO THE United States in the late summer of 1943, Archie Roosevelt went to work at the Office of War Information headquarters in Washington, DC, linking up again with his Muslim friend Muhammad Siblini to develop ideas for US propaganda in the Arab world. While in Washington, he often stayed with Kim and Polly Roosevelt in their home on the Willard family estate a few miles to the west in Fairfax, Virginia.

The Oyster Bay Roosevelts were a tight-knit family, and the cousins had seen each other quite often when they were growing up. Archibald Sr., a sentimental man despite his curmudgeonly tendencies, had kept one eye on his brother Kermit's children, making sure that they at least got regular baths at Sagamore while their father was off exploring and their mother was busy in Washington. For his part, Kim received special instructions from Archie's mother, Grace, to watch out for her son at Groton. "She seemed particularly worried about the way he is slanging everybody," Kim primly wrote his father. "I told her I would do all I could." Still, the two years that separated the cousins counted for a lot at hierarchical institutions like Groton and Harvard, and Archie appears to have spent less time with Kim than with Kim's younger brother Willard, his direct contemporary. It was not until the war, with both cousins involved in intelligence and raising young families (KW gave birth to a boy, Tweed, in 1942), that they really began to appreciate how much they had in common: "interests, tastes, and even sense of humor," as Archie put it later. Relaxing together over drinks after long days of war work, the two young men, neither yet thirty, talked late into the evening, Kim listening to Archie as he expounded what had become his personal theme, "that the Arab world would be of great importance after the war and deserved more attention now."[1]

Kim himself had not had any previous involvement with the Arab countries. The closest he had come was in September 1941, when Bill Donovan requested his views on Iran and he had taken himself off to the Library of Congress for a briefing on the subject by colonial affairs analyst (and future first black winner of the Nobel Peace Prize) Ralph Bunche. Around the same time, a family friend had suggested that Kim go out to China to join General Claire Chennault and his force of volunteer aviators, an idea that, if pursued, might well have led to his becoming a "China hand" rather than an Arabist, area specialisms with little in common except that they shared missionary pasts and would later both be reviled by many Americans.[2]

Instead, Kim moved sideways in Washington. In August 1942 he left Bill Donovan's outfit, which had just been renamed the Office of Strategic Services (OSS), for a post as an assistant section chief at the OWI, working on propaganda related to Lend-Lease, the program for sending war materials to US allies. He shifted jobs again in January 1943, this time joining the State Department, where he helped Dean Acheson, then assistant secretary in charge of economic affairs, in the actual implementation of Lend-Lease, attending a number of meetings with senior representatives of Allied governments. It was high-level stuff for one so young, yet Acheson, the quintessential East Coast patrician (and fellow Grotonian), was impressed with Kim's maturity, declaring that he possessed "a very able mind, an excellent educational and cultural background and an intense interest in governmental problems." Dining at the White House, Belle Roosevelt heard similar praise for her son's "mental attributes" and "virtues" from another Grotonian, undersecretary of state and family friend Sumner Welles. Kim was a rising star of wartime Washington.[3]

There is therefore something curious about his posting to Cairo in January 1944. Later, in his memoir *Countercoup*, Kim offered the fol-

lowing explanation for the move. In the course of the duties he was performing for Dean Acheson, he had recommended one James M. Landis
for the post of American director of economic operations in the Middle
East, responsible for overseeing the massive US Lend-Lease operation in
the region. Landis had duly been dispatched to Cairo, where he triggered
a diplomatic row by criticizing the British, still the dominant Western
power in Egypt. A furious Acheson had then ordered his assistant out to
the Middle East to clean up the mess he had indirectly created.[4]

Evidently, though, there was more to Kim Roosevelt's Cairo mission than the Landis affair alone. As he himself revealed in *Countercoup*,
Kim was still reporting to Bill Donovan as well as Dean Acheson when
he left Washington. Elsewhere, he wrote of "doing special intelligence
work" in Cairo, "originally with the State Department and later with the
army." Declassified official records suggest that, at least after April 1944,
when he was officially reassigned from the State Department to the OSS
and entered the US Army in the rank of private, Kim was a key player in
Project SOPHIA, a secret program for spreading OSS officers throughout the region under cover of Landis's economic assistance operations.[5]

Archie Roosevelt, for one, was skeptical about the official explanation of his cousin's presence in the Egyptian capital. "I don't believe his
mission came about by an arbitrary decision by his superiors," he stated
later. "Rather, it may have resulted from what I had said in Washington
about the future importance of the Middle East." Whether it was Archie
who planted the seed of Kim's first Middle East mission, it was not the
last time that the cousins' professional lives would intersect in ways that
were to prove momentous, both personally and historically.[6]

AS KIM ROOSEVELT OBSERVED LATER, the continuing influence
of British imperialism was everywhere in wartime Cairo, from the
"shabby grandeur" of Shepheard's Hotel and its famous Long Bar to
the "clipped British accent[s]" of many young Arab intellectuals. Kim
might also have mentioned the sizeable presence of British spies. Cairo
had been the headquarters of Britain's Arab Bureau in World War I,
and it performed a similar function in World War II, as home to the
British Political Intelligence Centre Cairo, a vast spy station that coordinated a region-wide espionage network not just in the Middle East but
in the Nazi-occupied Balkans as well (the British still lumped together

the countries of the eastern Mediterranean into one imperial zone, the "Near East"). The Balkan resistance movement was riddled with internal divisions, and these were replicated in Cairo itself, where, according to senior British official Bickham Sweet-Escott, "an atmosphere of jealousy, suspicion, and intrigue" prevailed. One common aim, however, did unite the British: keeping other Westerners out of their bailiwick. Small wonder, then, that Americans, especially those with a distaste for European imperialism, should have regarded the Egyptian capital with considerable misgivings. The wartime British minister resident, Harold Macmillan, summed up US attitudes in his diary: "Cairo is suspect—it is somehow connected in their minds with imperialism, Kipling and all that."[7]

Nonetheless, the Americans were not prepared to concede the Middle East entirely to their European allies, especially after the good show that Bill Eddy had put on in French North Africa. As early as the summer of 1942, Bill Donovan had proposed a plan for setting up an OSS station in Cairo to serve as a base for independent US operations in the Balkans and for sending an expedition to Lebanon to establish an American intelligence presence in the Middle East itself. Having gained the enthusiastic approval of the president, Donovan handed over the mission to Colonel Harold B. Hoskins, a textile executive with extensive Middle Eastern experience. Hoskins was a cousin of Bill Eddy, and the two men were cut from the same cloth, both Lebanon-born sons of Protestant missionaries and educators, Princeton graduates, and former marines. Hoskins's plan for Expedition 90 was premised on the assumption that, thanks to its past reputation for disinterested benevolence in the Arab world, the United States was in a far better position than its European allies to compete with the Axis powers for Middle Eastern hearts and minds. As a State Department telegram to the American ambassador in London explained, Hoskins envisioned that the expedition's headquarters in Beirut, supported by subsidiary stations throughout the Middle East, would orchestrate a massive campaign "of political warfare and of propaganda" specifically appealing to the unique history "of American missionary, educational, and philanthropic efforts" in the region. The mission would perforce cooperate with other Allied powers, but it was to operate "as an independent American organization and not . . . as a 'front' for the French and British."[8]

Not surprisingly, London did not take to Hoskins's plan. "It was, perhaps, an odd document to be shown to an Englishman," remarked the laconic Sweet-Escott. "Its main burden was that the British had done nothing for the Middle East and were, therefore, completely discredited throughout the Arab world." British apprehensions increased further when it was reported that the State Department was encouraging Hoskins to travel throughout the whole region and report back to Washington on political as well as intelligence matters. Interestingly, it was Kim Roosevelt's admirer, Sumner Welles, who was reputed to be behind these moves; Hoskins's Expedition 90 team included Welles's son Benjamin, Kim's Harvard classmate. Eventually, a combination of British foot-dragging and interdepartmental disagreements on the American side led to the quiet abandonment of the Lebanon station idea. Nevertheless, the irrepressible Hoskins still went on his tour in November 1942, provoking so many complaints that eventually Bill Donovan had to rein him in.[9]

The British were less successful at halting the American plans for an OSS station in Cairo. These culminated in May 1943 with the arrival in Egypt of Stephen B. L. Penrose Jr. Although not of Middle East missionary stock himself, Penrose was the next best thing: the son of the president of Whitman College, a small college founded in Washington state by New England missionaries. After spells of teaching at the American University of Beirut (where he would later return as president) and helping direct the Near East College Association in New York, Penrose had joined the coordinator of information's office in April 1942. He set off for Egypt the following year with "instructions to establish intelligence-gathering services in the Middle East."[10]

The task facing Penrose, a hard-driving worker with a wry sense of humor, was a daunting one. The Axis forces in North Africa had finally just surrendered, and the British were now able to focus on protecting their colonial regime from other threats. Although Anglo-American relations were often good on a personal level, the British Centre Cairo jealously guarded its agent networks and other local intelligence assets. "They were so sophisticated that they worked a great deal through the coffee shops and all sorts of things like this which were quite beyond us with our small staff," recalled Jane Smiley Hart, a Dartmouth graduate recruited by OSS/Cairo in June 1944 as a desk clerk (and later wife of eminent State Department Arabist Parker T. Hart). Security was another concern for the new station, which operated out of the basement of an ornate villa on Rustum Pasha Street; when given the address, taxi drivers would reputedly respond, "Oh, you want the secret intelligence headquarters!" Unfortunately, while Hart "realized that we were . . . inexperienced and had to be very discreet indeed," other American recruits failed to grasp the need for absolute secrecy. "Sometimes I can understand why the British think we are a bunch of enthusiastic amateurs," observed Stephen Penrose bitterly, after a "cluck" traveling from the United States "never once attempted to cover the fact that he was an OSS man."[11]

There was also the challenging environment of wartime Cairo itself, beginning with the usual inconveniences facing Westerners: "The heat, the dirt, the lack of modern plumbing . . . , the fact that not only the language but the alphabet and numbers are strange," as Kim Roosevelt summarized them. Added to these were the peculiar strains of clandestine war work, what Jane Hart called "the complications, the constant movement, our overall fear." For Hart, the atmosphere of the Egyptian capital had a surreal quality, very like that portrayed by the British novelist Olivia Manning in her semi-autobiographical *Fortunes of War*: "a strange mixture of glamour and long hours of hard work and very little sleep. And a great cloud hanging over our heads all the time, [as] we didn't really know what was going to happen."[12]

For all the problems confronting him, Penrose did have some resources on which to draw. To begin with, he had his own Arabist connections in the missionary and educational worlds. Shortly after arriving in Egypt, Penrose sent for several old colleagues at the American University of Beirut to join him in the command structure of the new OSS station. These included Archie Crawford, who became his chief assistant, and David Dodge, the great-grandson of AUB founder Daniel Bliss. Missionaries, meanwhile, were a potential reservoir of field agents. While still based in Washington, Penrose had leveraged his contacts on several American missionary boards for intelligence purposes, obtaining street maps of Kuwait, for example, and grooming a young evangelist about to depart for Iran to gather "whatever information" he could. He therefore already had a rudimentary espionage network in the field when he arrived to take charge in Cairo. Finally, one other group of private US citizens on the ground had expert local knowledge and unusual freedom of movement around the region. Ironically, it was the British who had pioneered the role of archaeologist-spy: T. E. Lawrence had used excavations at the Syrian site of Carchemish as a cover for surveying the new Berlin-Baghdad railroad before World War I. Now it was the turn of American archaeologists—who during the interwar period had established a presence in the Middle East to rival that of the British—to emulate Lawrence's example. Indiana Jones, it seems, was not a complete invention.[13]

SUCH WAS THE SITUATION THAT greeted Kim Roosevelt when he arrived in Cairo at the beginning of 1944. Thanks to his earlier travels, "dirt and germs were nothing new" for him, he recalled later, and "the Middle East came as no shock." Quite the reverse, in fact: like his father before him, Kim positively enjoyed the sensation of "what was formerly an abstract appreciation," based on "travel literature," gradually acquiring "real meaning." He also made a point of engaging in "frequent contact with local people," an approach that contrasted with "the isolationist views of the average American soldier." The latter attitude he blamed largely on army doctors, whose lectures to troops about the medical risks of fraternizing struck him as excessively alarmist, not to mention offensive to the local population. He was particularly irritated when a boorish medic whom he was accompanying on a US Army goodwill trip to Jeddah (Kim "had other business" in the Saudi Arabian city and was "along for the ride") upset the Arab hosts of a banquet held in the Americans' honor by loudly advising his companions not to touch any of the dishes in front of them. Kim tucked in with extra gusto. "Our prestige is clearly strong enough to survive an occasional descent of this sort," he wrote in his official report on the trip, "but I can see no satisfactory reason why it should be subjected to such a strain." Still, for all the cultural sensitivity Kim Roosevelt displayed in his dealings with Arabs during his 1944 Egyptian mission, there was not quite the same sense of romantic stirring that had accompanied Archie Roosevelt's first posting in the Arab world. Kim "found the land and people stimulating, full of challenging differences, encouraging and discouraging similarities," but he had not fallen in love, at least not yet.[14]

Kim's assignment in Egypt with SOPHIA, the OSS project for placing intelligence officers under cover of James Landis's economic mission, was a kind of covert version of Harold Hoskins's Expedition 90, and as such it involved considerable travel around the entire Middle East. From the point of view of his future career with the CIA, Kim's most significant sortie from Cairo occurred in March 1944, shortly after his Jeddah trip, when he flew to Allied-occupied Iran, ostensibly as a member of an economic team led by Landis. Landing in Tehran, a strategically crucial funnel of Lend-Lease aid to the beleaguered Soviet Union, the first thing Kim noticed was Red Army troops guarding the air field. After a few days of economic diplomacy and sightseeing in the city's bazaars, the "mysteriously undefined" Kim Roosevelt (as he himself put it) met secretly with a local OSS field agent, Joseph M. Upton, for a briefing on the US intelligence effort in the country as a whole.[15]

Upton was a Harvard-educated expert on Persian antiquities, and he was apparently in Tehran overseeing archaeological excavations by New York's Metropolitan Museum of Art. As such, his OSS cover was typical for the country. T. Cuyler Young, another operative based in Tehran, specialized in Persian language and history at Princeton University, eventually chairing that institution's Oriental Studies Department. A third OSS agent, Donald Wilber, had majored in art and archaeology at Princeton before embarking on a scholarly career in which he won note as an authority on Persian architecture. Wilber monitored German and, increasingly, Soviet activities in Iran while researching books on Islamic monuments of the Mongol period and Persian gardens. During one expedition to spy on Red Army troop movements in Azerbaijan, he visited a village reputed to contain the tomb of a Mongol ruler and stumbled on a particularly fine Seljuk dome chamber. His excitement at the discovery was tinged by fears that the village was also home to a nest of German agents.[16]

After further meetings with another OSS agent ("Roger Black," likely a pseudonym for T. Cuyler Young), and a side trip to Iran's beautiful old capital, Isfahan, Kim Roosevelt flew back to Cairo, where he was soon joined by a familiar face, that of his cousin Archie Roosevelt. Archie's return to the field after his expulsion from French North Africa had not been easy. He was still "owned" by military intelligence, G2, and, although the army blocked a request by the OSS research and analysis division for his services, it otherwise seemed unsure what to do with him, sending him back to military training camp, where, between comically inept drills, he studied Arab history and taught himself Hebrew. During an interview about possible postings in the Middle East, a G2 officer asked Archie whether he was "impartial on Arab questions." His response probably did not help his cause: "I think I am as impartial as possible," he said, "but as an aspiring orientalist I naturally have some sympathy with the Arabs." Eventually, G2 relented, and after further training by area specialists with Middle East experience, Archie was assigned to military intelligence in Cairo, well away from the French. He embarked from Miami in April 1944, shortly after learning from a civilian doctor in New York that he had a "systolic murmur," a heart condition that would have gotten him discharged if discovered in an army medical exam. He did not tell his superiors.[17]

In Cairo, Archie found himself under the supervision of another Middle East–raised American, Major Edwin M. Wright, "a former missionary and later an archaeologist in Southeast Turkey, Iraq, and Iran," as Archie described him. He also had the opportunity to reacquaint himself with his old North African travel companion Hooker Doolittle and with the Tunisian nationalist Slim Driga, now a fugitive from French justice, who introduced him to another exile, the famous Rif tribal leader and rebel 'Abd al-Krim. Most consequential of his meetings in Cairo, though, was Archie's reunion with his cousin Kim. "I have really grown very fond of him," Archie wrote his wife, KW, in June. "In spite of a certain small weakness I mentioned," he continued, with tantalizing vagueness, "[Kim] is a great solace and one of the few people I have confidence in 100%. . . . He does not, I think, go off the deep end, make stupid blunders, . . . , etc. as do so many people in this difficult atmosphere, and he is one of the infinitesimally small number of people I take with me in some of the more delicate interviews, without qualms." A glowing tribute (excepting the mysterious qualification), this statement nonetheless implies that, at this stage in their professional relationship, Archie saw himself as the senior partner.[18]

Archie's field of responsibility for military intelligence was the Levant states and Palestine, and he therefore was in Cairo itself only rarely, spending most of his time traveling around the eastern Mediterranean. As was his wont, Kim came along for the ride. Early one May morning, the Roosevelts left Cairo, drove through the Sinai desert, and arrived in Jerusalem just as the light was fading, unsure whether they felt more like pilgrims or crusaders as they approached the Holy City. Clearly the younger cousin was the one calling the shots. Using his "excellent contacts," Archie (as he wrote in his memoirs) "got into the swing right away," and the cousins "were soon swamped with interviews and invitations." High on their list of people to see were intelligence officers of the pre-Israel Jewish authority, the Jewish Agency, which was conducting its own clandestine war against the Axis powers. These included a tousled-haired "kibbutznik," the future mayor of Jerusalem, Teddy Kollek, who guided them on the next leg of their journey past the shore of the Sea of Galilee, up the Golan Heights, and into Syria. En route, they spent the night at Kollek's kibbutz and attended a banquet at which Jews dined with Arabs. After the "green oasis" of Damascus, it was on to Beirut, where Archie delighted the guests at an OWI party by addressing them in Arabic.

Although Lebanon would later play an extremely important role for Archie in both his professional and his private life, this was a hurried visit. The Roosevelts were soon back in Cairo, Kim no doubt grateful for the brief but instructive glimpse of Levantine life his cousin had provided. Rare photographs of the two men together depict them at various stages of their tour. Archie looks uncharacteristically dapper in his officer's uniform, while Kim is slightly disheveled in dark suit and tie. Otherwise, the cousins are remarkably alike: both of medium height and slight build, with similar, recognizably Rooseveltian features, although Kim's face is slightly ruddier and fleshier, his hair starting to recede.[19]

Although Archie and Kim managed to fit in one more trip to Palestine, during which they were guided into Transjordan by another OSS archaeologist, Rabbi Nelson Glueck, their time together was coming to an end. In June 1944 Archie received orders to make his way to Iraq, where he took up the vacant post of assistant military attaché in Baghdad, a position he held for the remainder of the war. Stephen Penrose's Cairo operation, meanwhile, was shifting its focus away from the Middle East and toward the Balkans, where Bill Donovan was renewing his efforts to establish a US intelligence presence independent of the British. A dashing young southerner by the name of Frank G. Wisner was brought in to run OSS/Cairo's satellite station in Istanbul and begin mounting parachute missions into the Balkan countries and Greece. Nonetheless, OSS suspicions of British imperial intrigues remained, even as the German threat receded and possible problems with the Soviets surfaced. Many Americans were, at this stage, more inclined to support local leftist insurgents than pro-British reactionaries.

Kim Roosevelt was redeployed to Italy, where Allied forces were moving northwards in a campaign of liberation, as an "economic investigator" for Central Europe. Just after Victory in Europe Day, a jeep accident left Kim with a badly broken ankle (an injury that meant he nursed a stiff leg for the rest of his life). Sent home to convalesce, he was put to work compiling the official wartime history of the OSS, a task that was not completed until the summer of 1947. It was only then that he would return to the Middle East. Archie, in the meantime, barely left it.[20]

The overall assessment of the OSS's performance in the Middle East contained in Kim Roosevelt's official history is surprising: the "effort in the theater in general must be considered a waste of time and money," it reads. This seems an unduly harsh verdict on Stephen Penrose's record. As the official history itself goes on to note, by the end of the war, "twenty-nine undercover agents had been placed in the Middle East, and in all but two countries (Afghanistan and Arabia) intelligence coverage was good." Using a variety of covers, these agents in turn built up chains of "over 500 sub-agents" who "helped turn in, by June 1945, more than 5,000 reports." Certainly Penrose faced considerable obstacles, among them British obstructionism, noncooperation from some US foreign service officers who resented the sudden appearance in their midst of these novice spies, and poor or nonexistent communications, which necessitated that agents in Arabia, for example, travel in person to Cairo in order to file their reports. Nonetheless, like Eddy earlier in the war, Penrose traded skillfully on his own local experience. "His knowledge of the area was of inestimable value to OSS in recruiting future representatives who were to operate in countries where strong religious, political and racial differences existed," noted a commendation by the OSS theater commander, John Toulmin, in November 1944. Considering that he was starting completely from scratch, Penrose's efforts "to lay a firm foundation for intelligence work in the Middle East" do not appear quite such a "waste" after all, Kim Roosevelt's critical verdict notwithstanding.[21]

As for Kim himself, his personal approach to the Middle East was deeply affected by his service under Penrose's command in Cairo. While he never went quite so far as his cousin Archie in his wartime identification with the Arabs, he did now have some real, lived experience of the region and its inhabitants, as opposed to the literary, Orientalist notions with which he had grown up. The impressions and relationships Kim formed during his World War II tour of Egypt were to prove crucial when it became his turn to assume the leadership of US Middle Eastern intelligence in the Cold War.

FOUR

Great Game Redux

IT WAS SUMMER 1945, the war was ending, and while Kim Roosevelt was home in the United States recovering from his accident in Italy, cousin Archie was still in Iraq, wondering about his peacetime future. His outstanding student record and natural scholarly bent seemed to mark him out for an academic career, and he had already begun sounding out various East Coast schools about possible positions. Try as he might, though, he could not muster much enthusiasm for the prospect. His experiences in the Arab world, including his current posting as assistant military attaché in Iraq, had awakened in him an appetite for a less cloistered, more active life. Moreover, there were signs that, even as one world war was ending, another was beginning, with the United States and the Soviet Union as the chief protagonists, and neighboring Iran as the new conflict's flashpoint.

It was as he was taking off on a sortie to the Iranian capital of Tehran, his plane rising from the yellow desert floor to the snow-capped peaks of the Zagros mountains, that Archie was struck by a revelation. "How can I go back from this to a university to study dead languages and old civilizations?" he asked himself. "I am a part of something new, something exciting." Although he did not realize it at the time, it was a pivotal moment in Archie's life. His decision to stay on in the Middle East after World War II launched him on "the process of becoming a committed intelligence officer," confirmed his new identity as an Arabist, and made him a firsthand witness to and participant in many of the key events of the Cold War, beginning with the Iran Crisis of 1946.[1]

WHAT WAS IT, EXACTLY, THAT had prompted Archie's momentous decision? One factor, clearly, was the fascination with the Arab world that he had developed in French North Africa and that grew even stronger during his tour of duty in Iraq. His mentor during his previous posting in Cairo, the former missionary and archaeologist Edwin Wright, had warned him not to expect too much of Baghdad, whose modern-day appearance was a notorious source of disappointment for travelers brought up on *The Arabian Nights*. Archie, however, was delighted to be "on the site of the splendor of Old Islam," regarding his assignment to Iraq as his first real step on the "Road to Samarkand," his quest for understanding the Arab and Muslim worlds. It perhaps helped that the Roosevelt family name won him easy access to the upper rungs of Baghdad society: he renewed his childhood acquaintance with the Hashemite prince Muhiddin ibn 'Ali al-Haidar and befriended the prince's cousin, the regent 'Abd al-Ilah, then ruling Iraq on behalf of the boy king, Faisal II. In May 1945, he even accompanied the regent to the United States on a state visit that included a side trip to the Roosevelt family seat in Oyster Bay.

But Archie did not just confine himself to the aristocracy of Baghdad; he also devoted a great deal of time to adventurous expeditions among the Arab tribes of Iraq's southern provinces and the rebellious Kurds of the country's mountainous northeast, a region he found instantly beguiling. His official reports on these trips, replete with minute ethnographic detail about Iraqi tribal life, soon earned him a reputation as an American authority on the subject, something from which he evidently derived great personal satisfaction. Looking back at his eighteen-month assignment in Baghdad many years on, Archie reckoned it one of the happiest times of his life.[2]

Another factor that contributed to Archie Roosevelt's enjoyment of Iraq—and his desire to become an intelligence officer—was less predictable, given his dislike of French colonialism in North Africa: the British imperial presence in the country. To a certain extent, Archie could not avoid dealing with the British. Although Iraq was nominally independent, the British mandate there having ended in 1932, its location astride land routes to India and its massive oil reserves meant that London continued to exercise a barely hidden hand in its affairs. Growing nationalist sentiment had erupted in a pro-Axis coup in 1941, which saw the regent briefly banished to Transjordan, but the British succeeded in quelling the insurgency and afterward only tightened their grip further. By the time Archie arrived in Baghdad, both court and cabinet were firmly under the sway of the British embassy, although the veteran prime minister, Nuri al-Sa'id (another of Archie's Iraqi friends), did manage to collaborate with the British on terms somewhat of his own making. In the tribal areas British political advisers wielded the power of, in Archie's phrase, "kinglets." To conduct any sort of intelligence business in Iraq, therefore, Archie Roosevelt had little choice but to cooperate with his British counterparts.[3]

Yet there was more to the young American's relations with British officials in Iraq than bureaucratic necessity. Like his uncle Kermit during World War I, Archie Roosevelt appears to have felt a strong attraction to the Arabist officers and advisers who manned Britain's imperial regime—its "Covert Empire"—in the Middle East. The day before he set off on his journey from the United States to Cairo in April 1944, he dined in Washington with Freya Stark, the famous Arabian explorer (and friend of the poet James Elroy Flecker, of "Golden Road to Samarkand" fame) now engaged in wartime British propaganda efforts in the Arab world, and the two "took to each other beautifully." Immediately after arriving in Baghdad, Archie visited the mud-brick headquarters of the British Counter Intelligence Centre, Iraq, where its staff of young RAF officers greeted him warmly. "The barrier of our different nationalities melted away," he recalled later, and "we formed these easy friendships of wartime."[4]

These friendly feelings, so different from Archie's frosty encounters with French colonial officials earlier in the war, sprang from several sources. In part, Archie was channeling the traditional attitudes of American visitors to the Middle East, especially the missionary and educator settlers of the Levant, who had tended to get on much better with British officials there than with the French. An additional factor was Archie's own upbringing and education. "My New England background had conditioned me to be an Anglophile," he confessed in his memoirs. "Philosophically, I found the [British] congenial; we were the same kind of people." Finally, as a budding Arabist himself, Archie was drawn to the British reputation for cultural immersion in the Arab world. Unlike the French, who "for the most part considered 'their' Arabs inferiors," the "Englishman . . . is broader minded, and seeks to find out what is right and true," wrote Archie in one of his attaché reports. This rather gushing judgment was probably colored by the air of Kipling-esque romance that surrounded many of the British Arabists in Iraq. Francis Grimley, for example, a political officer "with a merry, open face under fair hair" who guided Archie along the Lower Tigris, habitually wore Arab clothes, a sartorial choice that "won him the disapproval of some of the old colonial hands" but that the young American happily imitated during their expeditions together. And along with the hovering presence of Lawrence of Arabia, Kipling's India itself was not far from wartime Iraq: the British forces stationed there included a large number of Indian regiments, while its political officer system basically reproduced that of the Raj.[5]

In sum, for all his distaste for European colonialism and his desire that Americans should invent a new kind of Western relationship with the Middle East, Archie Roosevelt's ambition of becoming an intelligence officer, indeed his very conception of that role, was heavily influenced by the British imperial experience. "When I speak of an intelligence officer," he wrote later, "it is in the old-fashioned sense, perhaps best exemplified . . . by Kipling's British political officers in India." Even the fact that the revelation about his future had come to him while overflying Iran was telling: RAF aerial surveillance had been a crucial technique for enforcing the British mandate, so this was very much an imperial perspective from which to survey the Middle East.[6]

That said, Archie's decision to stay on in the region after the war was impelled above all by a consideration not mentioned so far: his hatred of communism. Often Cold War American anticommunism is characterized as a product of mindless conformism, a shapeless fear of the McCarthy era. What this picture omits is the deliberate ideological conviction with which many Americans had opposed the ideas and tactics of the communist movement long before Senator McCarthy appeared on the scene in 1950. Archie Roosevelt is a good example. The roots of his anticommunism can be dated to his school days, when he came across the *Daily Worker* in the Groton library "and found its message of class hatred a calumny on the ideals of America." A few years later, shortly after graduating from Harvard, Archie learned that communists were secretly involved in running the American Youth Congress (AYC), a national youth group prominently supported by his cousin, First Lady Eleanor Roosevelt. Although not a political activist by nature, in January 1940 Archie traveled with two friends to Washington to attend an AYC meeting and protest what he perceived as the organization's hidden communist agenda. In a piece published soon afterward in the *New York Herald Tribune*, Archie attacked those who "pretend to be defenders of democracy at home" while serving as "minions of tyranny abroad." He also criticized Eleanor Roosevelt for lending "her prestige and her eloquence" to the AYC's cause, echoing the common anticommunist complaint that "innocent liberals" were the unwitting dupes of the Soviet Union (while at the same time conjuring the ongoing family rivalry between the Oyster Bay and the Hyde Park Roosevelts).[7]

Despite the United States' wartime alliance with the Soviet Union, Archie's anticommunism intensified during World War II, especially in its later stages, when he began to perceive signs that Joseph Stalin intended to expand the Soviet empire after the war was over. The possibility appalled him: in his eyes, the Nazis had never really stood a chance of defeating the United States because the appeal of German nationalism was limited by its very nature, but communism was a philosophy that transcended national boundaries. Nowhere was the danger it posed greater than in the Middle East, where, despite British attempts to shore up its empire, the colonial powers were clearly overstretched and the Soviets had spied an opportunity to relaunch the old tsarist push toward, as Archie put it, "domination of the Straits of the Bosphorus and the Dardanelles, and a warm-water port on the Persian Gulf." Unfortunately, the Hyde Park Roosevelt in the White House was "apparently unaware of past Russian empire-building."[8]

Dismayed as he was by FDR's yielding approach, Archie was comforted to realize that some in government shared his more realistic view of Soviet intentions. One such was Edwin Wright, his supervisor in Egypt and a long-time foe of the Soviets; another was the US ambassador in Baghdad, Loy W. Henderson, a career foreign service officer who had previously served with distinction in Moscow and, indeed, was only in Iraq because his implacable anticommunism had made him persona non grata in Washington. Together with other officials such as George Kennan, chargé d'affaires in the Moscow embassy and father of the US Cold War strategy of "containment," these men formed a distinct anticommunist network within the State Department — and exercised a formative intellectual influence on the young Archie Roosevelt. Interestingly, Archie spent a lot of his time in Baghdad socializing with the Soviet representative there, Nikolai Klimov, an undercover officer of the NKVD (the predecessor organization to the KGB). His conversations with the Russian spy, conducted over numerous glasses of vodka, were friendly, even fraternal: Klimov once told Archie that he reminded him of his younger brother, who had died fighting the Nazis. Still, the American's hostility to communism was in no way softened by these encounters; Klimov, evidently a sensitive man underneath his pallid exterior, struck Archie as a pathetic victim of an inhumane system. Such perceptions were common currency among anticommunists in the US foreign service at the time. George Kennan, for example, hated the Soviet state yet loved the Russian people. Archie also shared with Kennan a profound admiration for high Russian culture, reading Dostoevsky and Pushkin for pleasure (in the original, of course, not in translation). Even before the end of World War II, then, Archie Roosevelt was looking at the world through a Cold War lens.[9]

Archie returned home a few months after the Japanese surrender, in December 1945, joining his wife, KW, and their son, Tweed, now a boisterous four-year-old, for a family Christmas in New Hampshire. It was not a festive occasion. After the desert sun, Archie found his snowy New England surroundings depressing, and he and his wife were soon arguing about their future together. Having expected that Archie would pursue a university career in the United States, KW was dismayed to learn that he had turned down a number of academic offers (including a personal invitation from the eminent Arab American scholar Philip Hitti to join him at Princeton) and was considering a return to the Middle East. She much preferred the contemplative to the active life, and she urged Archie to follow in the footsteps of her personal hero, the poet T. S. Eliot, not some crass power politician like Loy Henderson. "I don't think your comparison . . . is fair," Archie responded. "Eliot . . . can do nothing about Russia and . . . the coming crisis except to whistle in the dark." Biding his time (and turning down another job offer, this time of a State Department desk directly under Henderson), Archie waited for an assignment that would put him as close as possible to the coming battle with communism. In January 1946 he got it, thanks in part to the intercession of Ed Wright: another posting as assistant military attaché, this time in Iran, the scene of his revelation the previous year. He arrived in Tehran in March, having vaguely agreed with KW that she and Tweed would join him there some time afterward. Archie's marriage, entered into at a young age perhaps as much out of duty as out of love, was beginning to unravel. His mission to Iran was an act of both service to his country and flight from his domestic life.[10]

FOR A CENTURY AND A half before Archie's arrival there, Iran had been a playing field in the Great Game. Its location, adjoining Afghanistan (the classic arena of Anglo-Russian rivalry), British India, and Russia itself, ensured this. So too did its vast oil reserves, "a prize from fairyland beyond our wildest dreams," as Winston Churchill described them in the 1920s. After the Bolshevik Revolution, it was the British who held the upper hand in Persia, the Anglo-Iranian Oil Company reaping fabulous profits from its controlling stake in the country's petroleum industry. During World War II, Britain and the Soviet Union, now allies, marched into Iran and deposed the shah, Reza Shah Pahlavi, ostensibly because he had been courting Nazi Germany but really in order to protect their control of the country's oil fields and open a corridor for moving Lend-Lease supplies to the USSR (the operation witnessed by Kim Roosevelt when he visited Tehran in 1944). Ordinary Iranians, heirs to a millennia-old civilization that had nurtured some of the greatest leaders, thinkers, and poets in human history, felt a deep sense of national humiliation and dreamed of a future free from foreign depredations on their soil.[11]

As in the Arab world, Americans were initially seen as potential allies in Iran's struggle against Western imperialism. The United States' origins lay in a war of national liberation from British colonial rule, and individual Americans, such as the Presbyterian missionary Howard Baskerville, had defended Iran's own Constitutional Revolution of 1906–1911 against Russian-backed royalist forces. The early twentieth century had also seen several American economic missions visit the country, a practice repeated during World War II. (It was one such mission that provided Kim Roosevelt with cover during his 1944 visit.) Members of the Roosevelt administration even talked about the Allied occupation as a model of the principles enshrined in the Atlantic Charter, including the self-determination and territorial integrity of small nations. Small wonder, then, that there was friction between British and American representatives in wartime Tehran, rather like that witnessed in Cairo after the arrival of the OSS.[12]

By 1945, however, irritation with the British was giving way to alarm about the Soviets. Like its neighbor Iraq, Iran was troubled by secessionist movements in its outlying provinces, and the Soviets appeared to be trying to harness these centrifugal forces for their own expansionist purposes. In the fall, nationalists in the northern province of Azerbaijan, still under Soviet occupation, established a new communist government backed by Moscow. Meanwhile, Kurds in the mountains between Azerbaijan and Iraq began taking similar steps toward establishing their own independent nation-state. Were these developments portents of a Soviet annexation of Iran?

In hindsight, it seems clear that Stalin's postwar ambitions in Iran were in fact limited to protecting the Soviet Union's vulnerable southern borders and, possibly, obtaining an oil concession in the north of the country like that enjoyed by the British in the Abadan oil field to the south. Indeed, Moscow was quite prepared to rein in Azeri and Kurdish nationalists if they threatened to get carried away in their revolutionary zeal. In late 1945, however, observers in Washington, a city grown noticeably less friendly toward the Soviet Union since the death of FDR earlier in the year, were less inclined to give the benefit of any doubt to the Russians. "The Soviet Union seems to be determined to break down the structure which Great Britain has maintained so that Russian power and influence can sweep . . . across Iran and through the Persian Gulf into the Indian Ocean," observed Loy Henderson, now back in the State Department running its Near East and Africa division, in December. This analysis appeared to be confirmed in the first week of March 1946, when the date for the withdrawal of Allied forces from Iran passed without the Red Army leaving. Two weeks earlier, the State Department had received George Kennan's "Long Telegram," with its foundational Cold War assessment of the sources of Soviet conduct. On March 5, Winston Churchill, in the course of his "Iron Curtain" speech in Fulton, Missouri, had referred specifically to Russian designs on Persia. Against this background, the nonevacuation of the Soviet troops seemed to fulfill the worst predictions of the State Department's anticommunists. From having been a theater of the Great Game, Iran was fast becoming the battlefield for the first US-Soviet confrontation in the Cold War.[13]

"It was just after this dangerous week," recalled Archie Roosevelt later, "that my bold British pilot landed me through close, thick cloud cover in the caldron of Tehran." Archie had been able to observe the breakaway movements in northwestern Iran during the final days of his previous posting in Iraq, and his assessment of the situation there was every bit as dire as the prognostications of the State Department's Middle East hands. "The Russians appeared to be on the verge of realizing a centuries-old dream, the conquest of Iran," he wrote later. "I believed that I could somehow be a part of an effort to block them." Plunging into the fray, Archie immediately caught a ride north to observe Soviet troop movements for himself, flying in the same US military plane that had borne him to Tehran on his revelatory trip of the previous year. Piloted by air attaché Carl Garver, a flying ace of rugged character and appearance, the plane dipped to three hundred feet, and Archie "saw the white faces of Soviet soldiers looking up at us beside some twenty tanks."[14]

In the event, the evacuation crisis ended as quickly as it had arisen, with the Soviet leadership agreeing to withdraw a few weeks later. However, Iran was not out of danger yet. Azerbaijan remained under the rule of the communist-controlled government in the city of Tabriz, and Kurdish nationalists had established a similar entity in Mahabad. Meanwhile, in Tehran itself, the Iranian Communist Party, or Tudeh, was working to undermine the government of Reza Shah's successor, his son Mohammed Reza Pahlavi, "a weak, washed-out-looking young man" (in Archie's description) who seemed ill-equipped to withstand the terrible pressures on his country. It did not help that the new shah's prime minister was the (again, according to Archie) "devious" Ahmad Qavam al-Saltaneh, an old nationalist who was ready to appease the Soviets if it suited his personal interests, or that Qavam was in turn being advised by his even more slippery éminence grise, the "sinister" Mozaffar Firuz, whose main aim in life seemed to be to deliver Iran up to the Kremlin.[15]

Or such, anyway, was Archie Roosevelt's assessment of the situation. Historians writing today with access to records available only since the end of the Cold War tend to favor a more nuanced interpretation, with Iranian communists pursuing a somewhat different agenda from Moscow's, and Prime Minister Qavam attempting to steer a middle course between left and right, Tudeh and shah, designed to preserve Iran's independence and integrity. Little of this complexity, though, was evident at the time to Archie Roosevelt, who saw only an existential threat to Iran and, therefore, the West itself. His thoughts about US policy toward the Middle East were changing accordingly. A few years earlier, he had envisioned an American approach that was fundamentally different from the imperial European past. Now the threat of communist expansionism was such that Americans had no option but to throw in their lot with, if not France, then at least with Britain, whether that meant backing the British position in the region or having (as Archie put it) "to some extent [to] replace the power of a fading British Empire." Either scenario meant Archie compromising his earlier vision of a new kind of Western policy based on Americans' unique history of noncolonial engagement with the Arab and Muslim worlds.[16]

Archie's behavior changed as well. Whereas in Africa he had spent as much time as possible with local inhabitants, among them many future Arab nationalist leaders, during his tour of Iran he seemed instead to prefer the company of his American colleagues, who emerge from the pages of his autobiography as a small band of ideological brothers-in-arms. And while the tone of charming self-deprecation present throughout his memoirs is still detectable in these passages, a new note of masculine bravado, even swagger, has appeared. In one passage, for example, Archie describes a trip to Tabriz in the company of the US consul Robert Rossow, "one of a handful of men whose efforts halted Soviet expansion." With Carl Garver at the controls, the plane swooped down and buzzed some Azeri troops standing by their trenches. Detained briefly at the airport by a hostile group of officials, the Americans obtained their release when Rossow implied that Archie was a son of FDR. The party then proceeded to a Tabriz restaurant in the company of some British comrades and swigged champagne while an orchestra regaled them with wartime Western ditties. After this adventure, Archie was elected a member of Rossow's Azerbaijan Club. As he explained in his memoirs, admission was based on a points system. "There were points for days spent in Azerbaijan, hours under arrest, being targets of gunfire. Twenty points were required for membership, which could be attained at one stroke if you were killed trying out for it."[17]

It was as if Archie were now joining in the Great Game, both philosophically and emotionally. Some of the reasons for his doing so are obvious—his Anglophilia, his anticommunism, his Rooseveltian urge to be the first into this new world war—but another factor was also at work. Archie simply never developed the same love for Iranians as he had for Arabs. Indeed, in his memoirs, they suffer badly from the comparison. Whereas Arabs had a "democratic tradition," exemplified by the "majlis, the tribal deliberative body," Iranians had always been "dominated by an all-powerful khan" or "autocratic shah," and so had never known "anything like democracy." Worse than that, Iran was, Archie believed, the source of all things "slavish" and "oriental" in the Middle East: eunuchs, women's veils, self-abasement before the ruler—"all the despotic splendor of the East." The lesson for the present day was unpleasant but unavoidable. While the Arab world had potential for democratization, it was only "idealists who hoped for true democratic government in Iran."[18]

These sentences, which ignored such evidence of democratic aspiration in Iran's history as the Constitutional Revolution of 1906–1911, were written in the 1980s, not long after the 1979 Iranian Revolution had brought about the overthrow of the shah in favor of the Ayatollah Ruhollah Khomeini and the taking of fifty-two US embassy workers in a hostage crisis that lasted over a year. Archie Roosevelt's personal shock and anger at the events of 1979 are palpable in his memoirs—"How could we permit ourselves to become the victims of these fanatics, and undergo the humiliation of the seizure of our embassy and the ordeal of the hostages?" he asked—and it seems likely that his account of Iranian history was colored by these emotions. His reaction to Iran after his very first visit there, in January 1945, was far more positive, reminiscent of some of his observations of North Africa. Tehran was "a wonderful place, . . . a modern city with broad avenues" surrounded by "a beautiful range of mountains." A year later, however, with the Cold War brewing, Archie's impressions on returning to the country for his attaché posting, as recorded in his personal diary, were much less favorable, more in keeping with the mood of his autobiography. On closer inspection, the city's modernity proved to be superficial. The streets had developed a Russian appearance; the food was bad and the hotels crummy; even the shah's palace was disappointing, with many of the jewels on the legendary Peacock Throne either made of paste or missing altogether. Such signs of decrepitude, a source of charm for Archie in Baghdad, now just repelled him. Most significantly, in his eyes the Iranians lacked the personally attractive qualities he had discerned in the Arabs of North Africa. Some even had traits usually ascribed them by European Orientalists. Prime Minister Qavam's dastardly adviser Firuz, for example, was literally dehumanized in Archie's description: he had the "face of a fox [and the] movements of a snake." A combination of Cold War crisis and classic Orientalism had, it seemed, disposed Archie Roosevelt to see Iranians less as historical actors in their own right—worthy of American support in their struggles against domestic tyranny and foreign intervention—than as pawns in a new, Soviet-American iteration of the Great Game.[19]

Archie's assignment to Iran ended in February 1947. By then, the separatist governments in Tabriz and Mahabad had collapsed, as the shah's army retook the north of the country (in Azerbaijan, Iranian forces were preceded by two gung-ho US pressmen, Joseph C. Goodwin and Clifton Daniel, driving Archie's staff car). Moscow watched impassively as the Azeri and Kurdish nationalist movements were brutally suppressed. Meanwhile, American pressure on Prime Minister Qavam induced him to get rid of Firuz and purge the communist members of his cabinet. In December 1947, Qavam himself was dismissed by the shah, his fate prefiguring that of Mohammed Mosaddeq a few years later. Hence, by 1947, the United States was already moving toward support for the repressive rule of the shah and away from the idealistic principles it had earlier sought to uphold in Iran.

Although Archie returned to the United States feeling his duty was done, he was not without his regrets. Shortly before he left Iran, in January 1947, he learned that Mohammed Qazi, a well-educated Muslim judge who had helped set up the Kurdish republic government in Mahabad, was about to be executed, along with his brother. Rushing to the embassy, Archie begged the new US ambassador, George V. Allen, to intercede with the shah on the Qazis' behalf, explaining that (as Allen recalled later) they were Kurdish nationalists who had collaborated with the Soviets "only because Moscow alone had shown interest in supporting the Kurds." After teasing Archie that he was interested in the Qazis' fate mainly because he feared the extinction of Kurdish, one of his several languages, Allen agreed to raise the matter with the shah. When he began to do so during an audience at the palace later that day, however, the shah headed him off. "Are you afraid I'm going to have them shot?" he asked Allen. "If so, you can rest your mind. I am not." Allen expressed his relief and left, only to read in the following day's newspapers that the Qazis had just been executed, on the shah's orders. Archie, whose account of the incident rounds off the section of his memoirs on his time in Iran, bitterly concluded that the command must have been given "as soon as our ambassador had closed the door behind him." The original, handwritten draft of this passage, included among Archie's papers at the Library of Congress, contains a closing comment about the shah that did not find its way into the published version. "I never was one of his admirers," it reads. "Even so, neither he nor Iran deserved their miserable fate."[20]

FIVE

Zion

HAVING SEEN FOR HIMSELF THE first post–World War II Soviet-American confrontation in Iran, Archie Roosevelt arrived back in Washington just in time to witness the US government officially declaring Cold War. In March 1947, prompted by the news that an impoverished Britain could no longer afford to prop up teetering noncommunist governments in Greece and Turkey, President Harry S. Truman told Congress that the United States would henceforth provide aid to any countries threatened by communist takeover. A few months after the announcement of the Truman Doctrine, the new secretary of state, George C. Marshall, used a June commencement ceremony at Harvard as the occasion to outline what soon became known as the Marshall Plan, a multibillion-dollar aid package designed to shore up the war-devastated economies of Europe against communism. The anticommunist consensus that previously had been confined to an inner circle of senior foreign policy officials had now spread to the whole government.

This is not to say that the atmosphere in Washington was one of complete unanimity. Two controversies in particular roiled the nation's political establishment. One of these concerned the future of foreign intelligence in America. In the last days of World War II, OSS chief Bill

Donovan had begun lobbying the White House for the creation of a permanent civilian intelligence agency to help the United States cope with its greatly expanded role in world affairs. The internationalist-minded FDR was sympathetic, but he was also aware that many Americans would not care for the suggestion, smacking as it did of big government and Old World political intrigue, and so he avoided giving Donovan a clear response. Undeterred, Wild Bill pursued the proposal with Harry Truman, only to find the new president definitely opposed to it on the grounds that he wanted no hand in "building up a gestapo." The OSS was terminated on October 1, 1945, with its research and analysis branch hived off to the State Department, and most of its other divisions going to the military. Peacetime America, it seemed, would be no place for spies.[1]

But the matter did not rest there. Confronted by the threatening postwar environment, President Truman decided that he did need some sort of intelligence service after all, and in January 1946 he created the interim Central Intelligence Group (CIG). Meanwhile, Donovan carried on his campaign with the support of other former OSS-ers such as Allen W. Dulles, his wartime European deputy, now practicing corporate law on Wall Street. The Princeton-educated son of a Presbyterian minister and grandson of a secretary of state, Dulles was a card-carrying member of the Republican foreign policy establishment. Family friends included the Oyster Bay Roosevelts; indeed, Dulles's children had attended a small school run by Archie Roosevelt's parents, so he had known Archie and Kim since their childhoods. Although Dulles and his allies couched their pleas for the creation of a peacetime secret service in the language of political and bureaucratic necessity, what was most striking about their presentations was their appeal to the ethos of self-sacrificing public service—and aristocratic masculine privilege—fostered at exclusive East Coast institutions like Groton. "To create an effective Central Intelligence Agency, we must have in the key positions men who are prepared to make this a life work," explained Dulles in words that could well have been spoken by Endicott Peabody. "The Agency should be directed by a relatively small but elite corps of men [who] . . . must find their reward primarily in the work itself, and in the service they render their government, rather than in public acclaim."[2]

Donovan and Dulles's campaign, which received a valuable assist from the OSS Arabist Bill Eddy in his postwar role as head of intelligence in the State Department, encountered a good deal of resistance, both from those who objected to the proposed agency on principle as un-American and from institutional rivals such as J. Edgar Hoover's Federal Bureau of Investigation. Nonetheless, by July 1947 the atmosphere of international crisis was such that Congress was ready to swallow its qualms about executive tyranny and approve the National Security Act, at a stroke transforming the CIG into a centralized, independent secret service, the Central Intelligence Agency (CIA), and creating much of the rest of the modern US national security state besides. The intelligence reformers had failed to remove the new agency entirely from military control: the post of director of central intelligence would be occupied by a succession of admirals and generals until 1953, when Allen Dulles, always the reformers' preferred candidate for the job, eventually took over. In almost every other respect, however, they had prevailed.

The other controversy disturbing Washington at the time of Archie's return there in 1947 proved less susceptible to a quick resolution. More emotion-laden than the debate about foreign intelligence, it also had a much older and more complicated history.

TRADITIONALLY, AMERICAN OFFICIALS HAD TRIED to ignore the growing conflict between the Arab inhabitants of Palestine and the Jewish immigrants drawn to the country by the Zionist dream of a national homeland. The British were in charge there, as per the terms of their 1922 League of Nations mandate, so it was their problem to solve. By the time of World War II, though, this hands-off approach was no longer feasible. A second Arab Revolt, this time directed at British rather than Ottoman rule, had begun in 1936, leading to a series of violent clashes between Palestinians and Jewish settlers. Meanwhile, support for the Zionist project was growing within the United States among Jewish Americans who saw a new state in Palestine as a possible refuge for European Jews trying to flee Nazi persecution and among Christians who believed that Jewish restoration to the Holy Land was a fulfillment of biblical prophecy. The Zionist movement, its leadership increasingly radicalized by developments in Palestine and in Europe, was quick to act on this mood of public sympathy, taking out newspaper advertisements and lobbying Congress, many of whose members became active supporters. True to form, FDR lent a friendly ear to Zionist leaders while avoiding making any definite commitments, but even he was beginning to find it hard not to take a position on the issue.

One reason for FDR's reluctance to commit himself to the Zionist movement was the advice that the White House was receiving from the Middle East area specialists in the State Department who, almost to a man, advised against American support for a Jewish state. The phenomenon of anti-Zionism in the US foreign service was, and continues to be, deeply controversial. For example, Loy Henderson, the arch anticommunist who took over the State Department's Near East division after the war, was denounced vehemently at the time for his widely reported opposition to Zionism—one congressman from a heavily Jewish area of New York City, Emanuel Celler, called him a "striped-trousered underling saboteur"—and has often been accused since of having been motivated by anti-Semitism.[3]

In Henderson's case, this last charge is probably unfair, at least in the sense that his ruling emotion when running the Near East bureau was the same as it had been during his earlier postings as a "Sovietologist" in Eastern Europe and the Soviet Union: his hatred of communism. American support for the creation of a Zionist state in Palestine would, he feared, open up the Middle East to Soviet influence by turning its majority Arab population against the United States. The fact that many Zionist leaders came from socialist backgrounds also rankled with him, sowing the suspicion that a Jewish nation would naturally gravitate toward Moscow rather than Washington. For Loy Henderson, then, the debate about American support for Jewish statehood came down mainly to a question of Cold War strategy.[4]

That said, cultural and social factors did undoubtedly play some role in the US foreign service's lack of sympathy for Zionism. Like most elite American institutions prior to World War II, the State Department and its Near East office had a WASP-ish, clubby atmosphere that was not especially friendly to Jews, and during the war itself, foreign service careerists by and large failed to appreciate the transformative impact that the Holocaust had on Jewish attitudes toward the question of a national homeland. If not actually anti-Semitic, they were at least guilty of a serious failure of imagination. There was also an unmistakable hint of patrician hauteur about these mandarins' response to the democratic pressures on government that the Zionist movement was mobilizing. US foreign policy should be left to trained civil servants such as themselves, they believed, not to the whims of public opinion.

Whatever its origins, the anti-Zionism of the "overt" Cold War foreign policy establishment is well known. Less widely appreciated is the opposition to Jewish statehood of the individuals responsible for setting up the United States' *covert* apparatus in the Middle East, first Bill Donovan's OSS, and then the CIA—men like Kim Roosevelt's boss in Cairo, Stephen Penrose. Documents among Penrose's personal papers reveal him engaged in a variety of anti-Zionist activities at the same time that he was commencing his official duties with the OSS. In 1942, the militant Zionist Peter Bergson organized a campaign to raise US support for a "Jewish army" to fight in Europe alongside Allied forces. Penrose suspected that Bergson's proposal was a ruse to prepare the ground for Jewish statehood after the war, when the putative army would also probably be used to crush Arab resistance to Zionism. After Bergson had purchased a two-page advertisement for his campaign in the *New York Times* featuring a petition signed by an impressive list of prominent American citizens, Penrose wrote eight of the signatories who hailed from his home state of Washington, urging them to withdraw their support. All but one obliged.

Early the following year, when he learned that Rabbi James G. Heller, the Zionist president of the Central Conference of American Rabbis, was also advocating the army idea, Penrose stepped up his counteroffensive, obtaining letters from signatories of Bergson's petition stating their newfound opposition to the proposal, lobbying congressmen he thought might be receptive to his anti-Zionist message, and even contacting the State Department to discuss Rabbi Heller's plans to travel to Palestine, presumably with a view to placing some bureaucratic obstacles in his path. Although he was at pains to make it clear that he was acting in a private rather than an official capacity, Penrose also let it be known that his views were shared by his OSS colleagues. "Some pretty potent stuff is brewing in opposition to the Zionist," he told an anti-Zionist friend. "Although I am one of the chief cooks, I shall not appear in the dining room."[5]

There was an emotional edge to Penrose's statements about Zionism that raises the question of whether some deep-seated prejudice might have been at play. However, none of his papers contain any definite evidence of anti-Semitism, while other records point toward his having cooperated extensively with the pre-Israel Jewish authority, the Jewish Agency, when he was in Cairo. (The Agency, incidentally, shared some of Penrose's objections to Peter Bergson's activities in the United States.) Like the Sovietologist Henderson, Penrose's anti-Zionism was probably motivated first and foremost by a prior, overriding intellectual and emotional commitment. As a former American University of Beirut instructor of missionary and educator descent, Penrose was deeply concerned about the welfare of Palestinian Arabs and the tradition of American-Arab friendship that had developed since the nineteenth century, both causes that he feared might be harmed by US support for a Jewish state in Palestine. (Like other Arabists, Penrose also feared, apparently sincerely, for the future of the Jewish settlers themselves, believing that they would eventually be wiped out by their numerically superior Arab neighbors.) Doubtless, Penrose's anti-Zionism was reinforced by the fact that, like his area counterparts in the State Department, he moved mostly in circles in which there were few if any Jews. Still, there is no reason to disbelieve the claim he made explicitly to fellow anti-Zionists that his opposition to Jewish statehood in Palestine was driven by concerns about its likely consequences for Arab Palestinians and US-Arab relations rather than by a dislike of Zionism per se.[6]

In addition to pointing out the possible strategic and humanitarian costs of Jewish statehood, anti-Zionists in the State Department and the OSS appealed straight to the bottom line. The Saudi Arabian oil industry, which US companies had first broken into in 1933 with the help of the renegade British Arabist Jack Philby, had by the time of World War II assumed massive importance in the minds of not just American oilmen but also Washington's national security planners. The United States still had vast oil reserves of its own, but they were fast being depleted by the war effort, and experts had already forecast that the nation's postwar energy needs would exceed its ability to supply them. With the Axis powers clearly planning military strategy to ensure their access to foreign oil fields, and the British and Russians tightening their grip on Iran, the Roosevelt administration focused its attention on keeping Saudi petroleum—"the greatest single prize in all history," as one State Department analyst described it in 1943—firmly within the American grasp. To achieve this vital goal, it was necessary to maintain the goodwill of the Saudi king, 'Abd al-'Aziz Al Sa'ud, an aged but still fearsome warrior who had created his desert kingdom by killing in battle or driving from the Arabian peninsula all potential rivals to his rule. As the self-proclaimed leader of the Arab world—he was contemptuous of similar claims made by the British-backed Hashemite rulers of Iraq and Transjordan—Ibn Saud was implacably opposed to Zionism and deeply suspicious of American intentions in Palestine.[7]

To deal with this formidable personage, Washington turned to the Arabists, including two of the principal figures involved in the OSS's efforts to build up a US espionage presence in the Arab world: Harold Hoskins, the textile magnate picked to lead Expedition 90 in 1942, and his cousin, Bill Eddy. Hoskins returned from his controversial mission to the Middle East in the spring of 1943 reporting that the "most important and most serious fact" he had discovered on his travels was the danger of a "renewed outbreak of fighting between Arabs and Jews in Palestine before the end of the war." Although FDR did not act on Hoskins's recommendation that the United States declare a moratorium on the Palestine issue until after the war was over—a ploy to slow the momentum the Zionist movement was gaining in America—the president did call on Hoskins's services again in the summer of 1943, this time for a mission to sound out King Ibn Saud about the possibility of his entering into secret peace talks with the moderate Zionist leader Chaim Weizmann. Unfortunately, the plan reminded the Saudi ruler of a similar scheme involving Weizmann and an offer of £20 million in development money brought to him by the meddlesome Jack Philby a few years earlier, a proposal he had rejected angrily as an attempted bribe. Although Hoskins therefore made no progress with regard to Palestine, he otherwise got along very well with Ibn Saud, and the Arabist returned to Washington persuaded of the king's "fundamental honesty and his deep religious sincerity," as he told FDR during a one-and-a-half-hour meeting in the White House. Hoskins also used his audience with the president to restate the anti-Zionist view "that the establishment of a Jewish State in Palestine can only be imposed . . . [and] maintained by force"—in other words, that if the Zionists were to succeed, FDR would have to send American troops into the Middle East.[8]

While Harold Hoskins helped initiate the American alliance with Ibn Saud—scoring points against the Zionists as he did so—it was William Eddy who clinched it. Eddy was assigned to Saudi Arabia after returning from his triumphant tour of North Africa in 1943, first as a roving regional emissary for FDR, then in the impressive-sounding role of envoy extraordinary and minister plenipotentiary, specifically tasked with working his way into Ibn Saud's confidence. He was to prove very effective in this mission, accompanying the king as he progressed around the tribal Arabian hinterland and even sleeping in the royal tent. It helped that the two men's views on such questions as the Palestinian conflict were almost identical. Indeed, it was sometimes difficult to tell whether, in his dispatches to Washington, Eddy was merely reporting Ibn Saud's opinions or advocating them.

Meanwhile, with millions of Lend-Lease dollars starting to flow to Saudi Arabia after FDR declared the country of vital strategic interest to the United States in 1943, the American presence there grew steadily. In the oil town of Dhahran, the recently formed US consortium the Arabian American Oil Company (ARAMCO) built a company compound, American Camp, that reminded visitors of a Californian suburb. The construction of a neighboring American airfield, negotiated by Eddy, soon followed, providing the United States with a vital strategic base in the Persian Gulf. The climax of the courtship came in February 1945, when, returning from the Yalta conference, the ailing FDR hosted a reception for Ibn Saud on board the USS *Quincy*, Eddy acting in the symbolically appropriate role of interpreter. With bedouin tents and Persian rugs strewn on the steel deck of the US cruiser, the meeting had an improbable, even surreal quality, and the president was surprised to find his famous charm failing to sway the king from his hatred of Zionism. In every other regard, however, the conference was wildly successful, cementing the new US-Saudi "special relationship" just as a comparatively chilly encounter between Winston Churchill and Ibn Saud soon afterward captured the fading British influence on the Arabian scene. For Eddy, it was a supremely happy moment, a convergence of the two civilizations he had tried to bridge his entire life, the beginning of a new spiritual alliance between Christianity and Islam that harked back to the one forged centuries earlier during the Crusades by Richard the Lionheart and Saladin.[9]

However, the Arabists' anti-Zionist campaign was about to suffer a disastrous setback. The death of FDR brought to the White House a man who had stronger natural sympathies for Zionism than his predecessor—a legacy, in part, of his Baptist upbringing—and less skill at straddling conflicting political positions. As the full horror of the Holocaust began to sink in with the US public, the Zionism of the American Jewish community increased, especially among its Eastern European grassroots, and along with it the number of Gentile sympathizers. With Arab Americans and their advocates relatively few in number, arithmetic alone indicated that it made good political sense for elected representatives to support Zionist calls for the lifting of British restrictions on Jewish immigration to Palestine and the creation of a Jewish state. "I have to answer to hundreds of thousands who are anxious for the success of Zionism," Truman pointed out. "I do not have hundreds of thousands of Arabs [among] my constituents."[10]

Faced with what they saw as an increasingly disturbing domestic picture, Arabists in the foreign service, Eddy prominent among them, struggled to persuade Truman not to give in to Zionist demands. In addition to repeating Henderson's argument that US support for a Jewish state might drive Arabs into the arms of the Soviet Union, Eddy and the others harped on Ibn Saud's anti-Zionism, warning that Saudi Arabia might cancel ARAMCO's oil concession if the United States took a Zionist position on Palestine. Although prepared to bow to the advice of the foreign policy advisors he had inherited from FDR on other questions, Truman was unimpressed by these representations. Pro-Zionist members of his White House staff were telling him that the House of Saud needed US support just as much as Americans needed Saudi oil, and the sometimes pompous, lecturing approach of the "striped-pants boys" from Foggy Bottom needled the plain-spoken president. As congressional elections loomed in the fall of 1946, Truman chose the eve of Yom Kippur, October 4, to declare his public support for the notion of a Jewish state in Palestine, the first US president ever to do so.[11]

Meanwhile, the situation in Palestine itself was deteriorating rapidly. Terrorist attacks on British targets by Jewish groups hastened London's decision to surrender its authority to the United Nations, with May 1948 named as the date for final British withdrawal. The question of what was to follow the British Mandate could no longer be sidestepped. Zionists advocated what they represented as a compromise solution: the partition of Palestine into Arab and Jewish states, with Jerusalem under international control. Although a UN special committee that reported in September 1947 made a similar recommendation, Arab leaders rejected partition on the grounds that it violated the rights of Palestine's majority Arab population. In the meantime, the British authorities fueled the emotional atmosphere in the United States by turning away boatloads of displaced persons, many of them Holocaust survivors, seeking admission to Palestine. The UN, preparing to vote on the special committee's recommendation for partition in November, was the scene of frantic lobbying by both sides.[12]

It was at this point that the newly created CIA, in one of its earliest intelligence assessments—a seventeen-page paper on "The Consequences of the Partition of Palestine" dated November 28, 1947—made an extraordinary intervention in the debate. Its authorship is not known for sure, but Thomas W. Lippman, biographer of Bill Eddy, strongly suspects the OSS Arabist's hand in it. As Lippman points out, the tone is disconcertingly subjective, with the proposed partition portrayed as nothing less than an unmitigated disaster for all parties concerned. Specific predictions in the document, such as the likelihood that Arab forces would wipe out the new Jewish state within two years, were to prove seriously inaccurate. In other respects, however, the report was eerily prophetic, such as its forecast that partition would lead to prolonged "armed hostilities between Jews and Arabs," serious disturbance of the "stability of the Arab world," and damage to the United States' previously excellent standing in the Middle East. Accurate though it might have been in these predictions, "The Consequences of the Partition of Palestine" failed to change any minds in the Truman White House, or to affect the voting behavior of the UN General Assembly, which on November 29 approved the partition resolution.[13]

At almost exactly the same moment that the OSS had been revived in Cold War form as the CIA, the Arabist spies of World War II had gone down to defeat on Palestine. Their shock and anger were manifest. Eddy resigned from government service in October 1947, citing unhappiness about supposedly inadequate congressional appropriations for the new intelligence apparatus he had helped steer into being. Family members, however, testify that it was in fact despair about the Truman administration's unreceptiveness to the Arabists' viewpoint that drove his resignation. He went to work for ARAMCO in Saudi Arabia, as an "adviser on political relations in the Near East," beating a path to the oil companies that would be followed by many other former intelligence officers (although, as later events would show, he never entirely severed his ties to the CIA). Stephen Penrose, who after the OSS's dissolution had stayed on as an operations chief in the CIG and then in the fall of 1947 moved over to work as special assistant to the hardline anticommunist and anti-Zionist defense secretary James V. Forrestal, also eventually returned to the private sector, in his case taking up the presidency of the American University of Beirut in the summer of 1948, a post he held until his untimely death in 1954. Finally, the independently wealthy Harold

Hoskins, whose last official position had been that of James Landis's replacement running the wartime Middle East Supply Center in Cairo, carried on a Cassandra-like commentary on the government's Palestine policy while at the same time consulting with ARAMCO and serving on the AUB board of trustees. The OSS Arabists' most prominent ally in the State Department, Loy Henderson, was once again punished for crossing the White House by being shunted off to the diplomatic sidings, this time an ambassadorship in India, although he was to reappear in the Middle East at a crucial juncture a few years later.[14]

The Arabists had been taught a harsh lesson in postwar American politics. It did not matter that they were from Ivy League backgrounds, that they knew their field better than anyone else, or even that they held senior government posts. The emotional power of Zionism in Holocaust-era America and the skill of the Zionist movement's leadership in mobilizing the support of ordinary Americans were more than a match for these advantages. If anything, the Arabists' elite position seemed to count against them, as it enabled the Zionists to portray them as aristocratic, conspiratorial, and un-American. Indeed, the very meaning of the word "Arabist" itself shifted in these years, from a neutral term simply referring to an individual with area expertise to a pejorative epithet for someone who identified excessively with Arab culture and, by definition, was anti-Zionist, if not anti-Semitic, to boot. Meanwhile, at the same time that positive images of Zionists in Palestine began circulating in national media—the settlers were depicted variously as repeating the American frontier experience, cultivating a desert, and creating an oasis of democracy in an otherwise benighted region— Arabs were represented increasingly in Orientalist terms, as backward, fanatical, and cruel. One of the aims of Protestant missionaries in the 1800s had been to try to educate their fellow Americans about the many splendid achievements of Arab civilization. Their twentieth-century heirs were, it seemed, failing to tell the Arabs' story in similar terms.[15]

ARCHIE ROOSEVELT WAS KEEPING AN eye on developments in Palestine in the summer and fall of 1947, but they were not the main thing on his mind. Of far more pressing concern was his own personal future. Earlier in the year, immediately after his return from his tour in Iran, it had briefly seemed as if Archie might be quitting the spying game. His burgeoning reputation as a Middle East expert had earned him several different job offers, including a renewed invitation from Loy Henderson to come work with him in the State Department, and KW was hopeful that her husband might yet decide to stay and work in Washington. Just as he was about to take the foreign service oral examination (he had completed the written exams while still in Tehran, achieving the highest ever recorded score of 94 percent), however, Archie received a message via Kim Roosevelt from Michael G. Mitchell, head of the Middle East section of the Central Intelligence Group (the CIA's immediate predecessor), asking him to come for an interview. A few days later came another offer of employment: replacing Daniel C. Dennett Jr., a former AUB instructor and OSS officer who had just died in a plane crash, as chief of the CIG station in Beirut. The Lebanese capital had been the notional location of the OSS's regional headquarters under Harold Hoskins's Expedition 90 plan, and Archie found the prospect of heading such an important post in the new Central Intelligence Agency irresistible. After a summer of "pretty rudimentary" training in spy craft at CIG headquarters, he left for the Middle East on September 10, 1947, "full of foreboding" about the state of his marriage, with KW and his son, Tweed, waving forlornly at the departing plane.[16]

Sitting next to Archie was another young intelligence officer bound for a chief of station posting in the Syrian capital of Damascus, "a brilliant, talented extrovert from Alabama" (as Archie described him) whom Archie had befriended during training. Together, these two young station chiefs would blaze the CIA's trail in the Levant and, along with Kim Roosevelt, form an Arabist triumvirate that would dominate the Agency's first covert operations in the Middle East as a whole.[17]

SIX

The Guest No One
Invites Again

WILLIAM EDDY, HAROLD HOSKINS, AND Stephen Penrose, three Arabists of missionary stock, had pioneered the United States' intelligence effort in the Middle East while at the same time working to promote their deeply held Arabist and anti-Zionist convictions. Overall, considering the strong colonial hold that the British and French still exercised on the region, the OSS Arabists had been unexpectedly successful in their intelligence mission, reflecting their intimate experience and knowledge of the Arab world. Where they had failed—again, to some extent because of their partial detachment from US society and culture—was in converting their fellow Americans to their love of Arab civilization and opposition to a Zionist state in Palestine.

Now, with the passing of the OSS and creation of the CIA, a new generation of younger intelligence officers was appearing on the scene who, although not themselves Middle East–born, shared the Arabist values of their predecessors thanks to their wartime experiences serving in the Arab world. The main exemplars of this type were the Roosevelt cousins Kim and Archie. However, not all of the new CIA's Middle

Eastern hands were of such aristocratic lineage, nor did they necessarily have any experience of serving in the region prior to their posting there by the Agency. Indeed, several came from quite humble backgrounds and were drawn to the Middle East, at least initially, mainly for reasons of adventure—men like the young Alabaman seated next to Archie on the flight to Lebanon in September 1947.

MILES COPELAND PRESENTS THE HISTORIAN with a problem. After leaving the CIA, he wrote a series of books, culminating in his 1989 autobiography, *The Game Player*, that together constitute one of the most revelatory set of writings by a former US intelligence officer ever published. In addition to disarmingly candid confessions about their author's personality—*The Game Player* begins with an account of how, when quizzed by CIA psychologists, Copeland could not think of anyone he had ever disliked and then cheerfully owned up to his readiness "to ice someone"—these works also contain extraordinarily detailed accounts of CIA covert operations in, among other countries, Syria, Egypt, and Iran, making them an indispensable source about the secret history of America's involvement in the Middle East. As such, they present a stark contrast with Archie Roosevelt's autobiography, which is so tight-lipped about CIA operations that, in the words of British author John Keay, "its main title, *For Lust of Knowing*, invites a '*But Not of Telling.*'"[1]

The trouble is that it is very difficult to know how far one can trust Copeland's writings. Former colleagues, personal acquaintances, and even, tacitly, Copeland himself testified to his unreliability. When confronted about one wild claim, "he laughed, thought it was terribly funny," recalled one friend. Indeed, the consensus on this score is so unanimous that the skeptical researcher begins to wonder if it might not be a bluff concocted by CIA insiders to distract attention from Copeland's essential truthfulness. Then there are other possibilities to consider. Perhaps Copeland deliberately mixed fact and fiction in order to evade official censorship, a fate that would befall several other CIA memoirists. Was there a more mysterious, darker motive, as hinted by Jack Philby's son, the British double agent Kim Philby, who described another of Copeland's controversial books, *The Game of Nations*, as "itself a move in the CIA's monstrous game"? Or was it simply that Miles

Copeland enjoyed telling a tall tale, playing games with his readers? Whatever the explanation, this trait in Copeland obliges one to tread carefully, cross-checking his assertions when other records are available, and acknowledging when there is only his word to go on. "Miles Copeland," the irreverent, rollicking, and thoroughly amoral Game Player of Copeland's own writings, was a splendid literary creation—but was he real?[2]

To begin with what we know for sure: Miles Axe Copeland Jr. was born on July 16, 1916, in Birmingham, Alabama. His father, Miles Sr., was a distinguished local physician, his mother, Lenora, a professional cook who developed recipes for radio. According to *The Game Player*, young Miles was close to the warm-hearted Lenora, a gifted storyteller, but never got on with his father, a remote and severe disciplinarian (a parenting style he consciously rejected when raising his own sons). Although he would eventually grow into a robust, big-framed man, with "thick, sandy hair and . . . eyes that danced with excitement," as one acquaintance described him, Miles Jr. was a sickly, tubercular boy, forced to rely on his cunning to best his athletic younger brother, Hunter. Kept home for two years until his health improved, he eventually enrolled at Birmingham's Erskine Ramsay Technical High School, where, according to the 1933 yearbook, he sat on the school council and presided over his Session Room, and, according to his autobiography, plagued his teachers with devilish pranks while at the same time pretending to advise them on how to catch the perpetrator. From Ramsay High it was on to the University of Alabama, Tuscaloosa, which he attended until the spring of 1937, majoring in advertising and sales, playing in the ROTC band and Capstone Orchestra, and boxing for the varsity squad. He did not graduate, however, because of extracurricular distractions, the main one being his flourishing career as a jazz trumpeter.[3]

It is at this point that the record becomes hazier. In his memoirs, Copeland makes several impressive statements about his days as a jazz musician, claiming that, for example, in early 1932 he played with an all-black combo that later became Erskine Hawkins's big band from Tuskegee, Alabama, performing the hit "Tuxedo Junction" in Harlem's Cotton Club; also that in September 1940 he spent a week playing fourth trumpet in the Glenn Miller orchestra on the Roosevelt Hotel roof in New Orleans. Yet, in fact, Erskine Hawkins's band was from Montgomery, not Tuskegee, and never performed at the Cotton Club, while the nearest the Glenn Miller orchestra got to New Orleans in the latter part of 1940 was Washington, DC. Copeland's CIA personnel records say nothing about his having ever been a professional musician, suggesting instead that during the late 1930s he held a number of prosaic-sounding sales jobs in Birmingham while studying prelaw subjects at Birmingham Southern College.[4]

Still, none of this disproves Copeland's main claim to have been a good trumpet player. Several relatives and friends have testified to his musical ability, among them two sons, Miles III and Ian, who became major producers and managers in the rock music industry, and a third, Stewart, who played the drums behind front man Sting in the Police. There is also a hint of willful recklessness about some of his boasts—the movements and membership of the Glenn Miller orchestra are among the best documented phenomena in jazz history—as if he were deliberately courting correction by some earnest musicologist. Whatever the exact truth, it is clear that his early days as a jazz musician became an important part of the Copeland persona, lending him a bohemian, "wild man" reputation in the early CIA that helped compensate for his relative lack of education and social pedigree. Here was a rougher but more obviously authentic masculinity than the aristocratic sort manufactured by Endicott Peabody at Groton. And perhaps the jazz man's experience of crossing between the segregated worlds of white and black in the pre–Civil Rights era South gave Copeland skills of cultural adaptability that his social betters from the Ivy League schools lacked.

In any case, life as a salesman-cum-musician eventually began to pall, and in November 1940 Copeland joined the US Army, working in the divisional Finance Office of the National Guard Armory, not perhaps the best job for him given that his other great interest in life beside jazz was gambling. Various Bilko-esque escapades ensued (see *The Game Player* for details), and then, in the course of a routine army exam at Camp Livingstone, Louisiana, our hero was discovered to have supergenius-level intelligence, "roughly the same as the estimated IQs of Albert Einstein, Johann Wolfgang von Goethe, and Jesus Christ," as he helpfully explained later. Declaring himself "super-brain," Copeland wrote one of his congressmen requesting a transfer to a post better suited to his abilities, and he soon found himself in Washington, DC, sitting across a desk from Coordinator of Information Wild Bill Donovan, entertaining him with stories of maneuvers in the Louisiana swamps.

Shortly after his return to Camp Livingstone, a secret dispatch arrived at Private Copeland's pup tent ordering him back to Washington, where he was assigned as a "special agent" to the military counterespionage and subversion unit, the Counter Intelligence Corps (CIC), not quite the "Oh So Social" OSS but a step up nonetheless. After training by a young journalist, Frank Kearns, the former jazz man was let loose on the streets of the nation's capital to sniff out Axis spies. When none revealed themselves, Special Agents Copeland and Kearns resorted to "gaming out" possible acts of sabotage by German agents, causing consternation among the District of Columbia's regular police.

Again, the stories are obviously embellished, but the main elements ring true. The Washington field office of the CIC did get carried away in its wartime domestic investigations—for example, bugging a hotel where Eleanor Roosevelt was suspected of carrying on a romantic liaison with a communist army sergeant—and was eventually disbanded in November 1943. Also, despite the tomfoolery, something else was becoming clear: Copeland really was bright, and the emergency conditions of the early 1940s were creating opportunities for him to prove it.[5]

In the summer of 1942, the Counter Intelligence Corps began deploying overseas, starting with a detachment that joined the TORCH invasion force in North Africa. Miles Copeland's destination was London, where he took up residence in a flat near the Albert Hall with Kearns and another CIC officer, the writer and editor James M. Eichelberger. It was not long before he was up to his old tricks, testing security measures at US Army high command by stealing a safe from its headquarters on Grosvenor Square, and idly plotting the assassination of a rival for the affections of the piano prodigy Moura Lympany. "I would not actually have gone through with the murder plot," he reassured readers later. "I've killed, oh, perhaps half a dozen people since, but never anyone *with whom I've mixed socially*."[6]

Something of a Pauline conversion took place, however, when Copeland was sent on the tough Inter-Allied Commando training course in the Scottish highlands and then, on returning to London, met a young British woman at an English Speaking Union reception for US troops. Elizabeth Lorraine Adie, the daughter of an eminent Harley Street neurosurgeon, was herself engaged in intelligence work, researching the itineraries of French trains for the wartime British political warfare unit, the Special Operations Executive, "so the Resistance could blow them up," as she explained later. After a whirlwind Anglo-American romance, Miles and Lorraine were married in September 1942 (Frank Kearns was the best man) and settled down to life together in her mother's North London home, where they were joined in May 1944 by Miles III. Miles Jr. now applied himself to his work with rather more purpose, organizing and directing a CIC school for orienting American counterintelligence agents assigned to the European theater, an initiative that earned him the Legion of Merit.[7]

Copeland also began putting his interest in game playing to uses other than gambling, participating in Grosvenor Square war games intended to gauge likely German responses to Operation OVERLORD, the planned Allied invasion of occupied northwest France. Discussions about the possibility that Nazi scientists had developed atomic weapons brought him briefly into the orbit of Boris T. Pash, a Russian-born security officer for the US nuclear bomb research program, the Manhattan Project, who toward the end of the war led the American charge to beat the advancing Red Army to research facilities in Germany. Copeland's own war ended in Paris, which he and a few CIC colleagues had entered well in advance of the main OVERLORD invasion force, although he later admitted that they were not, as he had boasted for a while, the first Americans in the liberated city. They were merely "the first Americans to enter Paris with no particular good reason." Drinking champagne, eating caviar, and carousing with Ernest Hemingway consumed several days, after which the young American went to work interrogating leading French collaborators and German espionage agents and then compiling the "CIC Interrogation Manual" for the benefit of other agents. Impressed by his literary efforts, in February 1945 his superiors appointed Captain Copeland, as he now was, to write a history of US counterintelligence activities in Europe. It was, as he later wrote, a project that required him to interview various Nazi scientists and spies who, "once the Second World War was over and forgotten, would be valuable to us in facing any new enemies that might have grown out of it."[8]

Copeland returned to Washington in September 1945 and began work for the Strategic Services Unit, a stopgap agency that housed the orphan intelligence and counterespionage services of the defunct OSS. Lorraine joined him a year later after receiving her naturalization papers, and the family, augmented by the arrival of a daughter, Lennie, moved into the Parkfairfax development in Alexandria, Virginia. Over the next two years, Copeland shuttled between the temporary buildings on the Washington mall that housed the nation's nascent intelligence community, variously working on the German desk of the counterespionage branch, X-2; devising methods for recruiting agents to spy on the Soviets; and drawing up organizational charts for the handover of special operations to the new Central Intelligence Agency. Whether these contributions justified his subsequent self-depiction as a founding father of the CIA is a matter of interpretation. Kim Roosevelt, soon to be his boss in the Agency's Near East division, was, for one, "somewhat dismissive" of this claim. "That's Miles," he would say, with a mixture of amusement and irritation.[9]

The next big development in Copeland's picaresque career was his September 1947 posting to Damascus as CIA station chief. *The Game Player* records that it was Stephen Penrose, in his postwar role as head of special operations in the Central Intelligence Group, who first raised the possibility of a Middle Eastern assignment for Copeland. Nazi fugitives were resurfacing in the capital cities of the region, and Penrose believed that the former Counter Intelligence Corps officer's experience of interrogating potentially useful German prisoners of war, combined with his reputation for amorality—his "well-known glandular deficiency," as Copeland himself described it—made him the perfect man to go and investigate. His interest piqued, Copeland then read a report predicting that the Zionist-Arab clash in Palestine was bound to create chronic conflict in the Middle East and that, in these circumstances, the best the United States could do was limit the resulting damage to its own interests in the area, by covert means if necessary.[10]

Excited by "the prospect of engaging in a bit of clandestine hanky-panky with the justification that it was in the national interest," Copeland learned that the front-runner for the job of commanding the new CIA's station in Syria, "a rough and ready Marine captain," had failed to obtain the requisite security clearance because he had confessed to an experimental sexual encounter with a male RAF pilot during the war. Offered the post instead, Copeland hesitated only briefly before accepting. The factor that swung his decision, he explained later, was his meeting Archie Roosevelt, who had just been offered the equivalent job in Beirut. Although something of an odd couple—"me a New Orleans jazz musician and Tennessee riverboat gambler, he a member in good standing of what passes for nobility in America," as Copeland put it in a British newspaper obituary for Archie many years later—the two men got on famously, each delighted by the other's "wicked sense of humor" and united by their shared belief that the main threat to US national security now came from the Soviet Union.[11]

Hence it was that Miles Copeland, a clever young man from nowhere in particular—"The Guest No One Invites Again," as he described himself later—found himself sitting alongside a grandson of Theodore Roosevelt on his way to the Middle East. Arriving in Beirut on September 13, 1947, Copeland spent a convivial evening with Archie; the following day he traveled on to Damascus in the legation car. Archie, meanwhile, was joined in Beirut two days later by Kim Roosevelt, who was then passing through Lebanon on another of his slightly mysterious regional tours. The cousins rapidly fell into their old routine of traveling together, and on Thursday, September 18—the same day the CIA was formally established in Washington—they drove over the mountains to find out how Miles was faring in his new duties. The three men hit it off instantly, following in T. E. Lawrence's footsteps by setting out "on a tour of Crusader castles and off-the-beaten-path places," as Copeland described it later. First stop was Aleppo, where, according to Archie's diary, they climbed the steps of the ancient fortified citadel, stronghold of generations of foreign conquerors, including Greeks, Mongols, and Ottomans, and gazed out at "the whole city stretching green around us." The Orient lay awaiting a new wave of foreigners.[12]

Part Two

Warm-Up, 1947–1949

SEVEN

Game Plan

WHEN THEY CAME TO THE Middle East in the fall of 1947, the CIA Arabists found a region greatly but not entirely transformed by the fading of European colonial power. The French had reluctantly withdrawn from Lebanon and Syria the previous year (thanks in part to American pressure), although both countries would continue to be troubled by tribal and sectarian divisions left over from the divide-and-rule days of the French mandate. Also in 1946, the emirate of Transjordan had acquired its independence from Britain and become a Hashemite kingdom. Nevertheless, like its supposedly independent Hashemite neighbor Iraq, Transjordan remained under de facto British control. A similar situation obtained in Egypt, where, after a brief show of independence during the war that ended when he was humiliatingly slapped down by British ambassador Sir Miles Lampson, young King Farouk ruled in name only. Among the Arab world's monarchs, only the United States' new friend, Ibn Saud of Saudi Arabia, had really succeeded in emerging from under the sway of the European powers.

Such was the state of affairs awaiting the newly arrived Americans. How would they respond? Would they perpetuate Western imperialism in the Middle East, creating another "Covert Empire" like that of the

British, or would they honor the Arabist legacy of their OSS forebears and help the Arabs at last achieve true independence? It would not be until two years later, in 1949, when the first Arab coup of the Cold War era was launched in Syria, that the CIA Arabists' principles would be put to the test in the Middle East itself. In the meantime, however, an answer of sorts would be provided back in the United States, where Kim Roosevelt, his wartime fascination with the Arab world strengthened by a return trip there in 1947, was hard at work on two major projects: telling the story of the Arabs to the American public and building a movement capable of countering the growing influence of Zionism on US foreign policy.

WHEREAS ARCHIE ROOSEVELT AND MILES Copeland, in their new role as CIA station chiefs, were in the Middle East on official business in September 1947, Kim Roosevelt was traveling as a private citizen. Although he had enjoyed some aspects of his postwar assignment as OSS historian—commuting from Washington to New York to interview Bill Donovan and Allen Dulles, for example—Kim had resented the "horrible officialese language" in which he was compelled to write. With the project finally finished in May 1947, he promptly resigned from government employment and set about trying to live off his private income from the Willard family's real estate holdings, supplemented by occasional writing and lecturing engagements. He would carry on in this fashion for the next two years, recreating the lifestyle of his father, Kermit, a gentleman amateur who performed secret service for the state out of a sense of patriotic rather than professional duty. Meanwhile, as befitted a grandson of Theodore Roosevelt, Kim engaged conspicuously in public life, speaking at Republican Party meetings and writing about the Middle East in such venues as *Harper's* magazine (once a publishing platform for TR himself).[1]

It was just such a writing assignment—a book contract with Harper—that brought Kim back to the Middle East for the first time since the war in May 1947, only a week after his government contract had ended. Arriving in Cairo accompanied by his wife, Polly, who planned to sell photographs of the trip to the *Saturday Evening Post*, Kim headed for his old haunt, Shepheard's Hotel, to reacquaint himself with the passing American oilmen, archaeologists, and reporters who frequented the Long Bar. After nearly a month in Egypt, it was on to Lebanon—a happy development for Polly, who had been overwhelmed by the heat and dirt of Cairo and had once landed in jail when an angry crowd took exception to her photographing some street children. Beirut, like "a European Mediterranean town except for a few Arab costumes here and there," as a relieved Polly observed, became the couple's headquarters for the remainder of their half-year tour of the Middle East, which included excursions to Palestine, Syria, Transjordan, Iraq, Iran, and Saudi Arabia.[2]

In all these places, Kim met with an amazing range of local political, religious, and tribal leaders, including no fewer than four kings and one regent. This extraordinary degree of access to the region's elites reflected both the hard work he had put into cultivating Middle Eastern contacts during his wartime posting in Cairo—several, of course, the result of introductions by Archie—and the cachet of the Roosevelt family name. It seems also that Kim was acting as a "semi-official U.S. representative," as he wrote his mother, Belle, with the blessing if not the encouragement of the many powerful figures he still knew in the US foreign policy establishment. "We are royally received everywhere," he explained, after delivering a statement on US policy to the regent and prime minister of Iraq. "It's not exactly a reporter's job, but no one seems to care." Like his earlier undercover OSS mission, Kim's trip had more than one purpose.[3]

Be that as it may, the book that resulted from Kim's 1947 tour, *Arabs, Oil, and History*, was a remarkable document in its own right: part travelogue, part introductory survey of Middle Eastern affairs, part Arabist polemic, and part a personal manifesto by the man soon to take charge of the region for the CIA—a sort of blueprint for early US covert operations in the Arab world. As such, it is worth pausing the narrative briefly to consider the book's main points.

First, *Arabs, Oil, and History* was strikingly critical of earlier European imperialism in the Middle East and the legacy of autocracy and underdevelopment it had left behind. For example, whereas TR had praised the British in Egypt, Kim condemned the "faulty British tactics which rel[ied] upon stability imposed by a small, selfishly interested clique." Under the client king Farouk—a pudgy playboy, in Kim's pen-portrait—Egyptian society was characterized by a startlingly deep economic divide between the ruling class and the rest of the population,

summed up for Kim in the old Arab saying "Cakes for the Fat, an Onion for the Thin." A similar state of affairs prevailed in the Arab states
ruled by the Hashemites, "the most British-dominated of Arab dynas-
ties," as Kim put it. Transjordan, governed by the vain, slippery, and
overweight king 'Abdullah, was a "little artificial impoverished country." In Iraq the downtrodden masses so hated the Hashemites that, if
"it weren't for British protection (which allowed them to build up their
own secret police and army), Abdul Ilah and the others would be murdered in two hours"—a prescient observation, as later events proved.
Among the Middle Eastern countries within the British sphere of influence, only non-Arab Iran escaped complete condemnation in *Arabs,
Oil, and History*, and even here Kim's review was less than glowing.
The young shah was barely mentioned—Kim had far more to say about
the charismatic chief of the Qashqai tribe, Khosrow Khan—and the same
Iranian army that had just "liberated" Azerbaijan was dismissed as corrupt and ill-disciplined.[4]

Kim did compliment some individual Britons for their "wholly personal contributions" to Western relations with the Arab and Muslim
worlds, among them Lawrence of Arabia, Jack Philby, and the Orientalist adventurer Aubrey Herbert (the model for the master of disguise
Sandy Arbuthnot in John Buchan's *Greenmantle*), whom he described,
with a hint of envy, as "able to don native dress and vanish without trace
into quarters which no foreigner could enter." In short, *Arabs, Oil, and
History* was not altogether devoid of its author's earlier enthusiasm for
British imperial culture. Overall, though, the verdict on Britain's record
was surprisingly harsh: the main consequence of the British presence
in the Middle East was a profound sense of Arab "bitterness" toward
the West that was now "available to demagogues (and the Russians) for
whatever purpose they may choose."[5]

Fortunately, there was an alternative model for the Middle East–
West relationship and future American policy, one based not on "political domination and economic exploitation," but rather "on common
interests." Here Kim explicitly invoked the United States' distinctive
history of nongovernmental interaction with Arabs and Muslims: the
missions of nineteenth-century evangelists, the building of American
universities in Beirut and Cairo, and, most recently, the efforts of the
American oil industry to improve education, medicine, and communications in Saudi Arabia. These activities, which contrasted with the general

dearth of earlier official US involvement in the region (symbolized for Kim by the ineptness of the goodwill mission he had accompanied to Saudi Arabia in 1944), had caused Middle Easterners to adopt "a different attitude toward [Americans] as distinct from other Westerners." Together, these activities constituted "a national asset of incalculable value" and, potentially, "more effective bulwarks of national security than the imperialisms of Russia and Britain."[6]

Furthermore, a sizable group of Arabs were naturally disposed to friendship with the United States. The "Young Effendis," as Kim Roosevelt called them, using a term coined by Archie's friend British explorer Freya Stark, were Arab nationalists who wanted to rid the Middle East of the vestiges of European colonialism, including its client monarchies. Despite their anticolonial politics, these nationalists were no communists, Soviet Russia appearing to them in much the same guise as the imperial Western European powers. They had also resisted the urge taking hold among some groups of young Arabs—the recently created Muslim Brotherhood, for example—to reject all foreign influence in favor of a xenophobic form of Islamism. Instead, reflecting the fact that many of them had been educated at American-founded institutions in the region, and a few in the United States itself, the Young Effendis positively welcomed American interest in their countries. They identified with causes similar to those traditionally promoted by US visitors, such as education, health care, and women's rights. Although strongly associated with particular countries—Egypt, for example, where nationalist reformers had "made some real strides in the right direction," and Syria, home to "a very promising group of Young Effendis"—the phenomenon was a region-wide one, with "sober crusaders in education, government, and medicine . . . to be found from Istanbul to Aden, from Cairo to Teheran."[7]

Having identified the United States' main assets in the Middle East—its nongovernmental presence there and the potential local allies to be found among the ranks of young Arab nationalists—Kim Roosevelt went on to outline a concrete program for future American policy toward the region: "a little Marshall Plan" involving an alliance of US government and business that would promote "the social and economic advancement of Middle East peoples" and thereby foil "Communist infiltration and revolutionary tactics." Other Western powers, especially the British, could assist this effort by providing Americans with the benefit of their area expertise. Some traditional elements of Arab society could also be harnessed to the cause, as the example of Ibn Saud and his partnership with ARAMCO showed. (Kim had thoroughly absorbed the OSS Arabists' enthusiasm for the "Lord of the Desert," describing him as "proud and erect"—a real man, in other words, unlike the effete, corpulent Hashemites.) Nevertheless, looking across the whole region, its future clearly lay with the modernizing program of the Young Effendis and their efforts to turn themselves into a viable Arab middle class. And the inspiration for this movement should be not some faded European colonial power but rather the young, progressive democracy of the United States.[8]

Kim Roosevelt had a final point to make in *Arabs, Oil, and History*, and it concerned what he perceived as the main threat to his vision of future American–Middle Eastern relations: US support for Zionism. On this issue, Kim was no less outspoken than the OSS Arabists. In entertaining Zionist demands for a Jewish state in Palestine, Kim argued, the United States risked squandering the Arab goodwill carefully built up by generations of private American citizens. It was even possible that Arabs might end up rejecting democracy itself, the system of government that had produced this obviously wrongheaded policy. Nor did the Zionist cause necessarily benefit the Jews who espoused it, he continued, as it invited an anti-Semitic backlash in the West and exposed Jewish settlers in Palestine to the hostility of their Arab neighbors.

To these by now well-rehearsed anti-Zionist arguments, Kim added another that related specifically to his own dream of a US-Arab alliance for progress. By fuelling anti-Western feeling in the Middle East, American support for Zionism strengthened the hand not only of communist elements there but also of antiforeign zealots such as the Muslim Brotherhood, thereby isolating and marginalizing moderate, secular progressives like the Young Effendis. "The long-range danger," Kim concluded, in a statement remarkable for both its prophetic quality and, given some of his own later actions, its historical irony, "is that we encourage the creation of an isolationist, fanatically reactionary, and xenophobic force which will dominate an important segment of the world and constitute an always-festering wound in the side of peace."[9]

The arguments of *Arabs, Oil, and History* strongly resembled elements of US Cold War strategy in Western Europe—not just the Marshall Plan's emphasis on government-business partnership but also the identification of local progressives as potential American allies. (Early CIA operations in Europe often focused on strengthening the position of liberals and social democrats, the so-called Non-Communist Left, who were perceived in Washington as the most important strategic counterforce to Stalinist expansionism.) To a certain extent, then, Kim was simply paraphrasing the foreign policy wisdom of the late 1940s, which emphasized the role of US-led economic development as a weapon for defeating communism—an idea that would increasingly be applied to Third World theaters of the Cold War in the guise of modernization.

But *Arabs, Oil, and History* was more than just an echo of Washington Cold War planning discussions. It also bore definite traces of OSS-style Arabism, the result of its author's wartime experiences working under Stephen Penrose in Cairo. For example, Kim portrayed the Palestine issue less as a policy challenge for the United States than as a moral and humanitarian crisis within the Arab world. Writing at a time when Palestinian refugees were starting to flood into neighboring states, he described the situation as "a human tragedy, . . . public-health threat, . . . [and] very real political problem to the shaky Arab governments." He was also prepared to state the ethical case for the Palestinian Arabs. "It is, essentially, . . . very simple," he wrote at one point. "It rests on the assumption that those who have been living in a land have the strongest possible claim to that land."[10]

There was one respect, however, in which *Arabs, Oil, and History* differed from the pronouncements by the OSS and State Department Arabists of the previous generation: it was much more sensitive to the feelings of Jewish Americans. For example, Kim was quick to acknowledge the sincerity of the Zionist desire for a haven from persecution and the part played by past Gentile actions in causing that feeling. "To our shame, anti-Semitism in one degree or another has been a distinctive feature of Occidental cultures from Russia to America," he admitted. "You cannot blame Jews for deciding that they must learn from that bitter lesson." Anti-Semitism in the Arab world also attracted denunciation in *Arabs, Oil, and History*: Kim's pen-portrait of the Palestinian leader and notorious Nazi collaborator the Grand Mufti Muhammad Amin al-Husseini was an unflattering one, consistent with Kim's criticisms elsewhere of Islamist xenophobia. This last characteristic of *Arabs, Oil, and History* perhaps reflected the fact that, unlike some earlier Arabists, Kim personally knew many Jews, both in the Middle East itself—his wartime acquaintance, Teddy Kollek, became a lifelong friend—and within the United States. (Archie Roosevelt, incidentally, shared in several of these friendships.)[11]

In short, *Arabs, Oil, and History* seemed an ideal combination of reasonable argumentation, engaging personal reflection, and sensible policy prescription, all served up by a favorite son of one of America's most famous families. Americans might not have heeded the State Department and OSS Arabists, but surely they would listen now.

AFTER RETURNING TO THE UNITED States from his tour of the Middle East in the fall of 1947, Kim plunged into a nationwide lecture tour about his impressions of the region, taking as his theme the title of his 1946 *Harper's* article, "The Arabs Live There Too." Like his grandfather Theodore, Kim was not blessed with a strong public speaking voice, but he made up for this with an informal, relaxed style of delivery that appealed to audiences. He also possessed considerable verbal dexterity; one listener noted the fact that during a forty-minute-long talk in which he dwelt at length on the Palestinian situation, he did not use the words "Jew" or "Zionist" once. Meanwhile, Kim maintained a steady stream of publications, in venues ranging from scholarly journals such as the *Annals of the American Academy of Political and Social Science* to the mass-circulation *Saturday Evening Post*, as well as writing regularly to the *New York Times*. The previous year, a State Department memo had noted that while there was "a large and aggressive element in public opinion" that supported the Zionist line, American anti-Zionism had "not been articulate." It was as if Kim were now providing that missing voice.[12]

This was not, as he himself admitted, an easy task. In a January 1948 *Middle East Journal* article, "Partition of Palestine: A Lesson in Pressure Politics," Kim reconstructed the passage of events leading to the November 1947 UN vote in favor of a Jewish state—"an instructive, and disturbing, story," as he described it. Almost all Americans "with diplomatic, educational, missionary, or business experience in the Middle East" were fervently opposed to Zionism, he claimed. Nonetheless, the Zionist movement had been so successful in winning over the newspapers and Congress to its cause, while imputing its opponents with ignoble motives, including anti-Semitism, that the US government had eventually adopted a policy that was contrary to American interests in the region. The lesson, Kim concluded, was clear: "the partition of Palestine demonstrates the vital need of a foreign policy based on national rather than partisan interests." How this was to be achieved in the face of the growing power of Zionism was, unfortunately, less obvious.[13]

Part of the problem facing Kim was the lack of Arab representation in US politics. Some individuals and groups within the small Arab American community were prepared to speak out about Palestine— for example, Khalil Totah of the Institute for Arab American Affairs, a New York–based organization whose advisory board Kim had joined in 1946. (Kim's "Partition of Palestine" piece was reprinted as an Institute pamphlet in February 1948.) The Institute also put Kim in touch with the Arab Office in Washington, the foreign publicity arm of the recently formed regional organization of Arab states, the Arab League. The staff of the Arab Office were mostly Western-educated, moderate nationalists of the sort Kim referred to approvingly as "Young Effendis," and he did his best to help their cause, opening "many doors to us in the society of Washington and New York," as the Office's director Cecil Hourani (brother of the eminent Arab historian Albert Hourani) recalled later. But he was powerless to protect them when, having been accused in Congress of taking orders from the grand mufti and consorting with pro-Nazi elements in the United States, they were charged with violating the Foreign Agents Registration Act. In December 1947, a week after the UN partition vote, the Arab Office announced that it was closing down its American operation in the face of a "complete and arrogant disregard for Arab rights, Arab interests, and Arab feelings." The Institute of Arab American Affairs, whose director, Khalil Totah, developed an unfortunate (and probably unfair) reputation for emotional instability, suffered a similar fate, shutting up shop in 1950.[14]

In the absence of a viable Arab lobby, Kim turned elsewhere for allies in the anti-Zionist struggle, starting with the Protestant missionaries, educators, and aid workers whose contribution to Middle Eastern development he praised in *Arabs, Oil, and History*. The Protestant presence in the Arab world was backed up by a domestic-support apparatus consisting of mission boards and educational bodies such as the Near East College Association, and it had some effective spokespersons, most notably the venerable AUB president Bayard Dodge. In addition, a small but influential body of Protestant theologians challenged fundamentalist

Protestants' linking of Jewish restoration with the millennium, an argument expounded regularly by the Chicago-based weekly *Christian Century*. All this added up to a distinct tradition of Protestant American anti-Zionism available for mobilization by a would-be anti-Zionist organizer.[15]

Also ready to lend a hand was the American oil industry. The Arabian consortium ARAMCO depended for its access to Saudi oil fields on the goodwill of Ibn Saud, an irreconcilable anti-Zionist, and was developing plans for a trans-Arabian pipeline (TAPline) to the Mediterranean that would run through the Arab countries neighboring Palestine. Concerned lest US government policy hurt these ventures, the company launched a public relations campaign intended to bring American opinion around to the Arab viewpoint. Predictably, the ubiquitous William Eddy, now in ARAMCO employ, featured heavily, briefing Washington officials about the hazards of a Zionist foreign policy before taking off on periodic tours of Arab capitals. (Archie Roosevelt met Eddy for the first time shortly after arriving in Beirut in 1947 and quickly declared him "a truly great man.") Not as impressive in person as Eddy, but no less influential behind the scenes, was the ARAMCO vice president James Terry Duce, "a discreet and unostentatious man," according to company historian William Mulligan, with "the face and figure of a Kewpie doll." Duce set up an office in Washington, the Government Relations Organization, that functioned as a kind of ARAMCO State Department, with an Arabian affairs division reputedly modeled after OSS/ Cairo. He also worked with Eddy to make sure that deserving causes in the United States, such as the Princeton Middle East program, received unpublicized ARAMCO assistance. Kim Roosevelt, meanwhile, boosted the company's image to an American audience in *Arabs, Oil, and History*, describing its efforts to improve Arabian education, health care, and transportation as a model for the Marshall Plan–like program he hoped to see the US government enacting throughout the region. (This was, arguably, a more positive depiction of ARAMCO's Saudi operation than it really deserved.)[16]

If there was nothing terribly surprising about the anti-Zionism of Arabist Protestants and oilmen, that of a third group that would prove an important ally for Kim Roosevelt requires a little more explanation. In the 1940s a subgroup of Jewish Americans felt distinctly uncomfortable about the recent successes of the Zionist movement. Generally of high social status and old-stock, German descent, these Reform Jews questioned Zionism's insistence on a distinct Jewish national identity, seeing it as a denial of their Americanism and an invitation to persecution by anti-Semites. In 1942, goaded by the support of the Central Conference of American Rabbis for the Zionist plan to form a Jewish army, this group formed a breakaway organization, the American Council for Judaism (ACJ). With the chair of the Sears Roebuck board, Lessing J. Rosenwald, serving as president, day-to-day running of the ACJ fell to Executive Director Elmer Berger, a rabbi from Flint, Michigan. Despite a somewhat lugubrious appearance, Berger was an energetic and ingratiating young man who soon won the ACJ the support of a number of prominent lay Jews, among them George L. Levison, scion of an old and wealthy San Francisco family. Together with another well-connected anti-Zionist rabbi, Morris S. Lazaron, Berger and the others set to work trying to persuade the Jewish American community that Zionism was fundamentally opposed not only to American ideals but also to the universal, religious character of Judaism.[17]

It was an uphill struggle. No matter how hard they worked to craft compelling theological and practical arguments, the leaders of the American Council for Judaism simply could not compete with Zionism's raw emotional appeal nor with the organizational and polemical skills of the Zionist leadership. Increasingly isolated within the Jewish community, they looked elsewhere for support—and found it among the Arabists of the State Department. It was Morris Lazaron who initiated this alliance, reporting to his friend, Undersecretary of State Sumner Welles, on the ructions in the Central Conference of American Rabbis. Lessing Rosenwald, who served in the early 1940s on the War Production Board, accepted the ACJ presidency only after having satisfied himself that the State Department would not object, and helped bring Dean Acheson and Loy Henderson into the organization's orbit. The ACJ's main representative in government circles, though, was the gregarious George Levison, who, thanks to wartime service in the State Department, enjoyed "intimate associations," as Berger put it, with Acheson, Henderson, and Kim Roosevelt. Levison and Kim had roomed together in Cairo, where the former was serving as a special assistant in the Landis mission. After the war, when Kim was removed from the Middle East scene by his OSS history project duties, Levison worked with Henderson to counter the Zionist campaign for partition, pressing instead for a relaxation of federal immigration restrictions so as to permit more Jewish displaced persons to enter the United States, as opposed to Palestine. Elmer Berger also became involved in this effort, after Levison had introduced him around Washington. Given this tangle of connections — several of them traceable, like so much of the CIA's early program in the Middle East, back to OSS/Cairo — it was hardly surprising that Kim Roosevelt should have reached out to the Jews around the ACJ when he embarked on his anti-Zionist publicity campaign.[18]

It would be easy to view the collaboration that developed from these contacts as one in which a master spy used an apparently independent organization as a front for secret government purposes. There is an element of truth to this interpretation, but it also obscures a more complex, and interesting, reality. To begin with, correspondence between George Levison and Elmer Berger shows that it was the American Council for Judaism that first courted Kim Roosevelt, rather than vice versa; the anti-Zionist Jews clearly regarded the young American blue blood, with his combination of society connections and access to mass media like the *Saturday Evening Post*, as a potentially invaluable ally in promoting their cause. "Please keep your spies on the alert for the return from the Middle East of one young Kermit Roosevelt, Jr.," Levison wrote Berger in June 1947 in his customarily jovial style. "I think we should grab said aforementioned young man quickly."[19]

The plotting was successful. Soon after his return from his tour, Kim agreed to lecture in November 1947 to a local chapter of the American Council for Judaism in Houston, Texas. The run-up to this event revealed a service that the ACJ could perform in return for Kim. His reputation as an outspoken anti-Zionist preceded him to Texas, and Zionists there accused him of also being an anti-Semite, causing the Houston chapter to get cold feet about hosting his appearance. When word of this reached Levison, he was furious, writing the chapter president that he had known Kim "intimately for more than four years" and could "state without equivocation that there [was] not one iota of truth in the Zionists' accusation." The lecture passed off without incident, presumably because Kim, with his usual cool pragmatism, steered clear of comment about Palestine. Nonetheless, the episode showed the vulnerability of non-Jewish anti-Zionists to allegations of anti-Semitism. Henceforth, Levison and Berger deliberately offered the ACJ platform to eminent Gentiles wishing to go on record against Zionism as a means of deflecting such charges. "We might be cited as an example of a group of *Jews* holding this viewpoint," Berger wrote one potential spokesperson. "That fact has been found by some other people to be a reed upon which they could lean in the event that someone tried to make them anti-Semites 'by appointment.'"[20]

Another noteworthy aspect of the collaboration between Kim Roosevelt and the anti-Zionist Jews of the American Council for Judaism was the strong element of friendship involved. "My father had very few close friends, very few, but one of them was certainly George Levison," recalled Kim's son Jonathan years later. "As a youth, George . . . was very much part of my life, he came to the house, [and] I remember visiting him in California once. . . . He was a wonderful, kind, fatherly-type man." Kermit III had similar childhood memories: "I grew up knowing Elmer Berger, whom I liked, and I was surprised to discover later in life how controversial a figure [he] was." Kim and Polly socialized with Elmer Berger and his wife, Ruth, whenever they got the chance. Berger gave the Roosevelt children presents, and in 1953 Kim asked Levison to be godfather to his newest child, daughter Anne. This was not just an expedient political alliance; it was also an intimate personal relationship.[21]

Of course, the timing of Kim's enlistment in the ACJ's campaign proved to be far from propitious, with the UN vote for partition coming at the end of November 1947, a development that demoralized many of the organization's members and caused some even to consider disbanding. Berger, however, was determined to keep the ACJ flag flying and, by the end of the year, was detecting signs of a revival in anti-Zionist fortunes. Partition was running into trouble, the result of Arab opposition and growing intercommunal strife in Palestine, leading the State Department to suggest the creation of a UN trusteeship—effectively, a reversal of the November resolution. Meanwhile, Kim Roosevelt was busy networking in Arabist and anti-Zionist circles, trying to create the sort of movement momentum that had propelled Zionism in the run-up to partition. This was not the first time these disparate groups had interacted: for example, the anti-Zionist Protestants associated with the *Christian Century* and the Jews of the ACJ were engaged in ongoing dialogue. However, no one had ever attempted to give these sporadic connections organized form—until, that is, the launch of the Committee for Justice and Peace in the Holy Land (CJP) in February 1948.

The Committee for Justice and Peace was a broad alliance of individuals from a variety of backgrounds, oddly reminiscent of the Popular Front, the diverse coalition against fascism stitched together by the communists in the 1930s. Kim Roosevelt was clearly the spark plug, identifying himself as "Organizing Secretary" in a telegram sent on February 21 to "100 prominent Americans," inviting them to form a committee "to uphold international law and democratic principles" in the national debate about Palestine. Those subsequently listed as National Council members included an impressive assortment of religious figures, educators, and businessmen. Particularly striking were the names of the vice chairs—Morris Lazaron of the ACJ and Henry Sloane Coffin, the distinguished former president of Union Theological Seminary (and uncle of future CIA officer turned antiwar campaigner William Sloane Coffin)—and chair, Virginia C. Gildersleeve.

The long-serving dean of New York City's Barnard College, the redoubtable Gildersleeve was a pioneer in American women's higher education and the only female member of the US delegation to the 1945 founding conference of the UN. She was also a high-profile anti-Zionist, having become involved with the Arab cause through her association with the Arabist philanthropist Charles Crane and the historian of Arab nationalism George Antonius. It was presumably this last quality that most recommended her to Kim Roosevelt, who already knew her through his sister, Clochette, a Barnard student (there was a Roosevelt family correspondence with Gildersleeve not unlike that with Endicott Peabody). The simple fact that Gildersleeve was a woman might also have been a factor in her selection as the public face of the CJP: women were often preferred for such roles in this period because they were deemed to embody the American associational impulse and to transcend the masculine world of vulgar power politics better than men. Eleanor Roosevelt, who chaired countless committees in the postwar years, was the most famous personification of this putative feminine trait.[22]

Gildersleeve announced the CJP's formation on March 2, explaining that the Committee planned on pressing the UN Security Council to call a cease-fire in Palestine and then petition the General Assembly to reconsider its partition resolution. The same statement went on to identify Kim Roosevelt as the Committee's executive director and Garland Evans Hopkins, a Virginia minister who had traveled in the Middle East on behalf of the Methodist Board of Missions, as its secretary. Not included in

Gildersleeve's announcement was any information about the new organization's finances. Later, a Zionist source reported that an unidentified ARAMCO official had handed Hopkins $2,000 in a dark corridor of the Willard Hotel. Although there is no other evidence of this transaction, ARAMCO's record of donating to Arabist causes, and the appearance of James Terry Duce's name on the Committee for Justice and Peace's National Council roster, lends the claim some credibility. That said, the Committee's overheads were minimal, as it received free administrative support from the ACJ's Elmer Berger, who was more experienced in such matters than his aristocratic friend Kim Roosevelt. "He really is a swell guy but he is an innocent abroad in terms of organizational work," Berger told Levison before going on to recount how, after a meandering meeting of the CJP executive committee held at Belle Roosevelt's New York townhouse, he had coached Kim on how to prepare press statements and advertisements. (The two men then repaired to Berger's apartment and "proceeded to get sufficiently inebriated to forget about the trying day.") This was not the only service the ACJ provided for the CJP: Berger believed that Morris Lazaron's overt participation in the Committee helped "remove any basis for saying it is an anti-Jewish or anti-Semitic organization."[23]

At first, the Committee for Justice and Peace struck a responsive chord in Washington. In early March, Kim Roosevelt arranged an appointment for Gildersleeve, Daniel Bliss (grandson of the AUB founder), and the OSS ethnographer Carleton Coon to meet with George Marshall. The secretary of state "listened with interest" as the Arabists explained the Committee's purpose; Gildersleeve later gathered that Marshall "was rather in sympathy with our views." Shortly afterward, the CJP chair called on Warren R. Austin, head of the US delegation to the UN, to inform him about the Committee's work and offer "its services in helping to bring about peace and justice in the Holy Land." In the course of this meeting, she "was delighted to find that a new policy was being developed," one very like the one she had urged on Marshall. The American Council for Judaism also performed its part: Rosenwald, Levison, and Berger all liaised with Roosevelt and Henderson in an effort to run interference on the Zionist movement, which was campaigning hard to preserve partition. The tide appeared to be turning. On March 8, Truman authorized Marshall to advance a plan for UN trusteeship of Palestine; on March 19, Warren Austin asked the

Security Council to approve the proposal. The CJP and ACJ activists were jubilant. Thanks to Kim Roosevelt, American anti-Zionism was at last making some headway.[24]

But the rejoicing did not last. The president, it turned out, immediately regretted his new position on partition, writing privately that the State Department had "pulled the rug out from under" him and made him into a "liar and double-crosser." The trusteeship idea proved hard to translate into practice, and with the May deadline for the withdrawal of British troops approaching fast, Jewish forces in Palestine achieved a clear military advantage over their Arab opponents. Meanwhile, US Zionists cranked up the pressure on a White House increasingly preoccupied by the upcoming November presidential election, whose outcome, some observers predicted, would be determined by the voting behavior of East Coast Jews. The CJP and ACJ responded by redoubling their own publicity efforts. Kim Roosevelt in particular worked frenetically to counter the "renewed effort to bring about the partitioning of Palestine," traveling to San Francisco to address a number of meetings organized by George Levison, drafting news releases, and huddling about strategy with Loy Henderson. Nonetheless, he found the mood among his Washington allies "gloomy," as he reported to ACJ president Lessing Rosenwald, and access to the White House—"the key to the whole situation"—impossible. By early May, Kim knew that the game was up, even as he and his allies rushed between meetings and rallies. "The fact is I am afraid that present conditions are extremely inauspicious," he wrote Elmer Berger on May 10, with uncharacteristic despondency. "Right at the moment I am feeling rather discouraged." On May 14, following a series of extraordinarily tense and ill-tempered meetings between State Department and White House officials, and just eleven minutes after Zionist leaders in Tel Aviv had declared their independence, a spokesman for the president announced formal US recognition of the new state of Israel.[25]

For the second time, the anti-Zionists had failed to carry America with them. This defeat was all the more bitter because of the bloody Arab-Israeli war that followed, and the accompanying flight and expulsion of Arab refugees from Palestine. Other setbacks followed in short order. Allegations of anti-Semitism aimed at CJP officers began to stick, especially to Virginia Gildersleeve, who was not helped by her reputation for deliberately fostering a genteel, WASP-ish atmosphere at

Barnard that many Jewish students found hostile. The appointment of their old friend Dean Acheson as successor to George Marshall in January 1949 provided some encouragement to the anti-Zionists, but it soon became clear that the new secretary of state intended to keep the CJP and American Council for Judaism at arm's length. Nor did the publication of *Arabs, Oil, and History* in April 1949 have quite the impact that Kim had hoped it would, possibly because, as he informed Berger, Zionist pressure had induced major reviewers, such as the Sunday *New York Times*, to bury it. The grandson of TR and the anti-Zionist rabbi commiserated with each as they rode in the Roosevelt family car back to Washington after an ACJ lecture in Baltimore, their "eloquent moans" just audible "above the rattle of the ten-year old Ford." Berger summed up the feeling of being an anti-Zionist in the late 1940s rather well. It was, he told Kim in March 1949, like marching through the ranks of a parade "in the opposite direction."[26]

KIM ROOSEVELT AND HIS ALLIES had failed to prevent US recognition of Israel in 1948, much as the OSS Arabists had been unable to avert the partition of Palestine the year before. Where Kim had done much better than the previous generation of Arabists was in promoting the Arab cause to the American public and organizing the various forces of anti-Zionism in US society, including anti-Zionist Jews. Thanks to his efforts, there now existed a dynamic, well-coordinated, and deeply committed anti-Zionist network capable of being reactivated in more auspicious times.

Nor were the prospects for Arabism on the ground in the Middle East itself entirely gloomy. Indeed, in Syria, the new CIA station chief was having the time of his life.

EIGHT

The Right Kind of Leader?
Syria, 1949

MILES COPELAND WAS DELIGHTED. Told to expect a "hardship post" when he set off for Damascus in September 1947, he arrived to find a city felicitously located between the mountains of Lebanon and the Syrian desert, a harmonious blend of gracious French avenues and picturesque cobbled streets. His wife, Lorraine, and their two children joined him early in 1948, and the young family moved into a seven-bedroom villa with a staff of servants drawn from nearby Christian villages. While Miles went to work under his cover as a foreign service officer at the legation (the US post in Damascus was not yet a full-fledged embassy), Lorraine shopped in the city's bustling souks and hitched plane rides with the US air attaché to other parts of the region. The legation was tightly run by Ambassador James Hugh Keeley Jr., an Arabist with long area experience who had arrived in Damascus shortly after Copeland, and morale among American officials was high.

The Copelands socialized with Miles's colleagues and members of the Levant's expatriate European community. As a childhood fan of Lawrence of Arabia, Lorraine was particularly thrilled to meet his

World War I companion, Colonel W. F. Stirling. But they did not confine themselves to Western circles, finding a warm welcome among elite Damascenes still well disposed toward the United States after a century of American "disinterested benevolence" in the region, and the legation's recent assistance in expelling the French. On weekends, the Copelands went picnicking in the surrounding countryside, often receiving spontaneous offers of hospitality from villagers who turned out to greet them. Sometimes they were joined on these outings by Archie Roosevelt, or they would drive across the mountains to see him in Beirut, where he was settling down to an equally pleasant existence in a little house in the Manara quarter, overlooking the waterfront. One summer, Archie and the Copelands rented a stone cottage together in the mountains above Beirut, taking long walks among the olive groves during the day and watching the city lights begin to twinkle below them as dusk gathered. It was "a wonderful period in our lives," Lorraine recalled later.[1]

Professionally, Miles and Archie faced a formidable task: building an espionage network almost from scratch. In Archie's case, the challenge was all the greater because, as he soon realized, the principal Lebanese agent he had inherited from the previous Beirut station chief, Dan Dennett, was making up his reports (Archie caught him in the act by inventing a story about a nonexistent Soviet embassy official that the agent duly confirmed as true). It was not long, however, before the young Arabist, putting to good use the language skills and capacity for cultural immersion he had already demonstrated in North Africa, was receiving a steady stream of intelligence reports in French, Arabic, and Russian from credible local sources. Indeed, newly independent Lebanon, with its many ethnic and religious communities, turned out to be the perfect espionage environment for the eternally curious, multilingual Archie Roosevelt. It was as if Harold Hoskins's abortive wartime Expedition 90 had at long last arrived at its intended destination, only in one-man form.[2]

In Damascus, meanwhile, Miles Copeland was proving no slouch in the espionage stakes, rapidly acquiring good Arabic (although he always spoke it with an Alabama drawl), recruiting local agents (such as a Damascus loan shark, who in turn helped him cultivate sources in the Ministry of Defense), and building up contacts in the Syrian intelligence service, the Deuxième Bureau. Whether his reporting to headquarters ever matched the quality of Archie's, though, is doubtful. According to Miles's later recollection, Archie would chide him "for fabricating his reports." "What's the difference between my fabricating reports and your letting your agents do it?" Miles would retort. "At least mine make sense."[3]

As this last comment suggests, there was more than a hint of game playing about both Miles's and Archie's early CIA careers in the Middle East. Almost immediately after arriving in the Levant, the two young men incurred the ire of their divisional boss, Mike Mitchell, by questioning his negative assessment of another Middle Eastern station chief they had encountered en route. Mitchell, according to Archie a rather humorless, moralistic Arab American of missionary stock, responded with an "eyes only" cable to Archie, stating, "Such irresponsible free-wheeling will not be tolerated in the future." Future reprimands of this nature were also directed to Archie in Lebanon rather than Miles in Syria, reflecting, presumably, the higher status of the Beirut station. Yet there was no shortage of questionable behavior on Miles's part.

This included one occasion, clearly much embellished in Copeland family legend, when a bedouin merchant turned up at the Damascus legation with a roll of parchment that Miles carried to the building's roof for photographing with his CIA-issue camera, in the process losing several pieces to the wind, only later to realize that they were a portion of the Dead Sea Scrolls. "Most of my station chiefs test the ice, then move cautiously across the pool," Mitchell told a friend of Archie's. "Miles, though, is an architect by nature—he'd build a submarine. And Archie would just rush on across the thin ice to the opposite side, never mind the consequences." The assessment would seem unfair to Archie, except that there was often a whiff of mischief making in the air whenever he and Miles got together. "Miles appears," reads Archie's diary for October 14, 1947. "Stupid tel[egram] from Wash[ington]. Lots of fun as ever." Ten days later: "Miles appears. Usual confusion."[4]

Later, the phenomenon of US intelligence operatives freewheeling in the Middle East would acquire more sinister overtones. At this early stage, however, such antics had an innocent, even benign quality to them. In *The Game of Nations*, Miles Copeland described the first American covert operations in post-mandate Syria as being focused on the elimination of corruption and intimidation in national elections held in July 1947. As he went on to explain, these efforts arose out of the idealistic impulses of the first generation of US government officers in the Levant, "mostly former missionaries and romantics," who wanted to free the Arab world of the last shackles of "Turkish or French sub-jection," and believed "that changing the leadership in Middle Eastern countries . . . was a matter of removing certain artificial props which were keeping in power leaders who, by rights, shouldn't be there in the first place." Miles even suggested that Syria was consciously viewed by US officials as a "pilot project" for testing the American capacity for exerting a democratizing influence on Arab countries. Although there is little other documentary evidence of the existence of such a program, we have little reason to disbelieve Miles on this score, as what he said about the American desire to aid "the rise of 'the right kind of leaders'" fits with what else we know about OSS and CIA Arabism in the 1940s, including the program outlined in Kim Roosevelt's *Arabs, Oil, and History* for boosting the position of young nationalist reformers in Arab society. Miles's "right kind of leaders" sounds a lot like Kim's "Young Effendis."[5]

If this was the original American game plan, it was upset by the UN vote on Palestine in November 1947. In Syria, the consequences of partition were manifold, beginning with a precipitous decline in the United States' popularity. "Everyone was aghast," remembered Lorraine Copeland. A mob besieged the legation in Damascus, tearing down the US flag and burning cars. Legation officials responded by working frantically to salvage America's image, remonstrating with Washington about its Palestine policy and striving to mend bridges to Syrian politicians. The initial turbulence abated as a result but flared up again with the declaration of Israeli statehood the following year and with the first anniversary of the partition vote, which was greeted with a fresh round of rioting in Damascus.[6]

The Palestine crisis, particularly the rout of Arab forces in the 1948 war with Israel, also affected Syria's internal politics. Syrians already faced a number of political challenges, including the sectarian and tribal tensions nurtured by the French, as well as constant interference by their Hashemite neighbors, Iraq and Transjordan. Both nursed ambitions to take over a country long regarded as the commercial, intellectual, and even spiritual center of the Arab world and schemed accordingly with rival Syrian factions. These divisions were reflected in the results of the elections that took place in 1947 (the same elections that US officials had tried secretly to police) and produced a weak, minority government under the presidency of the Damascene aristocrat Shukri al-Quwatli.

Meanwhile, new parties, defined by ideology rather than by sectarian identity, and more in touch with "the street," were beginning to emerge, among them the Ba'ath ("Renaissance"), a movement of nationalist, socialist intellectuals; the Communist Party; and the Muslim Brotherhood. The Arab-Israeli conflict only fractured these fault lines further, discrediting the Quwatli government, which handled the 1948 war ineptly, and providing radicals with a rallying cry that was to prove more powerful than even the struggle against European colonialism.

Kim Roosevelt lamented these developments in *Arabs, Oil, and History*, remarking on how Palestine had rendered the position of moderate, American-educated Young Effendis in Syria almost untenable. Viewed with the advantage of hindsight, however, a more important consequence of the 1948 Arab-Israeli War was its role in politicizing the Syrian army, whose officer corps felt that the nation's honor had been besmirched by its battlefield defeat. Often from humble, minority-community backgrounds that contrasted with the landed and merchant Sunni families who had so far dominated the nation's politics, these soldiers had begun to feel a burning sense of grievance against Syria's civilian politicians.[7]

As Miles Copeland wrote later, "the game environment was undergoing a rapid transformation." Viewed from Washington, events in Syria were deeply worrying. Instability in the country spelled trouble for a number of wider US interests in the region: ARAMCO's pipeline to the Mediterranean, TAPline, whose successful completion depended on the cooperation of the Syrian government; the security of Turkey, a crucial US ally on the southern rim of the Soviet empire; the Arab-Israeli conflict, whose peaceful settlement required Syrian willingness to come to the negotiating table; and the containment of communism, an ideology that thrived on conditions of political unrest. More generally, as the first of the Arab countries to truly escape from under European colonial control, Syria could be seen as a test case for what might happen elsewhere in the Middle East in the postcolonial era. A secret policy statement of January 1949 summed up what was at stake: "Owing to Syria's strategic location, economic potentialities and importance as a center of Arab political and cultural activity, it is essential to our general policy of maintaining and strengthening the regional stability and well-being of the Near East that Syria . . . be a democratic, cooperative and internally stable member of the world community."[8]

How, though, to accomplish this in practice? As with much else that was to follow in US Middle East policy over the next few years, a clue was provided in Kim Roosevelt's *Arabs, Oil, and History*. To judge by the contents of the final chapter, which explicitly revise some of the arguments made earlier in the book, Kim must have tacked on "A Footnote to Americans" at the last moment before publication, possibly at the same time he wrote the dedication, in February 1949. In it, Kim added an important qualification to his thesis that the United States' main aim in the Middle East should be to promote moderate, Western-educated nationalists using democratic methods. American democracy was, he now pointed out, the product of a specific set of historical conditions that were not necessarily present in the modern Arab world, while the position of the Young Effendis had been severely compromised by recent events. In these circumstances, such universal human values as "dignity, decency, and individual liberty" might stand a better chance of being defended by a form of government other than "a self-styled 'democracy,'" even if that meant the United States supporting autocracies. "To favor democracy and oppose imperialism," Kim concluded, ominously, "cannot . . . entirely do away with the hard fact that empires have existed and, though abbreviated, still do exist."[9]

It is not clear whether Kim specifically had the situation in Syria in mind when he wrote these words, but they were oddly prescient of what was about to take place in that country.

NOT LONG AFTER MILES COPELAND'S arrival in Syria, another American—a tough-looking, muscular, "James Bond kind of character" (as one of Miles's sons remembered him)—appeared in Damascus. Major Stephen J. Meade had served in the elite First US Army Ranger Battalion, the legendary "Darby's Rangers," during World War II, taking part in the Allied invasions of North Africa, Sicily, and Italy. According to Miles, he had also worked for the OSS, undertaking escape and evasion operations in Iran while disguised as a Kurdish tribesman and accompanying Archie Roosevelt on a mission to rescue some American missionaries who had been kidnapped by a fleeing SS platoon. Whether or not these last claims are true, it is clear that Meade was a highly coveted covert operative, lent out by the army to the CIA whenever the need was felt for his peculiar combination of physical strength, language skills,

and (to quote Miles's *The Game Player*) "earthy charm." After Meade
was posted to Beirut as assistant military attaché, Miles was instructed to
stay away from him—evidently Mike Mitchell feared that if these alpha
males ever got together, "it would somehow be a case of one and one
adding up to more than two," as Miles put it. But their paths kept crossing until, at a Beirut legation function, they agreed to "stop the cha-
rade." "We've got a lot to talk about," Meade told Miles, "so who cares
what the bureaucrats think?" Shortly afterward, the American minister
Jim Keeley requested Meade's transfer to Damascus.[10]

As a military attaché, Meade had unique access to the higher eche-
lons of the Syrian army, including a clique of discontented officers gathered around the chief of staff, a fifty-year-old Kurdish colonel called
Husni al-Za'im. Even allowing for Orientalist prejudice in Western descriptions of him, Za'im appears not to have been a prepossessing figure.
Heavyset and florid, he was vain, bombastic, and utterly unscrupulous.
Nonetheless, to dismiss him as a buffoon lacking "the competence of
a French corporal," as one US official did, was a mistake. For, as Steve
Meade was about to discover, Za'im possessed not only a well-laid plan
for obtaining political power in Syria—hardly surprising given that, according to the British military attaché, he had been toying with the idea
of a coup since March 1947—but also a clear vision of how he would use
that power once he had it, including proposals for far-reaching political,
social, and economic reform.[11]

Meeting with Za'im for the first time on November 30, 1948, Meade
was immediately struck (as he informed Washington) by how well the
Kurdish colonel's "strongman characteristics" would lend themselves
to an "army-supported dictatorship." In subsequent interviews, the two
men skirted around this possibility, but by early March 1949, the Syrian,
possibly persuaded by the assurances of their mutual friend, the head of
the Lebanese secret service, or Sûreté, had decided to take the American
into his confidence. Summoned to his side on March 3 and then again
on March 7, Meade heard Za'im predict that "widespread internal disturbances" would take place over the remainder of the month, causing
"the fall of the incumbent government" and "leaving the military establishment in control of the country." After the army takeover, Za'im
continued, the country's communists and "'weak' politicians" would be
rounded up and placed in "desert concentration camps." Meanwhile,
with Za'im effectively in charge as defense minister, the new government

would embark on a three- to five-year period of reform, including "the breakdown of feudal power with re-distribution of lands," and modernization of the country's political, judicial, and social welfare institutions. With Syrians thus "properly educated and disciplined," there would, Za'im assured Meade, be "a gradual lessening of regimentation of the population" over the next decade. In the meantime, however, there was "only one way to start the Syrian people along the road to progress and democracy," the would-be dictator exclaimed, hitting the desk with his riding crop, and that was "with the whip."[12]

The US minister, Jim Keeley, deplored talk of a military dictatorship: the notion of illegal regime change offended him morally, and, as an Arabist, he believed in the fundamentally democratic aspirations of the Syrian people. But he also feared that Syria was on the verge of complete collapse, and he was therefore prepared to go along with Za'im's plan as a way of safeguarding what he thought were the long-term prospects of democracy in the country. Such, anyway, is the claim advanced in Miles Copeland's 1969 book, *The Game of Nations*, which goes on to recount how, acting on explicit orders from Keeley, a "'political action team'" headed by Meade "systematically developed a friendship with Za'im, . . . suggested to him the idea of a *coup d'etat*, advised him how to go about it, and guided him through the intricate preparations in laying the groundwork for it." Miles's later autobiography, *The Game Player*, fleshed out this statement with more detailed descriptions of how Meade rode around Damascus in Za'im's limousine pointing out facilities to be seized in the hypothetical event of a coup and of how Miles himself used his agents in the Ministry of Defense to obtain "certain information" that Za'im himself could not request "without exciting suspicion." Miles also claimed to have met periodically with one of Za'im's co-conspirators, Adib al-Shishakli, a tank commander with a reputation as an amoral political operator (the two men were together one night when Lorraine Copeland, heavily pregnant with her third child, Ian, fell ill with eclampsia, and Shishakli helped save her life by rushing her to the hospital). The total effect of these passages was, as Miles presumably intended, to create the impression that Za'im's coup plan was a CIA operation from start to finish.[13]

Predictably, this version of events has proven highly controversial, with several critics suggesting that Miles greatly exaggerated his own contribution to Za'im's coup planning. Certainly, there is an even stronger literary quality to Miles's account of events in Syria than usual, with the reader sensing that, as events in the life of a CIA officer go, coups lend themselves particularly well to subsequent storytelling. "As I review my varied past in search of materials suitable for bedtime stories to tell my grandchildren, I find myself dwelling inordinately on *coups d'etat*," Miles himself admitted later in *The Game Player*. It also has to be said that Miles did not exactly help his own cause when, for no apparent reason, he suddenly backtracked in one passage of *The Game Player*, flatly contradicting his earlier account in *The Game of Nations* by stating that, in fact, "it was Husni's show all the way."[14]

Still, for all the doubts about Miles's veracity, there is some historical evidence, besides his testimony, of covert US plotting in Syria. For example, a young political officer in the US legation, Deane R. Hinton, later went on record stating that Copeland and Meade had indeed conspired with Za'im. (Hinton, who like many foreign service officers disapproved of the CIA's activities, went on to state that Miles considered himself "a bigger bigshot than the Minister" and that "hyperbole was his middle name.") Some Syrian sources also alluded to clandestine American meddling: the foreign minister in the Quwatli government, for one, suspected the "American military attaché" of nefarious activities.[15]

Surprisingly, it is the most implausible-sounding story in *The Game Player* that turns out to be the best supported in terms of other evidence. Trying to come up with ways of embarrassing the Quwatli government, Copeland and Meade (so Miles wrote later) hit on the idea of staging an incident at the former's home intended to suggest that foreign representatives in Syria had no protection from the country's authorities. The plan was to spread rumors that Miles kept secret documents in his house, luring Syrian intelligence officers into raiding it when it appeared to be unoccupied. Miles, Meade, and some American accomplices would then emerge from hiding places and apprehend the housebreakers. Preparations for the sting proceeded smoothly, with Lorraine Copeland and the children packed off to Lebanon and the villa booby-trapped with klieg lights and teargas canisters. Things started to go wrong after a larger-than-expected team of government goons arrived toting guns and opened fire when called on to surrender. The Americans returned fire and a twenty-minute gun battle ensued, only ending when the raiders fled by car, leaving the house's occupants unscathed. While Husni Za'im was delighted that the incident was even more spectacular than originally planned, Miles's boss in Washington, Mike Mitchell, was characteristically unimpressed, sternly demanding a detailed report of the whole incident.[16]

Although this all sounds like another Copeland yarn, it has some support from an unexpected quarter: a *New York Times* story, dated March 10, 1949, describing "four muffled gunmen" firing on the home of one Miles A. Copeland Jr., "attaché in the United States Legation" and "crack shot," who fired back with his pistol. Indeed, the explanation offered in *The Game Player* is rather more convincing than the one offered at the time by legation officials, who, according to the *Times*, stone-facedly insisted that "the attack had no political motive." There is, in addition, a substantial body of Copeland family lore about the shoot-out, not all of it concocted by Miles himself. For example, Miles III vividly remembers himself as a five-year-old being whisked away from Damascus to a hotel in the mountains, where he had to eat poached eggs, which he hated, and returning to find his home pockmarked with bullet holes. A contemporary document, a legation report of March 18, 1949, also offers a hint of corroboration, referring to Za'im's interest in having US agents "provoke and abet internal disturbance which [is] essential for [a] coup d'état."[17]

Of course, none of this necessarily proves Miles's original claim in *The Game of Nations* that Za'im was acting as an American agent. In fact, most of the available evidence indicates that it was the Kurd himself who took the initiative in plotting his coup. In the middle of March, for instance, he produced what he claimed to be a list of communist assassination targets featuring the names of eight Syrian officials, the American minister, and the British ambassador. Officials in the US legation suspected that he had fabricated the document in order to stoke Western concerns about Syrian internal security, thereby preparing the ground for a change of government. It is also clear that Meade was not the only Westerner Za'im took into his confidence. Both Colonel Gordon Fox, a British military adviser employed by the Syrian army, and the UK military attaché met with Za'im in March and heard his predictions of a military takeover, although in these conversations Za'im placed less emphasis on the threat of communism and his plans for social reform than on his desire for closer relations with the governments of Transjordan and Iraq—both British-backed regimes. In other words, the Syrian was tailoring his message, telling particular Westerners what he believed they wanted to hear.[18]

The coup itself, when it came in the early morning hours of Wednesday, March 30, 1949, was a masterpiece of military planning, bloodless apart from the deaths of three bodyguards attached to a government minister. As Miles recalled in *The Game Player*, Za'im distributed secret orders to four other senior army officers, with instructions that they open them separately at midnight, having taken the precaution of locking the two secretaries who had typed them in a Defense Ministry closet. At two thirty AM, infantry units and armored cars stationed outside Damascus rumbled into the city and disarmed police and the normal security forces. What happened next was a scene that would repeat itself numerous times in years to come, described on this occasion by British journalist Patrick Seale: "One detachment of troops arrested the President in hospital where he was receiving treatment for a gastric ulcer and heart complaint; another the Prime Minister; a third secured the radio station; a fourth took over police headquarters; a fifth the headquarters of the gendarmerie; a sixth the central telephone exchange." As dawn approached, the populace of Damascus "awoke to the sounds of the Syrian national anthem on the radio," wrote Copeland, "followed by the recorded voice of Husni Za'im announcing that he had taken over the country." According to Miles, this clockwork-like operation became a standard reference point in US efforts to effect covert regime change in other Third World countries, "studied in CIA training classes for the next two decades."[19]

Whatever the precise extent of covert US collusion with Za'im prior to his coup, American reservations about him of the sort expressed by Jim Keeley remained after he assumed power, causing a delay in Washington granting the new regime formal recognition. In the absence of regular diplomatic relations, Steve Meade carried on his precoup role as the primary point of American contact with the military leadership. Hence, when the US legation learned that Za'im was considering "execution, accident, and poisoned food" as possible means of disposing of ex-president Quwatli, Meade was dispatched to entreat the dictator to spare the life of his predecessor. "What do they want me to do with him, let him free to plot against me?" Za'im angrily asked his American friend. "I could easily prove that he died from natural causes." Eventually, however, the new Syrian leader was prevailed on to telephone the military hospital where Quwatli was being held. "How is he?" Meade heard him ask. "Give him lots of milk [and] cheese. . . . And let me know how he keeps; I am interested." Reassured by this dramatic show of concern for Quwatli's welfare, Meade departed to report Za'im's apparent change of heart to Keeley.[20]

Strains remained in US relations with Za'im (the "unscrupulous desperado," as Keeley called him just after the coup). American officials remained personally wary of the Syrian dictator, the result of a combination of Orientalist stereotyping, the undoubted fact of his universally acknowledged egotism, and a tendency to view him in light of previous US experience of military juntas in Latin America (Steve Meade once referred to him as a "'Banana Republic' dictator type.") On his side, Za'im resented the delay in formal US recognition of his authority, retaliating by holding up the possibility of his favoring France as Syria's principal future Western ally. He also had occasion to offer a mild rebuke to Meade when he found out that an indiscreet American official at the Saudi court had bruited their relationship to Ibn Saud. It was probably these incidents, rather than, as Miles Copeland comically implied, Za'im's vanity, that explain why the Syrian strongman became more distant in his behavior toward Miles and Meade, brusquely demanding that they stand up when he entered the room, and address him with the formal form of "you" in French (*vous*) rather than the familiar (*tu*).[21]

By and large, though, US observers were favorably impressed by Za'im's performance as Syrian head of state—not surprising, given that his policies might have been designed specifically to please them. Immediately after assuming power, he proclaimed his desire to ratify the much-delayed TAPline concession (delighting ARAMCO's James Terry Duce and Bill Eddy in Washington). Later in April, Za'im also announced his plans to improve Syrian relations with both Turkey and Israel, telling Jim Keeley confidentially that he was willing to resettle a quarter of a million Palestinian refugees in Syria and even meet personally with the Israeli prime minister, David Ben-Gurion. This was proof, so Keeley reported, of "his earnest desire to liquidate [the] Pal[estine] debacle by pursuing henceforth [a] policy of give and take." Meanwhile, as promised to Meade, Za'im embarked on an internal security crackdown, rounding up some four hundred alleged communists and sending a squad of twelve boxers and wrestlers to execute "speedy and clandestine arrests" in Lebanon and Iraq. When this anticommunist drive lost steam, the Syrian army intelligence chief asked Meade to help him identify Soviet agents, promising to deal with them "immediately and harshly."[22]

In addition to these welcome efforts to improve internal and regional stability, Za'im embarked on an ambitious program of domestic
reform and modernization. He reinforced and reequipped the demoralized Syrian army, eliminated corruption and nepotism in the civil service, and launched various public works projects. Literate Syrian women
acquired the right to vote, the use of such titles as Bey and Pasha was
banned, and Sharia laws were replaced by civil, criminal, and commercial codes. "Za'im shocked Damascus society out of its stuffy puritan-
ism," observed Patrick Seale. "He let it be known that he disapproved
of traditional Arab clothing and headgear, and the streets blossomed
with a curious collection of aged European hats." Even allowing for the
comedic elements, it was an impressive record of progressive accom-
plishment. The uncouth Kurdish colonel was coming on like one of Kim
Roosevelt's Young Effendis.[23]

By late April, Za'im's good behavior had at last brought his government formal US recognition. (Jim Keeley still bitterly regretted the
"negation of democratic process" but salved his conscience by telling
himself that Americans might "accomplish more on [the] moral plane
by exercising our influence for moderation . . . after initial recognition.")
Thereafter, Syrian-American relations improved steadily. During a conversation on June 4, Keeley accepted Za'im's assurances that a presidential election due to take place on June 25 would be entirely democratic,
remarking afterward that the colonel's "driving will to serve his country's best interests" was a "marked contrast to the traditional indolence
[of] . . . his predecessors." The following month, after a predictable
victory at the polls (there was, after all, only one candidate), President
Za'im conferred high Syrian decorations on both Keeley and Meade, the
latter sniffily described by a British embassy observer as "one of Za'im's
cronies." Reporting on the event, the *New York Times* took the opportunity to review the recent achievements of the Za'im government,
among them the TAPline agreement, improved relations with Turkey,
and increased watchfulness for communist penetration in the Middle
East. Along with the decorations for American officials, these actions all
testified, so the *Times* reported, to "Syria's outspoken attitude of good
will toward the United States."[24]

Sadly for Husni Za'im, American approval alone was not enough
to save him from his enemies among his fellow countrymen. Various
elements in Syrian society already had reason to dislike the dictator

even before he was elected to the presidency: radicals, Muslims, and nationalists who objected to his accommodating attitude toward Israel.
There were also indications that Syrian allies of the country's Hashemite neighbors, in particular Iraq, had begun to scheme against him. The
turning point came when Za'im lost the support of his main power base,
the army. His fellow officers had begun muttering darkly among themselves when Za'im exchanged the title of president for marshal, adorning
himself with an elaborate new uniform and a baton the size of a rolling
pin, swathed in gold and green velvet. The muttering increased when he
appointed as his prime minister a former associate of Quwatli's, Muhsin
al-Barazi, who was perceived in military circles as a Rasputin-like figure,
an "evil genius" behind the throne. What really doomed Za'im, though,
was his government's role in aiding the July 1949 arrest and execution in
Lebanon of the influential Syrian nationalist Antun Sa'adah, a disgrace-
ful act of betrayal in the eyes of many army officers and another stain
on the nation's honor.[25]

On August 14, 1949, following weeks of rumors about assassination
plots, and just three days after Steve Meade had paid a farewell call on
Za'im prior to returning to his post in Beirut, the Syrian army again
moved on Damascus in the small hours of the morning. Awake in her
villa off the main road, Lorraine Copeland heard what was becoming a
familiar noise: "the sound of tank engines, indicating that 'something
was up.'" As the column of armored cars advanced, detachments began
fanning out down side streets headed for various government facilities
in a maneuver identical to the operation of four and a half months earlier. The main difference between the March and the August 1949 coups
was that, in the earlier one, both President Quwatli and Prime Minister
Khalid al-'Azm survived their fall from power. It is unclear whether,
as the conspirators claimed, there was a hasty military trial or simply,
as seems more likely, a summary execution, but early in the morning of
August 14, Marshal Husni Za'im was shot to death, along with his prime
minister, Barazi. The Za'im regime had lasted just 136 days.[26]

THE TRUTH ABOUT THE CIA'S role in bringing Husni Za'im to power
probably lies somewhere in between Miles Copeland's original claim
that the March 1949 coup in Syria was entirely an Agency operation and
his later statement that it was all Za'im's own doing. On the one hand,

there are sources indicating that the Syrian conceived of the idea himself, staged certain incidents without consulting with American officials, and juggled potential Western supporters. On the other, US government records indicate that Steve Meade did enjoy an exceptional degree of access to Za'im in the weeks leading up to the coup, and there is other, scattered evidence of direct American involvement in its preparation. Even better documented is Meade's extensive contact with Za'im *after* the coup, when official American and British observers concurred in identifying the on-loan CIA operative as the dictator's principal Western confidant. And while Za'im was in power, the Syrian government pursued a set of policies that bore an uncanny resemblance to Cold War American aims for Middle Eastern defense and development. Taking all this into account, the most sensible conclusion to draw is that the coup was the product of both internal and external factors, a coming together of Syrian initiative and American encouragement.

While its causes remain hard to pinpoint precisely, the consequences of Za'im's power grab for the subsequent course of Syrian history are abundantly and painfully clear: a legacy of instability, authoritarianism, and anti-Americanism. The regime that succeeded Za'im's survived until December 1949, when it in turn was overthrown in a third putsch led by another military strongman, Miles's friend Adib al-Shishakli, ushering in a period of revolving-door civilian governments and growing behind-the-scenes military influence, until Shishakli himself assumed the presidency in 1951. Meanwhile, as rumors of American legation involvement in antigovernment plots became commonplace, the United States saw its image in Syria, a country understandably sensitive to the threat of foreign meddling, start to lose its luster. Previously, Americans had been known in the Levant as missionaries, doctors, and professors. Now they were starting to be seen as spies.

Clearly, the CIA Arabists had underestimated the obstacles in the path of democracy and reform in Syria—the corrosive aftereffects of colonial-era sectarianism and the multiple forces acting on the country from without—and overestimated their own ability to bring about positive political change through external manipulation. According to Miles Copeland's later reflections on the subject, this was not the lesson that was drawn from the Za'im episode. Rather, Miles concluded that Middle Eastern societies such as Syria were inherently prone to "chronic political instability" and "self-destructive emotionalism"; therefore, the next time the United States set about the "business of 'interference in the internal affairs of sovereign nations,'" it would need to find a stronger leader than Za'im, one capable "of building a durable power base and of surviving." In other words, "the problem," Miles declared, "was not one of bringing about a change of government, but of making the change stick."[27]

It would be a few years yet before the CIA Arabists encountered a young army officer in Egypt who possessed the "sticking" power that Husni Za'im had lacked. In the meantime, however, a precedent had been set. The Arabists had not given up their dream of creating an independent, modern, democratic Middle East allied with the United States, but they had shown themselves prepared to countenance military rule as a means to that end, thereby compromising the moralistic idealism of the previous generation of Arabists.

Part Three

Winning, 1949–1956

NINE

American Friends
of the Middle East

SOME TIME IN 1949—THE exact date is not publicly recorded—the head of the CIA's Near East division, Mike Mitchell, attended a top-level, interagency meeting in Washington to discuss the staffing of a new Cold War covert unit, the Office of Policy Coordination (OPC). The OPC was not concerned with espionage, the clandestine gathering of foreign intelligence, which remained the business of the CIA. Rather its mission—as explained in its charter, National Security Council (NSC) directive 10/2, of June 1948—was "covert operations," that is, "all activities" carried out against "hostile foreign states or groups" in such a way "that, if uncovered, the U.S. Government can plausibly disclaim any responsibility for them." As in the run-up to the creation of the CIA the previous year, some officials had been loath to give organized form to covert operations, believing that they were un-American and an invitation to domestic tyranny. This view prevailed to the extent that NSC 10/2 decreed a bureaucratic separation of powers, with the Office of Policy Coordination housed within the CIA but obliged to seek policy guidance from the secretaries of state and defense. Otherwise, though, the new outfit was pretty much unaccountable, with an extraordinary degree of operational latitude, reflecting the climate of Cold War crisis in which it was born (1948 was the year of the communist takeover in Czechoslovakia and the launch of the Berlin blockade). The State Department Sovietologists and ex-OSS Wall Street lawyers who had been pushing for ever greater secret government powers to wage the Cold War had triumphed; deception and subterfuge now had official sanction.[1]

"I think that Kermit Roosevelt, not Archie, would be better fitted for this role." Thus spoke Mike Mitchell, when discussion turned to candidates for the job of Near East division chief in the new covert operations unit. According to the explanation that Mitchell offered to Archie at the time, his reason for making the recommendation was that he feared losing the valuable services of the younger Roosevelt cousin as his Beirut station chief. One wonders, though, whether Archie's perhaps undeserved reputation for freewheeling might also have been an issue. "His attempts to accomplish the most and best in the shortest time have made him very productive but, on [a] few occasions, have left something more to be desired," declared Mitchell in Archie's 1949 CIA performance report. "He does not take criticism easily."[2]

In contrast with the sometimes excitable Archie, Kim had a reputation for cool handling of work situations and colleagues. Successive CIA personnel evaluations described him as "level-headed" and "astute in his dealings with people." According to the British double agent Kim Philby, who was stationed in Washington between 1949 and 1951, his American namesake was "a courteous, soft-spoken Easterner with impeccable social connections, well-educated rather than intellectual, pleasant and unassuming as host and guest. . . . In fact, the last person you would expect to be up to the neck in dirty tricks." Philby even claimed to have dubbed Kim Roosevelt "the quiet American" several years before his friend Graham Greene wrote a novel with that title. (Kim quoted these "surprisingly kind" comments in his memoir Countercoup, apparently missing the irony in Philby's description: "the quiet American" of Greene's novel is a well-meaning but naïve idealist whose actions prove disastrous.)[3]

Also in Kim's favor were the "impeccable social connections" noted by Philby. Not only was he closely associated with the new secretary of state, Dean Acheson, but there were also his old family ties with leading figures in the intelligence community, including the influential Allen Dulles, who had known him since he was a boy and who happened to take a particular interest in Middle Eastern affairs. Thanks to his wartime posting in Cairo, Kim also knew the man named to run the Office of Policy Coordination, Frank Wisner, the adventurous Southerner who had taken over the management of OSS Balkan operations from Stephen Penrose. This is not to mention the strong sway that Belle Roosevelt still held in Washington society. Archie Roosevelt shared some of these connections, but lacking Kim's appetite for the Washington power game and removed from the scene for long periods by his overseas postings, he was nowhere near as well networked as his cousin.[4]

Whatever the decisive factor, the selection of Kim over Archie Roosevelt to head up US covert operations in the Middle East was another turning point in the lives of the cousins. Archie was devastated by Kim's nomination, which he regarded as "an unfair, unprincipled act" on Mitchell's part. "It seemed like a fatal blow to my hopes for a future as the mastermind of U.S. intelligence in the Middle East, the role I then felt sure I was destined to fulfill," he wrote later. Kim, in contrast, was quietly delighted. For a government post, his new salary of $10,000 was quite decent, and very welcome after two years of freelancing (at GS-15, Kim was two points above Archie on the government pay scale, despite the latter's longer CIA service). The vaguely defined powers of the OPC held out the possibility of translating the Arabist manifesto outlined in *Arabs, Oil, and History* into practice without having to answer to Zionist supporters in Congress. (It helped here that Kim could count on the support of Secretary of State Acheson, who happened to share his belief in economic and social development as an instrument of foreign policy, as did Acheson's pick for assistant secretary for Near Eastern affairs, the oilman George C. McGhee.) Last, but by no means least, the role offered Kim the chance to indulge his penchant for Kipling-esque adventure in a classic spy landscape. Miles Copeland's later statement that Kim "joined the CIA frankly for reasons of adventure" was an exaggeration—but it did have some truth to it.[5]

Hence it was that on November 10, 1949, Kim Roosevelt reported to OPC headquarters on the Washington Mall to take up his duties as deputy chief of the Near East and Africa Division (NEA). The years that followed would constitute a defining period in modern US–Middle Eastern relations, as Kim first worked secretly to support the Arab world's

leading nationalist—the Egyptian Gamal 'Abdel Nasser—and then personally led a covert operation to topple the region's other most prominent
nationalist leader, Iran's Mohammed Mosaddeq. Nor was Kim's influence confined to the Middle East. At home, in America itself, the CIA
would be increasingly drawn into the domestic debate about US policy
toward Israel, as Kim used his new position to provide covert US government support for a group of apparently private American Arabists
and anti-Zionists.[6]

KIM ROOSEVELT'S FIRST VENTURE IN anti-Zionist organizing, the
Committee for Justice and Peace in the Holy Land (CJP), had fizzled
out from a combination of its "straitened financial condition . . . and the
curious reluctance of the press to report our activities," as Kim explained
to members. Another organization featuring much the same personnel,
the Holyland Emergency Liaison Program, was launched in September
1949 with the twin aims of coordinating relief efforts for Palestinian refugees and publicizing the Arab cause to Americans, but it too failed to
generate public support. Kim's attempts to organize the forces of American Arabism and anti-Zionism were, it appeared, doomed to an endless
cycle of initial optimism and eventual disappointment.[7]

By 1950, though, the Arabist camp enjoyed two advantages it had
not possessed before. One was the backing of a genuine American celebrity, the journalist Dorothy Thompson. Described in 1939 by *Time*
magazine as the most influential American woman after Eleanor Roosevelt, Thompson wrote a thrice-weekly column, "On the Record," that
was syndicated to two hundred American newspapers, and during the
late 1930s she appeared nightly as a news commentator on NBC radio.
Patrician-accented and formidable in appearance, Thompson had some
of the instincts of a literary bohemian—she had once been married to
novelist Sinclair Lewis—and was drawn to political controversy. She
was reputed to have inspired the character of the foreign correspondent
Tess Harding, an archetypal role for actress Katherine Hepburn in the
1942 movie *Woman of the Year*. Most of all, Thompson was famous for
having been tossed out of Germany in 1934, the first American journalist to be so treated by the Nazis, after having personally criticized
Adolf Hitler. She subsequently became a prominent campaigner in the
United States on behalf of the victims of the Third Reich, a position she
combined with vocal support for Zionism.[8]

It was a surprise, therefore, when in the late 1940s Thompson began voicing objections to various aspects of Zionist behavior, both in Palestine and in the United States: acts of terrorism against the British, harsh treatment of Palestinian Arabs, and the growth of nationalist feeling among American Jews, which she perceived as a form of divided loyalty. In response, she was attacked in Zionist media, and pressure was brought on some of the newspapers that carried her column to drop it. Thanks to a mixture of intellectual conviction, ruffled personal dignity, and sheer cussedness, this treatment only stiffened Thompson's resolve, and she began to cast around for possible comrades in her new cause. Catching word of this interesting development, the ever-resourceful anti-Zionist activist Rabbi Elmer Berger wrote her in January 1949, offering her the American Council for Judaism (ACJ) as a platform to express her misgivings about Zionism to the American Jewish community, and apprising his friend Kim Roosevelt of this valuable new contact. Later in the year, in November, she spoke to the ACJ's Philadelphia chapter, another shot across Zionist bows. Meanwhile, officers of the Holyland Emergency Liaison Program attempted to rope her into their activities, and the following year William Eddy started regularly writing her from the Middle East. By the summer of 1950, Dorothy Thompson was a card-carrying member of Kim Roosevelt's anti-Zionist network and a potential organizational figurehead in the tradition of the CJP chair Virginia Gildersleeve, only much better known.[9]

The other advantage enjoyed by American anti-Zionists in 1950 was even more important than the involvement of Thompson but less apparent to the outside observer—indeed, deliberately hidden from public view: the covert financial support of the CIA. Two years earlier, the Office of Policy Coordination had begun making secret payments to US labor leaders involved in overseas efforts to counter communist "front" activities in the international labor movement. By 1950, the list of those receiving clandestine subsidies from the CIA had grown to include several other citizens' groups on the American Non-Communist Left, among them students and intellectuals, and the OPC was experimenting with various forms of funding pass-through to disguise its grants, including fake charitable foundations. Maintaining secrecy across this sprawling, tentacular operation was not easy for the intelligence officers involved, but they were helped by the anticommunist consensus that prevailed in early Cold War America and by the social deference they could generally count on others to show them on account of their elite backgrounds.

It would not be until 1967, with the anticommunist consensus badly undermined by the Vietnam War and the social power of old East Coast elites eroded by the cultural upheavals of the sixties, that the CIA's cover would be blown by the radical West Coast magazine *Ramparts*.[10]

Although the relevant official records remain closed to researchers, it is possible to assemble a quite detailed picture of CIA front operations from clues contained in papers left by the private citizens who participated in them. The first hint that Kim Roosevelt was thinking of using the front tactic to promote the causes of Arabism and anti-Zionism dates from June 1950, when his correspondence with Elmer Berger started to feature veiled references to the possibility of Berger taking on some official work in Washington. Later in the year, in December, with Berger still waiting for "clearance," the OSS Arabist Bill Eddy wrote Cornelius Van H. Engert, a retired foreign service officer and former US ambassador to Afghanistan, informing him of a plan to create "a small group . . . to promote fellowship and interest in the Near East." Engert responded enthusiastically, noting the possible interest in this suggestion of an old friend of his, Allen Dulles, who was in the process of joining the CIA as deputy director. In January 1951, around the same time that Dorothy Thompson was returning from a two-month tour of the Middle East (an idea originally suggested, according to one of Thompson's biographers, by Arabist acquaintances in the State Department), Berger was cleared to begin part-time consultancy duties with the CIA, which he carried out while continuing to work full-time for the American Council for Judaism.[11]

On March 16, 1951, Berger wrote Thompson asking to see her "at a very early date *privately* [emphasis in the original] on a matter of the utmost importance and confidence." At the end of March, Berger and Thompson (who was already friendly with Allen Dulles) traveled to the nation's capital for meetings about the "Washington project" with Kim Roosevelt and other, unidentified CIA officers. Early the following month, Thompson circulated a letter (probably drafted with the assistance of Berger and Engert) to a long list of prominent US citizens. Stressing the importance of "the spiritual and cultural bonds between the civilizations of the Middle East and our own" as a defense against "the onslaught which Communism is today preparing against us," this letter proposed the formation of a group to promote US–Middle Eastern friendship, adding that "some financial support would be forthcoming" for the initiative. On May 11, Allen Dulles instructed office staff at the CIA to expect a call from Engert, who was "engaged in setting up . . . a committee and [would] need office space and personnel." Four days later, on May 15, twenty-four people meeting at Thompson's spacious Manhattan residence on East Forty-Eighth Street formed a steering committee to launch a new organization, the American Friends of the Middle East (AFME).[12]

Despite all these signs of CIA involvement, as of summer 1951 the American Friends of the Middle East still had quite an ad hoc, amateurish feel to it. With Dorothy Thompson retreating from the New York heat to her farmhouse in the Vermont countryside, the spry former diplomat Cornelius Van Engert took up residence in her Manhattan home and began attending to such matters as the new group's legal incorporation and creating a checking account for it at Thompson's bank. There are also indications that, at least at this stage, ARAMCO was carrying on its role as a discreet benefactor of American Arabism. The company's chief Washington-based executive, James Terry Duce, corresponded frequently with Engert, while Bill Eddy continued to write Thompson on a regular basis. Eddy would later refer to himself as a member "of Dorothy Thompson's original advisory committee."[13]

It was not until October 1951 that the CIA took steps to give the American Friends of the Middle East a more permanent, professional basis, appointing a case officer for the organization and dispatching him to New York to set its affairs in order. Unusually for an Agency front group, it is possible to identify the case officer in question thanks to some unofficial correspondence discovered in a collection of family papers. As his name suggests, Mather Greenleaf Eliot was from an old WASP dynasty. His ancestors included William Greenleaf Eliot, the founder of Washington University in St. Louis, and one of his cousins was T. S. Eliot (as already noted, Kim Roosevelt's favorite poet). Born in 1911 in Berkeley, California, Mather graduated from Antioch College, Ohio, in 1933 and then spent several footloose years roaming from job to job—relatives describe him as a gregarious dilettante—before serving in the US Army during World War II and with American occupation forces in postwar Berlin. He joined the CIA early in 1950, finding it "something of a grind and not too rewarding" at first, until his transfer in June 1951 to the Near East division, where he discovered a team of "adventurous spirits" like himself.

After several months spent reading various classic works of Orientalist scholarship, Eliot returned from a vacation in October to "a big job" (as he proudly wrote his parents), "an organization with headquarters in New York, a promising program, but a wholly inadequate staff whose members, to boot, were in a sorry state of bad morale due to ill-assorted personalities and a sad lack of direction and care from Washington." After a month of "patient negotiating with scores of people," Eliot secured the services of the Virginia minister Garland Evans Hopkins, who since the demise of the Committee for Justice and Peace in the Holy Land had been working in Chicago as associate editor of the *Christian Century*. Promising him a princely annual salary of $12,000, Eliot installed Hopkins in new offices in midtown Manhattan, on East Fifty-Seventh Street, with "a staff about him who were transformed from gloom to confidence." The CIA officer then set to work steering "the revitalized 'project' through a hierarchy of committees . . . to approve its enlargement . . . into a size . . . that is realistic in relation to the job to be done."[14]

The fruits of these labors became apparent at a second meeting of the new organization's charter members on December 12, 1951, when Thompson announced that she had just received a gift of $25,000 from a donor who wished to remain anonymous, with a pledge of a further $25,000 if she matched the amount with donations from other sources. (Incidentally, $25,000 was exactly the amount paid by an anonymous donor to another CIA front group, a women's organization called the Committee of Correspondence, when it was launched in January 1953.) "Our situation is that we have friends who say 'Go ahead, but for God's sake don't tell that I gave you any money,'" Thompson informed those present, before revealing that "it certainly was not the oil interests who made this contribution" and that the mysterious patron was interested in "piping down some of the radical Zionists." Cornelius Van Engert, now acting as the American Friends of the Middle East's secretary-treasurer, rose to the donor's challenge and secured the additional funding during the spring of 1952. Later in the same year, the Dearborn Foundation, only just formed in Chicago, made the first of a series of regular grants to the organization that would, by 1957, add up to a recorded total of roughly $1.5 million. The Dearborn, whose other beneficiaries included the women's front group, the Committee of Correspondence, was one of the foundations identified in the *Ramparts'* revelations of 1967 as a CIA conduit.[15]

Although Kim Roosevelt had by this point retreated entirely from public view, there are occasional hints of his continuing to exercise a strong interest in the American Friends of the Middle East from behind the scenes. "One of his 'little boys' was up here on Tuesday," Elmer Berger wrote his and Kim's mutual friend George Levison from New York on December 20, 1951, probably referring to Mather Eliot, "and he tells me that Kim is involved more than ever."[16]

ITS FUNDING ASSURED, THE AMERICAN Friends of the Middle East now set about creating a permanent administrative structure for itself. In December 1951, at the same meeting that heard Thompson's announcement about the anonymous grant, the organization's charter members constituted themselves as a National Council, elected a board of directors to make policy, and formed an executive committee to carry it out, consisting of the president, Dorothy Thompson; the vice president (effectively, chief executive officer), Garland Evans Hopkins; and the secretary-treasurer, Engert. By April of the following year, Hopkins had established four executive departments: Intercultural Relations, Research and Publications, Public Relations, and Student Affairs. Volunteer branches sprang up around the United States—those in Chicago and Los Angeles proved especially active—as well as in the Middle East itself, the latter mainly attached to American colleges in the region. By the summer of 1953, the organization had begun setting up field offices in Middle Eastern cities: first in Tehran, under the direction of a former Presbyterian minister, Charles R. Hulac Jr., and then in Jerusalem under John W. Barwick, previously a YMCA worker aiding Palestinian refugees in Lebanon and Jordan. In October 1953, Mather Eliot himself traveled to Damascus to assume the post of AFME Middle East director.[17]

With this apparatus in place, and with its recorded annual budget rising to over half a million dollars by 1955, AFME embarked on an impressively wide-ranging program of activities. Annual meetings in New York, noted for their lavish standard of hospitality, were complemented by numerous lectures and other local events, many hosted enthusiastically by volunteer members. Distinguished Middle Eastern guests visited the United States on AFME grants, while American grantees and officers of the organization traveled in the other direction. Cultural exchange was also the theme of a thriving student program that included support for Arab student conferences and organizations in the United States and local screening of Middle Eastern applicants for American universities in Iran and Iraq. (The latter service was pioneered by Charles Hulac, who came to AFME from a position as international student director at Lafayette College, Pennsylvania, an institution with several other Middle Eastern links.) In addition to building a well-stocked library at its headquarters, AFME published its own books and pamphlets, a monthly newsletter, and remarkably detailed and handsomely produced annual reports; a subsidiary service, Phoenix, provided "background" news releases about and to the Middle East. The organization was also behind a well-publicized convocation of Christian and Muslim theologians that took place in Dhahran, Saudi Arabia, in April 1954, and led to the formation of the Continuing Committee on Muslim-Christian Cooperation, a separate entity that received AFME assistance and guidance through its co-secretary chair, Garland Hopkins.[18]

In all these activities, AFME's directors and officers consistently expressed a clear set of values. Perhaps the strongest of these was a sense of cultural and spiritual identification between America and the Middle East. In part, this reflected the prior engagement of many of the individuals concerned in missionary and educational work in the region, an experience that sensitized them to the interpersonal dimension of foreign relations. As Garland Hopkins put it in the organization's 1954–1955 annual report, citing John Barwick's aid work in Palestinian refugee camps as an example, "the personal element is of the essence." This emphasis on Americans' nonmaterial bonds with the Middle East also sprang from a deep historical consciousness of the area's role as a "cradle" of monotheistic world faiths, the "Religions of the Book," as writer, former OSS operative, and AFME director Harold Lamb called them—meaning not just Christianity and Judaism but Islam as well. The fundamental similarity between the religious beliefs of Christians and Muslims was a frequent refrain of the organization's supporters. "We . . . share with Islam many of our prophets and much of our Scripture," wrote William Eddy. "We [also] share the beliefs in reverence, humility, charity, the brotherhood of mankind, and the family as the sacred unit in society." Other statements from the AFME circle pointed out how Arab scholars had nurtured the "ideas of Western civilization" during the European Dark Ages, thereby implying a Western debt to the Arab world that had yet to be repaid.[19]

Those around AFME also shared the belief that, since the missionary endeavors of the previous century, Americans' relations with Arabs and Muslims had become clouded by mutual misunderstanding and ignorance. "Too often Americans are apt to think of the Middle East either in the romantic terms of the 'Thousand and One Nights,' or as a vast petroleum reservoir," explained an AFME statement in 1951. For their part, Middle Easterners generally failed to see through the superficial materialism of modern American life to the spiritual values that lay underneath, animating the nation's very existence. At a time when communism was seeking to portray itself as holding the same precepts as the great religions yet really was working "to capture and eventually destroy" both Christianity and Islam, this situation was downright dangerous.[20]

AFME's mission was clear. On the one hand, the organization had a duty to reeducate Americans about Arabs and Muslims' contribution to Western civilization, to "get away from thinking of the Middle East only in terms of strategy or oil or trade," as Cornelius Van Engert put it. On the other, AFME was charged with helping Middle Easterners understand that, for all the United States' obvious scientific and technical progress in recent times, still "Americans regard spiritual and cultural values as supreme." To be sure, there was a Cold War purpose to this program. By raising consciousness of a common spiritual heritage in the United States and Middle East, AFME would also be generating a shared awareness of "the same menace of atheistic communism or materialism that we ourselves fear and feel menaced by," as Engert told the December 1951 meeting of the organization's founders. In Bill Eddy's mind, the idea of a "moral alliance" against communism between Christianity and Islam was the key to winning the Cold War in the Middle East; he pushed this idea heavily throughout the early 1950s, both in Washington and the region itself, discussing it (as he informed Dorothy Thompson in June 1951) with the secretary-general of the Arab League, the grand mufti of Jerusalem, and Saudi Arabia's King Ibn Saud.[21]

AFME's purpose was not confined merely to gaining tactical advantage in a new theater of the Cold War. In keeping with Eddy's earlier vision of a great synthesis of Christian and Muslim civilizations, the organization's founders nursed notions of something much grander. America could settle the West's ancient debt to the East, they believed, by sharing with it the benefits of recent Western progress, political as well as material, and supporting new Arab nations as they moved toward democracy "in their own several ways." In return, the Middle East could convey some of the religious intensity of modern Islam back into the United States, helping "Americans themselves revive and reactivate the spiritual truths." (Anxiety about the materialism of modern American life was a nagging undercurrent in many utterances of the AFME Arabists, much as it had been for several nineteenth-century missionaries.)[22]

This is not to say that the Arabists of AFME envisioned a completely equal exchange between West and East. Admiration for the ancient glories of Islamic civilization tended to go hand in hand with perceptions of more recent "cultural stagnation," to quote Garland Hopkins, which in turn implied the need for benign American tutelage in the ways of modernity. It is also noticeable that, although their principal interest clearly lay in the Arab world, officers of AFME tended to favor a rather vague and elastic definition of the "Middle East"—according to Hopkins, it was "more a psychological than a geographical area," extending "from Morocco through Indonesia"—that arguably invited the maximum play of US power in the region. Still, compared with earlier colonial and Orientalist approaches, AFME represented a new departure of sorts, an effort to place Western relations with Arabs and Muslims on a more humane, engaged, mutually beneficial footing.[23]

Perhaps the clearest expression of this impulse was the vehemence with which AFME's leaders rejected the legacy of European colonialism in the Middle East. Garland Evans Hopkins was especially vocal on this score, telling the State Department in 1953, for example, that it should "support those seeking freedom from foreign-sponsored ... ruling cliques who are now in control in some of the Middle Eastern countries." As he went on to make clear, Hopkins was referring not only to the French but the British as well, whom he denounced for their continuing grip on the Suez Canal and Iran's oil fields. Dorothy Thompson went further still when, speaking in Iraq during the first official Middle Eastern tour by AFME representatives in 1952, she told an audience of American University of Beirut graduates that Britain was "an over-populated little island casting about for friends to keep her alive." A more measured statement by the organization from later in the decade, while noting the need for the United States to honor its commitments to its Western European allies, nonetheless insisted on "the premise that our sympathies

are with peoples seeking the national goals for which we struggled successfully," thus equating Arab nationalism with America's own history
of successful rebellion against colonial rule.[24]

Finally, while less immediately obvious as a motivating force for
AFME than it had been for some of its organizational predecessors, and
playing second fiddle to the more positive goal of promoting intercultural dialogue with Arabs and Muslims, anti-Zionism was clearly present in the organization's value system, detectable in vague references
to "special interests" subverting US foreign policy and in the absence
of Israel from the roster of Middle East countries included in AFME
exchange programs and other activities. This was perhaps unsurprising,
considering that, although there had been some changes in open leadership positions since the days of the Committee for Justice and Peace—
Kim Roosevelt's disappearance from the public eye, for example, and
Gildersleeve's replacement by Thompson—many of the same personalities were involved behind the scenes.

Elmer Berger had consulted extensively with the CIA as AFME was
set up in 1951, and he served as the new organization's "chief pamphle-
teer" in the first months of its existence. Thereafter, although he did
eventually join AFME's National Council the following year, Berger
kept a low profile, encouraging his American Council on Judaism colleague Morris Lazaron to play a more visible role. There was a danger
of AFME's Protestant leaders being tarred with anti-Semitism, Berger
told Lazaron, and this made it "extremely important for some Jewish
representation to be present." Berger also kept George Levison apprised
of developments, explaining that, because of "the difficulties of money
appropriated from Washington," the new organization was obliged to
soft-pedal on domestic activity until it was able "to build up some kind
of a segregated bank account." This was a reference, presumably, to the
provision of the 1947 National Security Act that explicitly prohibited
the CIA from operation within the United States.[25]

Was AFME's anti-Zionism related to anti-Semitic attitudes in the
organization's circle, as Zionist critics would allege later? This question
is impossible to answer categorically, but there are indications that at
least one AFME officer, Dorothy Thompson, held some problematic
ethnic and religious attitudes. "I am *seriously* concerned about the position
of the Jews in the United States," she wrote Virginia Gildersleeve in August 1951. "Everything on the surface seems to be going the Zionist way,

but underneath the country is beginning to seethe with resentment . . . and [people] are asking themselves the question: who is really running America?" Anti-Zionists had long used the argument that Zionist agitation in the United States invited an anti-Semitic backlash, but Thompson's expression of it lacked the tact and restraint of earlier statements by the likes of Kim Roosevelt. Nor was she any more sensitive in her remarks to Jewish anti-Zionists, complaining to Berger, for example, about "this self-centered insensibility of the Israeli (and the Zionists), this lack of any radio-receiving stations in their minds, ears or pores, so extraordinary among Jews, whom I have always thought to be possessed of, even afflicted by, hyper-sensibility." Not that she confined such characterizations to Jews: Arabs were also ascribed a "supersensitive" nature, the result, Thompson informed her British friend Rebecca West, of a collective "psychological trauma involving 'status' and inferiority, made more murderous by the fact that they damned well *are* inferior." Despite her record of courageous identification with the victims of Nazi racism, Dorothy Thompson appears to have harbored prejudiced attitudes that embraced all Semites, Arab as well as Jewish.[26]

Thompson was, however, unusual in AFME's inner circle in that she was neither an anti-Zionist Jew nor a thoroughgoing Arabist with long, firsthand area experience. There is no conclusive documentary evidence of individuals who fall into either of these two categories holding anti-Semitic views—unless, of course, one interprets anti-Zionism as prima facie proof of anti-Semitism or, in the case of anti-Zionist Jews, Jewish self-hatred. Equally, though, there is little sign that the upper-class Gentiles around AFME ever developed much consideration for the post-Holocaust emotions of American Jews, the more subtle example of Kim Roosevelt's anti-Zionism notwithstanding; Bill Eddy's willingness to consort with the anti-Semitic and pro-Nazi grand mufti is a case in point. Indeed, after the disappointments of Palestinian partition and US recognition of Israeli statehood, the anti-Zionism of older Arabists like Eddy only hardened further. There was also a growing sense of aristocratic irritation about the new influence of Zionist lobbyists on the domestic political process and, indirectly, on official foreign relations. "If U.S. policy, under our democratic system, must be determined by the need of politicians for funds and votes in our domestic elections," wrote Eddy to Thompson in October 1951, "then it should be necessary some day, as George Kennan has remarked, to take a second look at the alleged blessings of our American democratic system." Until some way of moderating the baleful effects of excessive democracy was found, so the reasoning went, American Arabists and anti-Zionists would have to resort to the stratagem of executive secrecy, in the form of covert CIA funding.[27]

WHILE IT IS HARD TO say for certain in the absence of the relevant CIA files, it is possible to infer from various other sources some of the tactical objectives that the Agency brought to its secret relationship with the American Friends of the Middle East. To start with perhaps the most obvious of these, the presence of AFME field offices in the Middle East provided CIA officers with nonembassy cover to carry out their espionage and covert action duties. There is scattered evidence from credible sources of AFME representatives in the Middle East performing such a function: one, based in Syria, would rendezvous with members of the embassy CIA station at night in "the 'safe houses' that the station maintained for clandestine contacts" to pass on the intelligence he had gathered; another, in Baghdad, would type up "at least weekly roundups" of local events and hide them in "a special bookcase with a secret compartment in its base." The presence of these "deep-cover" intelligence officers was convenient for Middle Easterners wanting to maintain a "back channel" to the US government. One AFME representative suspected that most local officials realized that the organization was a front but cooperated with it because it served their interests to do so.[28]

AFME's appearance as a nongovernment organization was also useful when it came to promoting cultural exchange. Middle Easterners were more likely to accept an invitation to visit the United States from a voluntary association than from a government agency, while Americans going the other way enjoyed more credibility in Arab and Muslim eyes when traveling with private as opposed to official sponsorship. "In a number of cases we have found it extremely helpful to call on AFME to sponsor certain visits which we as a government were unable to sponsor," one State Department officer informed another in 1959. "Exchanges under such auspices tend to give the individuals concerned an independent status which enhances their effectiveness." It was not just the unpopularity of Western governments in the Arab world that made the use of nonofficial instrumentalities so desirable there; the region's historical experience of benevolent actions by private American citizens meant that organizations such as AFME could draw on "the good will of their predecessors," as William Eddy put it.[29]

AFME had one more practical use for its covert official sponsors that belied its overt purpose: its mere existence testified to the existence of Arabist, anti-Zionist opinion in the United States, and therefore of the possibility of the US government adopting a Middle East policy less favorable to Israel and more so to the Arab countries. Whether or not this might happen in reality was, of course, very much open to question, not least given that AFME was launched while Harry Truman, the president who had recognized the independence of Israel just eleven minutes after its declaration, was still in the White House. Still, it was desirable to maintain the *impression* that such change might occur. "In the absence of any marked change in policy which would remove [Arab] political mistrust, we, as propagandists, can only do our best to keep alive the hope in the Arab world that a political solution on the part of the United States is possible," explained the US ambassador to Iraq, Burton Y. Berry, in 1952, before going on explicitly to describe the government's "channel to the activities of the American Friends of the Middle East" as holding "the greatest promise in this direction." In this respect, AFME was similar to other CIA front activities that enabled the US government to present more than one face to foreign audiences simultaneously—for example, the secret subsidizing of groups on the Non-Communist Left at a time when the US Congress was experiencing the conservative convulsions of McCarthyism.[30]

In addition to offering a glimpse of the CIA's tactical aims in running AFME, State Department records and other, privately generated documents throw light on the security arrangements the Agency used to "handle" its Middle Eastern front group. First, it assigned the organization a case officer, who helped manage its day-to-day affairs— a role performed initially by Mather Eliot, whose frequent meetings in New York with the organization's leadership were explained away by his adopting the guise of Dorothy Thompson's personal secretary. After Eliot moved into the field as AFME Middle East director in 1953, two other junior CIA officers, Jack Williams and Lorraine Nye Norton, "teamed up" as his "joint 'backstop'" in the United States. Norton, a native New Yorker who had spent much of World War II in occupied France as a doctoral student at the Sorbonne, was an accomplished literary scholar, former wife of a son of the eminent French Arabist Maurice Gaudefroy-Demombynes, and fluent French speaker who had joined the CIA as a North Africa specialist in 1950. Later, in 1956, when Eliot left AFME altogether and began a new cover assignment as an oilman in Iran, Norton took over the job of the organization's case officer from him, making her one of very few women to command such responsibility in the CIA at this time. (Much later, Eliot and Norton would marry.)[31]

The case officer was not the CIA's only channel to AFME. The board of directors was an important medium of communication, with men styled as representatives of the Dearborn Foundation attending meetings in order to pass on decisions about general policy or particular projects made elsewhere, which were then relayed by board members to the organization's executive officers. (The Committee of Correspondence, the CIA's all-woman front group, received similar visits from "the Dearborn.") According to Lorraine Norton, her commanding officer, H. Ben Smith, would often be in attendance, and sometimes Kim Roosevelt himself would sit in. AFME's executive officers, all of whom had sworn official secrecy oaths and, according to Norton, received payment for their services, also communicated directly with senior Agency personnel. For example, Dorothy Thompson's personal papers include a copy of a letter from Garland Evans Hopkins addressed to a Harold U. Stobart (probably a code name or "funny name") at a post office box in Washington containing confidential information about the Continuing Committee on Muslim-Christian Cooperation, laying out various financial requirements, and identifying "people fully to be trusted to cooperate" whose participation should "allow the maximum opportunity for guidance." Although one of her biographers denies it, Thompson herself was clearly "witting"—operational terminology for private citizens who were privy to details of the CIA's relationships with front groups—judging not only by her coy remarks about the anonymous donor of $25,000 at the organizing meeting in December 1951 but also by her advice to Garland Hopkins during the 1954 search for someone to direct the Phoenix news service that "nobody should be hired without previous and unequivocal clearance." Thompson was, however, reluctant to take money from the CIA, Norton recalls, presumably because she feared damage to her journalistic reputation if word ever got out.[32]

Finally, there is evidence that some AFME field station workers besides Mather Eliot were career intelligence officers. For example, "Keith

Williams" (probably another code name), an AFME representative in Damascus, was later identified as an undercover CIA man, as was "Eugene Burns," an AFME relief worker in Baghdad. Meanwhile, at its domestic headquarters in New York, AFME took on administrative staff who had previously worked for other groups later revealed to be CIA fronts, often women graduates of the Seven Sisters colleges. Vassar-educated Nancy Spofford, for example, came to the organization from Radio Free Europe; Alice B. Whelen, AFME's general factotum in its earlier days, was a graduate not only of Smith but also of the OSS, for which she had worked "in the psychological warfare field in connection with the Italian and North African campaign." Again, the same practice took place in the Committee of Correspondence.[33]

There is, then, evidence aplenty of the CIA using AFME for tactical purposes in the Middle East and keeping a tight hold on the organization's affairs at home. But it would be a mistake to leap to the conclusion that the organization was merely an inanimate instrument of the Agency's will—a puppet on a string, as it were. A number of considerations weigh against such a view of AFME: the long history of private-citizen engagement in the Middle East that preceded its creation, its immediate organizational origins in spontaneous anti-Zionist activism by nongovernment actors, and the fact that the man in overall charge of the CIA's Middle Eastern program, Kim Roosevelt, had himself participated in that tradition. Historians of CIA front operations on the Non-Communist Left have noted how many of the intelligence officers involved naturally shared the liberal political values of the citizen groups they were secretly subsidizing. A similar pattern seems to have prevailed in the case of AFME, except that the values concerned were Arabism and anti-Zionism. Indeed, the hold of these values appears to have been so strong that even CIA officers who lacked a prior history of engagement with the Arab cause, such as Mather Eliot, soon developed an Arabist and anti-Zionist mind-set after becoming involved with the organization. Writing to his parents in December 1953 following a tour of "the front lines of Jordan and Israel," Eliot lamented the lot of the Palestinians evicted from land that was "their whole life and their whole inheritance," predicting that the "Jews who took easily will live to rue . . . the day they did this taking."[34]

In other words, the relationship between the CIA and the American Friends of the Middle East was less like that of a patron and client than an alliance of partners united by a shared purpose and outlook. That said, there was a fundamental contradiction involved in the arrangement. AFME professed to represent a private tradition of disinterested American engagement with the Arab world, yet it was secretly dependent on US government support for its very existence. Moreover, while the CIA might have naturally shared AFME's agenda and therefore have been disinclined to meddle in the group, its control of the purse strings did give it the ultimate say in the affairs of its Arabist front organization—the power to call the tune, as it were.

WHILE KIM ROOSEVELT WAS AT last realizing his long-held ambition of creating a viable Arabist citizen group, Archie Roosevelt, the man he had beaten out for the Office of Policy Coordination job, was in crisis. In addition to his strained relationship with his boss, Mike Mitchell, Archie had clashed with the US ambassador in Lebanon, Lowell C. Pinkerton (a not uncommon occurrence in the early history of the CIA, as jurisdictional disputes arose between veteran diplomats and novice spies). His family life offered scant consolation, as he and KW, who had eventually gone out to join him in Beirut with young Tweed, remained trapped in a loveless marriage. To cap it all, in the summer of 1949, Archie had nearly died from endocarditis, a bacterial infection of his faulty heart valve, only surviving thanks to treatment he received at the American University of Beirut hospital. In an implicit protest at the wretched state of his life, Archie took the unprecedented step, for a Roosevelt man, of growing a beard, attracting the disapproval of his militaristic father and causing children in Cold Spring Harbor to run after him, laughing and pointing.[35]

Archie's fortunes eventually began to turn around after he returned home from his Beirut tour of duty. In November 1949 he went on loan from the CIA to work at the New York offices of the Voice of America, overseeing the launch of US broadcast operations in the Middle East. He and KW at last began divorce proceedings, and he moved into a small midtown apartment in Manhattan. Then, one Saturday in June 1950, while Archie was catching up on paperwork at his office, there was a knock on his door. A Vassar senior, Selwa "Lucky" Showker, had been sent to see him by his wartime mentor, Edwin Wright, to discuss the possibility of working on the Voice's Arabic service—and perhaps be assessed for recruitment by the CIA. The daughter of Lebanese Druze immigrants who spoke with an accent that reflected her upbringing in Tennessee—very different from the clipped East Coast tones Archie was used to hearing—Lucky instantly captivated the young Arabist. Although it soon became evident that she did not have enough Arabic to be useful to either the Voice or the CIA, Archie, in a moment of romantic impetuosity, asked her to lunch. After flirting outrageously over cocktails, the two contrived to spend the rest of the afternoon and all of Sunday together as well, Archie accompanying Lucky back to Vassar, unable to tear himself away. The following week he could hardly contain his excitement as he lunched with Miles Copeland, also now based back in the United States, rhapsodizing about the "semitic" beauty of the Lebanese woman from the South. "She's even got a dolichocephalic head!" he exclaimed—a reference to the supposedly long crania of Semites. ("Christ, I thought, the boy is in love!" recalled Miles.) Lucky, for her part, was charmed by Archie's mixture of old-world gallantry and boyish sense of fun. Three months later, on September 1, 1950, the couple were married at Belle Roosevelt's New York home on Sutton Place, overlooking the East River, with cousin Kim, apparently forgiven for taking the OPC job, serving as best man.[36]

Archie's marriage to an Arab American meant that, in order to avoid charges of bias, he would henceforth recuse himself from intelligence postings in Arab countries. But this seemed a small price to pay for his new state of domestic bliss. And in any case, the Arabist cause appeared safe in the hands of his cousin. Indeed, having just secretly come to the financial rescue of pro-Arab, anti-Zionist elements within American society, Kim Roosevelt was about to throw the support of the CIA behind the greatest Arab nationalist leader of his generation.

TEN

In Search of a Hero: Egypt, 1952

KIM ROOSEVELT'S SHIFT TO THE Office of Policy Coordination was a smart career move. The new covert operations unit, propelled by such Cold War shocks as China's turn to communism and the outbreak of war in Korea, grew at a prodigious rate, from slightly over three hundred employees in 1949 to just under six thousand by 1952. Exempted from congressional accounting requirements by the Central Intelligence Act of 1949, the CIA was awash with unvouchered funds for new projects. Miles Copeland, now assisting Kim as his deputy chief for intelligence, calculated that the Near East division (NEA), whose geographical territory also included Africa and Southeast Asia, needed a budget of roughly $20 million. Kim, not wanting to be outdone by other division heads, requested five times that amount—and got it. Miles insisted later that the uses to which this money was put were quite harmless. "We were *not* a lot of evil geniuses plotting to brainwash the world," he wrote in his memoirs. Nevertheless, some of the "W&W" ("Weird and Wonderful") NEA projects he went on to describe—attempting to slip hallucinogens to the Indonesian leader Sukarno, for example, or employing a medium in Richmond, Virginia, to send telepathic messages to Istanbul—hardly suggest a measured, disciplined approach, even allowing for Copeland narrative license.[1]

There were some efforts to rein in the OPC's game-playing tendencies, especially after the widely respected general Walter Bedell Smith, Dwight Eisenhower's chief of staff during World War II, became director of Central Intelligence in October 1950. The notoriously irascible "Beetle" fired many of the Agency's more flagrant society types and established a "murder board" to weed out particularly hare-brained projects, thoroughly intimidating OPC chief Frank Wisner in the process. However, he did not halt the CIA's underlying drift away from its original mission of intelligence gathering and analysis toward covert action. Moreover, thanks perhaps to the influence of his friend Belle Roosevelt, Beetle nursed a soft spot for Kim, who had moved to within a few doors of his home in the upmarket Washington neighborhood of Wesley Heights. So too did Smith's deputy director, the genial, pipe-smoking Allen Dulles. Dulles cared a great deal about social pedigree, and Kim's was impeccable. Better still, he was "an Oyster Bay Roosevelt," as Dulles joked when introducing him to fellow Republicans, "not one of those Hyde Park liberals." Even the literary association of Kim's nickname counted in his favor: Dulles had spent several years of his youth in India, counted *Kim* among his favorite books (a copy was by his bedside when he died), and "imagined himself a character in a John Buchan novel," as Kim once told Miles Copeland. Combined with the shortage of Middle Eastern area expertise in US government circles, Kim's high standing with his seniors meant that he and his small circle of Arabist intimates increasingly enjoyed "what amounted to a show of our own," as Miles put it later.[2]

Kim had used the operational latitude and resources available to him at the OPC to accomplish one element of his Arabist program: the creation of a domestic counterforce to American Zionism. His ambitions for the Middle East itself, though, were as yet unfulfilled. Syria's Husni Za'im had briefly shown promise as "the right kind of leader," an enlightened strongman committed to modernizing his country and even seeking a modus vivendi between Arabs and Israelis, yet in the end he had been found wanting in the personal qualities necessary for the role. Now Kim turned elsewhere in his search for an Arab hero.

WHEN KIM ARRIVED AT CAIRO'S King Farouk Airport in February 1952, he did not head for his usual accommodation. A few weeks earlier, on January 26—Black Saturday, as it became known—nationalist protestors had reduced Shepheard's Hotel to a heap of smoldering rubble, along with Barclays Bank, the Turf Club, and several other landmarks of British colonialism. The rioting in Cairo, which left seventy-six dead and countless more injured, had come in response to the killing of fifty Egyptian policemen during a British army raid on police barracks on the Suez Canal, which had itself followed a series of attacks by nationalist guerillas (fedayeen) on the British canal base. Watching from Washington, Dean Acheson despaired at Britain's inability to contain the spiraling violence, tartly observing, "The 'splutter of musketry' apparently does not stop things as we had been told from time to time that it would." If the United States was to prevent chaos from overtaking Egypt and spreading throughout the region, thereby opening it up to communist penetration, it would have to act now, independently of the British—"break the embrace and take to the oars," as Acheson put it. As a first step, the secretary of state did the same thing he had done in 1944 when he learned that the Landis mission in Cairo had gotten into difficulty: he sent for Kim Roosevelt.[3]

Kim had been back to Cairo several times since the war, beginning with the 1947 research trip that resulted in the *Harper's* article "Egypt's Inferiority Complex" and the chapter "Cakes for the Fat, an Onion for the Thin" in *Arabs, Oil, and History*. These writings had condemned Egypt's social and economic inequalities, portrayed young King Farouk as a feckless playboy unmanned by the constant humiliation of kowtowing to the British, and praised the reform efforts of the country's Young Effendis. Small wonder, then, that the Egyptian authorities detained Kim when he attempted to pass through Farouk Airport in January 1951 on charges of making anti-Arab statements. Eventually, however, "after some high-level activity," the young CIA officer was released.[4]

Despite these frustrations, Kim was acutely conscious of Egypt's strategic importance as, to quote *Arabs, Oil, and History*, "a communications center, close to oil, [and] as a key state in the Arab world where democracy and Communism meet face to face." Moreover, for all his reservations about the contemporary state of the country, Kim was fascinated both by Egypt's pharaonic history and its more recent past as the headquarters of Britain's "Covert Empire" in the Arab world. In the summer of 1951, during a tour of CIA stations in the region, Kim dallied in Cairo so that his oldest son, Kermit, could absorb the atmosphere of empires ancient and modern, climbing the pyramids and sailing on the Nile.[5]

Kim's ambivalence about Egypt was reflected in the mission on which Dean Acheson dispatched him in February 1952. According to an account offered in Miles Copeland's 1969 book *The Game of Nations*, and later verified by Kim himself, the secretary of state had charged Kim with persuading King Farouk to implement a reform program that would defuse the "revolutionary forces" in Egyptian society and thereby save his throne. (In his later memoir, *The Game Player*, Miles also volunteered the information that the mission was "approved by Allen Dulles over tea in his Georgetown house on the Sunday afternoon following Black Saturday," and that it was informally known within the CIA's NEA division as "Project FF" for Farouk's unkind nickname, "Fat Fucker.") If, Miles continued, the effort to bring about a "peaceful revolution" should fail, then Kim was to abandon Farouk and cast around for other leadership elements capable of bringing stability to the country—"a handsome front man, a strong man, or some formula combining the two."[6]

Kim returned from Cairo pleased with the outcome of his mission. "He really did have a successful time in Egypt and is keeping his fingers crossed . . . that the result of his labors will last and be of some benefit to the situation," Kim's wife, Polly, wrote his mother, Belle, in early March. It soon became obvious, however, that Farouk lacked the good sense to follow through on Kim's concept of a "peaceful revolution" and save himself (he "would not even build up a security force!" Kim later explained disgustedly). Instead, there unfolded a series of events very similar to those that had occurred in Syria three years earlier.[7]

The Egyptian army, whose officer corps included a number of alienated young men from provincial, lower-class backgrounds, had become a seedbed of nationalist opposition to Farouk's semicolonial regime. The continuing presence of British troops in Suez was a cause of burning resentment; so too was the corruption of the country's pasha class of civilian politicians, who were blamed for the army's defeat in the 1948 Arab-Israeli war. After years of conspiratorial planning, the crisis of 1952 provided the pretext the so-called Free Officers needed to make their move. Overnight on July 22–23, army units rolled into the center of Cairo, occupying strategic positions. Two days later, on July 25, Farouk abdicated his throne and set sail from Alexandria for exile in Italy. The Free Officers constituted themselves as a Revolutionary Command Council (RCC) under the leadership of the popular, avuncular General Muhammad Naguib, who assumed the post of minister of war. Informed observers knew that power really resided in the hands of a quiet-spoken thirty-four-year-old colonel by the name of Gamal 'Abdel Nasser.

The similarities between the Syrian coup of 1949 and the Egyptian Revolution of 1952 do not end there. Just as with the earlier event, there has been a long-running dispute about the degree of clandestine US involvement in Farouk's ouster—and, once again, Miles Copeland's books are the main cause of the controversy. On the one hand, there is Miles's assertion in *The Game of Nations* that in March 1952 Kim Roosevelt met three times with members of the Free Officers, who apprised him of their plans to carry out a coup and establish a dictatorship that would foster the eventual emergence of democracy in Egypt. There is also Miles's further testimony in *The Game Player* that he himself set up the meetings between Kim and the Free Officers during a trip of his own to Egypt in March 1952; that he was assisted in this work by "Rupert," an Arabic-speaking American agent of Kim's; and that the officers with whom Kim met included none other than Nasser himself.[8]

As with the Syrian putsch, some circumstantial evidence seems to corroborate Miles's claims. In January 1952, an interdepartmental committee established by Dean Acheson to study the problems of the Arab world and chaired by Kim Roosevelt had recommended that the US government "encourage the emergence of competent leaders" in the Middle East, by covert means if necessary, "even when they are not in power." Other documents show that prior to the July Revolution there was contact between the Free Officers and officials at the American embassy in Cairo, in particular the US-trained air force intelligence chief, Wing-Commander 'Ali Sabri, and Lieutenant Colonel David Evans III, the American assistant air attaché, who performed a role not unlike Steve Meade's in the run-up to Husni Za'im's coup in Syria. Russian records show that contemporary Soviet intelligence officials suspected a hidden American hand in the revolution. And Kim Roosevelt's own *Arabs, Oil, and History* makes some eerily pertinent observations about the shakiness of Farouk's hold on power and Egypt's unreadiness for democracy. Finally, Miles's Rupert invites tentative identification as Richard Paul

Mitchell, a young Syrian American graduate student who had come to Cairo in 1951 on a Fulbright scholarship to research the Muslim Brotherhood. According to the later recollection of William Lakeland, a junior political officer at the US embassy at the time, Mitchell "proved very useful in Cairo, because he could pass for a local . . . and report on what was going on in the town." Unfortunately, Lakeland's testimony does not shed any light on the truthfulness of Miles's story that he first encountered Rupert disguised as a whirling dervish in a Cairo nightclub called Milo's Den, a scene straight out of John Buchan's *Greenmantle*.[9]

Perhaps inevitably, though, other sources contradict the Copeland scenario of a coup carried out according to a plan agreed on by Roosevelt and Nasser. Interviewed recently, William Lakeland, who himself had close links to Nasser and the Free Officers, expressed doubts that Miles and Kim met with leading members of the movement before the revolution. (Lakeland's general attitude to Miles is rather cool, similar to that of the junior political officer in the Damascus embassy, Deane Hinton.) In a second echo of March 1949, when Za'im approached British military adviser Colonel Gordon Fox prior to launching his coup, there is evidence of the Egyptian Free Officers courting Western suitors besides the Americans. In December 1951, another British military instructor, former RAF intelligence officer Group Captain Patrick Domville, wrote the Conservative member of Parliament Julian Amery telling him that friends in the Egyptian army and air force had asked him to seek secret British support for a plot "to overthrow . . . the King and then to set up a military dictatorship." Perhaps most damaging to Miles's claims, both Kim Roosevelt himself and several of the Free Officers allegedly involved later denied any CIA role in the conspiracy to depose Farouk, Kim explicitly rejecting the suggestion that he returned to Egypt after his February trip to meet with Nasser and the others—although he did admit that the Agency was "informed indirectly" of the coup plot (and family correspondence indicates that he might in fact have traveled to Cairo in April).[10]

Of course, it is hardly surprising that both Kim and the Free Officers should have denied Miles's claims, the former because he later developed business relationships with several Arab monarchs and would therefore want to avoid any appearance of having once been involved in a republican conspiracy, the latter because the suggestion that a Western imperial power was present at the creation of Egypt's revolutionary government was politically embarrassing. Moreover, there is a considerable amount of evidence that, whether or not the CIA dealt directly with the Free Officers *prior* to their July 1952 coup, there was extensive secret American-Egyptian contact in the months *after* the revolution. As in 1949, when Steve Meade had provided a key channel to the Za'im regime during the early months of its existence, Air Attaché David Evans was the Free Officers' first point of contact. Within hours of the revolution, Evans received an invitation to Military Intelligence headquarters, where he learned of the new government's desire for cooperation with the United States and its plans to crack down on Egyptian communists. William Lakeland, too, stayed close to the officers; befriended Nasser's favorite reporter, the up-and-coming journalist Muhammad Haikal; and regularly hosted Nasser himself for supper at his apartment overlooking the Nile. Although the American ambassador, Jefferson Caffery, a stately Southerner approaching retirement, preferred to deal only with the nominal Egyptian premier, General Naguib, he quietly encouraged Evans and Lakeland to build on their contacts with Nasser. A long-time critic of British imperialism, Caffery was keen to promote American friendship with the Free Officers; he boosted the new regime in his reports to Washington.[11]

According to Miles's later recollection, Kim Roosevelt was weary of military dictatorships after the Za'im debacle, and he therefore "refrained from any direct contact with Nasser" in the early days of the Egyptian Revolution. This did not prevent him, though, from sending out indirect probes to the Free Officers, as revealed in an extraordinary document discovered among the personal papers of AFME president Dorothy Thompson. In September 1952, while preparing for a trip to Egypt, Thompson received a note bearing Kim's handwriting, instructing her to raise with General Naguib the fate of former prime minister Hilali and two other members of the previous government "with reputations for honesty and independence (and . . . a pro-American bias)" who had been imprisoned since the revolution. Naguib, the note explained, had "shown himself to be an able, efficient, and determined leader," but such political arrests had the potential to "cast a poor light on his whole program." Interestingly, this indirect call for clemency, reminiscent of Meade's intervention with Za'im on behalf of the deposed Syrian president Quwatli in 1949, specifically excluded certain Egyptian politicians who had been so closely associated with the Farouk regime that they now seemed beyond rehabilitation. One such was Murtada al-Maraghi, a former government minister and, if Miles is to be believed, an accomplice in Kim's earlier plot to foment a "peaceful revolution," who was quietly abandoned to his fate.[12]

In an accompanying note on "The Background" to Thompson's mission, Kim expanded on the reasons for his desire to improve Naguib's image, in doing so providing a revealing glimpse of his general feelings about Egypt's new government. Since gaining power, Kim explained, the Free Officers had initiated "a number of reform measures which began to raise the hopes of informed friends of Egypt." These included the abolition of such titles as "Bey" and "Pasha," a "house-cleaning" of the "corrupt . . . parliament," and the institution of a badly needed "land-reform program" combined with measures to attract "foreign investment." These socially and economically progressive steps had all been taken at the same time that the new government had adopted measures "to strengthen the basis of Egypt's internal security." (Kim was possibly referring here to the military's brutal repression of a strike by textile workers in Alexandria the previous month, and a subsequent roundup of communist leaders.) In short, the Free Officers offered short-term stability while holding out the long-term possibility of democratization and modernization carried out under American guidance. A further visit to Cairo in October 1952 by a new member of the AFME circle, Edward L. R. Elson, a Presbyterian minister from Washington, DC, only served to strengthen this impression. In answer to a series of pointedly political questions posed by Elson, Naguib confirmed his regime's respect for individual liberties, receptiveness to foreign assistance, and ambition to develop the Egyptian economy. "Everything indicated that we now had at the board a new player who was exactly what we were looking for," wrote Miles Copeland later.[13]

On their side, the Free Officers were, it seems, highly receptive to these American overtures. With its founding in a successful struggle against colonial British rule, and its more recent history of relatively benign missionary activity in the Arab world, the United States looked to the Egyptians like a potential partner—more so than the godless Soviet Union. Intelligence chief 'Ali Sabri and journalist Muhammad Haikal had been to the Land of the Free and returned with an appreciation of American popular culture that they shared with their compatriots. Haikal encouraged Bill Lakeland to serve Nasser hot dogs and show him Hollywood movies, both of which he consumed enthusiastically (according to Lakeland, Nasser was a particular fan of "aquamusical" star Esther Williams). The young Egyptians also warmed to the democratic informality of American manners, a refreshing change from the starchy British. The appreciation was mutual. Americans noted with approval the earnestness and self-discipline the Free Officers brought to the task of governing Egypt, traits also reflected in their private lives—Nasser, a dedicated family man, led a particularly modest existence—all very different from the licentious Farouk. Even the young men's physiques—"clean-cut . . . slim, and athletic looking," to quote Copeland—contrasted favorably with the pot-bellied generals of the Farouk era. Americans, too, were young and virile, unlike the old and feeble British. Nasser reportedly referred to the United States as *al-gāyin* ("the coming") and Britain as *al-rāyihin* ("the going").[14]

Not surprisingly, British observers did not much care for these signs of Egyptian-American camaraderie. During World War II, the British had condescended to OSS officers in Cairo; now, they were just plain angry. The Americans were being disloyal to their old friend and ally, complained the British ambassador in Cairo, Ralph Stevenson, and were encouraging the Egyptians to make unreasonable demands. They were also being naïve, failing to detect the deviousness of Arabs who professed friendship yet in truth, according to veteran Arabist Sir Alec Kirkbride, regarded them with "hidden contempt for being so easily deceived." ("Sooner or later, the local associates go too far and the connexion has to be broken, so that the Americans end with their erstwhile friends as their enemies," the sour Kirkbride went on to observe, with, as it turned out, some prescience.) Resorting to amateur psychology, the British blamed these tendencies on "semi-conscious feelings and emotions about the Arabs and ourselves latent in the American mind" (Roger Makins, British ambassador in Washington) and on "the underlying fixed, even if almost subconscious, ideas which they have of us as 'imperialists' and oppressors of backward races, as distinct from themselves, whom they feel to be the liberators and uplifters of the oppressed" (Robin Hankey, Foreign Office official in Cairo). The Americans, in other words, were allowing themselves to be ruled by irrational, emotional forces, rather like the Oriental Arabs, in fact, and not at all like the sensible, hard-nosed British. "The most pathetic aspects of the question are the belief of the average American that he deserves to be liked, and his inability to understand why he is not when that fact becomes too obvious to be overlooked any longer," concluded Alec Kirkbride, now pretty much resorting to abuse.[15]

With his various British associations, Kim Roosevelt proved, at least at this stage, something of an exception to this attitude; the principal targets for British attack were instead the "sentimental" William Lakeland and the "dreadful" Jefferson Caffery. Yet, in truth, if any one individual cemented the growing alliance between the United States and the new Egyptian government, it was Kim. His first trip to Cairo after the revolution came in October 1952, when Caffery introduced him to both Naguib and Nasser at the Mena House Hotel, looking out to the pyramids. Thereafter, while the ambassador continued to conduct formal diplomatic business with the "handsome front man" Naguib, the CIA officer and Nasser would meet independently of the embassy, sometimes at the latter's suburban home, at other times in various secret locations, where they would discuss more substantial yet sensitive matters, such as US military assistance for the new government. The clandestine nature of these meetings was not a problem for the Egyptian, who had spent years concealing the existence of the Free Officers' association from Farouk's regime. Shortly after the July Revolution, Nasser was asked whether he was a "leftist" or a "rightist." Neither, he replied. "I'm a conspirator."[16]

Beyond their shared love of subterfuge, how are we to explain the rapport that developed between these two men, one the descendant of a US president and archetypal Washington insider, the other the son of a provincial post office clerk who dedicated his life to nationalist struggle? Nasser, it seems, quickly realized that Kim could be useful to him politically, providing a top-level back channel to Washington whose secrecy would protect him against accusations from fellow Egyptian nationalists that he was currying favor with the Americans. But he likely also preferred the personal company of this soft-spoken, unostentatious thirty-six-year-old to that of the rather grand, elderly Caffery. One senses an element of genuine personal sympathy in this relationship missing from Nasser's dealings with other Western officials.[17]

For his part, Kim was thrilled with Nasser. Like Husni Za'im in Syria, the Egyptian combined an idealistic commitment to modernizing reform with a realistic understanding of the need for short-term authoritarian measures, but unlike the Syrian he was personally clever and charismatic enough—Western observers commented frequently on his tall, powerful frame, impressive profile, and meltingly dark eyes—to stand a chance of actually remaining in power. Not only that, Nasser was also showing signs that he could take on a leadership role beyond Egypt, in the wider Arab world. "Col. Nas[se]r is the one man I have met who has impressed me with the feeling that he possesses the capabilities to lead the Near East—not only Egypt but through Egypt her Arab friends and neighbors—out of the barren wilderness," Kim wrote Miles Copeland. "I am sure that provided with inspiring leadership the Near Eastern peoples are capable of a great Renaissance," Kim continued. "Without it, present weaknesses and unreasoning national passions and despairs will further ravage the area."[18]

There were, perhaps, some unfortunate echoes here of earlier would-be kingmakers, imperial agents who had also searched for a strong leader capable of uniting the supposedly chaotic Arab race. T. E. Lawrence, for example, had come to Arabia to "consider its great men" for the role of "necessary leader," a mission that eventually yielded the Hashemite prince Faisal. In one sense, then, Kim Roosevelt was merely repeating Lawrence's quest for "a force transcending tribe," a "master-spirit" who "would set the desert on fire" and "bring the Arab Revolt to full glory."[19]

In fairness to Kim, though, he was not the only one consciously thinking about casting the part of Arab hero. As Nasser would explain a couple of years later in his *Egypt's Liberation: The Philosophy of the Revolution*, he himself believed that "within the Arab circle there is a role, wandering aimlessly in search of a hero," and that "this role . . . has at last settled down, tired and weary, near the borders of our country and is beckoning to us to move, to take up its lines, to put on its costume, since no one else is qualified to play it."[20]

For the time being, at least, Kim Roosevelt and Gamal Nasser were reading from the same script.

THINGS WERE MOVING KIM'S WAY closer to home as well. In late 1952, as part of Beetle Smith's reorganization campaign, the OPC was removed from the direction of the State and Defense Departments and folded into the command structure of the CIA, uniting covert action and espionage in a single overseas secret service. Kim took over the combined Near East/Africa divisions, edging out Archie Roosevelt's old nemesis, Mike Mitchell (who, according to Miles Copeland, was sent "off to a minor job in Registry"). This put Kim in charge, to quote Miles again, "not only over intelligence operations in the Middle East, South-east Asia and Africa but also over our budding political action, psychological warfare, economic warfare and paramilitary operations in those areas."[21]

Even domestic electoral politics were playing out to Kim's advantage. In November 1952, with Harry Truman declining to run for reelection, Republican presidential contender Dwight D. Eisenhower handily defeated the Democratic candidate Adlai Stevenson. Although outgoing secretary of state Dean Acheson had shared Kim's broad vision of Middle Eastern development and, in particular, his perception of Egypt as the region's leading power, the Truman White House's support for Israel had conflicted with another major component of Kim's Arabist program, his anti-Zionism. Ike, however, had achieved victory without having to court the so-called Jewish vote, and his administration appeared set to adopt a more even-handed approach to the Arab-Israeli conflict than its predecessor. Moreover, the new president's pick to succeed Acheson was none other than Allen Dulles's elder brother, John Foster. With Allen himself taking over from Beetle Smith as director of Central Intelligence in early 1953, Kim now stood a reasonable chance of seeing *all*, not just part, of his Arabist vision translated into practice.

Sensing that change was in the Washington air, Kim's state-private network of Arabists and anti-Zionists rallied around in a concerted effort to secure his appointment as assistant secretary of state for Near Eastern affairs, thereby moving him from a covert position of influence in the CIA to an overt one in the State Department. Kim was "highly intelligent, well-informed, energetic and personally agreeable," so Virginia Gildersleeve assured the new secretary of state. Appealing to Foster Dulles "as a writer of history to a maker of history," AFME director Harold Lamb stated his belief that "the grandson of Theodore Roosevelt" could "hold to the line of American interest . . . in the troubled Middle East." And so on. Dulles's papers contain a sheaf of commendations for Kim from the private citizens in the AFME circle, testifying to the collaborative, reciprocal nature of the relations that bound the CIA to its Arabist front group.[22]

As it turned out, AFME's representations were in vain. After reportedly offering the position to Kim's former OSS boss, Stephen Penrose, who turned it down in order to carry on as president of the American University of Beirut, Foster Dulles decided to retain the services of Henry A. Byroade, the assistant secretary he had inherited from the Truman administration. The reasons for Kim losing out in this fashion are not altogether clear. Later, a story developed that he was secretly offered the post but rejected it after receiving advice from senior officials that he should stay at the CIA, "'where the action is.'" However, there are contemporary indications that his candidacy was derailed by other factors, including his youth and an equally concerted-looking campaign of protest from his old Zionist enemies.[23]

Still, AFME's supporters could take heart in the fact that the job had been offered to Penrose, suggesting as it did that the new administration was basically friendly to the values they espoused. As for Kim Roosevelt himself, with the distraction of the abortive assistant secretary campaign out of the way, he was now free to focus his considerable clandestine powers on a cause that had grown personally dear to him: supporting his new friend Gamal Nasser as he consolidated his hold on power in Egypt. The year 1953 would prove a busy one in the life of the young Arabist—his own, TR-like "crowded hour."

ELEVEN

Mad Men on the Nile

IN MAY 1953, JOHN FOSTER DULLES became the first US secretary of state to visit the Middle East. A tall, somber Presbyterian who lacked the naughty twinkle of his brother Allen, Foster Dulles was preoccupied with what he perceived as the existential threat of the Soviet Union to the Christian West. Nonetheless, he grasped that the focus of the Cold War was moving away from Europe toward the postcolonial Third World, where communists were already trying to harness the growing power of revolutionary nationalism. His decision to go on a three-week tour of twelve countries in the Near East and South Asia reflected "the strategic location of these lands," so he explained to the American press, and their bearing on "the freedom and the security of the entire free world."[1]

The secretary was especially keen to see Egypt, a country he regarded as "the key to development of our strength in the Middle East," and made it the first stop on his itinerary, arriving in Cairo on May 11. After a pleasant meeting with the titular head of the revolutionary government, Muhammad Naguib, Foster Dulles spent most of the next day closeted at the US embassy with Naguib's deputy—and power behind the throne—Gamal Nasser. The secretary used the opportunity to express his "real enthusiasm for the new regime in Egypt" and confidence that it would "set an example to the other Arab states," adding, rather casually, "that it was interesting to note that the Republican Administration does not owe the same degree of political debt as did the Democrats to Jewish groups." Nasser, responding in English so quietly that the Americans present had difficulty catching all that he said, observed simply that "the objectives of the U.S. and Egypt are the same." The only area of disagreement appeared to be Dulles's plans for a regional defense pact to repel possible Soviet expansion into the Middle East. As Nasser pointed out, a far more pressing concern for Egyptians was ridding their country of the last traces of British colonialism, in particular the troops occupying the Suez Canal base.[2]

Despite this and some other misunderstandings—Dulles was mystified by Nasser's constant allusions to previous conversations with "Bill" until he was introduced to the embassy's young political officer, William Lakeland—both sides considered the meetings a success. The secretary returned to Washington more convinced than ever of the need to carry on courting Arab nationalists in general and Nasser in particular. As National Security Council directive 155/1 of July 14, 1953, explained, the Eisenhower administration aimed "to guide the revolutionary and nationalistic pressures throughout the area into orderly channels not antagonistic to the West, rather than attempt merely to preserve the status quo." In the case of Egypt, this meant seeking a resolution to the Arab-Israeli dispute that would be acceptable in Cairo as well as in Tel Aviv. The first priority, however, was the same as the Egyptian government's: bringing about the orderly departure of the British.[3]

Hence it was that Kim Roosevelt at last achieved a goal that had eluded the OSS Arabists a decade earlier: dislodging the British from their position of dominance in Egypt, dumping "Kipling and all that" for distinctly American techniques of covert power borrowed, like so many new ideas of the 1950s, from Madison Avenue. To understand how he did this, it is necessary to reintroduce the man who, having already invented one new identity for himself—that of Arabist spy—was now about to return to the Middle East disguised as a Mad Man.

THE DECADE HAD NOT BEGUN promisingly for Miles Copeland. After his assignment to Syria ended in 1950, he found himself back in Arlington, Virginia, living in cramped quarters with his growing brood of children (Stewart, the future Police drummer, arrived in 1952) and a large number of unruly dogs, all a far cry from his palatial surroundings in Damascus. His new position as Kim Roosevelt's deputy assistant had its moments of fun—helping Kim select young women operatives for a "honey-trap" program known informally as Mrs. McMurty's Charm School, for example—but none of it quite measured up to the glamor and intrigue of Syria. The merger between the Office of Policy Coordination and the CIA was yet to take place, and Miles's post was based, as he put it later, on "the wrong side of the house": the Agency's espionage branch, the Office of Special Operations (OSO). Compared with the Ivy League-ish, dashing OPC, where Kim and other regional barons ran covert operations, the intelligence-gathering OSO had a rather humdrum feel to it that belied its exciting-sounding name. Moreover, while Kim was in many respects an excellent boss, his patronage had more than a hint of aristocratic condescension about it. "It would be to his own advantage if he could curb his impetuousness," Kim wrote in a 1953 personnel evaluation of Miles. "In Headquarters he is most effective while working under the tempering influence of one in whom he has confidence."[4]

Things began to look up for Miles after the OPC and OSO were merged into the Directorate of Plans and he moved to a new position: chief of the combined Near East divisions' Information Planning Staff, plotting covert propaganda operations from a suite of offices next door to Kim's. US government use of "psychological warfare"—the preferred official term for actions intended to bolster the morale of allies and undermine that of enemies—dated back to World War I, but it had never been an exclusively official business. From the beginning, psy-war had drawn heavily on ideas and methods pioneered in the American advertising industry, particularly the public relations theory of Sigmund Freud's nephew Edward Bernays. It made sense, therefore, that Copeland's new venture should rope in executives from Madison Avenue, such as his old Counter Intelligence Corps comrade James "Eich" Eichelberger, who had gone to work for advertising giant J. Walter Thompson in Chicago after the war, acquiring a reputation as an "idea man." During the day Miles and Eich would concoct stories for Middle Eastern audiences and then reconvene in the evening for discussion of "highbrow literary topics."[5]

Partly so that he could hold his own intellectually with the likes of Eichelberger, and partly so that he could develop some ideas about revolutionary leadership that had begun forming in his mind during his time with Husni Za'im in Syria, Miles now embarked on a self-taught crash course in social theory. Although he read widely in the founding texts of modern sociology, including classic works by Marx and Weber, it was two more recently published books that really captured his interest. One was *The Machiavellians* (1943) by James Burnham, a former Trotskyist who had broken with Marxism and, on his way to becoming an important figure in post–World War II American conservative thought, had taken on a job as a consultant for the OPC. The other was *The Anatomy of Revolution* (1938) by the eminent historian and ex-OSS analyst Crane Brinton, who had cast a strong intellectual influence on the generation of students he taught at Harvard during the 1930s, among them Kim Roosevelt. According to Miles's later recollection, Kim made *Anatomy* "compulsory reading for all members of his staff."[6]

From Burnham's book, basically a primer in non-Marxist social thought for budding conservatives, Miles absorbed a Machiavellian sense of pessimism about human nature and the prospects for modern democracy. Brinton's *Anatomy*, which compared four modern revolutions in an effort to detect similar underlying structures, alerted him to both revolutionary governments' tendency to eventual collapse and the wisdom of governing elites preempting potential threats to their power. Behind Burnham and Brinton moved the figure of Vilfredo Pareto, an Italian sociologist sometimes referred to as the "Karl Marx of the bourgeoisie." Pareto's writings borrowed concepts from the natural sciences to depict human societies as closed systems that, after temporary disturbances, return to a state of equilibrium, rather like a body recovering from disease (Brinton repeatedly used the metaphor of fever to describe revolutions in *Anatomy*). This idea caught on at Harvard in the 1930s among professors of a conservative bent, giving rise to talk of a Harvard "Pareto circle"; it also influenced Italian fascists like Benito Mussolini.[7]

Miles was clearly excited by the Paretian concepts he encountered in Brinton and, especially, Burnham. He based a lecture to new CIA recruits on *The Machiavellians* and sought its author's advice about ways to shore up revolutionary governments. Later, Miles identified three principles he had learned from Burnham: that "the first task of any ruling group is to keep itself in power . . . instead of trying to please everybody"; second, that "the behavior of a nation's leaders must be 'logical'—i.e. they must have a 'deliberately held goal, or purpose'— but the leaders must never forget that they are dealing with a populace

whose motivations are mostly illogical"; and, finally, that a revolutionary government "cannot avoid the use of *some* repressive action . . .
but as rapidly as possible it must systematically go about winning the
support of influential groups and classes." The successful revolutionary
government, therefore, was "one that succeeds in balancing the 'repressive' with the 'constructive,' concealing the former while publicizing
the latter." Nor was Burnham's influence on Copeland confined to specific lessons in power politics: Miles's whole approach now had a social
scientific, clinical feel to it that owed a great deal to Pareto's notion of
societies as contained, self-regulating organisms. "You can't get angry at a
diphtheria germ, it does what it does, it's not its fault," Miles Copeland III
recalls his father saying. "You just have to understand how it works."
It was all a far cry from the fundamentally moralistic discourse of the
previous generation of missionary-descended OSS Arabists.[8]

Intellectual historians have identified the 1930s Pareto vogue as
crucial in shaping the evolution of organization theory and industrial
psychology, so it was no coincidence that Miles should have become
interested in another new "applied" social science, management engineering. He had already demonstrated an interest in organizational dy-
namics in the late 1940s, when he drew up charts to manage the complex
transition to the CIA from its predecessor intelligence groups. In the
early 1950s, OPC boss Kilbourne Johnston introduced him to the growing body of professional literature on organization and management,
or "O&M." Combining what he read there with his new sociological
knowledge and personal observations of revolutionary governments in
the Middle East and Africa, Copeland wrote a thirty-page report in late
1952 on Third World leadership and bureaucracy that came to the attention of executives of the leading US management consulting company,
Booz, Allen & Hamilton. Shortly afterward, he lunched with the BA&H
Washington office's director, who offered him a job helping set up the
firm's new international division. Lured by a salary double what he was
being paid by the government, and perhaps only too glad for some re-
spite from the company of old Grotonians, Miles decided to take a sabbatical from the CIA, thus becoming the first of the Agency Arabists to
enter the "revolving door" between the public and private sectors.[9]

Miles had not, however, left the government behind altogether. "You
can take the boy out of the CIA, but you can't take the CIA out of
the boy," as he explained later. Following conversations with Kim Roo-

Theodore Roosevelt and his grandson, Kermit "Kim" Roosevelt Jr., in the year of Kim's birth, 1916.
LIBRARY OF CONGRESS

The implacable TR and Kim's father, the romantic adventurer Kermit Sr., shortly after their 1909 safari in East Africa.
LIBRARY OF CONGRESS

Kim Roosevelt hunting in the Brazilian rain forest between his freshman and sophomore years at Harvard.

KERMIT AND BELLE ROOSEVELT PAPERS, LIBRARY OF CONGRESS

Kim with wife, Polly, and sons, Kermit III and Jonathan, in the summer of 1940, marking time in California. The following year, Kim would join the unit that became America's wartime secret service, and precursor to the CIA, the OSS.

KERMIT AND BELLE ROOSEVELT PAPERS, LIBRARY OF CONGRESS

Kim's cousin and future CIA colleague, Archie Roosevelt, Jr., during a childhood family tour of the Mediterranean.

Faculty of the missionary-founded American University of Beirut, the most important early US institution in the Arab world. Second and third from the left in the back row are the fathers of Harold Hoskins and William "Bill" Eddy, two pioneers of the American intelligence effort in the Middle East.

A Middle Eastern childhood: a young
Bill Eddy (left) in Lebanon.

Archie Roosevelt, with his host's son on his knee, and fellow US Army officers in
Rabat, Morocco, in 1942, shortly after Archie first arrived in the Arab world.

Archie Roosevelt
en route to his military
intelligence posting in
Cairo in 1944.
ARCHIE ROOSEVELT PAPERS,
LIBRARY OF CONGRESS

The OSS's notoriously conspicuous headquarters in Cairo.
RECORDS OF THE OFFICE OF STRATEGIC SERVICES, NATIONAL
ARCHIVES

Stephen Penrose, chief of OSS/Cairo, and another US trailblazer in Middle Eastern
intelligence, in his later role as president of the American University of Beirut.
STEPHEN B. L. PENROSE JR. PAPERS, WHITMAN COLLEGE AND NORTHWEST ARCHIVES

Kim and Archie Roosevelt in
wartime Jerusalem, May 1944.
ARCHIE ROOSEVELT PAPERS,
LIBRARY OF CONGRESS

Iran, 1946: Archie Roosevelt preparing for
a daring air sortie in one of the opening
skirmishes of the Cold War.
ARCHIE ROOSEVELT PAPERS, LIBRARY OF CONGRESS

Harold Hoskins (center) with King Ibn Saud of Saudi Arabia.
HAROLD HOSKINS PAPERS, PUBLIC POLICY PAPERS DIVISION, DEPARTMENT OF
RARE BOOKS AND SPECIAL COLLECTIONS, PRINCETON UNIVERSITY LIBRARY

The famous 1945 shipboard meeting between Ibn Saud and FDR that launched the
US-Saudi alliance, with Bill Eddy (left) acting in the symbolically appropriate role of
interpreter.

Miles and Lorraine Copeland wed in
London, 1942.

Military strongman Husni al-Za'im during his inauguration as president of Syria in July 1949. Behind him are various officers and officials who had supported him when he seized power in a coup earlier in the year, with CIA foreknowledge and, possibly, assistance. A month later, he was himself overthrown and murdered.

Steve Meade, the roving, Bond-like CIA operative who befriended the Syrian dictator Za'im.

CIA officer Miles Copeland and wife, Lorraine, under diplomatic cover.

LENNIE COPELAND/JERRY DAVIS

A fresh-faced Mather Greenleaf Eliot, the CIA case officer for Kim Roosevelt's Arabist, anti-Zionist citizen group, the American Friends of the Middle East.

ELIOT FAMILY PAPERS, UNIVERSITY OF PITTSBURGH LIBRARY

Kim Roosevelt's close friend and fellow anti-Zionist activist, Rabbi Elmer Berger.

WISCONSIN HISTORICAL SOCIETY

The celebrity journalist Dorothy Thompson visiting Iraq as president of the CIA-funded American Friends of the Middle East.

Garland Evans Hopkins, the ardently pro-Arab and anti-Zionist chief executive officer of the American Friends of the Middle East. The CIA removed him from his position after the Eisenhower administration abandoned its policy of support for Arab nationalism.

Edward Elson traveling with the American Friends of the Middle East. The Presbyterian pastor of both John Foster Dulles and Dwight Eisenhower, Elson courted controversy with his criticisms of Israel and support for Arab nationalism.

The September 1950 wedding of Archie and Selwa "Lucky" Roosevelt, the personally happiest expression of the early CIA's romance with the Arab world.

ARCHIE ROOSEVELT PAPERS, LIBRARY OF CONGRESS

The overt and covert faces of US foreign policy during the Eisenhower years: John Foster Dulles (left) and brother, Allen.

A nighttime meeting in Cairo: Kim Roosevelt (center) confers with the head of Egypt's revolutionary government, Muhammad Naguib (right), and the man soon to replace him—and carry the CIA's hopes for the Arab world—Gamal 'Abdel Nasser (left).

Gamal Nasser and Kim Roosevelt, friends and rivals in America's Great Game.

Iranian prime minister Mohammed Mosaddeq touching the Liberty Bell in
Independence Hall during a 1951 visit to the United States. Two years later, Mosaddeq
would be overthrown in a coup carried out, on the American side, by Kim Roosevelt.
DEPARTMENT OF STATE, HARRY S. TRUMAN LIBRARY

The shah and empress of Iran arriving at
Rome Airport on August 18, 1953, after the
apparent failure of Kim Roosevelt's coup
operation. A few days later, the shah would
return to Iran in triumph.
CORBIS

James Eichelberger, the former ad man who coached the leadership of Egypt's revolutionary government while running the CIA station in Cairo.
ANNE TAZEWELL EICHELBERGER

Gamal Nasser. "He is very good at chess," said a friend. "It's never easy to know his intentions."
GETTY

Wilbur Crane Eveland (right), Allen Dulles's personal Middle East operative during the late 1950s and perhaps the most reckless American game player of them all.

Lucky, Archie, and Kim Roosevelt in Portugal in the late 1950s.

A rare picture of James Jesus Angleton (center), chief of CIA counterintelligence and the Israeli "account," with the Zionist leader David Ben-Gurion. As Arabism waned after the mid-1950s, the CIA-Mossad "Connection" thrived.

The Game of Nations: the board game designed by Miles Copeland in his retirement. "Skill and nerve are the principal requirements in this amoral and cynical game," Miles explained on the box. "There are neither winners nor losers—only survivors."

sevelt and Frank Wisner, Miles agreed to become what Wisner called a "loyal alumnus," carrying out particularly sensitive duties for his former employer under the cover of his new job. BA&H did not object to this arrangement. The firm already had a history of working for government agencies, having helped the navy streamline its command structures in readiness for World War II and after the war carrying out a study of guided missile production capabilities for the air force. Later on, BA&H would become the federal government's management consultants of choice, with a campus next door to the CIA's Langley headquarters in Mc-Lean, Virginia. It was perhaps telling that the company's first assignment outside the United States came in 1953, when it was contracted to carry out a land-ownership study by the Philippines government of Ramón Magsaysay, who had just come to power with the assistance of the CIA's legendary counterinsurgency operative and "nation builder," Edward G. Lansdale (another ad man and, allegedly, the real-life inspiration for Graham Greene's *The Quiet American*). BA&H's work in the Philippines might be seen as a precursor to a broader, government-business effort to win the Cold War in the Third World by conferring on it the benefits of Western modernity, American-style—in short, by modernizing it.[10]

Miles Copeland's dual mission was worked out over the spring and early summer of 1953, as he shuttled between meetings with officials in Washington and the New York offices of BA&H. Both his old and his new bosses wanted him in Cairo—BA&H so that he could prepare the ground for a survey of the tangled holdings of the Egyptian national bank, the Banque Misr, and the CIA so that he could follow up on discussions between the air attaché David Evans and chiefs of the Egyptian intelligence agency, the Mukhabarat, about possible American assistance with officer training. In April, Miles was introduced to Hassan al-Tuhami, a Free Officer sent to Washington by Nasser to inspect the US intelligence services on their home ground and establish an American-Egyptian liaison. Shortly afterward, Kim Roosevelt and Nasser met in Cairo and formalized the liaison arrangement. Miles, Lorraine, the children, and dogs decamped to Egypt in June 1953.[11]

The Copelands were delighted to be back in the Middle East, leading an existence that combined elements of Britain's passing imperial regime—the sort described by novelist Lawrence Durrell in his *Alexandria Quartet*—and the new American order. Hassan Tuhami installed them in a sprawling villa, and himself in the guest house, on the east bank of the Nile in Maadi, a village about thirty minutes' drive from Cairo. The house, which came with formal gardens and a kidney-shaped swimming pool, had earlier been home to the commander of British troops in Egypt, General "Jumbo" Wilson, and Maadi had a British school and country club, where the Copeland children learned to swim. With a full staff, Lorraine had the time to visit all the nearby antiquities, snap up bargains in oriental bric-a-brac, and enjoy evening parties in a canvas-sailed *felucca* on the Nile. It was, she admitted, "a cocooned life," made all the more pleasurable by the fact that, because of Miles's move to BA&H, she did not have to submit to the authority of Ambassador Caffery's fearsome wife, Gertrude, who insisted on "white gloves, hats and straight stocking seams" for the "Embassy wives." This left Lorraine free to indulge her growing interest in archaeology, which had been whetted during a "red-carpet" tour with Kim and Polly Roosevelt, when she was allowed to go into a pit by the Great Pyramid and look through a peephole at the just-discovered Khufu ship. The Copeland children, meanwhile, romped through the villa, ate figs and drank goat's milk, and explored the streets on bicycle.[12]

It was proving a good move for Miles professionally, too. A BA&H task force of five management engineers set up shop in Cairo's Garden City, a wealthy neighborhood originally designed around the citadel-like British embassy, and got to work at the Banque Misr, "cutting through both organizational chaos and . . . the 'petrification of tradition,'" as one team member put it. Meanwhile, two other new arrivals from Washington were on hand to support the work Miles was doing for the CIA: Jim Eichelberger and another London roommate from Counter Intelligence Corps days, journalist Frank Kearns. Kim Roosevelt had sent Eich to Cairo undercover as economic attaché to advise the revolutionary government on matters of organization. Kearns, who had recently contributed to Earl Warren's campaign for governor in California, was in Egypt simultaneously working as a CBS reporter and, according to Miles, "giving Nasser a bit of free public relations advice ('Just get him to *smile* a bit more,' Kim told him)." (A third operative, Miles's Syrian playmate Steve Meade, also passed through Cairo on Kim's orders, assessing the Nasser regime's prospects for survival, but he had moved on by the time of Miles's arrival.)[13]

It was not long before Copeland was in regular contact with Nasser himself, lunching on soup and sandwiches in the latter's office or the mess of the Revolutionary Command Council's headquarters. The Egyptian

appreciated Miles's knowledge about covert affairs in other Arab countries, especially Syria, and his sense of humor; the American reckoned
it was his "store of anecdotes about Syrian coups" that made him "*persona grata* in Nasser's household." On his side, Miles clearly enjoyed
Nasser's company. "I know of no one with whom I would rather spend
a long evening of conversation and joking," he wrote later. The two men
were surprisingly indiscreet about their friendship. Lorraine Copeland
remembers Nasser roaring up to the villa in Maadi "with a motor-
cycle escort and an entourage," and running into him one evening at
a Cairo movie theater in a knot of bodyguards. "He saw Miles and
slapped him on the back, grinning." Nasser would continue to meet
with Miles confidentially for years, even after he stopped talking to most
other Westerners.[14]

After seeing Nasser, Miles would rendezvous with Eichelberger and
Kearns in the latter's luxurious apartment in the Badrawi Buildings in
the affluent Zamalek district on Gezira Island, which served as a kind
of informal CIA station. The three old CIC comrades were delighted to
be reunited and often partied together with their wives at each other's
homes. Another gathering place was the Gezira Sporting Club, previously the exclusive domain of the British army but now, under Nasser,
open to elite Egyptians and, so it seems, to spies of various nationalities.
According to one Israeli agent, "the Americans had colonized a place
near the entrance to the restaurant," where the British glowered at them
from "their own corners near the billiard room." The Mad Men were
taking over.[15]

ALTHOUGH MILES COPELAND AND MUHAMMAD Haikal, the eminent Egyptian journalist-cum-Nasser mouthpiece, did not always see
eye to eye, they agreed on one thing. When seeking a word to describe
the interactions between the CIA and the Nasser regime that took
place in the years 1953 to 1955, they both reached for the language
of romance. This was, they wrote separately, a "honeymoon" period.
Not only was the Eisenhower administration better disposed toward the
Arab cause than its predecessor, but it also was prepared to give freer rein
to CIA covert operations as part of its "New Look" national security
policy (the Truman White House had always seemed rather queasy about
the use of dirty tricks). Better still, the president was a great personal

believer in psychological warfare, even appointing Time-Life executive
C. D. Jackson as a special presidential adviser on the subject—and Jackson happened to agree entirely with Kim Roosevelt's views on the Middle East. In short, every possible element on the American side was lined up in favor of Kim's policy of secret support for the revolutionary Egyptian government, even down to the Dulles brothers, old Roosevelt family friends, occupying the two most powerful positions within the US foreign policy apparatus. As for the Egyptians themselves, the United States was easily the most appealing of the potential candidates for the role of great-power ally; in Kim Roosevelt it had a personal representative much more attractive to Gamal Nasser than the other foreign officials with whom he was dealing. Of course, the word "honeymoon" carries with it the possible implication of an eventual cooling of ardor, but at this stage of the relationship there were few if any signs of marital discord.[16]

So what exactly did the CIA do to strengthen the Nasser regime during this initial period of American-Egyptian harmony? First, it set about schooling Egypt's new rulers in Western political theory. It was Jim Eichelberger, described by Lorraine Copeland as the "academically educated philosopher of our group," who took over this task, writing a series of theoretical papers that were translated into Arabic for circulation within the Revolutionary Command Council. In the course of follow-up conversations with Nasser, Muhammad Haikal, and others, Eichelberger formed the impression, as reported to Ambassador Caffery, that the Free Officers were "embarked on a policy of drift and compromise," overly concerned with their "popularity" and lacking "confidence in the efficacy of their repressive powers." In response, Eichelberger produced a new essay, "Power Problems of a Revolutionary Government," which Miles Copeland later included as an appendix to his *Game of Nations*. Rather than seeking "mere popularity," Eichelberger advised, revolutionary leaders should concern themselves with the more serious business of building a "constructive base" for their power, using the instruments of government to win the people's support "by *appealing to their self-interest* as well as to their emotions." This task, however, was not the most pressing order of business. The revolutionary government's first priority was survival, and that meant securing its "repressive base," quelling counterrevolutionary threats by outlawing opposition movements, and strengthening the state police and intelligence service. History was littered with examples of revolutions that had reversed these steps, relying excessively on constructive means at first and then, when those failed, resorting to intense repression, or terror, to cling to power. "This is a disease of revolutions," warned Eichelberger, echoing Crane Brinton, "and one that can be fatal."[17]

If Eichelberger supplied the theory for the CIA's Egyptian "coup-proofing," Miles Copeland provided the practice. While other members of the BA&H office in Cairo dealt with identity cards "and other 'home office' problems" for the Egyptian interior ministry, Miles busied himself drawing up organizational charts and outlining new courses for the national police school. To help him with the latter task, he flew in two former FBI agents and a New York policeman who had managed security for VIPs visiting Manhattan. Realizing that the existing intelligence apparatus was inadequate, the Free Officers created a new General Investigations Directorate (GID) modeled partly on the CIA. Miles arranged US training for senior GID officers, instruction from the CIA's Office of National Estimates in the writing of daily intelligence summaries for the head of state, and provision of "the complete range of electronic equipment then being developed by American industrial espionage and counter-espionage organizations" (to quote *The Game of Nations*). Miles even spent hours sequestered with his liaison Hassan Tuhami, gaming out possible attempts by the Muslim Brotherhood and other opposition elements to overthrow Nasser. Quite what all this added up to is still a matter of debate. In *The Game of Nations*, after implying that the CIA invented much of the modern Egyptian security state, Miles suddenly grew modest, declaring that "despite all their foreign advisers," Nasser and Interior Minister Zakaria Mohieddin "built the intelligence and security services with remarkably little outside help." A veteran Egyptian intelligence officer, Abu al-Fadl, concurs in this judgment. Yet the former intelligence analyst Owen L. Sirrs, having recently reviewed all the available evidence, writes of the "CIA's ascendancy" in this period, "the heyday of [its] early involvement in Egypt."[18]

There is another, even more controversial claim in *The Game of Nations*: that the CIA helped import Nazi war criminals to Egypt to assist with the construction of Nasser's "repressive base." Here, the continuing controversy about Miles Copeland's reliability takes on an almost surreal quality, as the man himself voluntarily confesses to past behavior of spectacular moral questionability—and later writers point to evidence that contradicts his confession. According to *The Game of Nations*, the key figure in this operation was Otto Skorzeny, a former SS-Sturmbannführer who in 1943 had led a daring raid to rescue Mussolini from Allied captivity. Captured at the end of the war, Skorzeny befriended several Counter Intelligence Corps officers before escaping from prison in 1948 and setting up in business in Madrid. Some time in 1953 or 1954, so Miles claimed, the CIA brought Skorzeny to Cairo to advise Nasser about training the Egyptian army and to recruit former Gestapo officers to help build up the new GID. Eventually, several hundred ex-Nazis made the journey to Egypt, where, according to Miles (now characteristically pouring a little cold water on his earlier inflammatory statements), they were generally ignored and underpaid.[19]

There is indeed considerable proof in contemporary diplomatic records of an extensive German presence in Egypt at this time, including that of some egregious war criminals, such as Alois Brunner, a former assistant of Adolf Eichmann with a particular reputation for cruelty to Jewish children. One unofficial British observer told Conservative MP Julian Amery that a Munich restaurant had been physically transplanted to Cairo to cater to these expatriates, who also enjoyed such perks as access to untaxed German goods. "This is the revenge of the Africa Corps on Alamein," an ex-Nazi gloatingly told the dismayed Briton.[20]

Whether this was all the work of the CIA, though, is debatable. Ties between Egyptians and Germans dated back to World War II, when they had shared a common enemy in the British, and the Free Officers clearly had their own links with the West German intelligence chief, former Wehrmacht general Reinhard Gehlen. Indeed, the business of spiriting ex-Nazis into Egypt actually began while Farouk was still on the throne, with Wilhelm Voss, a former SS officer and close associate of Heinrich Himmler, blazing the trail later followed by Skorzeny. US records from the late 1950s, recently declassified in compliance with the Nazi War Crimes Disclosure Act of 1998, reveal CIA officials as ignorant of key aspects of the German penetration of Egypt.[21]

On the other hand, the same records also show that in 1959 a CIA officer based in Madrid requested that a visa be issued to Skorzeny so he could enter the United States on official business; there is plentiful evidence of the CIA collaborating with Reinhard Gehlen's "Organization" on other Cold War operations; and, like many former Counter Intelligence Corps officers, Miles Copeland did have experience of working with "useful" Nazis immediately after the war. At the very least, it seems likely that, as Owen Sirrs has concluded, "the CIA knew of and condoned the Egyptian-West German intelligence liaison relationship" —

hardly a record to boast about and one that would undoubtedly have incurred the moral disapproval of the OSS Arabists.[22]

In addition to these repressive actions, CIA officers also had a hand in building Nasser's (as Eichelberger put it) "constructive base," meaning principally that they helped him to wage psychological warfare. In part, this was a matter of defaming enemies of the RCC with either half true ("grey") or entirely made-up ("black") allegations of misconduct, usually of a sexual or religious nature. Although the powerful pro-Nasser publishers Mustafa and 'Ali Amin (old friends of Kim Roosevelt's) had made a good start on this front, flooding their newspapers with stories denouncing the old regime, the CIA decided that more was needed and called in one of its foremost psy-war consultants, Paul M. A. Linebarger. An army colonel and professor of Asiatic politics at Johns Hopkins University, Linebarger was the author of the seminal 1948 text *Psychological Warfare* (and, under the pen name Cordwainer Smith, a series of influential science fiction stories). During the early 1950s, he was a frequent presence in the Far and Middle East as, in his own words, "a visitor to small wars"; Edward Lansdale's counterinsurgency campaign in the Philippines benefited from his input. Traveling as Lawrence W. Teed, Linebarger arrived in Cairo in December 1954 for "operational appointments" in Maadi and Zamalek. While in Egypt, he provided the Free Officers with guidance about black and grey propaganda, including the technique of publicizing apparently positive information about individuals and groups that actually did long-term damage to their reputations. He also drew on the latest US communications research to coach the Ministry of National Guidance in public opinion surveying, the aim being to mobilize positive popular support for the revolutionary government.[23]

There was always the danger, of course, that such methods might not work, or even backfire, in a Third World environment. BA&H efforts to rationalize the Egyptian civil service, for example, foundered in the face of an entrenched culture of political patronage, while the CIA's decision to provide broadcasting equipment and training to Nasser's radio station, the Voice of the Arabs, would return to haunt it a few years later, when Cairo became the Arab world's main purveyor of anti-American propaganda. Miles and the others had to tread carefully in Cairo as, for all the shiny modernity of their principles and methods, their role as technical assistants to the revolutionary government harked back to the earlier colonial practice, particularly associated with the much hated proconsul, Lord Cromer, of posting British advisers to native ministers. For that matter, there were also similarities between the consultancy work Miles was doing for the Nasser regime and T. E. Lawrence's relationship with the Hashemites, or Jack Philby's with the House of Saud. Still, for all these echoes of earlier empires, the Free Officers do seem, at least between 1953 and 1955, to have been genuinely receptive to the newfangled ideas being touted by the American ad men and psy-warriors.

THE FINAL SERVICE PROVIDED TO Egypt's revolutionary government by the CIA was definitely evocative of an older era, involving as it did Kim Roosevelt acting like an eighteenth- or nineteenth-century court envoy. After his May 1953 meeting with the Free Officers, John Foster Dulles had realized that his first priority with regard to Egypt was solving its disruptive dispute with Britain over the Suez Canal. It soon became clear that all the main parties involved wanted a settlement, even the British, who had begun to feel the economic pinch of defending the canal base. The prospects for negotiation were blighted by several factors, though, including the potential for Nasser's internal enemies to make mischief if he were seen publicly dealing with the detested British. It did not help in this regard that Muhammad Naguib was becoming fed up with his role as figurehead for the Revolutionary Command Council, demanding a greater say in policy decisions and building bridges to the Muslim Brotherhood. Another problem was that John Foster Dulles had failed to hit it off with his British opposite number, the aristocratic, languid foreign secretary, Anthony Eden, who discomforted Americans with his habit of addressing men as "My dear." The British, likewise, did not much care for the dour Dulles; after meeting him for the first time in January 1953, Prime Minister Winston Churchill retired to bed muttering about his "great slab of a face."[24]

The solution was worked out, according to Miles Copeland, in a meeting between himself and Nasser in August 1953: the enlistment of Kim Roosevelt as a secret Anglo-Egyptian mediator. Kim readily agreed to this role, as it appealed to his taste for intrigue, and he was in any case already spending a lot of time with the British for reasons that were just about to be revealed. Within a few weeks of Miles and Nasser's conversation, he was shuttling between Washington, London, and Cairo, leaving an unusually wide documentary wash in his wake. On January 25, 1954, the *New York Times* reported, with a surprising lack of discretion, his appearance in Cairo for a conference at the RCC headquarters with Naguib and Nasser. In March, the British ambassador in Washington, Roger Makins, informed London that Nasser had just sent Kim a message "through secure channels" urging a quick resolution of the dispute before Naguib began "a competition in anti-British declarations which would make a settlement impossible." Later in the spring, with London signaling it was ready to withdraw all UK troops from Suez within twenty months in return for the right of reentry should war break out in the region, it was Kim's turn to tell Nasser that Washington would not pressure the British to make any more concessions. The young Arabist was clearly enjoying his secret access to the highest levels of government in three world capitals. When he was asked by President Eisenhower, in the hearing of White House press secretary James C. Hagerty, "if he had the right to make decisions on subjects that should properly be in the [Anglo-Egyptian] treaty," Kim "replied, rather annoyed, 'Why yes—eh, yes.'"[25]

Heads of Agreement between Britain and Egypt were initialed in Cairo at the end of July and the treaty itself signed in October 1954, paving the way for final British withdrawal from Suez by June 1956. While the Eisenhower administration congratulated itself on having defused one major threat to regional stability and prepared to tackle another, the Arab-Israeli conflict, Nasser's supporters rejoiced at the prospect of the British occupation ending after so many years. Later in October, a member of the Muslim Brotherhood, which saw the Anglo-Egyptian settlement as a capitulation to Western imperialism, shot at Nasser while he was giving a speech in Alexandria. The would-be assassin missed his intended victim, who immediately declared in a voice that rang out above the roar of the crowd, "Gamal 'Abdel Nasser is of you and from you and he is willing to sacrifice his life for the nation." Whether or not the incident was staged—Hassan Tuhami later claimed that the CIA equipped Nasser with a bulletproof vest before the event—it provided the RCC with the pretext it needed for a savage crackdown on the Brotherhood. The following month, President Naguib himself was arrested and sentenced to house arrest.[26]

Within two short years, Nasser had consolidated the July Revolution, eliminated his main rivals, and emerged as the hero of Egyptian nationalism. The role of regional Arab leader was now beckoning. Not even James Burnham's Machiavellians could have scripted a performance better than this. [27]

TWELVE

Authoring a Coup: Iran, 1953

AT PRECISELY THE SAME TIME that Kim Roosevelt was working covertly to remove the British and shore up Gamal Nasser's nationalist government in Egypt, he was also embroiled in another plot not far to the east. This one, however, would have a dramatically different effect on both the nation in question—Iran—and on the region as a whole. Whereas Kim's Egyptian operation advanced the anticolonial, pronationalist goals of American Arabism (albeit by supporting a military government), this one set back the cause of Middle Eastern nationalism and helped revive the power of the old imperial regime. It would also leave a legacy of suspicion and resentment of the United States in the region that threatened to destroy Americans' earlier reputation for disinterested benevolence.

The story of this plot—the August 1953 coup that removed Iranian prime minister Mohammed Mosaddeq and secured the throne of the young shah—has been told many times before, in countless books, articles, documentaries, and even recently a graphic novel. This is perhaps not surprising, given that, quite apart from its historical importance, the coup had a dramatic, thrilling, almost literary quality that lends itself very well to storytelling. However, in all the accounts of the event, one topic has received less attention than it deserves: Kim Roosevelt's personal motivation. Why did this young Arabist, the advocate of nationalism and anticolonialism in the Arab world, lead an operation that is now widely seen as having profoundly damaged these same causes in Iran?[1]

The answer to this question lies partly in grand strategic considerations relating to communism and oil that influenced US Middle East policies generally in the early Cold War period. But equally important for Kim Roosevelt personally were much more specific factors having to do with his cultural background and family history—and with the act of storytelling itself.

TO UNDERSTAND WHY KIM ROOSEVELT found himself in 1953 in charge of a covert effort to topple one of the Middle East's leading nationalists, it is necessary to go back several years in Iranian history, to long before Kim himself became involved in the operation.

The Cold War skirmishes of 1946 and 1947 witnessed by Archie Roosevelt—the withdrawal of Soviet troops and the suppression of separatist movements in Azerbaijan and Kurdistan—had apparently left Iran firmly tethered within the Western camp. A major source of instability remained, however. Despite the example set by ARAMCO in Saudi Arabia, where oil revenues were split fifty-fifty with the Saudi government, the British Anglo-Iranian Oil Company (AIOC) was refusing to share the profits from its drilling operations with Iranians. As the country's communist party, or Tudeh, began gaining support among the exploited workers in AIOC's massive Abadan refinery, a broad coalition of reform-oriented groups, the National Front, emerged under the leadership of Mohammed Mosaddeq, a veteran champion of Iranian independence and constitutional rule. Bowing to public pressure, the young shah appointed Mosaddeq as his prime minister in April 1951; a few days later, the Iranian government seized control of the nation's oil industry from the British.

Initially, the United States tried to take a neutral position in the Anglo-Iranian oil dispute, blocking a British plan to retake the Abadan refinery with military force and sending emissaries to Tehran and London to broker a negotiated settlement. Truman administration officials were irritated by the colonial mind-set of their British counterparts and, at this stage, saw the hugely popular Mosaddeq, a professed anticommunist, as a barrier against possible Soviet expansion into Iran. They were justified in doing so. The prime minister was no less opposed to Soviet than to British colonialism; like many nationalist leaders in Iran before him, his primary objective was putting an end to the Anglo-Russian Great Game on Iranian soil. In any case, just as in the 1946–1947 crisis, it was far from clear that the Soviets desired the communization of Iran. Recent research in Iranian and Russian archives has suggested that neither Moscow nor the Tudeh saw the country as ready for communist takeover.[2]

Gradually a number of factors undermined American neutrality. Although it is not altogether clear whether US petroleum interests coveted the Iranian oil fields for themselves, they definitely did not like the example set by Mosaddeq's seizure of AIOC assets and applied subtle pressure against him in Washington. The prime minister was a flamboyant figure, given to conducting government business from his bed and to theatrical fits of weeping and fainting. While this behavior delighted his Iranian supporters, it unnerved US officials, who tended to blame it on "Oriental" emotionalism and irrationality (in its 1951 "Man of the Year" article, *Time* magazine, adopting a prose style clearly intended to evoke an *Arabian Nights* tale, described Mosaddeq as a "dizzy old wizard"). The British, who made much of their greater experience in Persian affairs, did little to discourage this Orientalizing tendency. Finally, with the oil dispute dragging on and pressure on the Iranian economy mounting, the National Front coalition began to fragment. Emboldened opposition elements mounted street demonstrations in Tehran, causing Mosaddeq to resort to authoritarian measures. Observers in Washington were alarmed by what they perceived as a weakening of Iran's capability to resist Soviet influence. It did not help that, with Senator Joseph McCarthy riding high, the domestic political atmosphere in the United States was virulently anticommunist; moreover, as of September 1951, the US ambassador in Tehran reporting on developments there was none other than the archetypal foreign service Cold Warrior Loy Henderson.[3]

Although US officials continued to work for a negotiated settlement of the oil dispute, behind-the-scenes support for drastic action against Mosaddeq was growing. Following the events of 1946–1947, the CIA had carried on anti-Soviet covert operations in Iran, including BEDAMN, a psychological warfare program run by the archaeologist and former OSS officer Donald Wilber, now a half-time Agency consultant. After

1951, BEDAMN's principal agents, Ali Jalali and Faruq Kayvani (CIA code names Nerren and Cilley), increasingly focused their attentions on Mosaddeq himself, trying to turn leading Muslim clerics and other members of the National Front coalition against the prime minister. CIA intelligence estimates, meanwhile, emphasized Mosaddeq's "incompetence and dictatorial tendencies," as well as his vulnerability to communist adventurism. It was partly in response to such reporting that in November 1952 the Truman administration adopted NSC 136/1, directing US officials to expand "special political operations" to thwart a possible communist coup.[4]

As yet, no one in Washington was proposing an operation to get rid of Mosaddeq—that idea originated with the British. Somewhat improbably, it was two professors of Persian, Ann "Nancy" Lambton of London University and Oxford's Robin Zaehner, who first proposed, in 1951, the anti-Mosaddeq plot that culminated in the 1953 coup. The idea received the enthusiastic blessing of new prime minister Winston Churchill—a firm believer in both clandestine warfare and Britain's right to Iranian oil—and was turned over to the British Secret Intelligence Service (SIS, also known as MI6) for development in Tehran. MI6 station chief Christopher "Monty" Woodhouse mobilized British agents such as the three Rashidian brothers—merchants with excellent connections to opposition politicians, clerics, and journalists—in a campaign of anti-Mosaddeq intriguing. The prime minister responded in October 1952 by expelling all British personnel from the country. Undeterred, MI6 reassembled its Iranian team on its base in Cyprus under the command of Woodhouse's assistant, Norman Darbyshire. Before quitting Tehran, Woodhouse himself handed over the Rashidians and other British assets to Roger Goiran, head of the CIA station there. Woodhouse had believed from the first that US support was necessary if the British were to remove Mosaddeq, and in November 1952 he departed for Washington bearing a detailed plan for a joint Anglo-American operation code-named BOOT. While State Department representatives reacted coolly, CIA chiefs Allen Dulles and Frank Wisner both expressed guarded interest. As he confessed later, Woodhouse deliberately tailored his presentation to emphasize "the anti-Communist element in our plans" and avoided any hint that Americans "were being used to rescue Britain's oil interests." This tactic was effective, he believed. "At that date the CIA was a fairly new establishment, and willing to accept professional advice and even influence from the British."[5]

It was at this juncture that Kim Roosevelt appeared on the scene. Passing through London on his way back from one of his periodic trips to Tehran, Kim was collared by a group of British officials who presented him with BOOT. Intrigued, he pursued the idea with Allen Dulles, now slated to serve as CIA director in the incoming Eisenhower administration. As he explained later, he and Dulles "were in quiet disagreement with the outgoing administration's positions and had in fact already begun studying possible action in support of the Shah, and testing of agents with such action in mind."[6]

In February 1953, an MI6 team arrived in Washington and proposed Kim as the operation's "field commander." Miles Copeland was dispatched to Iran to assess the likelihood of a successor to Mosaddeq "sticking"; he returned in April with a positive estimate. Kim, meanwhile, was in Tehran meeting with the Rashidian brothers and a retired army major general, Fazlollah Zahedi, the man identified as the best bet to replace Mosaddeq. In May, Donald Wilber and Norman Darbyshire convened in Cyprus to thrash out details of the coup plan, now called TP-AJAX. "TP" was the CIA country prefix for Iran, while "AJAX" seems, rather prosaically, to have been a reference to the popular household cleanser, the implication being that the operation would scour Iran of communist influence.[7]

Following final planning meetings in Beirut, London, and Washington, Churchill granted official British approval for AJAX on July 1; Eisenhower signed off on the plan on July 11. On July 19, with both the CIA BEDAMN and MI6 Rashidian networks fomenting disturbances on the streets of Tehran, Kim slipped over the border from Iraq. He went into hiding in the hills just outside the capital, at the Tajrish home of Joseph Goodwin, one of the journalists who had preceded the shah's army into Azerbaijan seven years earlier and had since gone to work for the CIA. In the run-up to the coup, Goodwin acted as a replacement for station chief Roger Goiran, who on August 2 abruptly returned to Washington from Tehran. Various explanations for Goiran's departure have been offered, but the most likely seems his reluctance to participate in what he called an act of "Anglo-French colonialism." Such misgivings were not uncommon among mid-level CIA officers and the Persian experts who consulted with the Agency.[8]

With a team at CIA headquarters in Washington handling the propaganda and military aspects of the coup, and the British base in Cyprus providing three-way communication, Kim now set to work turning

Operation AJAX into reality. The crux of the plan was to provoke a constitutional crisis in which Iranians were forced to choose between Mosaddeq and the shah. Kim and his fellow conspirators were confident that, in a confrontation between the prime minister and the king, the most powerful elements of Iranian society—the merchants of the bazaar, Muslim religious leaders (with their ability to summon urban crowds), and army officers—would rally to the latter. The problem was that the young shah, while no friend of his turbulent prime minister, was reluctant to sign the royal decrees, or *firmans*, dismissing him and appointing Zahedi in his stead—hardly surprising, given the personal risk involved. Kim responded by applying pressure on him through various third parties, first the shah's famously strong-willed sister, Princess Ashraf (the supposedly irresistible Steve Meade was enlisted in the effort to win her over), then, when that ploy failed, General H. Norman Schwartzkopf, the highly regarded former head of a wartime US gendarmerie mission to Iran (and father of the Desert Storm commander). With the *firmans* still not forthcoming, finally Kim himself went to see the shah, hiding under a blanket as he was driven through the palace gates. The shah eventually signed the orders on August 13, after retreating to a royal resort on the Caspian Sea. With arrangements in place for the arrest of Mosaddeq and his supporters in the army, August 15 was set as the day for the coup.

Then everything went wrong. Alerted by at least one security leak, Mosaddeq ordered the arrest of the soldiers charged with arresting him. Zahedi concealed himself in a CIA officer's basement, the shah fled to Baghdad and then to Rome, and Washington ordered the evacuation of AJAX operatives from Tehran. August 17 found Walter Bedell Smith, now undersecretary of state, telling the British ambassador in Washington that the Eisenhower administration was taking "a new look at policy towards Persia" and even considering technical assistance for the Mosaddeq government. "Whatever his faults, Musaddiq [*sic*] had no love for the Russians and timely aid might enable him to keep Communism in check," Smith explained.[9]

Kim Roosevelt, however, had other ideas. The evacuation orders were slow to reach him, reportedly because the MI6 communications team held them up deliberately, and he took advantage of the time this brought him to improvise—using the Rashidians' contacts and US journalists to publicize the *firmans* and sending messengers to pro-shah army commanders stationed outside Tehran, urging them to march on the capital. According to one account, he even threatened to have the BEDAMN agents Jalali and Kayvani killed if they did not carry on with their anti-Mosaddeq activities.[10]

The tide turned on the morning of August 19, when a crowd gathered in Tehran's bazaar and then began marching toward the center of the city, waving pictures of the shah and chanting his name. Royalist army units joined in the procession, which began attacking buildings associated with the Tudeh and, early in the afternoon, occupied Radio Tehran. Zahedi emerged from hiding and went on air declaring himself the rightful prime minister. Following a pitched battle in which at least two hundred Iranians died, pro-shah forces subdued the last army battalion loyal to Mosaddeq outside his residence, which was then ransacked by the mob while the erstwhile premier fled over the garden wall. Informed of these developments at his hotel in Rome, a dazed shah chokingly declared, "I knew that they loved me," and hurriedly prepared to return to Tehran. Kim Roosevelt, meanwhile, was addressing a jubilant crowd of royalist army officers. "You owe me, the United States, the British, *nothing at all*, except, if you would like to give them, brief thanks," he told them, a little gracelessly. The shah arrived home in triumph on August 22, at the same time that Mosaddeq was apprehended and sentenced to house arrest, and Zahedi granted $5 million by the CIA so that he could meet month-end payrolls (regular subsidies would follow later). At a secret midnight meeting the following day, the shah raised a glass in toast to Kim with the words, "I owe my throne to God, my people, my army—and to you!"[11]

Whether Kim deserved such fulsome thanks is open to question. Later, other Western participants in the planning of AJAX would claim their share of the credit. While quite generous toward Kim personally, Monty Woodhouse's 1982 autobiography, *Something Ventured*, implicitly criticized the CIA for slighting the contribution of MI6 and taking "total responsibility for the disposal of Musaddiq [*sic*]" On the American side, Donald Wilber, in a rather peevish memoir published in 1986, was less kind to Kim, accusing him of monopolizing credit for the coup within the CIA, and asserting that "the plan was basically mine." (Wilber also complained about the victory celebration Kim laid on for the AJAX team after returning from Iran: "a Dutch treat lunch at a Chinese restaurant on Connecticut Avenue, which did not serve liquor.") Never one to miss an opportunity for a joke, Miles Copeland teasingly joined

in the competition for credit in his memoir, *The Game Player*, reporting that the words spoken by the shah to Kim immediately after the
coup were in fact, "I owe my throne to God, my people, my army, to
you and, of course, to that undercover assistant of yours whom I shall
not name."[12]

More recently (and more seriously), attention has focused on the
part played in the 1953 coup by another set of actors: Iranians themselves. According to a 2010 book by a former Iranian diplomat, it was
not Kim Roosevelt who was behind the crucial events of August 19—
the gathering in the morning of the pro-shah crowd in the bazaar and the
mobilization of the army units that joined in the demonstrations later in
the day—but rather royalist officers in the Tehran garrison and Muslim
clerics, in particular the Grand Ayatollah Boroujerdi in Qom, who had
decided that the drift of events under Mosaddeq was dangerous to Islam.
In this scenario, Kim's actions in the days immediately after the abortive
coup attempt of August 15 were geared less toward having a second stab
on the nineteenth, as was claimed later, than putting in place stay-behind
networks as part of the planned CIA evacuation of the country. These
measures had little bearing on the events of 28 Mordad (August 19 in the
Iranian calendar) but subsequently enabled Kim to claim responsibility
for the day's outcome.[13]

Certainly, it is striking that neither of the two major American
sources about the Iran coup—Kim Roosevelt's own memoir, the 1979
Countercoup, and a 1954 internal CIA report on the operation by Donald Wilber leaked to the *New York Times* in 2000—explicitly claim that
Kim played any part personally in the raising of the bazaar crowd or
the royalist army units. The chaotic and bloody events on August 19
bore little resemblance to other Middle Eastern putsches in which the
CIA had previously been implicated—the carefully planned and largely
bloodless military takeovers in Syria and Egypt. And it is evident on its
face that, whatever the role of Ayatollah Boroujerdi, players other than
Kim Roosevelt and his CIA colleagues did contribute to Mosaddeq's
downfall, including the Iranian prime minister himself, who made a series of crucial errors of judgment on 28 Mordad.[14]

Still, to correct the earlier exclusive focus on Western actors in the
Iran coup by denying all credit (or blame, depending on one's perspective) to Kim Roosevelt and his CIA team seems excessive. The constant
agitation of the political atmosphere in Tehran by Kim's agents Jalani

and Kayvani and their network of subagents surely helped to destabilize the Mosaddeq government, and it is difficult to imagine the events of August 19 taking place at all without the constitutional crisis that had been produced by the shah's dismissal of Mosaddeq and subsequent flight, events in which Kim incontrovertibly had a hand. When all is said and done, the causes of the 1953 regime change in Iran were probably similar to those of the Syrian coup of 1949: that is, the ouster of Mosaddeq was produced by a combination of Iranian, American, and British actions, with the Westerners' intervention helping produce a set of political conditions in Iran that slightly, perhaps crucially, advantaged some local elites over others.

While it may never be possible to establish definitively the precise balance of factors that caused Mosaddeq's fall, the consequences of the 1953 coup were all too clear. With CIA backing (including the assignment of Steve Meade to Tehran to help train the Iranian secret police), the shah established an authoritarian regime that, by brutally repressing both the Tudeh and the National Front, staved off possible communist influences at the cost of generating profound currents of internal opposition. Lacking any democratic outlets, these eventually surged in the Revolution of 1979 with the exile of the shah and the establishment in Iran of an Islamic republic under the leadership of the Ayatollah Khomeini. Already deeply sensitive to foreign meddling in their country, Iranians needed little encouragement to resent the suspected US role in the 1953 coup, and street demonstrators in 1979 chanted Mosaddeq's name and burned effigies of the American president. For these protestors, "the thread of memory led clearly from the Great Game to the Great Satan," as Yale scholar Abbas Amanat memorably put it. Iran now became a breeding ground for anti-Americanism in the wider Middle East and for Islamist acts of violence against US troops and civilians.[15]

Ironically, the possibility of such "blowback" seems to have been anticipated by Kim Roosevelt himself in 1949, when he concluded his manifesto *Arabs, Oil, and History* with the warning that the "danger of Russia versus the United States is . . . the seen danger," yet the "danger of Orient versus Occident seems as yet unseen; it could be ruinous; we may succumb to it from not seeing." In light of this prophetic statement, the question has to be asked: Just what was Kim Roosevelt thinking when he carried out the Iran coup operation of August 19, 1953?[16]

TO BE SURE, KIM ROOSEVELT shared in the dominant American view that Iran was dangerously vulnerable to Soviet influence. *Arabs, Oil, and History* portrays the country's political institutions as fragmented and weak, and his later account in *Countercoup* depicts Mosaddeq (inaccurately) as in "alliance . . . with the Soviet Union." Yet neither of these works ever conveys the sense of intense, ideological anticommunism detectable in statements by other US Middle East hands from the early Cold War—Loy Henderson, for example, or, for that matter, Archie Roosevelt. Other factors, of a cultural and psychological rather than political nature, seem to have been more important in shaping Kim's behavior toward Iran.[17]

To begin with, there was Roosevelt Anglophilia. Although again not quite as pronounced as in Archie's case, there was a palpable sense of cultural identification between the upper-class British spies who conceived of Operation BOOT and the patrician American who eventually carried it out. "Kim Roosevelt was quickly seen as an important ally in our plans," wrote the MI6 Tehran station chief Monty Woodhouse, an Oxford-educated classicist and future baron. "Like his grandfather, and also his father, he had a natural inclination for bold and imaginative action, and also a friendly sympathy with the British." Family connections doubtless played their part: when Kim passed through London, he tended to stay at the Chester Square residence of the Herberts, the aristocratic British family into which his aunt, Belle's sister Elizabeth, had married. Another of Belle's trans-Atlantic connections was the Duchess of Devonshire, Lady Mary Alice Gascoyne-Cecil ("Moucher" to Belle and other intimates), whose brother Robert ("Bobbety"), Fifth Marquess of Salisbury, was a Conservative Party grandee and, at the time of the Iran coup, acting foreign secretary. There were, admittedly, some strains in the intelligence dimension of the "Special Relationship": perhaps mindful of the recent exposure of Soviet moles—Kim Philby's accomplices Guy Burgess and Donald Maclean—Kim Roosevelt was reluctant to divulge the identity of the CIA's principal BEDAMN agents to his MI6 counterparts, while the latter could not hide "a faint note of envy . . . that the Agency was better equipped in the way of funds, personnel, and facilities than was SIS." Overall, though, the CIA's collaboration with MI6—"our cousins," as Kim tellingly referred to the British in *Countercoup*—was conspicuously harmonious, so much so that it was immediately seen as a precedent for future joint operations. "The lesson here is clear," concluded Donald Wilber's CIA report on AJAX, which drew heavily on briefings with Kim Roosevelt. "As in the larger world picture, U.S.-U.K. interests and activities must be coordinated."[18]

If culture helped make Kim receptive to the plans of the British, it set him against Iranians. Despite his affinity for the Arab world, Kim, much like Archie in this regard, viewed Persia through an Orientalist prism inherited from the British. His description of Mosaddeq in *Countercoup* went through the checklist of supposed Oriental character flaws: deviousness, inconsistency, and emotionalism. The "wily" prime minister "was like an ill-tempered, erratic old peasant, . . . judging all problems from his emotional standpoint," wrote Kim, ignoring Mosaddeq's aristocratic background and European education. "His great strength lay in his ability to mesmerize crowds," the description continued. "His wild exaggerations . . . led his listeners into almost insane hysteria." Hence Kim, who not much earlier had hailed Arab nationalism as a spontaneous, potent force in its own right, now dismissed its Iranian equivalent as irrational and susceptible to manipulation—exactly the British view of the same phenomenon.[19]

The main exception to this Orientalist representation of Iranians in *Countercoup* was Kim's portrayal of the shah. Whereas in the run-up to the coup many Western observers perceived the vacillating young king as a "mesmerized rabbit," to quote Monty Woodhouse, Kim in contrast portrayed him as a rather heroic figure, on one occasion bravely foiling an assassination attempt, on another piloting a crippled plane to safety, and fleeing Iran in August 1953 not out of cowardice but rather in a premeditated move to stimulate popular anti-Mosaddeq feeling. Yet it seems that this image of the shah was constructed after the fact. At the time of the coup, Kim was no less impatient with the king than other Westerners, at one point threatening to quit Iran "in complete disgust unless the Shah took action within a few days." Moreover, Kim's claim in *Countercoup* that the shah had left "a lasting impression" on him when they first met during his 1947 Middle Eastern tour is belied by the fact that the king is barely mentioned in the 1949 *Arabs, Oil, and History*. Interestingly, this process of reinventing the shah as a more decisive, virile, Western-like leader seems to have begun immediately after the August 19 coup, when Loy Henderson described him to Washington as showing newfound "vigour, decision, and clear thinking," and Kim called him "a new man."[20]

The argument here is not that Kim Roosevelt staged the 1953 coup because he disliked Iranians. Rather, it is that, as for other Anglo-American observers at this time, Orientalist attitudes clouded his judgment of Persian politics and encouraged his tendency to view Iran as a place for personal adventure, a playing field for spy games. This last impulse, which for Kim was strongly associated with his identity as a Roosevelt man, is evident throughout the narrative of events offered in *Countercoup*. As Kim set off from Beirut for Iran in July 1953, for example, he remembered what his father, Kermit, "wrote of his arrival in East Africa with *his* father, T.R., in 1909 on *The African Game Trails* trip. 'It was a great adventure, and all the world was young!'" The implicit comparison of TP-AJAX to one of his father's or grandfather's hunting expeditions was reinforced by "the traditional French hunter's sendoff" that Kim received from a Lebanese friend. The connection to earlier Roosevelt foreign adventures was not lost on contemporaries. Writing Washington shortly after the coup, the chief of the US military mission to Iran, Robert A. McClure, observed, "Frank W[isner]'s boys did a grand job, and wielded a big stick."[21]

Other incidents described in *Countercoup* add to the impression that Kim regarded his mission to Iran as a Kipling-esque adventure. He entered the country in July not bothering to conceal his identity; he showed his passport to a border guard, who mistakenly recorded his name as one of his distinguishing physical characteristics (a suitably swashbuckling one): "Mr. Scar on Right Forehead." On August 19, he belatedly responded to Walter Bedell Smith's cable ordering his return home, explaining that the tide had just turned in the shah's favor and then cheekily signing off, "Love and kisses from all the team." The sense of spying fun-and-games is heightened by the frequent references to actual games, especially card games, that populate *Countercoup*. Even the operation's "theme song," a tune Kim played repeatedly in the weeks before the coup, was about games: "Luck Be a Lady Tonight," the gambling song from the musical *Guys and Dolls*.[22]

The more one reads Kim's account of TP-AJAX in *Countercoup*, the more one is struck by its resemblance to an adventure novel or spy thriller. There are the allusions to Kipling, both implicit and explicit, as when Kim (Roosevelt) likens some bearded, roaming tribesmen in eastern Iran to Mahbub Ali in *Kim* (the novel). Then there is the narrative's main framing device, Kim's journey from Washington to Tehran, which both builds suspense and enables him to set the scene for the coup by recounting his previous experience of Iran. *Kim*, too, is basically about a journey that culminates in a decisive play in the Great Game. One also thinks of John Buchan's *Greenmantle* and its hero Richard Hannay's perilous trek across World War I Europe to the novel's climactic battle scene in Turkey.

If *Countercoup* reads like a novel, this was no coincidence: by the time Kim wrote the book in the 1970s, he had been telling the story of Operation AJAX for years. The process of emplotting the chaotic events that had taken place in Tehran, turning them into a coherent story to tell others, began immediately after the coup, when Kim stopped off in London on his way home and met with MI6 officials for debriefing. Both *Countercoup* and Donald Wilber's 1954 report on AJAX are surprisingly frank on this score. "They wanted the whole story, . . . concentrating on the glamorous features of the operation," Kim wrote of his meetings with the British spies, who clearly viewed Mosaddeq's removal as an opportunity to improve their standing with the Foreign Office. Kim obliged by telling his tale over dinner at the grill room of the Connaught Hotel "as elaborately and excitingly as [he] possibly could," including "all the names and numbers of the players, every suspicion, hope or anxiety [he] had known." The following day, with his "routine down cold, in living color," Kim visited the Foreign Office, where, as requested by his friends in MI6, he gave acting foreign secretary Lord Salisbury (Moucher's brother Bobbety) "the full treatment": "a vivid account of the recent disturbances in Iran," as Salisbury himself described it after the meeting. According to the Wilber coup report, Salisbury "appeared to be absolutely fascinated." As he left the Foreign Office, Kim encountered an MI6 official clutching "a folder covered with red ribbons, sealing wax, and other *objets d'art*" who excitedly told him that the acting foreign secretary had just given the go-ahead to another Secret Service operation he had previously been reluctant to approve.[23]

From the Foreign Office, it was on to the final appointment of the day, at Number 10 Downing Street. Led to a living room by a military aide, Kim found Prime Minister Winston Churchill lying in a bed, propped up by pillows. The old adventurer had recently suffered a stroke and was clearly in bad shape. "He had great difficulty in hearing; occasional difficulty in articulating; and apparent difficulty seeing to his left," so Kim reported after the meeting. Nevertheless, the young

American was greeted enthusiastically and instructed to pull up a chair on the right-hand side of the bed. There he sat for the next two hours, telling the story of the coup as the ailing prime minister, "consumed alternately by curiosity and by sleepiness," slipped in and out of a doze. At the tale's end, Sir Winston grinned, shifted himself up on his pillows, and addressed his visitor. "Young man," Kim recalled him saying, "if I had been but a few years younger, I would have loved nothing better than to have served under your command in this great venture." "Thank you, sir," replied Kim, deeply moved by "what was, coming from this man, the supreme compliment." The scene, which resembled nothing so much as a man telling a child a bedtime story, could not have been more poignant: Kim had gotten to rehearse his latter-day enactment of the Great Game narrative for a living relic of Britain's imperial heyday.[24]

The storytelling carried on in America, where Kim now returned, trailing clouds of glory. Fearful of arousing unwelcome press interest by visiting President Eisenhower in his Denver retreat—too "radio active" for the president's "gold-fish-bowl," as he told a British official—Kim spent the last days of August with his family in Nantucket, contenting himself with writing a report for the president that contained personal messages from the shah, General Zahedi, and Prime Minister Churchill. (As in the case of Egypt, it is easy to imagine Kim reveling in the role of personal envoy between kings, presidents, and prime ministers.) The following month, he at last got his chance to tell the president his story in person, presenting a briefing on Operation AJAX at a White House meeting attended by Eisenhower, the Dulles brothers, and other senior figures. "The substance of my report had nothing new," he wrote in *Countercoup*; "it was simply a combination of what I had told our British allies and the story I had given to the dozing Winston Churchill." Nevertheless, the reception was enthusiastic. John Foster Dulles, in particular, "seemed to be purring like a giant cat," Kim observed. The president, too, was impressed but shrewdly noted a literary quality in the reports he was receiving about Iran. They "sounded more like a dime novel than historical facts," he wrote later.[25]

Indeed, this was too good a story to keep completely secret. In the fall of the following year, after another successful CIA coup operation in Guatemala, Allen Dulles authorized Agency cooperation with the *Saturday Evening Post* on a three-part report by Richard and Gladys Harkness, "The Mysterious Doings of CIA." The boosterist story, which appeared around the same time that a presidential commission charged with reviewing the CIA's performance to date reported to the White House, paid particular attention to the "stranger-than-fiction circumstances" in which "the strategic little nation of Iran was rescued from the closing clutch of Moscow." Specific sentences, such as the reporters' insistence that, despite the CIA's enabling role, "the physical overthrow of Mossadegh [*sic*] was accomplished by the Iranians themselves," sound uncannily like formulations of Kim Roosevelt's—who, it will be remembered, had contributed several articles to the *Saturday Evening Post* before he joined the Agency. Kim, meanwhile, was delighting in telling the tale to guests at his Washington home. Normally a "very quiet, private person," he would, so his son Jonathan recalled later, become quite "garrulous" on the subject of Iran. When the story was published, many retellings later, as *Countercoup*, the intelligence commentator Thomas Powers remarked on the "golly-gee-whiz air" that pervaded the book. It was, he wrote, "the sort of story an old man might set down for the pleasure of his grandchildren," echoing Miles Copeland's observation in *The Game Player* that coups lent themselves particularly well to family storytelling.[26]

The Arab historian Albert Hourani once wrote of T. E. Lawrence and his self-mythologizing memoir of the Arab Revolt, *Seven Pillars of Wisdom*, that Lawrence deliberately acted like an epic hero during World War I and then after the war wrote an epic book about his actions. There was something of this circular, literary quality to Kim Roosevelt's involvement in the Iran coup. His actions were shaped, at least in part, by a cluster of ideas and emotions derived from Roosevelt family lore and earlier literary works. Afterward, indeed even before he had returned home from Iran, Kim was turning the operation into his signature story, his own charge up Kettle Hill or River of Doubt expedition, a real-life Kipling adventure. Others in the CIA (and, for that matter, MI6) encouraged him in this process because it suited their bureaucratic purposes to do so, with the result that the story entered the Agency's own canonical history as one of the signal successes of the Allen Dulles "Golden Era."[27]

If only Kim and his superiors in the CIA had heeded the words spoken by the lama to his fictional namesake in the Kipling novel: "Thou hast loosed an Act upon the world, and as a stone thrown into a pool so spread the consequences thou canst not tell how far."[28]

THIRTEEN

From ALPHA . . .

IT WAS A COOL SPRING morning in the nation's capital, but Kim Roosevelt was glowing with pride. With him in the White House were his wife, sons, and mother, Belle, as well as both Dulles brothers and Loy Henderson. "In a situation grave and menacing to our security, Mr. Roosevelt demonstrated the highest order of courage, resourcefulness, and determination," declared Dwight Eisenhower, reading a citation composed eighteen months earlier, shortly after the Iran coup. "His achievement is in keeping with the highest traditions of service to the United States and merits the gratitude of his Government." With these words, the president stepped forward to pin the National Security Medal to Kim's chest.[1]

The award, created in the final days of the Truman administration, was a rare honor, reserved for a select few in the intelligence community. Only two officers of the CIA had received it before Kim: his fellow nation builder and "quiet American" Edward Lansdale and Ike's former chief of staff, Walter Bedell Smith. For Kim, it was the latest in a series of personal triumphs, including TP-AJAX (the disastrous long-term results of which were yet to become apparent), his contribution to the Anglo-Egyptian settlement of the Suez dispute, and, most recently, his promotion from chief of the Near East division to assistant deputy director of plans, just under Frank Wisner in the CIA chain of command. Although the ceremony was marked as "Off Record" on the White House calendar, and therefore unaccompanied by the sort of press attention that would be paid to FBI director J. Edgar Hoover when he received the same honor in May 1955, this probably did not bother Kim. He was used to slipping in and out of the offices of presidents and prime ministers unobserved. Indeed, the lack of hoopla rather suited his growing reputation as a youthful éminence grise and his Grotonian sense of noblesse oblige.[2]

The timing of the ceremony—March 24, 1955—seemed propitious as well. With one of the two greatest threats to Middle East peace, the Suez issue, now apparently resolved (thanks in no small part to Kim), the Eisenhower administration was turning its attention to the other: the Arab-Israeli conflict. The obstacles in the path of a settlement were huge, of course, and new problems presented themselves almost daily, but there were some reasons for cautious optimism as well. No longer preoccupied with maintaining their position in Egypt, the British were ready to throw their weight behind the push for peace. Nasser, who had just proclaimed himself Egyptian prime minister, now enjoyed the internal stability and regional standing necessary to bear the weight of a negotiated settlement in the Arab world (something that Husni Za'im, an earlier candidate for the role of Arab "necessary leader," could never have claimed). And the Israelis, with the British buffer between themselves and the Egyptians about to go from Suez, were in an unusually accommodating mood. Most important, the Eisenhower administration, thanks to its Middle Eastern policy of "friendly impartiality," appeared much better placed than its predecessor to play the role of umpire or broker between the two sides. Indeed, the main concern of US officials was less to do with the substantial issues in the conflict than with domestic time constraints. The presidential election of 1956 was looming, meaning that before long the administration would have to steer clear of the controversial Palestine issue, potentially so costly in terms of pro-Israel votes. If the United States was to secure a settlement that would be acceptable in the Arab world, it would have to act quickly.

Such was the background to the launch of Project ALPHA, a comprehensive Anglo-American effort to resolve all the outstanding points of contention between Israel and its Arab neighbors. Formulated by a team of US and British negotiators in early 1955, the ALPHA proposals appeared on paper as strikingly fair, not least with regard to the two most divisive issues: the Palestinian refugees and territorial borders. According to the plan, Israel was to repatriate seventy-five thousand refugees and pay compensation to the remainder, who were to be absorbed by the Arab states. Meanwhile, Israel's borders would be fixed, with some minor adjustments, at the 1949 armistice lines, not those of the 1947 UN partition. As an incentive to both parties to accept these terms, the United States would commit the vast sum of $1 billion of aid to the area over the next five years. The ALPHA plan has since struck some Middle East experts as representing a moment of genuine promise in the history of the Arab-Israeli conflict, coming as it did before the piling up of grievances caused by later wars and the rise of such contentious issues as the Occupied Territories.[3]

With his new global role as the CIA's assistant deputy director of plans, Kim did not take part personally in the ALPHA negotiations, which in any case were at this stage the responsibility of State Department and Foreign Office diplomats. Nonetheless, his standing in Washington was so high that he retained his reputation as the CIA's "Mr. Middle East" and would still be summoned at a moment's notice by both Dulles brothers to proffer his advice or undertake some special mission to the Arab world. Later in the year, when ALPHA ran into serious difficulties, Kim would be dispatched to Egypt to reprise the role of covert envoy he had already performed to such good effect in helping to solve the Anglo-Egyptian dispute. Prior to that, his most important contribution to the peace plan came in the United States itself, as the state-private network he had helped create after World War II rallied once again to fight American Zionism and buy the Eisenhower administration some crucial time ahead of the 1956 election.[4]

FOR THE ANTI-ZIONIST JEWS AROUND the American Council for Judaism (ACJ) and the Arabist Protestants of the American Friends of the Middle East (AFME), the two years since Dwight Eisenhower entered the White House had been good ones, at least when compared with the accumulated disappointments of the Truman era. The change in the Washington air had first been noticed by the ACJ. In April 1953, Council president Lessing Rosenwald and Kim Roosevelt's old friend George Levison visited the White House to meet with the new president and leave a memorandum for his secretary of state explaining the organization's principles, including the all-important distinction between Judaism as a religion and Zionism as a political movement. The meeting was a great success. Eisenhower "was extremely attentive and gave . . . the impression that what he heard was in general agreement with his views," a delighted Levison reported to ACJ executive director Elmer Berger. Even better was to follow. Word reached Berger and his confreres that Secretary Dulles had taken their memorandum with him on his May 1953 tour of the Middle East. The famous speech that he gave after his return on June 1 announcing a more even-handed American policy in the region contained passages that bore a striking resemblance to statements of the ACJ—for example, a sentence calling on Israel to become "a part of the Near East community and cease to look upon itself . . . as alien to this community." (Shortly afterward, AFME, having apparently lost some of its earlier reticence about tangling with Zionists, gave this phrase a provocative reformulation, with Vice President Garland Evans Hopkins stating that "Israel is in the Middle East and of the Middle East, and must eventually conform to the pattern, or it has no other alternative but to cease to exist.")[5]

As the Eisenhower administration made clear its abandonment of Truman's policy of preferential treatment for Israel, the ACJ consolidated its links to government, both overt and covert. An important figure in this process was Henry Byroade, the man Kim Roosevelt had tried to dislodge as assistant secretary for Near East affairs. A brilliant and handsome young military officer whose previous foreign service experience lay mainly in the Far East and Germany, Byroade had a different background from most of the State Department Arabists, but he soon proved a surprisingly enthusiastic ally of the Jewish anti-Zionists. Elmer Berger, again displaying his gift for cultivating Washington insiders, developed an especially close relationship with him, the two men addressing each other affectionately as "Hank" and the "mad rabbi." Under Berger, the ACJ worked to help Byroade win domestic support for the new Middle East policy, promoting it "to Jews particularly and to Americans generally"; in return, the Council enjoyed special access to the State Department, including privileged information about American Zionist organizations suspected of acting illegally as publicity fronts for the Israeli government. Berger once joked to Levison that he was becoming a "kind of a Jewish FBI."[6]

Meanwhile, Berger kept up his close contacts with "Kim's outfit," as he coyly referred to the CIA. Although Kim himself was increasingly preoccupied by other matters — "He's almost as frenzied as you and I," Berger told Levison in May 1953, shortly before the Mosaddeq operation in Iran — he still found time to see Berger during the latter's frequent sallies to Washington. Berger was also a frequent dinner and overnight guest at the Roosevelt family's home in Wesley Heights. Correspondence in the American Council for Judaism's records makes clear that these contacts included discussion of possible CIA support for ACJ projects that were separate from the AFME operation, although the details were kept vague. The most conspicuous public expression of this burgeoning state-private alliance came in May 1954, when Henry Byroade addressed the ACJ's annual conference in Philadelphia, urging Israelis to "drop the attitude of the conqueror" and repeating the now familiar refrain that Israel should reconcile itself to being "a Middle Eastern state." The speech, which had been drafted with the help of veteran State Department Arabist Edwin Wright and delivered with the blessing of Foster Dulles, was an unprecedented gesture of official approval for the ACJ's anti-Zionist platform.[7]

Also clearly benefiting from the new dispensation in Washington were the American Friends of the Middle East. Garland Hopkins enjoyed several audiences with Secretary Dulles and Assistant Secretary Byroade, using them as opportunities to press the organization's pro-Arab and anti-Zionist agenda; AFME returned the favor by rallying around the Eisenhower administration on such occasions as the 1954 congressional elections, urging candidates to ignore Zionist calls on them to repudiate current US Middle East policy. This relationship was personified by another relative newcomer to the organized anti-Zionist struggle, Edward L. R. Elson. Raised by devout Presbyterian parents in Pennsylvania and ordained by the Presbytery of Los Angeles, Elson had served as an army chaplain during and after World War II, drawing the attention of General Eisenhower for his postwar work in Germany. After returning to the United States, he was named pastor of what later became the National Presbyterian Church in Washington, DC, in which role he baptized the new president in 1953 (despite his religiosity, Ike had never formally joined a church). President Eisenhower henceforth attended Elson's services regularly, along with that most conscientious of Presbyterians, Secretary of State Dulles.[8]

Reverend Elson joined AFME's board of directors in 1954, having earlier toured the Middle East as holder of the organization's first annual lectureship, speaking on the themes of "The Spiritual Significance of the

World Crisis" and "Resources for Dynamic Democracy." His interest in the region, he later explained, had grown out of reading the Bible in his childhood and touring the Arabian peninsula as a young man. These experiences left him with a profound admiration for the Arab world and, evidently, a strong antipathy toward "political Zionism," attitudes he was not shy about sharing with his politically powerful congregation. His sermons, famed for their skillful delivery and mixing of Calvinism with ardent patriotism, often alluded to the Middle East. He also wrote frequently to both the president and the secretary of state, offering spiritual and practical guidance about their handling of the region, urging the former to resist pressure from "a minority segment" of the American population to pander to Israel, and the latter to visit Cairo personally so that he could renew his acquaintance with Nasser. (Elson himself did just this in 1957, again with AFME sponsorship, coming away from a meeting with the Egyptian premier full of praise for his thoughtfulness and sincerity.) The Presbyterian pastor made a particular point of boosting AFME in his correspondence with Eisenhower, describing it as "the most effective instrument for promoting friendship on both sides." In 1955 he even managed to work in a reference to the work of the American Council for Judaism during the Thanksgiving Day celebrations at the Eisenhower family home in Gettysburg.[9]

This is not to say that AFME and the ACJ were so preoccupied supporting Eisenhower's Middle East policy that they forgot altogether about other aspects of their respective programs. The Council, for example, launched a successful religious education program in the early 1950s, founding ten schools dedicated to teaching the principles of classical Reform Judaism. As for AFME, something of the importance it still attached to its mission of promoting spiritual dialogue between Americans and Arabs can be inferred from the fact that CIA case officer Mather Eliot was assigned to lay the "administrative foundation" for the Christian-Muslim Convocation called by Garland Hopkins in Lebanon in 1954. Edward Elson proved an especially keen advocate of this dimension of AFME's work. "The people of the Middle East will understand us if we communicate in spiritual terms," he wrote his congregant, President Eisenhower. "It will help to acknowledge our indebtedness to the Middle East for contributing to the world the three great religions of Semitic origin." (An early draft of this letter had referred specifically to "Arabs" rather than "people of the Middle East," but Elson presumably decided this risked the appearance of special pleading and deleted the reference.) Eisenhower's response to his pastor's "fine memorandum" was also telling. "I am greatly impressed by your belief as to the relations we should maintain with the Arabs, as people," he wrote. The president's words reflected the deep importance his administration attached to what it called "People-to-People" diplomacy: the cultivation of mutual understanding and sympathy between ordinary American citizens and their counterparts overseas, as well as his own personal belief in the capability of religious faith to defeat communist atheism. In other words, it was not just AFME's anti-Zionism that struck a responsive chord in the Eisenhower White House; so too did the organization's positive interest in American-Arab friendship and Christian-Muslim dialogue.[10]

Still, at this point in its existence, AFME's primary focus was on the domestic front—in 1954 it reported that twenty-seven of its current projects were devoted mainly to "spreading information" about the Middle East in the United States, as compared with a mere four concerned with "interpreting" America to the Middle East—and this tendency only increased with the inauguration of Project ALPHA in the winter of 1955. It is clear from declassified State Department records that John Foster Dulles considered the management of domestic US opinion about the Arab-Israeli conflict an important adjunct of his peace plan. "The Secretary inquired how the group expected to keep Jewish leaders in this country quiet during this period of preparation," read the minutes of a planning meeting of ALPHA's Anglo-American team of negotiators in January 1955. "The Administration had succeeded in deflating Israel in order to make a reasonable settlement possible," Dulles went on to explain. "As a result the Israeli position was now weaker than it ever had been, but by 1956 it was likely to gain new strength." This last point about the impending presidential election, which Dulles repeated to the chief British representative, Evelyn Shuckburgh, later in the month, was partly intended to create tactical pressure on the Arabs to settle quickly. But it also reflected a real concern about the potential of American Zionists to derail ALPHA.[11]

Dulles was not alone in this concern. "Zionist influence in America is a force that cannot be ignored," Kim Roosevelt and Henry Byroade told the Egyptian ambassador Ahmad Hussein during a four-hour meeting in Washington in December 1954. Egyptian Foreign Ministry records show that Kim met frequently with Hussein during the year that followed, often expressing strong American support for the Nasser regime. (Nasser himself used to joke that Kim was so friendly to his government, and the US-educated ambassador Hussein so pro-American, that the two should swap jobs.) Edward Elson, identified only as the pastor of the church attended by the president and secretary of state, also featured in Hussein's reports to Cairo, assuring the ambassador that Eisenhower would be liberated in his approach to the Arab-Israeli conflict by victory in the 1956 election. A document from another Egyptian source (the papers of Miles Copeland's friend Hassan al-Tuhami), a "message from K to Big Brother" dated December 23, 1954, is even more revealing. In it, K (Kim Roosevelt, presumably) warns Big Brother (Nasser) that he, Nasser, is "in danger of walking into some well-laid Israeli traps, . . . with results which will handicap seriously the ability of [his] friends in the United States to counter Zionist pressure here." The following summer, Tuhami reported to Nasser that he and "Jones" (Miles's cover name in Cairo) had discussed "Egypt's need for . . . organized propaganda in America aimed at the purpose of opposing Jewish propaganda." Tuhami added that "they" (the CIA) "are completely ready to work with us in planning this program," hoping that Nasser would return the favor by softening some of his more anti-Western pronouncements.[12]

"I myself have been deeply involved in a number of things in Washington which I hesitate to put on paper," Elmer Berger wrote ACJ colleague Morris Lazaron in late December 1954. Although the documentary record is scant, it is possible, using scattered clues from a variety of sources, to assemble a detailed picture of the domestic campaign carried out by Kim Roosevelt's state-private network in support of the Eisenhower peace plan. First, there was the AFME group's support for Henry Byroade at a crucial stage of the ALPHA planning process. Prompted by an expectation that, as a young military man, Assistant Secretary Byroade would get on better with Nasser than the veteran diplomat Jefferson Caffery, Kim advised the White House to name him the new ambassador to Egypt, which it duly did in December. However, as Foster Dulles warned Eisenhower, there was bound to be resistance in Congress to the appointment because of Byroade's reputation for friendliness with Arabists and anti-Zionist Jews, and an unrelated vendetta against him by a senator from his home state of Indiana. Shortly afterward, Edward Elson and Dorothy Thompson swung into action, writing and meeting with the senator in question, William A. Jenner. In late January 1955, with his assignment to Egypt confirmed, a grateful Byroade wrote Thompson, "I hope you will continue . . . your good work with the American Friends of the Middle East . . . and, *inshallah*, that we meet in Cairo."[13]

As this was a battle for American public opinion, print media were a primary target of the AFME and ACJ activists. In addition to putting out their own newsletter and pamphlets, they worked hard to find publishers for books that would promote the Arabist, anti-Zionist cause to a wider audience. One such was *Violent Truce*, an exposé of Israeli violations of the 1949 UN armistice lines by navy commander Elmo Hutchison, the disgruntled former chair of the Israel/Jordan Mixed Armistice Commission. In New York, Elmer Berger pushed Hutchison's book with Devin-Adair, the publisher of his own *Partisan History of Judaism*; from Lebanon, Bill Eddy wrote Devin-Adair on "Hutch's" behalf and petitioned his ARAMCO colleague James Terry Duce for a grant to support the first printing; in Washington, Garland Hopkins heralded the book's appearance in AFME's fifth annual report. *Violent Truce* was eventually published in 1956, albeit to a muted public response.[14]

The AFME network's most remarkable publication of the period, at least from the point of view of Project ALPHA, came courtesy of Public Affairs Press in March 1955, when Dorothy Thompson contributed an introduction to the first English-language edition of Gamal Nasser's *Egypt's Liberation*. This work, a brief, autobiographical statement of Nasser's brand of revolutionary nationalism, later developed a reputation in some Western circles as a sort of blueprint for Third World demagoguery. For Thompson, however, the Nasser revealed in *Egypt's Liberation* utterly lacked "personal egotism and power-lust"; his most remarkable characteristics were rather "painful, humble, self-searching and self-analysis. . . . So far this man remains pure," she concluded, lyrically. "Pure, faithful, and brave."[15]

Nasser's reputation in the United States was clearly a major concern of the AFME circle, and as such it became a bone of contention between the group and the *New York Times*. The organization had long claimed that the newspaper failed to give its activities sufficient coverage, implying that this was due to its nervousness about the feelings of pro-Israel readers. To this complaint was now added another: that the *Times*' consistently anti-Nasser editorial statements conflicted with the more balanced reportage of the paper's own correspondent in Cairo, Kennett

Love. In his memoirs, Elmer Berger described with relish the visible embarrassment of the haughty *Times* managing editor Turner Catledge when confronted with this contradiction by the inexorable Dorothy Thompson. Unfortunately, there was no discernible improvement in the *Times'* editorial-page treatment of Nasser.[16]

For a more flattering portrayal of the Egyptian prime minister, Thompson and Berger had to turn instead to *Time* magazine. Henry Luce and C. D. Jackson had already intimated their support for AFME's agenda, the latter in conversation with Kim Roosevelt, the former by gracing the platform of the organization's first annual conference in 1953. This perhaps reflected both men's close identification with the Eisenhower administration; one also wonders whether Luce, the China-born son of a Presbyterian missionary, did not recognize some kindred spirits in the AFME Arabists. *Time* was as positive about Nasser as the *New York Times* was negative, granting the Egyptian leader the signal honor of a cover story in September 1955. "Egypt: The Revolutionary" presented a stark contrast to the Orientalist portrayal of the "dizzy old wizard" Mosaddeq that had appeared in *Time*'s pages a few years earlier. Nasser, a "dedicated soldier of only 37," was portrayed as a kind of idealized Western man in Arab guise: cool-headed, self-controlled, tough, "with the lithe grace of a big, handsome All-America fullback." The accompanying cover portrait, which depicted the Egyptian prime minister in a crisp officer's uniform against a background of pyramid-style wall murals, managed to associate him simultaneously with Egypt's glorious ancient past and its current promise of modernity and democracy. Having so emphatically declared its support for Nasser, two months later, in November 1955, *Time* nailed its anti-Zionist colors to the mast by reprinting an editorial from the anti-Zionist *Jewish Newsletter*, a publication also boosted by AFME and the ACJ. Current attitudes toward Israel among American Jews, so this piece alleged, were characterized by a "brand of hysteria" that had been "manufactured by Zionist leaders" as part of "a propaganda campaign in behalf of a foreign government."[17]

As usual, it was Elmer Berger who provided the single most imaginative contribution to the state-private drive behind the ALPHA peace plan. The anti-Zionist rabbi had long wanted to travel in the Arab countries but had never been able to obtain the necessary visas. In the spring of 1955, following contacts with State Department officials and, reportedly, Kim Roosevelt, he was able to cut through the red tape and, in May, launch himself and his wife, Ruth, on a two-month, AFME-sponsored tour of Egypt, Iraq, Lebanon, Syria, Jordan, and Israel. Predictably, the Bergers encountered their share of problems, including skepticism from some Arabs about the sincerity of their anti-Zionism and, as Ruth wrote home, "all possible annoyances and bad behavior" in Israel. Nonetheless, with the help of local AFME representatives and supporters such as Mather Eliot and Bill Eddy, they managed to win over some Arab audiences and even establish friendships with individual Arabs they met, including senior figures in the Egyptian government (although not Nasser himself). Indeed, US government officials monitoring their performance reckoned they had done a surprisingly effective job of informing Arabs about the existence of non-Zionist American Judaism and the Eisenhower administration's policy of friendly impartiality. Nor did their efforts end on their return home. Elmer, more persuaded than ever that US support for Israel actually worked against the interests of American Jews and the Israelis themselves, collected copies of the letters he had written his ACJ colleagues during the tour and published them for a domestic audience as a sort of polemical travelogue, *Who Knows Better Must Say So!*[18]

Although the activities of the ACJ and AFME in 1955 are strongly suggestive of a coordinated, directed campaign, there is no actual evidence of the CIA explicitly ordering the two organizations to mobilize in support of ALPHA—no "smoking gun," as it were. In an important sense, though, this does not matter, as the relationship between the US government and these Jewish anti-Zionists and Arabist Protestants was not (at least at this stage) one of simple, one-way control. It was indicative that, after returning from his tour of Israel and its Arab neighbors, Elmer Berger used debriefing sessions with Allen Dulles and officers of the State Department's Near East division not to ask what he could do next for the government, but rather to "spell out . . . the detrimental effects on American interests of the . . . Zionist apparatus" and urge officials to show the Arab world that US foreign policy was "not inevitably subject to Zionist pressure." Like other citizen groups with strong links to the CIA in the early Cold War period—for example, the American Friends of Vietnam, an organization created in 1955 to stimulate US support for the anticommunist regime in South Vietnam— the AFME-ACJ network was both a government front and a lobby group with an agenda of its own. Berger and his friends did not see Kim Roosevelt as their boss; rather, he was a partner working in a common cause.[19]

THE EFFORTS OF THE ARABISTS and anti-Zionists to bolster the Eisenhower administration's Middle East policy at home did not meet without resistance. After giving his speech before the ACJ—an organization reputedly known in Israel as "a traitor within the family"—Henry Byroade was told by the president of the World Jewish Congress, Nahum Goldmann, that he would never hold a good job again. With Byroade replacing Loy Henderson as the Zionists' most hated figure in the State Department, a new coinage, "Byroadism," meaning a toxic mix of anti-Semitism and Arabphilia, gained circulation. Private citizens in the AFME circle did not fare any better. Dorothy Thompson was a frequent target of Zionist denunciation, perhaps not surprising given her celebrity, sensitivity to personal criticism, and habit of making statements that flirted with anti-Semitism—although insinuations that her husband, the émigré Austrian artist Max Kopf, was a Nazi sympathizer were patently unfair. Edward Elson, too, came under attack, especially after a letter he wrote to a Zionist critic, drawing an inflammatory comparison between "Political Zionism" and the Nazi German-American Bund as movements that were "out of place in American life," fell into the hands of Zionist newspapers and the columnist Drew Pearson. When this incident was followed shortly after by another ill-advised move on Elson's part—an invitation to the State Department Arabist Edwin Wright to speak at the National Presbyterian Church—the extent of the pastor's influence on the Eisenhower White House became "one of the unanswered questions in Washington," or at least Zionist publicists made sure that it did.[20]

Clearly, some of this Zionist counteroffensive against the AFME-ACJ network was being coordinated from Israel. As soon as Eisenhower was elected in November 1952, David Ben-Gurion, the great Zionist leader and first Israeli prime minister, acknowledged the need to step up publicity or *hasbara* work in the United States. "Until now there was only one conduit to the White House—the Israeli; from now on, there will be an Arab one as well," he wrote privately. "Eisenhower adores his young brother Milton who is close to the pro-Arab group of Dorothy Thompson. Efforts must be made to influence Milton in our direction." Such activities appeared to intensify in late 1954, at the same time that American officials were beginning to formulate the ALPHA plan for Arab-Israeli peace, with *hasbara* officials at the Israeli embassies in Washington and New York confirming their twin desires "to try to reach the public directly, over as broad a front as possible," and "influence the

'molders of public opinion' in important specific spheres." The same year
saw the beginnings of a process of reorganization among Zionist groups
in the United States that included the founding by I. L. "Si" Kenen of the
American Zionist Committee for Public Affairs, subsequently renamed
the American Israel Public Affairs Committee (AIPAC). Launched a few
years later, Kenen's *Near East Report*, "A Washington Letter on American Policy in the Near East," routinely criticized AFME and its various Arabist and anti-Zionist associates in a special column, "Propaganda
Pressures." Indeed, so clearly were the lines of ideological battle drawn
that it is tempting to see the confrontation between the AFME-ACJ network and Zionist organizations such as AIPAC as part of a covert war
between the Israeli and US governments for control of American public
opinion concerning the Middle East.[21]

The hostile response of American Zionists to the AFME-ACJ
network's domestic campaign in support of ALPHA was predictable.
More concerning was evidence of a new determination on the part of
the Israelis themselves to resist the Anglo-American peace plan. Already casting a shadow over the initiative was the so-called Lavon
affair of summer 1954, an Israeli plot to have Egyptian-born Jewish
agents provocateurs attack Western targets in Egypt with the intention of wrecking the Anglo-Egyptian settlement and any consequent
UK-US efforts to impose an Arab-Israeli peace. The conspirators were
apprehended and the resulting Egyptian trials carried on into January
1955, embarrassing the government of Ben-Gurion's successor as prime
minister, the relatively moderate Zionist Moshe Sharett. However, Israelis still fretted about the dangers of a settlement negotiated by the
Americans and the British, especially the dreaded prospect of having to
give up territory in the Negev so that Egypt could have a common land
border with its Arab neighbor, Jordan. This was the backdrop to the
return to power in February 1955 of David Ben-Gurion and the Gaza
raid of February 28, when Israeli forces led by Ariel Sharon attacked
the Egyptian-controlled Gaza Strip, destroying its military headquarters and killing some forty soldiers. Although ostensibly carried out in
reprisal for earlier raids on Israel by Egyptian fedayeen, the Gaza raid
was perceived by some observers as a calculated attempt to antagonize
Nasser and strangle the Anglo-American peace plan in its cradle.

Israel was not the only party to the proposed settlement behaving
problematically. A few days before the Gaza raid, on February 25, 1955,

Iraq had signed a security treaty with Turkey, the so-called Baghdad Pact. As well as being a clear play for regional leadership by the veteran Iraqi prime minister Nuri al-Sa'id, the pact was a thinly veiled move by the British to restore their position in the Middle East through their Hashemite proxies in Baghdad and Amman. John Foster Dulles resisted British pressure to join the new security league but otherwise did little to indicate American disapproval, as the pact basically fit with his developing strategic vision of a "Northern Tier," a chain of Western-aligned states girding the southern borders of the Eurasian communist heartland. Nasser, in contrast, was appalled by the spectacle of the quisling Hashemites consorting with the Arabs' ancient Ottoman foe; he turned to Syria and Saudi Arabia in an effort to create a countervailing power bloc, thus joining an internal struggle for dominance in the Arab world that historians would later refer to as the "Arab Cold War."[22]

Obviously, none of this was good news for ALPHA, premised as it was on the idea of Nasser commanding unified Arab support for a probably unpopular settlement with Israel. This consideration seems not to have bothered the British, who had never much cared for the upstart Egyptian leader. Indeed, a gang of backbench Conservative members of Parliament known as the Suez Group was already calling on Anthony Eden, who succeeded Winston Churchill as prime minister in April 1955, to "bash the Wog," as the racist language of the day had it. Long overshadowed by Churchill, Eden was extremely sensitive to charges that he was "scuttling" the empire, and keen to assert his political manhood in the Middle East. The new British leader was already set on a collision course with Nasser.

But perhaps most worrisome of all for ALPHA's planners were unmistakable signs that Nasser himself, the Arab hero on whom their hopes for peace were pinned, was not acting according to his script. The Gaza raid and the Baghdad Pact were both blatant provocations, and it was understandable that the Egyptian should have been in a prickly mood in early 1955. Yet something else about his demeanor that spring was even more disquieting: a new determination to forge an independent course of his own.

FOURTEEN

Crypto-Diplomacy

"HE IS VERY GOOD AT chess," 'Abdel Hakim 'Amer, Nasser's friend and army chief of staff, told a *Time* reporter in 1955. "If he tries to win, he does. He is a fox. It's never easy to know his intentions." As Nasser consolidated his hold on power, the imagery of courtship and marriage that had previously characterized US-Egyptian relations, and in particular the relationship between the Free Officers and the CIA Arabists, was being replaced by gaming metaphors. This was perhaps not surprising, given the extent to which the British imperial narrative of the Great Game spilled over into the American encounter with the Middle East during the first years of the Cold War. However, the rules of the game were changing. Whereas previously British and Russian spies had, at least according to the logic of the Great Game, faced each other across a central Asian game board of passive chess pieces, now the game was growing more complicated and difficult, with local players starting to make moves of their own. Of course, the colonized peoples of Asia had long nursed nationalist aspirations, and these had eventually proved far more dangerous to the British Empire than Russian imperialism, in either its czarist or its Bolshevik incarnations, ever did. But this was not the lesson taught by Kipling: in *Kim*, the conspiracy threatening the Raj comes from without; of Indian resistance to British rule, there is no hint whatsoever.[1]

The issue that eventually ended the honeymoon period in the CIA Arabists' relationship with the Free Officers was a surprising one, considering how important military assistance would later become as an adhesive in US-Egyptian relations. Despite repeated attempts, Washington and Cairo proved unable to agree on the terms of a deal that would provide Nasser with arms to protect Egypt's new government from possible threats, both internal and external, thereby leaving the door open to deals with other powers. As before, during the Anglo-Egyptian dispute over the Suez base, Kim Roosevelt and his assistant Miles Copeland were called in to solve the problem by using their CIA back channels to broker an agreement in secret. In this instance, however, CIA "crypto-diplomacy," as Miles called it, did not work. Indeed, if anything, it aggravated the situation, mixing up the messages that Washington was sending Cairo through regular diplomatic channels. Ironically, the ultimate effect was to strengthen Nasser's position— but not in a way intended by the Arabists.[2]

THE INITIAL PROSPECTS FOR A US-Egyptian arms deal had seemed favorable enough. Nasser badly needed equipment for his armed forces, not just to defend Egypt against its external enemies but, no less importantly, to boost officer morale so as to proof himself against further military coups. On the American side, John Foster Dulles had already hinted at the possibility of military assistance by presenting General Naguib with a brace of pistols when he visited Cairo in May 1953, and other US officials had bandied around various dollar sums. The trouble was that any major appropriations for arms for Egypt were bound to run into resistance in Congress from American supporters of Israel and economic isolationists, while also likely arousing British fears of US-supplied weapons being turned against the Suez canal base before its final evacuation in 1956 (Winston Churchill was reportedly furious about Foster Dulles's gift to Naguib). For his part, Nasser strongly objected to requirements in the US legislation governing foreign military aid, the Mutual Assistance Program, that he sign a security pact with the United States and admit American military advisors to Egypt. After their experience with the British, Egyptians did not want uniformed Western officers on their soil again.

After a series of meetings in Cairo and Washington in late 1954, Kim Roosevelt came up with a plan. As a reward for signing off on the Suez treaty, the Egyptian government was to receive $40 million of economic aid for infrastructure improvements, a fraction of what had originally been implied, but with the tacit promise of more to come in the future. Of that sum, $5 million would be secret Defense Department money earmarked for the purchase of military equipment, thus circumventing the requirement for advisors. In addition to the public gift of $40 million, a further, nonattributed payment of $3 million would be made from the president's executive budget directly to Nasser himself so that he could buy such morale-building items as new army uniforms, again without the need for any overt US involvement. Nonetheless, two Pentagon negotiators in civilian clothing would be dispatched to Cairo to agree on how the disguised $5 million of military aid was to be spent.

The Pentagon mission duly arrived in Cairo in November 1954 and met with leaders of the Revolutionary Command Council in the guest-house occupied by Hassan Tuhami next to the Copeland villa in Maadi. Although the mood of these meetings was friendly, even convivial in a gruff, soldierly way, it soon became clear that Kim's plan had failed to resolve the underlying problems in US-Egyptian relations. "Colonel Abd-el-Nasr [sic] explained, for the thousandth time, . . . why he could not accept military aid unless we could conceal the fact that it was grant aid," Miles reported to Kim. "The Pentagon officials, in their turn, explained why we could not give aid unless Egypt would agree to certain minimum terms and that, moreover, we would find it extremely difficult to keep this fact secret." The gap between the two sides grew even wider when, in a turn reminiscent of the May 1953 meeting between Foster Dulles and Nasser, the conversation focused on regional defense issues, with the Pentagon representatives insisting on the need for collective security pacts to ward off Soviet adventurism and the Egyptians, rather bemusedly, pointing out that the more likely source of attack on their country came from across its border with Israel.[3]

Nor were these the only sources of US-Egyptian misunderstanding. Kim regarded the $3 million direct grant to Nasser as a very generous gesture. As he explained to Miles, "we have no funds for 'foreign aid' in the first place, and in the second place our budget is figured on an extremely tight basis." Moreover, simply getting the money to the Egyptian leader proved a challenge. Issued by the CIA's regional finance office in Beirut, the cash was then smuggled in the diplomatic pouch to

Cairo. There it was transferred to two suitcases by Miles, transported along the bumpy road to Maadi jostling against some groceries of Lorraine's, counted in the presence of Hassan Tuhami ($10 was missing), and eventually driven in Tuhami's Mercedes to Nasser's home on the other side of the Nile.[4]

Far from being gratified by all this trouble, however, Nasser was offended by the gift, interpreting it as a crude Western attempt to bribe a supposedly venal Oriental. When word of this response reached Kim back in Washington, it was his turn to react angrily. "We have made every effort to understand the Egyptian position but we are doubting that they are making any effort whatsoever to understand ours," he wrote Miles. "They have gotten some things from us, but we have gotten *nothing* from them." Nasser, meanwhile, had decided what to do with the perceived bribe. Instead of military hardware, he ordered the money to be spent on a public monument of considerable ostentation and questionable taste: a great concrete tower on Gezira Island in the center of Cairo, rising up in vertical, silent reproach to his would-be American corrupters. The Cairo Tower, which still looms above the city's skyline today, was referred to within Nasser's circle as *el wa'ef rusfel* or "Roosevelt's foundation." Wags at the CIA, however, chose to translate the Arabic as "Roosevelt's erection" and began calling it instead "Nasser's prick."[5]

The language indicated a clash of masculine wills developing between Kim and his putative Egyptian protégé. Nonetheless, the CIA Arabist continued to back Nasser in Washington, and the prospects for an arms deal appeared to brighten briefly as 1954 turned into 1955. Miles carried on his meetings with "Angrylion" (his code name for Tuhami) — "'We must never give up hope,' Angrylion always says," Miles told Kim — and took advantage of a trip home to present the Free Officers' perspective on the issue to a joint State-CIA meeting in John Foster Dulles's office. The launch of ALPHA and accompanying arrival in Cairo of US ambassador and Arab sympathizer Henry Byroade seemed to promise a new phase of US-Egyptian cooperation. Most important, the pressure on Nasser to acquire arms increased suddenly in February 1955 with the twin shocks of the Baghdad Pact and the Gaza raid. Now military assistance was desirable not just for psychological reasons: the Egyptian government had to have the means to defend its citizens against further attacks from Israel and to keep up with its Arab rivals. As if to reinforce the Egyptian feeling of defenselessness, Israeli warplanes were appearing regularly in the skies over Cairo. Sitting outside with Miles during one of the noisy overflights, Nasser complained, "I have to sit here and take this—and your government won't give me arms."[6]

Unfortunately for the CIA Arabists, an even more important effect of the Gaza raid and Baghdad Pact was to foster a growing sense of disillusionment with America in Nasser's circle. Not only did the Free Officers suspect the Americans of conniving in the British effort to build up the Northern Tier, they also began to doubt the sincerity of the Eisenhower administration's policy of friendly impartiality, even speculating about a possible US hand in the border incidents that continued to trouble Egyptian-Israeli relations. Far from allaying such concerns, the CIA's extensive penetration of the Egyptian government now served only to strengthen them. Was Kim Roosevelt plotting to install a new, more biddable pasha in Cairo, just as he had in Iran in 1953? Despite his soon establishing warm personal relations with Nasser, the new ambassador, Henry Byroade, was badly hampered by these suspicions, having to spend much of his time with the Egyptian leader reassuring him that US embassy officials were not spreading rumors against him. With the Cairo air thick with conspiracy theory, Byroade got short shrift when, as instructed by Foster Dulles, he attempted to link the promise of American military assistance with progress in Arab-Israeli peace talks. If anything, this crude bargaining ploy only served to turn the Egyptians against ALPHA.[7]

Nasser had sought US support as he strove to rid his country of the British imperialists for a number of reasons, among them America's anticolonial origins and nonimperial history in the Middle East; the unstuffy friendliness of its representatives in Cairo, young men like William Lakeland and Miles Copeland; even the seductive appeal of its popular culture. This did not mean, however, that he was prepared to go along with measures that he perceived as likely to turn Egypt into a US satellite. "Nuri Pasha may be willing to make his decisions on a basis of whether or not they fit your world strategy," Nasser once explained to Miles, referring to Iraq's pro-Western prime minister. "I intend to . . . make my decisions only on a basis of what's good for Egypt." The same applied to the regional role Nasser was expected to play now that he had consolidated his domestic base. "A strong and independent Egypt could take the lead . . . towards Arab unity," he went on to tell Miles, but only if that unity was "meaningful," not the kind "which the British and

Secretary Dulles [speak] of in connection with military alliances, and with an outdated, Lawrence of Arabia . . . understanding of the Arab mentality."[8]

Nasser's growing sense of his own importance as a national and regional figure was strengthened by his attendance at the conference of nonaligned nations that took place in April 1955 in Bandung, Indonesia, where he was acclaimed as a great future leader of the postcolonial world. If the CIA Arabists were unnerved by these developments, John Foster Dulles was appalled: in his view, anything other than wholehearted support for the United States in its crusade against communist atheism was an offense against God. But Bandung was significant for another reason: it was the first occasion on which the CIA picked up signals that Nasser was talking with communists (in this particular instance, Chinese premier Zhou Enlai) about a possible arms deal. In fact, Free Officers such as Hassan Tuhami had already been meeting with Soviet officials, in both Cairo and Moscow, for several years, as first Naguib and then Nasser explored alternatives to Western military assistance. By the time of Bandung, with the American avenue apparently closing down and the recent provocations of Gaza and Baghdad, the Egyptians had begun to negotiate in earnest. They found the Soviets in an accommodating mood. Stalin had died in 1953, and his successor, Nikita Khrushchev, was much more interested than Stalin had been in building the Soviet position in the Third World generally, and the Middle East in particular.[9]

"We in the CIA kept telling our State Department colleagues that Nasser was going to make this move, simply because as game players we had to admit that it was precisely the move any one of us would have made had we been in his place," Miles wrote later. With the foreign service insisting that the Egyptian was bluffing, the CIA Arabists made a last effort to salvage the situation themselves. Kim and go-betweens such as Ike's pastor, Edward Elson, met with Ambassador Hussein in New York; in Cairo, Miles tried to reassure his liaison, "Angrylion" Tuhami, about American intentions (and, if Miles's later testimony is to be believed, smuggled a lion cub into Egypt as a gift for him). In the summer, it briefly seemed as if a US-Egyptian deal was back on the table—Free Officer 'Ali Sabri even handed Byroade an arms "shopping list"—but it soon became obvious that Nasser was going through the motions. Byroade, seeing the American position in Cairo collapsing before his eyes, frantically lobbied Foster Dulles. The moralistic secretary of state, who in July attended an unprecedentedly amicable East-West summit in Switzerland, simply refused to believe talk of a secret Soviet arms deal, explaining (in the somewhat contemptuous recollection of Kim Roosevelt) that such a move would contravene "the spirit of Geneva." When on September 21, 1955, Byroade confirmed that the Egyptian government had just agreed to take delivery of a consignment of Russian arms, including fighter planes, tanks, and submarines, Dulles was dumbfounded. The communists had leaped over the protective barrier of the Northern Tier right into the heart of the Arab world. Suddenly, ALPHA's prospects seemed the least of the secretary's concerns.[10]

Dulles's next move was decided in conversation with his undersecretary of state, Herbert Hoover Jr., the son of the former US president and a forbidding, rather irritable man. "H[oover] thinks we should make one further, final try," read a secretary's notes. "Apparently there are misunderstandings and difficulties with respect to our man who is there"—Hoover was referring to Ambassador Byroade—"and H. would not feel satisfied we had done everything in our power unless Kim could go himself and talk with [Nasser]." Such a mission carried with it considerable risks: although Kim "could move without its being picked up," Hoover reckoned, there might well be "an explosion on the part of our man there"—in other words, a confrontation between the CIA officer and the ambassador. However, if Byroade was recalled to Washington, this would be widely interpreted as a sign that the State Department had lost confidence in him. "We have to weigh what [Kim] can do as against discrediting . . . our own ambassador," reflected Dulles. In the end, the decision was taken to "leave him there and shoot this boy out," as Hoover put it—to take the risk of sending Roosevelt without recalling Byroade. Kim was called back from a family vacation in Nantucket and instructed by Dulles to "Go and tell your friend [Nasser] this would be a foolish thing to do." Kim later claimed that both he and Allen Dulles thought the mission futile—the latter reportedly told his brother, "if he goes, he goes for you, not for me"—but there is no contemporary evidence of such a disagreement.[11]

Accompanied by his sidekick Miles Copeland, Kim Roosevelt arrived in Cairo on Friday, September 23, 1955. It was Miles's first time back in Egypt since July, when his sabbatical with Booz, Allen & Hamilton had ended and he had returned to Washington to work in CIA headquarters. The two men were collected from the airport and whisked straight to the Revolutionary Command Council headquarters and the Egyptian prime minister's second-story private quarters. "Nasser was in a teasing, 'I told you so' mood," Miles wrote later, "very cheerful and all set to enjoy hearing the famous Roosevelt persuasion grapple with his own unanswerable arguments." The precise content and sequence of the discussions that followed are not completely clear: accounts by Nasser's journalist friend Muhammad Haikal differ from American sources in claiming that Roosevelt did try to dissuade Nasser from dealing with the Soviets and that the Egyptian leader rebuffed the CIA man. That said, official US records back up Miles Copeland's claim that Kim, having accepted the deal as a fait accompli, then made a clever play to soften its impact (and give a boost to ALPHA) by suggesting to Nasser that he announce that the arms were intended purely for defensive purposes and that, with its borders secure, Egypt would be in a better position to reach a peace settlement with Israel. According to a cable sent from the Cairo US embassy on Monday, September 26, probably by Kim and Miles, Nasser "drew [the] line at making [an] outright conciliatory gesture . . . but agreed to go along with [the] suggestion to issue [a] public statement . . . stating [his] desire [to] discuss directly with Secretary Dulles concrete steps to reduce Arab-Israeli tensions." Although the Egyptian prime minister wanted it to be understood that he was "not a stooge," he was "willing [to] follow our advice to [the] extent such advice made sense to him."[12]

This agreement came in the course of a three-and-a-half-hour meeting in Nasser's RCC apartment that seemed to augur a dramatic recovery of the American position in Cairo—"a bold new era of friendship and economic development," as Miles put it. The high point of the evening came when, just after the prime minister had produced the bottle of Scotch he kept for Western visitors, the telephone rang. The British ambassador, Sir Humphrey Trevelyan, had gotten wind of the arms deal and was requesting an urgent meeting with Nasser. While the Egyptian and his American companions watched from a window as Trevelyan's Bentley pulled out of the British embassy compound and made the short journey across the Nile to RCC headquarters, they discussed what Nasser should tell him. Kim suggested that he stress the literal truth that the arms were being shipped not from the Soviet Union but from Czechoslovakia, the same nation that had in the past supplied Israel. (Whether this means that Kim invented the concept of the "Czech arms deal," as was later claimed, is doubtful: the ruse had already been suggested to Nasser by the Soviet ambassador to Egypt.) The prime minister, his mind possibly going back to the moment in 1942 when Trevelyan's predecessor, Sir Miles Lampson, had deliberately humiliated King Farouk in his palace, descended to receive the ambassador. Kim and Miles, meanwhile, stayed in his private quarters, nursing the whiskey. The meeting was brief, Trevelyan issuing a warning from Foreign Secretary Harold Macmillan that the deal could "not be allowed to go on," and Nasser stating simply that there was now no going back on it—few echoes here of Lampson and Farouk. After Trevelyan had left disconsolately, Miles's old associate Zakaria Mohieddin and Chief of Staff 'Abdel Hakim 'Amer arrived to take Nasser and the CIA men off to a dinner hosted by Kim's friend Ambassador Hussein, who was in Cairo on leave. The atmosphere by now was positively lighthearted, with the Egyptians imagining the expression on Trevelyan's face had the Americans come downstairs to ask Nasser for some soda to mix with their drinks. What better way to bond than over the mocking of a British ambassador, and a knight of the realm to boot?[13]

But then the mood of the evening changed dramatically. Waiting at the dinner party were three other Americans—CIA station chief James Eichelberger, the businessman and special presidential representative Eric A. Johnston, and Hank Byroade. The US ambassador was in a bad way. From the moment he had arrived in Cairo, his mission had been undermined by misunderstandings with Nasser, lack of support from Washington, and suspicions about the activities of the CIA. Rumors had also begun to circulate about his personal life, that he was hitting the bottle and "skirt-chasing." Earlier that day, Byroade had learned that a member of his embassy staff, the labor attaché, had been subjected to a brutal beating by a mob in Ismailia, probably because he was suspected of spying. Now, having had no intimation that Kim Roosevelt was even in Egypt, the ambassador was treated to the sight of the senior CIA officer walking into the room arm in arm with the prime minister, laughing at some private joke. Miles Copeland and Muhammad Haikal both described what happened next. After silently brooding over his whiskey, Byroade snapped. Interrupting a rambling anecdote by Johnston, he "launched into a tirade against the 'Egyptian police state'" that ended with the words, "I thought we were in a civilized country."

Nasser stubbed out his cigarette, turned to his fellow Egyptians with the words "Let's go," and stalked out.[14]

It was a calamitous performance by Byroade, and he regretted it instantly, the next morning enlisting both Miles Copeland and Haikal in an effort to appease Nasser. Meanwhile, Kim, assisted by Johnston, was reporting the whole incident to Washington, suggesting that perhaps the ambassador "needed a rest." As Miles explained to Eichelberger, Byroade's rant threatened to undo Kim's good work of turning the arms deal to American advantage by linking it with the cause of Arab-Israeli peace. When Byroade learned that Kim and Johnston were using his embassy's facilities to cable the State Department urging his recall, he was incandescent, yelling down the phone at Kim: "If you don't bring that goddamn cable here I'm coming over with my Marine guard." Egyptians with some inkling of these events were greatly amused. "Intrigue and rivalries among the Americans in Cairo had . . . reached an almost Byzantine pitch," recalled Haikal.[15]

The plot was about to grow even more convoluted. Dwight Eisenhower had suffered a heart attack on September 24, leaving the Dulles brothers in complete charge of US foreign policy while he recovered. In New York City two days later for the opening of the UN General Assembly, the secretary of state met with his UK counterpart, Foreign Secretary Macmillan, who was furious about the nerve of the upstart Nasser. "Dulles and H[arold] M[acmillan] got more and more worked up against the prospects of a Soviet arms deal with Egypt as they warmed to the subject," recorded London's point man on ALPHA, Evelyn Shuckburgh. "We could make life impossible for Nasser and ultimately bring about his fall by various pressures," ruminated Macmillan, the first recorded time the British had aired such a possibility before an American. With his brother Allen and trusted Middle Eastern lieutenant Kim Roosevelt still behind the Egyptian leader—"Our conviction . . . is that Nas[se]r remains our best, if not our only, hope here," declared the CIA cable from Cairo of September 26—Foster was not ready yet to entertain such talk seriously. He was, however, persuaded of the need for some sort of reprimand, especially after the public announcement of the arms deal came on September 27 sans the passage about peace with the Israelis, confirming the failure of the Roosevelt/Copeland mission and generating a wave of nationalist excitement around the Arab world. George Allen, Byroade's successor as assistant secretary for Near East affairs, was delegated with the task of writing a stern message to Nasser. But now the secretary of state faced another problem: how to deliver the note given that his ambassador in Egypt was, according to Roosevelt and Johnston, persona non grata with the Egyptian leader? The solution was decided in conversation with Herbert Hoover: Dulles would send George Allen to Cairo so that he could hand over the message personally. The assistant secretary was duly placed on board a Pentagon transport plane and arrived in Egypt the morning of Friday, September 30.[16]

Now the American handling of the Soviet-Egyptian arms deal descended into farce. The Associated Press had reported that a high-ranking US official was on his way to deliver an ultimatum to Nasser. Enraged at the prospect of being treated like some colonial satrap, the Egyptian premier told Kim that, if the story proved true, "he would ring the bell on his desk and have the Chief Chamberlain of the Presidency show the American out." After explaining to Washington that it was "most important not to put [Nasser] on the public spot," Kim scrambled to warn Allen himself not to tangle with the Egyptian leader. As the State Department official was preparing to exit his plane, Henry Byroade rushed through the crowd of waiting reporters and bounded up the aircraft steps. "If you say anything about an ultimatum," he warned Allen, "your ass is out of here right now." Then, while the two Americans were getting ready to descend together, up came an Egyptian messenger (Hassan Tuhami, according to Miles Copeland) with a note stating, "Advise extreme caution in whatever y[ou] say. Kim." By now, Allen had presumably gotten the message.[17]

After running the gauntlet of crowds of reporters and protestors chanting anti-American slogans, Allen arrived at the American embassy, where in a hastily convened meeting he discussed his next step with Kim, Miles, Johnston, and Byroade. Assuming he got to see Nasser—by no means a certainty, as the Egyptian leader was currently refusing him an appointment—what was he to do with Dulles's letter, which, if Nasser saw it, might very well cause him to break off diplomatic relations with the United States? Perhaps he could simply rip it up, suggested Johnston. No, said Allen, he had his orders. Eventually, after a discussion Miles Copeland recalled as "one confused rumble," it was decided that, rather than handing it over, Allen would read the message aloud to Nasser, possibly mumbling during the most objectionable passages. Kim, by now thoroughly disgusted with the whole affair, left to play tennis.[18]

Nasser relented the next day and agreed to see both Allen and By-roade, the latter for the first time since the fateful dinner party (Kim later claimed credit for engineering the meeting). The prime minister smiled his forgiveness at the ambassador, Allen recited the message, con-cealing the fact that it was a personal letter from Dulles, and Nasser used the opportunity to recount the unhappy history of Egypt's efforts to obtain American arms, concluding "that, in all frankness, he had the conviction that U.S. Government was trying to keep Egypt weak, and that this resulted from Jewish influence in U.S." Overall, the meeting was surprisingly friendly—Allen's report to Washington was noticeably sympathetic to the Egyptian leader, suggesting that yet another Amer-ican visitor had fallen under his spell—and the special emissary left Cairo a few days later having at least averted a complete breakdown in US-Egyptian relations. Still, from the US point of view, there was very little else to show for "Allen's lost weekend," as Miles Copeland took to calling it.[19]

WITH JOHN FOSTER DULLES ROUTINELY resorting to the secret channels provided by his brother Allen, crypto-diplomacy became the Eisenhower administration's preferred method for dealing with Middle Eastern leaders, and Kim Roosevelt the chief crypto-diplomat. "When someone had to hop on an aeroplane and go to Iran, Egypt, Jordan or Saudi Arabia to talk to the Shah, Nasser, King Hussein or King Saud, the Dulles brothers would think of either Kim or myself, sometimes together, sometimes singly, and sometimes in the company of some pro-fessional VIP," Miles Copeland explained later. "Throughout Secretary Dulles's time, an ambassador lived with the fear that one morning, be-tween his residence and the Chancery, he would encounter . . . [a] VIP crypto-diplomat riding by in the opposite direction, in a guest Cadillac, on his way to the palace."[20]

Crypto-diplomacy undoubtedly had its advantages, not least of which was that it afforded Middle Eastern leaders the opportunity to conduct conversations in private that they would have been unable to hold publicly, leading to negotiated breakthroughs like the Anglo-Egyptian Suez base agreement of 1954. But it also involved a number of risks: crossing wires with foreign service professionals, who understandably resented Secretary Dulles's constant use of nondiplomatic channels; distracting the intelligence professionals from their core mission, the gathering and evaluation of foreign intelligence; and sowing confusion and suspicion in the minds of foreign heads of state. When Dulles resorted to crypto-diplomacy to solve the arms-to-Egypt problem, he not only undermined the effectiveness of Ambassador Henry Byroade but eventually embarrassed Kim Roosevelt himself.

If American crypto-diplomacy clearly benefited anyone in 1955, it was Gamal Nasser. The Egyptian "was delighted with the whole thing," Miles recalled: "with the arms deal itself, with his public's reaction to it, with the talk of an 'ultimatum' from us, with his own performance in response to the ultimatum, with his public's reaction to his response, and with the fact that, in the end, there was no ultimatum. Not only had he made a play which raised his standing in the Arab world . . . but he had managed to dramatize it in the most advantageous way possible—and with our help."[21]

The Great Game in the Middle East had found its most skillful player yet, and he wasn't British, Russian, or even American—he was Arab.

FIFTEEN

Peacemakers

IN THE DESERT ARAB KINGDOM of Al Khadra, the prime minister, Brigadier Mustafa ibn Mabrouk, has been in secret negotiations with the Soviet Union. When he finds out, Calvin Hampshire, the American secretary of state, is livid, as Mabrouk is jeopardizing his grand strategic vision of a defensive ring encircling the communist bloc. Ignoring his ambassador in Al Khadra—the veteran foreign service Arabist Sean Fitzgibbon—Hampshire sends for his Harvard classmate Paul Pullmotor, a shadowy but vastly influential Cold War troubleshooter. Assisted by his sidekick, a Southern-born, multilingual master of disguise, Cornelius MacFlicker, Pullmotor sets about orchestrating a bedouin tribal uprising to topple Mabrouk.

Such is the plot of a highly entertaining 1964 novel, *Kingdom of Illusion*, by the American journalist Edward R. F. Sheehan. Based on Sheehan's experiences serving as a press officer in the US embassy in Cairo in the late 1950s, as well as, in all likelihood, later conversations with Miles Copeland about Gamal Nasser's 1955 Soviet-bloc arms deal, *Kingdom of Illusion* abounds in detail drawn from satirical observation of real personalities. The Nasser figure, the humbly born Mustafa ibn Mabrouk, is a brilliant but cynical young soldier, a "Borgian" (as opposed to Machiavellian), who runs Al Khadra "the only way he knew how: . . . by *plotting*." Mabrouk tries to get along with the moralistic Secretary of State Hampshire (Foster Dulles), but the two men fail to "find a common language," principally because Hampshire's "firm grasp of European problems did not always extend to the complexities of the world beyond." Instead, it is the ambitious and ruthless Paul Pullmotor (Hasty Pudding, tennis-playing, non–Arabic-speaking—Kim Roosevelt, in other words) who really understands Mabrouk, and vice versa. Indeed, the two men are close friends, Pullmotor having earlier helped Mabrouk shore up his nationalist revolution against British colonial rule, introducing him to "the latest gobbledegook of progressive government" and "the most modern methods of spy detection." Even after they quarrel and the American begins plotting against his erstwhile protégé (with the help of Cornelius MacFlicker—a thinly disguised Miles), the powerful connection between them remains. Mabrouk, who likes nothing more "than to play games of chance," positively relishes the prospect of taking on his old friend and fellow Borgian. "Plotting against Pullmotor is the most sublime pleasure I have in life," he declares. As for Pullmotor himself, "overthrowing governments was a game, and a good game was always very, very funny."[1]

The main difference between the events of fall 1955 and their imaginative rendering in *Kingdom of Illusion* is that the Soviet-bloc arms deal was not in fact followed immediately by a decisive American move to get rid of Nasser the way Mosaddeq had been removed two years earlier. Certainly, John Foster Dulles was angry, and the British were beginning to press for drastic measures against Egypt, but Washington still had too much invested in Nasser to give up on him quite so easily. In fact, by enhancing Egypt's regional prestige and increasing the pressure on Israel to yield to Western demands, the arms deal had, if anything, strengthened American hopes for an Arab-Israeli settlement with the Egyptian leader as a key player.

Consequently, what happened next was not another TP-AJAX–style coup but rather a last-ditch attempt to salvage Project ALPHA, with CIA crypto-diplomats Kim Roosevelt and Miles Copeland appearing in the perhaps unlikely guise of would-be peacemakers. In retrospect, this effort to rescue ALPHA might appear doomed from the start, so numerous and massive were the obstacles in its path. But at the time, it seemed to contain its moments of promise, and it deserves at least to be included in any historical reckoning of the CIA Arabists, alongside the coups and spy games with which their names are more commonly associated.

OPERATION GAMMA, AS THE POST-SOVIET arms deal iteration of the Eisenhower peace plan was code-named, differed from ALPHA in two important respects. With the United States no longer able to hold out arms as an incentive for Egyptian cooperation, another form of American assistance was now on offer. Key to Nasser's plans to transform Egypt into a modern economy was the building of a dam at Aswan, a giant engineering project that would bring flood control, irrigation, and hydroelectricity to the upper Nile valley. The projected cost of the dam's construction was astronomical, in excess of $1 billion, and the penurious Egyptian government was obliged to raise a foreign loan of $400 million. In December 1955, the World Bank agreed to lend Egypt half that amount, with the US and UK governments pledging to provide the remainder, on the tacit understanding that Nasser would seek no more aid from the communists and would advance the cause of Arab-Israeli peace. There was one further sweetener for the Egyptian premier. Zionists were calling on the Eisenhower administration to counter the Czech arms deal by selling a similar quantity of arms to the Israelis. With Miles Copeland in Cairo warning that such a move would drive Egypt further into the communist embrace, Foster Dulles let it be known that, for the time being, the United States was not going to arm Israel, even if that meant incurring the displeasure of Jewish American voters in the forthcoming elections.

The second major difference was that, whereas ALPHA had been a joint Anglo-American venture, this time the Americans were going it alone. The British had never gotten over their resentment at the United States' evident determination to replace them in Egypt, and they suspected that, for all its protestations of impartiality, the American government was still inclined to treat Israel preferentially. The Americans, for their part, were irritated by the United Kingdom's obvious ambition to hang onto its dominion in the Arab world by expanding the Baghdad Pact. Not only was this strategy antagonizing Nasser, and thereby damaging the prospects of Arab-Israeli peace, it was also inviting instability in countries such as Jordan, where Nasserite agents were fomenting nationalist unrest against the British-backed monarchy. Added to these tensions, the English-speaking powers were at loggerheads in the

Arabian peninsula, where the Saudis, allegedly funded by ARAMCO and the CIA, were fighting with the British-backed sheikhdoms on the Persian Gulf over ownership of the strategically valuable Buraimi oasis. Despite, or perhaps because of, his Anglophile credentials, Kim Roosevelt became a particular focus of British recriminations about Egypt and the Gulf. According to one rumor, Kim was trying to bribe sheikhs in Buraimi with air-conditioned Cadillacs.[2]

GAMMA would be an exclusively American—and, more specifically, a CIA—operation. Although not previously involved in the ALPHA negotiations as such, except in the sense that his Arabist and anti-Zionist citizen network had tried to protect the Eisenhower administration's domestic flank while the peace plan was rolled out in the Middle East, Kim Roosevelt had earlier been involved in another American effort to settle the Arab-Israeli dispute. Launched in late 1954, Operation Chameleon (also known as Mirage or Camelot) envisioned Nasser secretly meeting an "'opposite' [Israeli] representative" (as "K." told "Big Brother") to discuss a possible settlement, with an "American representative" (Kim himself) also in attendance to ensure "that the 'opposite' representative pull[ed] no tricks." Knowledge of the meeting would be confined to a tiny circle of senior officials in Egypt, Israel, and the United States, in the latter case consisting of (as Kim also explained) "myself, the President, the Secretary of State, and his brother." Although the plan advanced sufficiently far that the former Israeli chief of staff, Yigael Yadin, was tapped for the role of "opposite representative," Chameleon was eventually scuppered by the 1954 Lavon affair (Israel's plot involving attacks on Westerners in Egypt), and an attempt to revive it in the early summer of 1955 failed. Nonetheless, the CIA lines of communication that had facilitated the earlier covert contacts were still in place when the decision was made in the wake of the Soviet-bloc arms deal to relaunch the ALPHA peace process. GAMMA, then, represented a merging of ALPHA, hitherto run through overt foreign service channels, with CIA crypto-diplomacy.[3]

With Kim Roosevelt going to cover the Egyptian end of GAMMA, another CIA officer of equal if not even greater stature was selected to deal with the Israelis. James Jesus Angleton is best known to history as the long-serving counterintelligence chief who led the CIA in an increasingly obsessive, some would say paranoid, mole hunt until being eventually forced to retire in 1975. A less remarked-on facet of Angleton's career was his equally long ownership of the "Israeli account," the

CIA's intelligence-sharing arrangement with Israel's secret service, Mossad, which dated back to a series of high-level meetings in Washington and Tel Aviv in 1951. Quite why the Agency's Israel desk was hived off from the Near East division in this fashion is unclear. According to some accounts, the NEA's Arabists feared the possibility of Zionist sympathizers in their midst passing secrets to the Israeli embassy. Others suggest the opposite: that Israeli officials did not want the CIA-Mossad connection compromised by the Arabists in the NEA, and that Agency chiefs such as Allen Dulles complied with their wishes because Israel, with its large Soviet-bloc émigré population, was such a valuable source of Cold War intelligence about the communist world. Whatever its origins, the split led to a curious bifurcation in the Agency's Middle East operations, with Jim Angleton, who was as pro-Zionist as Kim Roosevelt was anti, jealously shielding his Israeli sources and assets from the Arabists. GAMMA, in which Angleton was to perform a support role in Israel similar to what Kim would play in Egypt, was therefore a rare moment of professional cooperation between these two CIA legends.[4]

Partly because of this institutional divide between the CIA's Arab and Israel desks, but chiefly because Nasser felt he could not risk the exposure of a direct meeting with Israeli representatives, the GAMMA plan involved a third American party besides Roosevelt and Angleton: a special presidential representative to serve as a secret intermediary between Cairo and Tel Aviv, moving to and fro until an agreement was reached in a manner that anticipated Henry Kissinger's "shuttle diplomacy" of the 1970s. Various candidates were suggested for this role, including the president's brother Milton Eisenhower and Eric Johnston, the VIP crypto-diplomat present in Cairo during the abortive Allen mission, but the choice eventually settled on a complete newcomer to the Middle East scene: former secretary of the navy and undersecretary of defense, Texan businessman Robert B. Anderson, not coincidentally a very close friend of the president's. In December, while Anderson traveled to London to get a feel for the British position, CIA officers working with Israeli and Egyptian leaders (or the "northerners" and "southerners," as Foster and Allen Dulles referred to them in telephone conversations) prepared the ground for a series of meetings to take place in Cairo and Tel Aviv in January 1956. Henry Byroade, still the US ambassador to Egypt, was not informed.[5]

The final piece in the GAMMA jigsaw was Kim Roosevelt's domestic state-private network. The deteriorating US position in the Middle East and, in particular, the September 1955 arms deal had, it seems, produced a bout of introspection in the American Friends of the Middle East. "AFME Takes a New Look," announced the organization's 1955–56 annual report, echoing the famous phrase adopted by the Eisenhower administration to describe its high-tech, low-cost strategy for waging the Cold War. "Should we continue as before, believing that the kind of human relations program we had built up for four years would, in the long run, meet the needs we wished to serve?" asked the report, summarizing the policy choices that now faced the organization. Or "should we scrap our basic program and expend all our energies in a frontal attack on those who were subverting America's interests in the Middle East?" In the end, the AFME board decided to soft-pedal on its Arabist, cultural diplomacy mission in the Middle East for the time being and adopt "a more positive approach" to the task of "combating special interests' propaganda"—in other words, to ramp up its anti-Zionist campaign within the United States.[6]

This new militancy, which coincided precisely with the CIA's assumption of responsibility for the implementation of the Eisenhower peace plan, found its most outspoken exponent in Garland Evans Hopkins. Returning home from a three-and-a-half-month tour of the Middle East in October 1955, Hopkins told a New York press conference that "it was the 'height of cynicism' to criticize Egypt for buying Communist weapons while saying nothing about alleged Israeli arms purchases from both Western and Iron Curtain countries." He went on to predict "a wave of anti-Semitism in this country" if Zionist pressures continued to jeopardize "America's best interests" in the Middle East. Following Hopkins's example, in early January 1956, Mather Eliot, just returned from Syria for his annual consultation at AFME headquarters, convened another press conference and, specifically addressing the prospects for an Arab-Israeli settlement, stated his belief "that what chances existed for peace in the Near East would have to be based on substantial concessions by Israel." Like Elmer Berger before them, both Hopkins and Eliot also made a point of seeking meetings with State Department officials, ostensibly to pass on their firsthand impressions of the Middle East but in fact to urge the adoption of a more pro-Arab, anti-Zionist US foreign policy. Eliot (lest it be forgotten, not just a member of Kim Roosevelt's state-private network but himself a CIA officer) was "in Washington for a week, 'lobbying' with members of Congress, labor officials, newspaper men and others." In short, all evidence indicates that the "New Look" taken by AFME in the winter of 1955–56 was closely linked to the new GAMMA peace initiative in the Middle East.[7]

With the main elements of GAMMA in place by the New Year, all the operation's principal players had to do now was wait. Hank Byroade was at last informed about GAMMA on January 6. ("He seemed to take it all right," Foster told Allen Dulles.) On January 11, Robert Anderson and Foster Dulles met with the president, who made clear his absolute confidence in his special envoy. "He is one of the most capable men I know," Ike wrote in his diary that night. After a brief delay caused by a cabinet reshuffle in Cairo, the day of departure at last arrived. Boarding a flight to Cairo on January 15, 1956, the GAMMA team joined the growing line of hopeful American peacemakers in the Middle East.[8]

THE PROBLEMS STARTED ALMOST AS soon as the plane touched down in Egypt. Mindful of the fate of Jordan's King 'Abdullah, gunned down in 1951 by a Palestinian who feared he was about to betray the Arab cause to the Israelis, Nasser demanded that the talks take place in absolute secrecy. The GAMMA team had already taken steps to conceal its mission, planning to shuttle Anderson between Cairo and Tel Aviv via Rome or Athens on disguised flights and to communicate with Washington in coded messages using CIA transmission channels. For his part, Nasser insisted on meeting only at night, so that he could be seen during the day carrying out his normal duties, and employed no support staff whatsoever—hardly ideal conditions for detailed negotiations. The only other Egyptians included in the talks were Interior Minister Zakaria Mohieddin and Director of the Prime Minister's Office 'Ali Sabri. Despite all these precautions, security lapses occurred. When the names of two non-CIA members of the GAMMA team, State Department experts on Palestine, appeared on the passenger list of a Pan Am flight from Rome, they were told not to board the plane and to await further orders. On another occasion, sources in New York and Washington informed some Cairo newspapers that the United States and Egypt were working toward a settlement with Israel. Nasser was furious.[9]

In addition to GAMMA's security woes, it soon grew obvious that, despite his president's faith in him, Robert Anderson was not particularly well-suited to the role of Arab-Israeli go-between. The first meeting between him and Nasser took place during the evening of Tuesday, January 17, in the Zamalek apartment of Zakaria Mohieddin. As usual on these occasions, the atmosphere was cordial, with the Egyptian leader nodding amiably as the American envoy described his hopes for a settlement. As the meeting broke up, however, and Kim Roosevelt talked on his own with Nasser, it emerged that the prime minister had been nodding in bafflement rather than agreement. Anderson's "Texas drawl was so thick that Nasser couldn't understand a thing he said," Kim explained later.[10]

At follow-up meetings between Anderson and Nasser, Kim acted as a kind of interpreter, "translating" the Texan's utterances for the Egyptian (Roosevelt's accent was closer to the upper-class English tones Nasser was used to hearing). The resulting discussions, combined with Anderson's opening talks the following week in Tel Aviv, revealed the true gulf that still separated the Arabs and Israelis. Nasser wanted a return to the UN partition lines and Palestinian refugees offered a choice between repatriation or compensation; the Israelis were prepared to offer some restitution but refused to recognize a Palestinian right of return and rejected talk of territorial concessions except for some minor border readjustments. As ever, the main sticking point was the Negev, the contested desert region between Egypt and Israel whose acquisition by the Israelis following the 1948 war had severed land contact between African and Asiatic Arabs. According to Haikal, Nasser scornfully dismissed American proposals to solve the problem by building a two-level highway linking Egypt to Jordan. What, asked the Egyptian prime minister, if an Arab on the overpass decided to relieve himself on Israeli traffic using the lower level? Might this not lead to war? Anderson discovered that the two sides could not even agree on what form negotiations should take, with the Israelis demanding a promise of face-to-face talks, and Nasser arguing it would be suicidal for him to make such an undertaking. The Texan Methodist was starting to learn the limits of American goodwill.[11]

But there were some glimmers of hope, including a suggestion from Nasser that, rather than merely "working with a Presidential representative for a 'few days,'" he lead an effort to create "a 'Secret Committee' of Egyptians and Americans" to discuss the Palestine conflict and other problems affecting the Middle East over a longer time period. The author of the CIA cable that reported this proposal—most likely Kim Roosevelt, judging by his obvious familiarity with the Egyptian leader and confident, assertive tone—endorsed this proposal enthusiastically. "We have a chance of solving the Palestine problem provided we are able to give Nas[se]r the capability of doing so," he told Washington. "If we are not able to work on this basis, . . . the Palestine problem will not be solved for many years to come." Mindful of the approaching US elections, and fearing that Israel might try to launch a preemptive attack on Egypt before Nasser's army had been able to absorb the Soviet arms, John Foster Dulles balked at the request for extra time. Nevertheless, on his return to Cairo at the end of January, Anderson did establish something that looked very like Nasser's secret committee: a working group made up of his CIA associates and 'Ali Sabri, tasked with agreeing on a package of negotiating points to put to the Israelis.[12]

Meanwhile, back home in the United States, the American Friends of the Middle East was preparing its boldest gesture yet in support of the Eisenhower administration's Middle Eastern policy. The previous October, Foster Dulles had spoken with senior officials about his desire to deal with the Arab-Israeli conflict "on a bipartisan basis" and "keep the matter out of politics . . . during the coming campaign." On January 25, 1956, AFME published "An Open Letter to Every American Citizen" in the New York Times and several other leading newspapers, demanding, "Take the Middle East Out of Domestic Politics!" The day after the statement appeared, the organization's annual conference opened at New York's Delmonico Hotel. The program had been revised at the last moment to address the controversy swirling around the issue of a possible Israel arms deal, and several speakers urged candidates for political office to rise above the partisan fray. "What we need in this issue, as in all others, is a disinterested American foreign policy," declared Dorothy Thompson.[13]

At the same time AFME was cranking up its New Look, Kim Roosevelt was fighting another fire in Cairo. Talks between Nasser and the president of the World Bank, Eugene R. Black, about the terms of the Aswan dam loan had stalled. Foster Dulles and Herbert Hoover Jr. were dismayed by this news, as it threatened to remove the major incentive for Egyptian cooperation with their peace plan, and on January 31 they cabled Black, urging him not to present Nasser with "a take it or leave it proposition." Shortly afterward, Kim was recalled to Cairo from Athens, where he had retreated with Anderson, with instructions to get the dam negotiations back on track. "The assignment put quite a strain on my persuasive powers," he remembered later, but on February 2 he was able to report that the "dam talks have taken [a] turn for [the] better, with both sides giving ground." The loan was quickly finalized, and announced on February 9.[14]

With one blaze damped down, the CIA's crypto-diplomats now returned their attention to extinguishing the Arab-Israeli conflict. Reinforced by the arrival from Athens of the chief American ALPHA negotiator, Francis Russell, the secret CIA-Egyptian working group knuckled down to its task. With no recent leaks to worry Nasser, and Sabri appearing "unusually interested and cooperative," the omens for once appeared auspicious. By February 8, Kim and Miles had produced a lengthy memorandum identifying the causes of Arab-Israeli tensions, suggesting measures for building up mutual confidence (including improved "Border Control" and "Positive Propaganda Measures"), and proposing an eight-step timetable culminating in meetings between heads of state and the announcement of a settlement. It was an ambitious yet pragmatic—even hardheaded—plan, as befitted the CIA men's self-professed Machiavellianism. "It appears almost certain that no formula for change can ever come as a result of resolving the problem of guilt and responsibility for the past," the document stated. "The alternative is a solution on grounds of self-interest and convenience." Although Sabri was "gloomy" about the prospects for specific elements of the plan, the memo nonetheless served as the basis for all the working party's subsequent discussions. On February 20, in a "business-like meeting," the Egyptian indicated his agreement to measures for easing Arab-Israeli tension and reducing area frictions generally—in other words, to the first three steps of Kim and Miles's plan. A corner, it seemed, had been turned.[15]

As ever, though, events elsewhere were conspiring against the CIA Arabists. In the United States, public calls for the government to supply arms to Israel were gaining in volume, partly because the president had just lifted an embargo on a shipment of tanks to Saudi Arabia. In their most blatantly political intervention to date, AFME representatives gamely tried to defend Ike's decision, Dorothy Thompson pointing out the strategic importance of the Arabian peninsula and Garland Hopkins insisting that criticism of the shipment showed "the extent to which partisans of Israel in this country [would] go in putting Israel's interests ahead of those of America and the free world." CIA officer Mather Eliot, meanwhile, was carrying on his campaign to sway American opinion, securing introductions from Thompson to various publishers and editors, and submitting an article to the *Christian Century*, "Arab-Israeli Peace Still Is Possible," in which he called on the US government to "pressure Israel into a reasonable compromise" or "risk delivering the whole of the Muslim and ex-colonial world into the Russian orbit." Despite these efforts to relieve the Zionist pressure on the Eisenhower administration, Foster Dulles was starting to buckle, asking his team in Cairo whether GAMMA could survive the fall-out from a US arms deal with Israel.[16]

The response from Egypt was unambiguous. Word had reached Nasser that an American deal with Israel was imminent, and during a meeting with the CIA team and Interior Minister Mohieddin on February 21, he blew up. Such a move "would put an end not only to the Anderson operation but to 'Everything,'" he exclaimed. The author of the CIA report on the meeting, most probably Kim Roosevelt, had "never seen Nas[se]r and Zacharia [sic] so upset about anything." An arms grant to Israel would, he predicted, "produce a fearsome reaction" that would be impossible "to avert or soften." At the end of the meeting, as the CIA man was preparing to leave, the Egyptian leader grasped his sleeve, imploring him to prevent a "catastrophe" that would "shatter all the hope we have been nursing along over the past three years."[17]

There was a growing sense that the Arabist project featuring Nasser in the role of pan-Arab "necessary leader" was in terminal crisis. Miles Copeland followed up Kim's report with a message stating the Cairo team's "unanimous opinion" that military assistance for Israel would result in an immediate end to the Anderson mission, the suspension of the Aswan dam loan, and, most likely, a further Egyptian arms deal with the communist bloc. Then, on the twenty-third, Henry Byroade, who had already sent a strongly worded cable to Herbert Hoover on the subject, dispatched an impassioned personal letter to Foster Dulles, urging him "to take the initiative domestically" and "break the back of Zionism as a political force." The ambassador concluded on a poignantly autobiographical note: "All this comes from an ex-Indiana farm boy who has never had the slightest feelings about race or creed—yet who now is labeled anti-Semitic. Believe me, I make these recommendations in what I consider to be the best interests of the United States—and in the firm conviction that they are in the long-range best interests of Israel—whether they agree or not."[18]

If any hope remained of rescuing both GAMMA and the larger hopes of the Arabists, it was about to be dealt a coup de grâce, with the blow coming from a predictable quarter. The British had always been half-hearted in their commitment to the ALPHA peace process, preoc- cupied as they were with the Baghdad Pact and their grievances against both the Americans and the Egyptians. Prime Minister Anthony Eden, in particular, nursed a festering personal hatred of Nasser. Reports from an MI6 source in Egypt, LUCKY BREAK, purported to show that the Egyptian premier was moving ever closer toward the Soviets while scheming to overthrow other Arab leaders. In December 1955, a cabinet reshuffle saw Harold Macmillan become chancellor of the Exchequer, leaving the Foreign Office in the relatively inexperienced hands of Welsh lawyer Selwyn Lloyd and stimulating Eden's inclination to intervene in foreign affairs, just as his predecessor Winston Churchill had while Eden was foreign secretary. Most concerningly, the prime minister's health was deteriorating, the legacy of a badly botched operation on his gall bladder, and he was increasingly prone to outbursts of violent temper.

Events came to a head on March 1, 1956, when 'Abdullah's successor as king of Jordan, his grandson Hussein, dismissed his British chief of staff, Lieutenant-General Sir John Bagot Glubb. "Glubb Pasha," who had first come to the small Hashemite kingdom when it was founded after World War I, was a legendary figure, the very archetype of "the old Kipling servant of the British monarchy deputized to a lesser ruler," in the words of one historian. His dismissal, which was viewed in London as the result of meddling by Nasser, seemed tantamount to a final evic- tion notice for the British in the Middle East, and Eden was beside him- self with rage. It did not matter that Hussein's action was in large part intended to placate Jordanian nationalists angered by British efforts to compel their country to join the Baghdad Pact, nor that the young king, a Sandhurst graduate, rather fancied himself in the role of commander of the Arab Legion, Glubb's Jordanian army. Eden, also fuming about a perceived snub to Selwyn Lloyd during a recent trip to Cairo, blamed Nasser personally. Dining with Evelyn Shuckburgh at Chequers, the prime minister's country residence, Eden, famed for his opposition to appeasement before World War II, compared the Egyptian to Mussolini, "and a sort of 1940 look came into his eye." Shuckburgh understood im- mediately what this meant: there would be no further efforts to appease the would-be Arab Hitler, no "Munich on the Nile."[19]

John Foster Dulles was not as disturbed by events in Jordan as Eden; indeed, Kim Roosevelt rather suspected that the secretary of state was enjoying the discomfiture of the British. Nonetheless, with GAMMA already running into problems, Dulles was far from unreceptive to British complaints about Nasser. Realizing this, Eden never missed an opportunity when in American company to denigrate that "awful fellow," and he made sure that the LUCKY BREAK reports were routinely passed on to Washington. It helped that Anglo-American tensions over the Arabian peninsula were easing and that the United States was showing greater interest in supporting Britain's Iraqi-Jordanian axis. As in Iran three years earlier, the Americans were moving slowly but inexorably toward the British position.[20]

On March 3, a dispirited Robert Anderson traveled to Cairo for what proved to be the last time. During a meeting on March 6, Nasser effectively killed off GAMMA (as Anderson reported to Washington) by announcing that there was no possibility of his meeting with the Israelis for security reasons (he referred to the fate of King 'Abdullah four times); that he was unwilling to spell out a timetable for his discussions with Americans; and, finally, in "a completely new and discouraging" development, that he was not prepared to take a leadership role in promoting any peace settlement to the wider Arab world. As this last notion was a fundamental premise of the American negotiating strategy in ALPHA and GAMMA, there seemed little point in Anderson remaining in Egypt, and he departed a few days later, having canceled a last meeting with Nasser.[21]

If any one day marked the end of Kim Roosevelt's Arabist dreams of Nasser, it was Thursday, March 8, 1956, when Anderson's final cables eventually reached Washington along with reports that the Egyptian government was bidding for more communist arms and preparing for an attack on Israel. "Today," Evelyn Shuckburgh recorded in his diary, "both we and the Americans really gave up hope of Nasser and began to look around for means of destroying him."[22]

Part Four
Losing, 1956–1958

SIXTEEN

... to OMEGA

AFTER MANY YEARS SPENT OBSERVING politics in the Middle East and United States, Miles Copeland posited a general theory of political behavior. "Both leaders and doers in a given society play three games at the same time," he wrote in his autobiography: "the personal, the domestic, the international—and sometimes a fourth, the bureaucratic."[1]

According to Miles's scheme, his old boss Kim Roosevelt had performed remarkably well during his first half-decade as a CIA officer. Personally, he had earned the sort of honor expected of someone from his family and educational background, achieving legendary status within the CIA. Domestically, he had scored a significant victory against Zionism by launching the American Friends of the Middle East, thereby accomplishing an important element of the Arabist agenda he had inherited from the first generation of OSS spies in the Middle East. Internationally, he had pulled off a spectacular covert action success in Iran while quietly building up the American position in the traditional British stronghold of Egypt, forging a personal friendship with the most important leader in the Arab world, Gamal Nasser. Bureaucratically, his supremely high standing with the Dulles brothers, combined with the general atmosphere of executive privilege that prevailed in 1950s Washington, meant that, to a great extent, he could do as he wished.

By mid-decade, however, the game environment, and with it Kim's performance, was deteriorating. At home, the Zionists, backed by supporters in the legislative branch of government as well as from abroad by Israel, were fighting back. In the Middle East, the British were likewise staging a comeback, mixing diehard imperialism with a tactical cleverness born of years of area experience and a readiness to resort to drastic measures if circumstances demanded them. Meanwhile, the Arabs were proving surprisingly uncooperative, not least Nasser himself, who had emerged as an outstandingly clever game player in his own right, upsetting Kim's carefully laid plans for Arab-Israeli peace. These setbacks had translated into some significant communist victories that, while they did not bother Kim particularly, horrified John Foster Dulles, whose highly personal handling of US foreign policy, and bureaucratic tendency to use the CIA as a tool of crypto-diplomacy, now began to work against the Arabist agenda. And, finally, there was always the danger that Kim's larger purposes might be undermined by his own personality, in particular by his desire for adventure—for game playing in the old-fashioned, Kipling sense.

In addition to his notion of multiple, overlapping games, Miles Copeland's experience serving under Kim Roosevelt in the Middle East led him to one other general conclusion. "An intelligent person, agency, political party or even nation can get so caught up in the interplay," he wrote, "that he, she or it is stuck with a source of action leading, inevitably, to disaster." And so it would prove for the CIA Arabists, as the game moved into a new phase, one featuring some familiar players and a few new ones, too.[2]

EARLY ON THE MORNING OF Wednesday, March 28, 1956, James Eichelberger, the ad man turned CIA Cairo station chief, knocked on the door of a suite at the exclusive Connaught Hotel in Mayfair, London. Eich had been ordered to England in the wake of the collapse of the Eisenhower peace initiative as part of a new Anglo-American program in the Middle East, OMEGA. Whereas ALPHA had accorded Nasser a leadership role in the Arab world, OMEGA sought to reduce the Egyptian's influence in favor of more reliably pro-Western leaders in the region. Eich's mission was to prepare a joint intelligence estimate of the prospects for this scheme with Britain's MI6, and to pave the way for the arrival in London on April 1 of Allen Dulles and Kim Roosevelt, at which point the discussions would shift up to the ministerial level. On his way to meet with the MI6 liaison officer Dan Debardeleben at a secret location in the West End, Eichelberger had stopped off at the Connaught to collect his American partner in the talks, Wilbur Crane Eveland.

Among the American adventurers attracted to the Middle East in the first years of the Cold War, Wilbur Eveland had traveled the furthest, both literally and figuratively. Born in 1918 to a poor, pioneer family in Spokane, Washington, young Bill soon grew bored with his isolated, circumscribed existence. In the mid-1930s, the depths of the Great Depression, he drifted, hobo-like, around America, eventually landing in Boston in the winter of 1940. Walking the streets looking for work during the day, and sleeping nights at South Station, he desultorily took some university extension classes on the Harvard campus (his CV would later claim full-time attendance) and then enlisted in the US Army. As for so many men of his generation, World War II proved the turning point. In no time, Eveland's native intelligence and ability to ingratiate himself with senior officers earned him promotion to sergeant and then recruitment by the army's Counter Intelligence Corps, the same route into wartime espionage work followed by that other self-made spy, Miles Copeland.[3]

Apart from a spell after the war working in a New York import-export business, Eveland would stay in the army through the mid-1950s, serving as assistant military attaché in Iraq (the post earlier occupied by Archie Roosevelt) and as Defense Department representative on the Operations Coordinating Board, the covert Cold War planning unit. Along the way, he acquired the trappings of an Arabist, including excellent Arabic and a sympathy for the Palestinian cause, an attitude he later claimed was strengthened by his strong sense of identification with his distant relative, the famously pro-Arab and anti-Zionist Charles Crane. (In fact, it is unclear if there was any connection between the two men beyond a shared name.) Meanwhile, Eveland also developed a taste for expensive hotels, as shown by his choice of the Connaught for his London lodgings, and high-end English-style clothing, a fact noted by Eichelberger and Copeland when they met him for the first time

at Cairo airport in 1954. "'Jeezus,' said Eich, 'he's in fancy dress!'" as
the tall, slender Eveland descended the airplane steps, clad, according to
Miles's later recollection, in "striped pants, tailored Oxford grey waist-
coat of the kind one wears to diplomatic funerals, [and] homburg hat."
This "apparition" earned Eichelberger's instant mistrust, but Copeland
took to Eveland as a fellow "kibbitzer" after hearing him casually drop
the name Foster into a conversation about the secretary of state.[4]

Americans with Eveland's knowledge of Arabic and facility for cultivating top-level contacts were rare in the early Cold War, so despite
his eccentricities, in June 1955 he was personally selected by Kim Roosevelt to undertake a particularly sensitive mission to Syria. Early in
the previous year, the former French colony had cast off the military
dictatorship of Miles's old friend, Adib Shishakli. Now, with the nationalist and socialist Ba'ath gaining in influence, and the local Communist
Party acquiring a reputation as the most active outside of the Eastern
bloc, the country was fast drifting leftward, raising American fears of a
Soviet takeover similar to those that preceded the 1953 Iran coup. It did
not help that the new president was none other than Shukri al-Quwatli,
the notoriously weak-willed politician Husni Za'im had overthrown in
March 1949. Unfortunately, the American ambassador in Damascus,
veteran Arabist James S. Moose, was having difficulty keeping up with
the pace of political developments—he was in "way over his head," Kim
told Eveland—while the CIA's own station chief had so far failed to
recruit any agents among Syria's new political elites. Eveland's mission,
code-named WAKEFUL ("WA" being the CIA prefix for Syria), was
to use his Arab contacts to, as he put it later, "expand the horizons of
the Damascus embassy for a few months" and then return to his desk
at the Operations Coordinating Board. Basing himself in neighboring
Lebanon, Eveland rapidly established links to right-wing Syrian mal-
contents conspiring against their country's leftist government. Although
he never actually joined the CIA, he reported directly to Allen Dulles,
becoming in effect the director's point man in Syria, thereby adding a
further layer of complexity to the United States' crypto-diplomatic ma-
neuverings in the Middle East. It was in this role that Eveland traveled
to London in March 1956, his presence at the Anglo-American talks
alongside Eichelberger ensuring that Syria would receive equal attention
to Egypt.[5]

After a briefing session with Dan Debardeleben, Eveland and Eichelberger carried on by Tube to St. James's Park station and then walked

the short distance to MI6 headquarters at 54 Broadway Buildings. There they were greeted by two surprises. One was the cramped, dreary condition of the glamorous spy agency's accommodations. Riding an ancient, rickety elevator to the top floor, the two Americans emerged into a gloomy conference room whose walls showed clear signs of rain damage. Seated around a table were six MI6 officers all attired in identical crumpled, stained suits that made them look less like aristocratic Oxbridge graduates than humble office clerks. "There wasn't a James Bond in the bunch," recalled Eveland later, sounding disappointed.[6]

The other surprise for the Americans was the acrimonious nature of their reception. Setting the tone was MI6 deputy director George Kennedy Young, a large, looming Scot with a reputation for brash Cold War activism. In a torrent of recrimination recalled later by Eveland, Young accused the absent Kim Roosevelt of "boasting about returning the shah of Iran to power," creating "a monster in Nasser," and passing on intelligence about Egypt that was "pure rubbish." As Eveland and Eichelberger listened with mounting dismay, Young then proceeded to outline a three-stage plan for preventing the further spread of Nasserite neutralism and communism in the Middle East. The first phase, so urgent that the United Kingdom was prepared to undertake it alone within the month, was a "complete change of government of Syria." Although Young deliberately concealed operational details of the projected coup, it was clear that Britain's principal Arab ally, Iraq, would play a major role, including mounting a possible invasion. Second, MI6 wanted "to discuss CIA political action potential" against Nasserite elements in Saudi Arabia; again, if the Americans were not prepared to go along with them, the British might mobilize the Iraqis as well as the Saudis' enemies in the sheikhdoms along the Persian Gulf. Finally, with Nasser's friends in Syria and Saudi Arabia removed from the picture, the time would be right "to tumble [the] Egyptian government" itself, if necessary "by force (both British and Israeli)." As if this scenario of clandestinely induced mayhem was not disturbing enough, Young liberally sprinkled his presentation with colonial-style references to "Wogs" and "Gyppos." "Don't be offended, Old Boy," another MI6 officer whispered to Eveland, "George is out of patience with the blasé attitude you chaps have taken to a situation which to us means life or death." After their final meeting, on the morning of April 1, Young stood menacingly at Eveland's shoulder as he composed a cable to Washington summarizing the talks. Far from demurring at the American's frank description of the British position, Young demanded the insertion of such apocalyptic phrases as "No matter what the cost we will win" and, even more ominously, "Britain [is] now prepared to fight its last battle."[7]

Something was rotten in Whitehall. This was no mere case of post-imperial malaise, the "wispy, enveloping" melancholy that another CIA liaison officer, Chester L. Cooper, had detected on arriving in London the previous summer. The British appeared enraged, vengeful, irrational. Jim Eichelberger claimed even to have heard Young say that MI6 was plotting an attempt on Nasser's life. "He talked openly of assassinating Nasser, instead of using a polite euphemism like 'liquidating,'" the CIA man reported after his return to Cairo. Years later, the renegade former British intelligence officer Peter Wright would reveal in his memoir *Spy-catcher* details of MI6 plans to place canisters of nerve gas inside the ventilation systems of the Egyptian leader's headquarters; when that plot fell through, the spies debated using a packet of cigarettes containing darts tipped with poison. With Prime Minister Anthony Eden consumed by a murderous hatred for Nasser, and MI6 practically unsupervised by the Foreign Office, there seemed to be no limits to the imaginings of Broadway Buildings' spies. Not surprisingly, gaming imagery abounded, although there was a growing sense that the old rules had ceased to matter, giving way to a sort of nihilistic free-for-all. "What bothered us most," Miles Copeland wrote later, "was the fact that the British weren't reacting at all like seasoned, cold-blooded gameplayers. . . . It was as though a chess Grand Master, embarrassed at having been outmaneuvred by an opponent whom he considered an inferior player, wanted to kick over the table."[8]

There were, however, several elements in the British proposals that also featured in US plans for OMEGA, which Foster Dulles had laid out before the president during a meeting at the White House on March 28, 1956. Still smarting from the Czech arms deal and the failure of ALPHA, the Americans agreed on the need to bring Nasser to heel, or at least show him he could not carry on dealing with the Soviets and expect "most-favored-nation treatment from the United States." Meanwhile, the United States would help Britain build up the Baghdad Pact nations as a counterweight to Nasserite and communist influence in the region; one proposal called for American assistance for Iraqi radio so that it could respond in kind to Egyptian broadcasts denouncing the pro-Western prime minister, Nuri al-Sa'id. Most significant was American acceptance of the need for secret joint planning with the British to bring about a "possible change of Government in Syria to one more friendly to Iraq and the West." It helped that the hectoring George Young was not the only British voice urging action on the Eisenhower administration. Prime Minister Eden, Foreign Secretary Lloyd, and Ambassador Roger Makins all joined in what Foreign Office Undersecretary Ivone Kirkpatrick patronizingly described as "an educational process through various channels." As in Iran three years earlier, the British noted that the "main United States preoccupation in the Middle East [was] the threat of Russian expansion" and adjusted their message accordingly.[9]

Still, for all this common ground, there were several important differences between the US and UK versions of OMEGA. The American preference for Syria was for regime change by internal opposition groups of the sort Bill Eveland had been cultivating in WAKEFUL, not some crude military intervention by a hostile neighboring power like Iraq, Turkey, or Israel, which might serve British interests but was bound to antagonize the rest of the Arab world. Young's call for a joint operation against Saudi Arabia was unacceptable on its face. Granted, the Saudis were less desirable allies since Ibn Saud's death in 1953: the old king's successor, his son Saud, lacked his father's prestige and abilities, and was proving far too accommodating toward Nasser's Egypt. Nonetheless, with its oil fields and US military bases, the desert kingdom, described by Allen Dulles during one National Security Council meeting as "right out of the Arabian Nights, with the addition of Cadillacs," remained crucial to US strategy in the region; Dwight Eisenhower in particular hoped that Saud might yet turn into a great spiritual leader capable of challenging Nasser for leadership of the Arab world. As for Egypt, the Eisenhower administration's emphasis was less on getting rid of Nasser—although such action was not ruled out in the long term— than on subtly bringing pressure to bear on him, by withholding aid and applying sanctions, for example, so that he would eventually be induced to mend his ways. "We would want for the time being to avoid any open break," Foster Dulles explained to the president, "and . . . leave Nasser a bridge back to good relations with the West if he so desires." Predictably, the British did not care for this show of independent American thinking. When Lloyd wrote Eden a note describing the "U.S. unwillingness to admit that we have a common policy," the PM recorded a one-word response in the margin: "Folly."[10]

Where did the CIA stand on these questions? Evidently, the British, perhaps thinking back to the 1953 Anglo-American operation in Iran, believed they could count on Washington's spies to back their latest schemes within the Eisenhower administration. "It will be easier to align the President and Foster Dulles in a new policy towards the Middle East if we have first convinced Allen Dulles and secured his cooperation in the practical measures which might be necessary," Selwyn Lloyd euphemistically wrote Roger Makins. There are no records of the meetings between MI6 and Kim Roosevelt that took place in London during the first week of April 1956 (Allen Dulles had decided to stay home, pleading his gout, although this might well have been an excuse to avoid exposing himself to unwelcome British pressure; Makins reported that Dulles "was very reluctant to go"). It is clear, though, from various sources that Kim disappointed British expectations, pouring cold water on STRAGGLE, as Young's plan for an Iraqi-assisted coup in Syria was code-named. In early May, Lloyd told Foster Dulles, "on the basis of conversations which he had had during Kermit Roosevelt's visit in London," that the "CIA was obviously more dubious than the British . . . that the operation could be carried out." "Their plans do not seem to us wholly realistic or likely to achieve the desired results," Allen Dulles explained to his brother a few days later, after Foster had quoted the Iran operation TP-AJAX as a possible precedent. "The situation does not lend itself to the same type of operation."[11]

Kim's diffidence about STRAGGLE was not an isolated phenomenon. Not long after TP-AJAX, Foster Dulles had invited the CIA Arabist to take command of PB-SUCCESS, a paramilitary operation to overthrow Jacobo Arbenz Guzmán, the democratically elected president of Guatemala, who was upsetting Washington with his supposedly communist-inspired efforts to expropriate land owned by US corporation United Fruit Company. Kim declined. AJAX had succeeded, he believed, chiefly because the CIA's aims were shared by large numbers of Iranians, and it was obvious that the same condition did not obtain among Guatemalans. The operation went ahead without Kim, and Arbenz resigned in June 1954, principally because blatant signs of American hostility had convinced him that a full-scale US invasion was imminent. "We had our will in Guatemala," Kim commented later, "[but] it wasn't really accomplished by clandestine means."[12]

There was perhaps a hint of self-boosterism in Kim's unflattering comparisons between AJAX and SUCCESS, but his objections to the more crudely interventionist aspects of the Guatemalan operation seem sincere enough and help explain his reluctance to rally behind British plans for STRAGGLE. It is possible to detect a similar wariness, even moral squeamishness, in the Arabist's response to another MI6 proposal: the elimination of Nasser. According to the then deputy director of the CIA, Robert Amory, "Kim was absolutely terrified at the thought of . . . arranging for the overthrow of Nasser with the support of the Egyptian army" because he "knew something of their torture methods." Whether Kim put him up to it is not clear, but after returning to Cairo from London, Jim Eichelberger leaked some of MI6's plans to his Egyptian contacts, warning them that the British "were determined to 'do a Mossadeq' [sic] with Nasser." True to form, Miles Copeland went one step further. According to his later account, no doubt embellished but probably still containing a grain of truth, the Dulles brothers sent Miles to Egypt to investigate the possibility of murdering Nasser on the tacit understanding that he would reach a negative assessment and thereby, it was hoped, discourage any British attempt. Arriving in Cairo, Miles immediately confessed his mission to Nasser, whereupon the old friends began gaming out possible assassination plots. "How about poison?" the American asked the Egyptian. "Suppose I just wait until you turn your head and then slip a pill into your coffee?" "Well, there's Hassan standing right there," replied Nasser. "If I didn't see you Hassan would." "But maybe we could bribe a servant to poison the coffee before bringing it in?" "The coffee would only kill the taster." And so the conversation carried on—at least in Miles's recollection.[13]

Not even the relatively restrained anti-Nasser plans of the Eisenhower administration found much favor with the CIA Arabists. Reacting to the State Department's March 28 OMEGA planning paper, Kim complained that it failed either to allow for the resumption of direct talks with Nasser should he show signs of reform or to make clear that "direct intervention" was, at this stage, only one of several possible courses of action. After returning from his meeting in London with MI6, Kim began attending the Middle East Policy Planning Group, a top-level interagency committee originally formed to discuss the ALPHA peace plan but now devoted to OMEGA. The group spent just as much time considering positive proposals for improving the Western position in the Arab world, including Allen Dulles's idea for a "Near East Development Institution," as it did punitive measures. The notion of a Middle

Eastern Marshall Plan, which Kim had proposed in *Arabs, Oil, and History*, was, it seemed, still not entirely dead.[14]

Meanwhile, far from putting "the squeeze on Nasser," as enjoined by OMEGA, the CIA station in Cairo appeared, if anything, to be growing closer to members of the circle around the Egyptian leader, in particular 'Ali Sabri and Zakaria Mohieddin. To a certain extent, these contacts were intended to expose the Egyptians to American arguments against Cold War neutralism and thereby engender some Nasserite "soul-searching." (Such exchanges, often "heated, but always friendly," according to a CIA cable from Cairo, usually ended with Zakaria cheerfully offering the advice that the United States "should not worry so much about the situation.") On other occasions, the spies seemed to be acting in direct contravention of OMEGA, as when they blamed recent Egyptian-American "misunderstandings" on Zionist and British meddling, rather than on Nasser himself. The most remarkable expression of dissent from the Eisenhower administration's new line came courtesy of Jim Eichelberger in a cable of May 2, 1956. The United States would be making a huge mistake, the CIA station chief warned, if it engaged in "direct combat with Arab nationalism," as such a course of action would almost certainly "lead to the defeat of Western interests in this area." As regards the specific measures contemplated by Washington, Eichelberger argued that anti-Soviet propaganda was unlikely to have much effect on Middle Eastern opinion; sanctions against Egypt would likely push the Nasser regime, and possibly other Arab nationalist governments, into accepting yet more assistance from the Eastern bloc; and "covert political action, particularly that involving the use of force, would run more than the usual degree of danger of boomeranging, even if successful at the outset." In places, Eichelberger's cable sounds more like a critique of 1950s US foreign policy by a modern-day liberal academic than a CIA message of the era itself. As such, it found a strong echo in reports to Washington from the US ambassador in Cairo, the Arabists' old ally Henry Byroade, who throughout the first half of 1956 grew increasingly strident in his criticisms of John Foster Dulles's policies toward Egypt. At times, the Cairo embassy was in almost open rebellion against Washington.[15]

The main effect of the mixed messages the United States was sending Nasser was probably to confuse him about American intentions, but they at least indicated that, in some quarters, America had not yet abandoned its traditional sympathy for Arab nationalism. Moreover, Kim's opposition to MI6's plans for Syria and Egypt showed that there were limits to his Anglophile and adventurist instincts: he was not going to tag along with the British in their ever more reckless campaign to restore their imperial position in the Middle East. In fact, next to MI6's saber-rattling George Young, who once described spies as "the main guardian[s] of intellectual integrity" in modern society, Kim looked distinctly cautious and conservative. An incident described in Bill Eveland's memoirs is telling. Passing through London again in May 1956, Eveland made a secret recording of a conversation with Young to pass on to the CIA. Far from applauding Eveland's initiative, Kim declared his subterfuge "perfidious": he had "breached all the rules of spycraft among allies." Apparently, the old Grotonian still believed in playing by the rules of the game, even if the public school boys of MI6 did not.[16]

AND YET KERMIT ROOSEVELT COULD not resist the call to *Kim*-like adventure altogether. With almost all CIA officers at the deputy director level or above preoccupied with one Cold War challenge or another—Frank Wisner, for example, with the liberation of Eastern Europe—Kim had an almost free hand in the Middle East whether he wanted it or not. TP-AJAX had transformed him into the Agency's "Mr. Political Action," one of the first to be consulted if some Third World leader was deemed in need of replacing, be it in Iran, Guatemala, or Indonesia. Kipling-esque imagery followed him around, trailing like an invisible cloud. "Kim Roosevelt is in the game," the British diplomat Evelyn Shuckburgh wrote excitedly in his diary in January 1956, after learning that the American was taking over the ALPHA negotiations in Egypt. His very name, conjuring as it did both the Great Game and the Rough Rider president, created certain expectations.[17]

Then there was Kim's lieutenant, Miles Copeland. By 1956, Miles was taking game playing to a whole new level. When not joking with Nasser in Cairo, the Alabaman was helping run a five-member CIA unit under Kim's direct command, the Political Action Staff, whose brief—thinking up new projects to counter Soviet political and psychological warfare—extended beyond the Middle East to cover all Third World theaters of the Cold War. Assisted by the former naval intelligence officer Robert S. Mandelstam, Miles explored such promising possibilities as "OHP" or "Occultism in High Places," a plan to plant astrologers, witch doctors, "and other exegetes of the occult" on superstitious Third World leaders with the aim of influencing their actions in a pro-Western direction. According to *The Game Player*, Mandelstam's OHP project involved a number of private American consultants with an interest in the occult, including Scientology founder L. Ron Hubbard. If these claims sound fanciful, they receive some independent confirmation in the less widely read memoirs of Donald Wilber, the Persian archaeologist who had helped plan TP-AJAX. Wilber recalled serving on "Kim's special group" during the 1950s, alongside the "most stimulating" Miles Copeland. Among the "fresh approaches to political action and psychological warfare" explored by the group was the possible use of hypnotism in political speech making, which Wilber investigated in some depth with the assistance of a leading US stage hypnotist. Although the idea was eventually rejected as operationally impractical, Wilber at least learned how to hypnotize dinner party guests with the cue "Rug Weaving in Iran."[18]

But Miles was not only playing games metaphorically; he was also doing so literally. Soon after he was recalled from Cairo to Washington in 1955, the CIA officer became a regular guest at a twelfth-floor State Department office overlooking Connecticut Avenue where, according to *The Game of Nations*, "a carefully selected assortment of super experts 'gamed out' international trends and crises to predict their outcome." In a typical "Games Center" exercise, teams representing particular nations assessed their responses to a fictional scenario on the basis of real information teletyped to them hourly by various US intelligence sources and then compiled a report that was either fed into a computer or passed to the relevant country desks in interested departments. Miles's task in these games was always the same. He played the part of Gamal Nasser, a role he was also often called on to perform at strategy-planning meetings in the offices of John Foster Dulles and Herbert Hoover Jr. So convincing was his "Nasser act" that senior officials would sometimes forget he was just pretending. During one crisis in American-Egyptian relations, Allen Dulles angrily told him: "If that colonel of yours pushes us too far, we will break him in half!"[19]

Historians of US government "War Games" have sought in vain for records documenting Miles's Games Center. Nonetheless, the existence of some such entity in the mid-1950s seems likely enough. War games developed at the RAND Corporation, a Cold War think tank, and following a format much like that described in *The Game of Nations* were just starting to catch on at elite East Coast research centers with links to the CIA, State Department, and Pentagon. Miles was an obvious choice to take part in such exercises. In addition to his uncommon familiarity with Nasser, he was intrinsically interested in game theory, the complex system of mathematical and social scientific thought on which RAND's original game designs were based. Indeed, important game theory concepts like "optimality"—a game outcome that cannot be improved without hurting at least one player—were derived from the writings of Vilfredo Pareto, the Italian thinker who had influenced Miles's intellectual mentor, James Burnham. The very notion of international relations as a game, self-contained and governed by rational rules, echoed the Paretian conception of society as a closed system or organism that naturally sought equilibrium. In other words, Miles's account of taking part in State Department war games intended to predict Nasser's behavior has the ring of truth about it (even if his accompanying claim to have written a "monumental textbook for the CIA, *Non-Mathematical Games for Innumerate Intelligence Officers*" does not). It was as if the Great Game had been reinvented for the Cold War, in glossy American social-scientific packaging.[20]

Yet, as both Miles and later historians pointed out, there was always a tension in the American government's war gaming between theory and lived experience, between scientific rationality and the often irrational behavior of real historical actors. A case in point was John Foster Dulles's growing personal animus against Nasser, fuelled by a mixture of Calvinism, Orientalism, and clever British goading. "We kept hearing that 'the Secretary is mad,'" Muhammad Haikal recalled. "We heard it so often that eventually . . . Nasser began to think he really was mad." The tipping point came on May 16, when, in Foster Dulles's equivalent of what the sacking of Glubb Pasha had meant to Anthony Eden, the Egyptian government formally recognized communist China. Ironically, this move was partly motivated by a desire on Nasser's part to exploit the emerging Sino-Soviet split for Egyptian tactical advantage, but such a possibility appears not to have occurred to the secretary of state, who only saw in it further evidence that Nasser was hitching his wagon to the international communist movement. Calling Ambassador Hussein into the State Department for a dressing down, Foster Dulles, sounding more and more like Eden, raged that "Nasser had made a bargain with the devil with the hope of . . . establishing an empire stretching from the Persian Gulf to the Atlantic ocean."[21]

The following week, on May 23, it was Kim Roosevelt's turn to be summoned to the secretary's office, for a conference with the State Department's Middle East hands to discuss "an expansion of the Omega program." Among the measures on the agenda for consideration at this crucial meeting were the clandestine distribution of "informational material pointing up Nasser's identification with the communists," "efforts in Saudi Arabia playing upon King Saud's . . . latent distrust of the Egyptians," and, most important, planning with the British "for possible covert action" in Syria "to bring into power and maintain a pro-Western government." Kim's contributions to the discussion have been redacted in the official records, although it is easy to imagine his spirits sinking as he contemplated the further slide of American relations with Nasser's Egypt and the rush to action with the British in Syria. Shortly after the meeting, Foster Dulles approved "a 'probing operation' involving contacts with selected Syrians and Iraqis to determine the extent of pro-Western strength which may be mustered in Syria." Raymond A. Hare, State Department deputy director and former ambassador to Saudi Arabia, then called Bill Eveland to his office. "You're to be the 'prober,'" Hare told Eveland.[22]

Shortly afterward, Eveland quit his OCB desk job and left Washington on a one-way ticket to Beirut, taking up permanent residence in the city that, with Cairo now increasingly off-limits to American spies, was becoming the cockpit of the US espionage effort in the Middle East. In his remarkably revealing memoir *Ropes of Sand*, published in 1980, Eveland tried to portray himself as a contemporary critic of Cold War American covert operations who was almost tricked into becoming Allen Dulles's point man in Syria. Yet a careful reading of this work (which otherwise seems to be quite reliable), combined with documentary evidence from the era itself, suggest the opposite—that Eveland positively jumped at the chance to relocate to Beirut to work for the CIA director. "I'd now dealt with chiefs of state and international policies," he wrote in *Ropes of Sand*. "The thought of returning to a routine existence appeared less attractive each day."[23]

And there was another personal factor involved. Eveland was married to Marjorie, a nurse from Kansas who did not share his love of glamorous international travel, preferring to stay in the United States raising their adopted son, Crane. In 1954, during a trip to Cairo, Eveland had become infatuated with a Pan Am stewardess, Mimosa "Mimi" Giordano, who happened to be based in Beirut. Shortly before leaving on his Syrian "probing operation," Bill Eveland announced his intention of divorcing Marje and marrying Mimi. "It was," he admitted later, "a heady atmosphere in which I was living, [and] my juices were flowing." For the 1950s American male spy, the Middle East could be a playground in more ways than one.[24]

THE SHIFT IN US MIDDLE East policy from ALPHA to OMEGA might have created new opportunities for masculine adventure, but it also spelled the beginning of the end of the CIA Arabists' project of backing Nasser as the nationalist hero of the Arab world. The baleful consequences of OMEGA would soon become evident not only in the Middle East itself, where there would be a surge of covert operations intended to combat rather than support Arab nationalism, but at home in the United States, where Kim Roosevelt's state-private network of Arabists and anti-Zionists would be purged of its most outspoken Nasser supporters.

First, though, would come the most audacious game-play yet: Nasser's nationalization of the Suez Canal.

SEVENTEEN

Increasingly a Vehicle
for Your Purposes

ON JULY 19, 1956, FOLLOWING months of growing American-Egyptian discord caused by the Czech arms deals, the collapse of the GAMMA peace talks, and Cairo's recognition of communist China, John Foster Dulles informed Ambassador Ahmed Hussein that the United States was withdrawing its offer to help finance the Aswan High Dam, thereby effectively declaring the Eisenhower administration's three-year court-ship of Egypt's nationalist government at an end. The move had been preceded by several clear signs that a decisive break was imminent, the most obvious of which was the transfer of the Arabist ambassador Henry Byroade from Cairo to South Africa. (One of Byroade's last acts in Egypt was to present Nasser with a copy of the Frank Capra movie *It's a Wonderful Life*, the gift a pathos-filled reminder of the Egyptian leader's love for sentimental, democratic American popular culture.) Nonetheless, the harsh State Department announcement accompanying the loan's cancellation, which explained the decision in terms of a lack of US confidence in Egyptians' ability to complete the dam, did come as a surprise. "This is not a withdrawal," a furious Nasser told his journalist friend, Muhammad Haikal. "It is an attack on the regime and an invitation to the people of Egypt to bring it down."[1]

The CIA Arabists were no less taken aback than Nasser. In Washington for a meeting about Syria, Bill Eveland encountered an ashen-faced Miles Copeland pacing a State Department corridor. "The Secretary of State has gone mad!" Miles informed Eveland, reporting how he had heard firsthand from Ahmed Hussein that "Dulles had insulted Nasser, the ambassador, the Arabs, and Arab nationalism." A few days later, the Jewish anti-Zionist Elmer Berger, also in the nation's capital for meetings, discovered (as he told another of Kim Roosevelt's Jewish friends, George Levison) a state of "utter confusion and consternation" in government circles. "I could not find any working officer who . . . was willing to say he agreed with the way in which the decision was made and announced." (Berger's personal view, perceptive as ever, was that the administration was playing "cat's paw for the British," who were "spoiling for a chance to go back into Egypt with force.")[2]

Outside Arabist and anti-Zionist circles, however, the move was greeted as a masterly diplomatic game-play. The day after the announcement, Dulles lunched with Eisenhower loyalists Henry Luce and C. D. Jackson. The usually granite-faced secretary of state was positively skittish, telling the Time-Life executives that the dam decision was "as big a chess move as U.S. diplomacy had made in a long time" and that Nasser was now "in a hell of a spot." The metaphor of a chess match between Dulles and Nasser, which at least granted the Egyptian leader the status of an actual player rather than an inanimate chess piece in the Great Game, was taken up by the previously pro-Nasser *Time* in its next issue. "On the broad chessboard of international diplomacy, the U.S. moved decisively last week in a gambit that took the breath of professionals for its daring," declared the magazine, portraying the secretary of state, in an unusually glamorous light, as cool, masterful, and manly. "It was highly possible," *Time* concluded, "that Chessmaster Dulles already had his opponents in check."[3]

No one, not even the CIA Arabists, predicted Nasser's countermove. On July 26, the day marking the climax of celebrations of the fourth anniversary of the 1952 Revolution, the Egyptian president, as he now was, told a crowd of some 250,000 in Alexandria that his government was nationalizing the Suez Canal Company, until then largely owned by British and French shareholders, and using the proceeds from the operation of the canal to finance the building of the high dam. At a stroke, Nasser had produced a brilliantly simple solution to his country's financial woes and an electrifying gesture of defiance against Western domination. To add insult to injury, in a lesser-noted passage of his two-and-a-half-hour speech recounting the history of "imperialistic efforts to thwart Egyptian independence," he mischievously referred to the events immediately following the Czech arms deal of the previous year, including his "special interview" with an unnamed "American official" who had told him to disregard the "strong note" carried to Cairo by Assistant Secretary of State George Allen. According to Allen's later recollection, this disclosure set off a flurry of speculation in Washington about the identity of the "despicable traitor," which was fuelled further when Allen told the *Washington Post* that the official in question was "a CIA employe[e]" with "a long-time interest in the Arab world." Allen further disclosed that the CIA officer—obviously Kim to anyone in the know—had been "reprimanded" for taking "it upon himself to become a diplomat" and thereby perform "a major disservice to State." Whether Nasser enjoyed the resulting embarrassment to his old friend and adversary (who later described Allen's action as "very naughty") is not recorded, but what is clear is that he did relish the apoplectic reaction of Secretary of State Dulles, who now looked as foolish as a week earlier he had looked clever. Checkmate.[4]

The earth-shaking ramifications of the nationalization of the Suez Canal in the Middle East itself—the secret British collusion with the French and Israelis to seize back the canal, their joint invasion, and their eventual humiliating withdrawal—are world-famous events. Far less well known are the repercussions of the July 1956 crisis within the United States, where Kim Roosevelt's Arabist citizen group, the American Friends of the Middle East, would experience a series of upheavals that would change its character forever, from that of a state-private alliance into something more akin to a simple tool of US foreign policy.[5]

FOR THOSE WHO CARED TO look, there were already signs of trouble brewing around AFME, not just among its old enemies in the Zionist movement but, more worryingly, within its own camp. In March 1954, for example, and then again in May 1955, the organization had come under attack from retired businessman Benjamin H. Freedman, a convert from Judaism to Roman Catholicism and anti-Zionist zealot. Freedman had offered AFME vice president Garland Evans Hopkins a $100,000 donation and then, when Hopkins declined the offer, decided that he must be dealing with a cunning Zionist front operation designed to lure Arabs and Muslims "into a situation inimical to their best interests." It followed logically that the Dearborn Foundation (later revealed, of course, to be a funding conduit created by the CIA) must be a fence for some shadowy pro-Israel interests. Zionist publicists had already begun to ask awkward questions about AFME's financial arrangements—in April 1953 a contributor to the *American Zionist*, James H. Sheldon, demanded to know just "who has been financing" this "elaborate propaganda machine"—so Freedman's allegations, although wide of the mark, were unwelcome nonetheless.[6]

While Freedman was a rather disreputable figure, another anti-Zionist critic of AFME, Alfred A. Lilienthal, was less easy to dismiss. A descendant of a prominent Reform Jewish family and a State Department lawyer, Lilienthal had served in Cairo with George Levison during World War II, and in the late 1940s he helped run the Holyland Emergency Liaison Program (HELP), successor to Kim Roosevelt's Committee for Justice and Peace in the Holy Land (CJP). Afterward, he had developed a career as a freelance anti-Zionist publicist, in 1953 writing the widely reviewed *What Price Israel?*, a deliberately intemperate tract that established his reputation as the highest-profile Jewish critic of Zionism next to Elmer Berger. He also became something of a gadfly to AFME, constantly chiding it for being too restrained and polite in its anti-Zionism. "The inconsequential continues to be done with a big noise, while the essential is ignored in complete silence," he claimed in a January 1955 report, blaming the organization's chronic "self-censorship" on "the terms of certain contributions to remain neutral in the United States." Another complaint of Lilienthal's was that AFME was undemocratic, a self-elected cabal whose wealth and connections were serving to stifle genuine, organic opposition to the Zionists. On more than one occasion, the young firebrand tried to reform the core group of anti-Zionists who made up the CJP and HELP into a new, more "democratic" and "virile" organization that would truly carry the fight to Israel's supporters in the United States.[7]

Meanwhile, mutterings of discontent were becoming audible in AFME's other main constituency besides Jewish anti-Zionists, Protestant

Arabists. Officers of the Middle East Institute, an independent research and training institution founded in Washington, DC, in 1946 (and another recipient of subsidies from ARAMCO), resented the implicit suggestion in some publicity materials produced by AFME that it was the only organization interpreting the Arab world to the American people, and protested when AFME set up a Washington chapter without first consulting them. There was also disquiet in Arabist circles about Garland Hopkins's 1954 Muslim-Christian conference in Lebanon, which some saw as an alien graft on the American missionary tradition in the area. Alford Carleton, president of Aleppo College, vigorously opposed the venture, which he feared might stir up rather than ameliorate sectarian tensions in the Levant, while back home the National Council of Churches' Division of Foreign Missions discreetly investigated the Dearborn Foundation. As for some Jewish anti-Zionists, there was a nagging sense that AFME, with its vast yet mysteriously derived resources, was slowly colonizing a field previously occupied only by experienced volunteers acting with the clearest, and purest, of intentions.[8]

Nor were such concerns limited to nongovernment actors: AFME's fuzzy background and mission were also causing misgivings in the State Department. In February 1953, Middle East hand Richard H. Sanger, observing the organization's first annual conference, detected "an undercurrent of feeling that AFME did not quite know where it was going, should rethink its role in the United States, and reassess the value of its activities abroad." Perhaps sensing that there was more to the group than met the eye, foreign service personnel were unsure how much overt US government agencies should do to promote it in the Middle East. "These are delicate and complex questions," declared Near East information officer G. H. Damon. By February 1954, State's unease about the CIA-funded group had grown into definite disapproval. AFME was in danger of becoming "merely a mouth-piece for pro-Arab and anti-Israel sentiments," opined Sanger. "We plan to discuss this problem with . . . ARAMCO and certain other financial supporters of AFME who also have indicated their unhappiness."[9]

As Sanger's last statement implies, even AFME's old backers in ARAMCO were growing dissatisfied with AFME. For Bill Eddy—the ex-OSS officer now working for the oil corporation—the problem was not the organization's outspokenness on the Arab-Israeli dispute; if anything, the old Arabist thought that AFME was not doing enough to counter Zionist publicity in the United States. A long-time correspondent of Alfred Lilienthal's, Eddy urged Garland Hopkins to boost sales of *What Price Israel?* At the same time, he seems to have doubted the efficacy of AFME's cultural diplomacy efforts overseas, sharing the missionaries' concerns about newcomers to the Middle East muscling in on territory that had previously been the exclusive reserve of private volunteers. "This is . . . only one of many complaints" and "just another reason for me to doubt that Aramco should continue any generous support to the organization," Eddy wrote Dorothy Thompson in February 1954, the same month that Sanger was proposing to discuss AFME with him.[10]

Increasingly, criticisms of AFME focused on one person: Garland Hopkins. Part of the problem was Hopkins's high-handed management style, which appears to have antagonized a number of AFME employees. His relationship with Kay Sisto, the director of AFME's Phoenix news bureau, was particularly bad—"our weekly editorial meetings have to date merely amounted to a series of proclamations by Mr. Hopkins," Sisto complained to Thompson—and contributed to the discontinuation of the service in December 1954. There also seems to have been a personal element in the tensions between AFME and other Arabist and anti-Zionist activists, especially Alfred Lilienthal, who repeatedly singled out Hopkins in his criticism of the organization, accusing him of frittering away the considerable funds at his disposal on self-seeking showmanship. In fairness to Hopkins, tensions over editorial freedom and the resentment of rival groups with scarcer resources were far from unusual in the affairs of CIA front groups. That said, AFME's chief executive officer does appear to have been an exceptionally "controversial figure," as Richard Sanger put it in January 1955. "AFME is a good idea," continued Sanger, "but it would seem not to have worked out well recently, partly due to Hopkins's personality and characteristics."[11]

Hopkins remained in charge of AFME for the time being, but changes were afoot that would eventually end his reign as executive vice president. These were heralded in late 1954, when ARAMCO suspended its subsidies to the organization. The precise circumstances are unclear, although it seems likely that Bill Eddy's growing dissatisfaction with AFME's domestic anti-Zionist record played a part. But this was probably not the only reason. With the increasing tendency of Middle Eastern leaders to nationalize their countries' primary assets, some US oil executives were growing nervous about the possible threat to their interests posed by Arab nationalism. AFME's support of Gamal Nasser, along with Garland Hopkins's past record of speaking up on behalf of Mohammed Mosaddeq in his confrontation with the Anglo-Iranian Oil Company, might therefore have begun to count against the organization. In any event, at the same time that the Arabian-based ARAMCO was retreating from the picture, new foundation donors with links to the Texas oil industry were appearing in AFME's annual accounts. The San Jacinto Fund, created in March 1954 by Houston oilman John W. Mecom, now became the group's second most generous patron after the Dearborn. In 1967, the year of the *Ramparts* revelations, the San Jacinto was identified as a CIA conduit, along with several other Houston-based foundations.[12]

These events were the backdrop to a major shake-up of AFME that began in July 1956, at precisely the same time John Foster Dulles decided to dump Nasser once and for all. First came a policy review initiated by the board of directors "in the light of the great political changes which have recently taken place in the Arab World" and "with the assumption that it was unlikely that AFME would . . . receive sizable contributions from other-than-Foundation sources." The board's main conclusions, as reported to Dorothy Thompson by Secretary-Treasurer Cornelius Van Engert, were that AFME should henceforth avoid "any activities which smack of propaganda and might be considered provocative"; scale down its domestic program to "the minimum required to support its overseas efforts"; and divorce itself altogether from specific projects such as Hopkins's Continuing Committee on Muslim-Christian Cooperation. In case Thompson was in any doubt as to the authority of these recommendations, Engert explained that the board had made them "knowing the repeatedly expressed preferences" of the "one or two Foundations" that were AFME's "principal supporters." In other words, these were orders straight from the CIA.[13]

An even more blatant intervention in AFME's affairs occurred on the morning of Tuesday, September 16. During a meeting with "Harold U. Stobart"—clearly a pseudonym for a CIA officer, likely Kim Roosevelt himself—Garland Hopkins was asked to resign. After considering his response for a few days, an overwrought Hopkins wrote "Harold" a remarkably bitter letter expressing "a deep sense of hurt at the summary way in which it has been proposed I leave AFME," demanding that Stobart continue to fund the Continuing Committee on Muslim-Christian Cooperation "as long as the essentially religious nature of that organization was not compromised," and protesting that his treatment violated "the old concept of the dual nature and operation of the organization. . . . The conception of AFME has greatly altered since its [launch] in 1951. It has increasingly become simply a vehicle for your purposes." Evidently, the CIA must have granted Hopkins's request concerning the CCMCC, as he resigned the AFME vice presidency in January 1957 ostensibly "in order to devote more time to his work with the Continuing Committee on Muslim-Christian Cooperation," receiving for his pains a parting gift of a silver plate presented him by the Presbyterian minister Edward Elson.[14]

The final upheaval in AFME's leadership during what the organization's 1956–1957 report described as "A Year of Test" occurred in April 1957, when Dorothy Thompson stepped down as president. Unlike Hopkins, Thompson had not been coerced into resigning (although she had consulted with Bill Eddy before taking the final step). Rather, her decision, which came in the midst of an AFME-sponsored tour of the Middle East, shortly after she had conducted a three-hour interview with President Nasser, reflected her growing despondency about Zionist attacks on her and her husband, and pressure from the syndication service that handled the distribution of her newspaper columns in the United States to choose between the roles of reporter and Arabist spokesperson. Increasingly isolated, cantankerous, and exhausted, the former golden girl of US journalism reflected despairingly on the personal costs of her commitment to the anti-Zionist cause. "It has lost me thousands of previous admirers and scores of personal friends. . . . It has mobilized against me one of the most powerfully organized and zealous groups in American public life. . . . And it has often filled my heart with tears."[15]

Although not imposed from without, Thompson's resignation was propitious for those seeking a new direction for AFME. Combined with the departure of Executive Secretary William Archer Wright for a Virginia pastorate, it signified a complete clearing out of the executive leadership since the previous year. The organization that emerged from the long crisis of 1956–1957 was different from the AFME of the early 1950s. After an interregnum during which the well-liked director of the Iran field office, Charles Hulac (once codedly described by Hopkins to "Stobart" as "related to you"—in other words, an undercover CIA officer), returned to the United States to run the national headquarters, former ambassador to Lebanon Harold B. Minor assumed the presidency in January 1958. The board of directors was reshuffled and departments restructured to reflect the more "constructive" priorities communicated by Engert to Thompson. Three new field offices opened in Amman, Jordan; Arab Jerusalem; and Karachi, Pakistan. And in the fall of 1958 AFME's headquarters, "Middle East House," relocated from New York to a handsome four-story brownstone on New Hampshire Avenue in Washington, DC.[16]

It is reasonable to assume that these changes were intended, at least partly, to make AFME more amenable to government direction. Certainly, the organization's new leadership was preferred by the State Department to the old: an official observer of AFME's 1957 annual conference approvingly noted Charles Hulac's "intelligent and modest attitude on the future role of AFME" and the "obvious effort made to get away from concentration on the Arab-Israel dispute." Later in the same year, President Minor displayed an un-Hopkins-like pliability when the new assistant secretary for Near East affairs, William M. Rountree, took exception to the pro-Nasser thrust of a statement he had prepared for the Senate Foreign Relations Committee. "Mr. Rountree pointed out that the usefulness of the American Friends of the Middle East . . . might be greatly impaired . . . if Ambassador Minor took a position of greater partisanship for President Nasser than we considered wise," the official minutes of the conversation recorded. "Minor acknowledged the validity of this point and indicated that he would make an effort to amend or modify his remarks."[17]

The changes to the leadership, structure, and location of AFME were accompanied by a subtle but definite shift in the organization's program. While continuing to engage in some cultural exchange activities— indeed, the spring of 1959 saw the introduction of Operation Insight, an "experiment in citizen democracy" involving a regular group tour of Arab countries by thirty or so American civic leaders—the organization increasingly emphasized what its annual reports referred to as "Technical Services," meaning the placement of Middle Eastern students at US universities and industrial training in the region itself. This new emphasis reflected a growing concern that the lack of a modern economic base in much of the Arab world was rendering student exchange programs useless, if not actually harmful, as they had the unintended effect of creating a pool of "over-educated and under-employed Middle Easterners," a situation ripe for exploitation by the communists. After discussions with H. Ben Smith of "the Foundation," AFME turned to Transworld Management Corporation (Tramancor), a consulting firm based in Long Beach, California, with extensive contacts in the Middle East (among them Sheikh Muhammad bin Laden of Saudi Arabia, father of Osama, whom Tramancor president William T. Dodson personally represented in the United States). Having completed a successful pilot scheme in Iran, AFME-Tramancor mounted a series of similar technical projects in Egypt, Jordan, Libya, and Afghanistan. The organization was especially proud of its part in training the Egyptian engineers who had taken over the management of the Suez Canal, some of whom were flown to Panama—the nearest US equivalent of the French-constructed waterway—for the purpose.[18]

This is not to say that AFME had abandoned its pro-Arab and anti-Zionist advocacy altogether, as was shown by its choice of Elmo Hutchison, friend of Bill Eddy and critic of Israel, to succeed CIA officer Mather Eliot in the role of Middle East director. Having discussed with Eddy "the need [for] a riot squad to shoot holes in Israeli and Zionist claims," in August 1956 the boisterous Hutchison set up shop in Cairo, rapidly earning considerable goodwill among Arab nationalists, including Nasser himself. Correspondingly unpopular with American Zionists, his reputation hit rock bottom in 1962, when, during a press conference, he declared that "the Israel of Ben-Gurion, the belligerent army of world Zionism, is not here to stay." Meanwhile, such luminaries as Elmer Berger and Edward Elson kept up an intermittent fire on Israel supporters in the United States, earning in return denunciations in Zionist organs such as the *Near East Report*. These did not deter the rabbi and the minister from still performing the occasional discreet service for the government when the anti-Zionist cause demanded it. When in February 1957 Secretary Dulles asked his pastor to provide "some pulpit support on Sunday" for the administration's latest Middle East initiative, which had attracted criticism "from the Jewish population," Elson "said he was preaching on an Old Testament subject and he thought he could do something about it." Six years later, Berger was on hand to offer J. William Fulbright his expertise about Israeli-financed lobbying efforts in the United States when the Arkansas senator chaired a Senate Foreign Relations Committee inquiry into foreign agent registration in the United States.[19]

Still, as even the *Near East Report* was prepared to admit, AFME's main focus had "veered away from explosive and controversial centers to distant, peripheral and picturesque oases." The main emphasis was no longer on promoting Arabism and anti-Zionism to American audiences; now the organization's chief objectives were development and technical training in the Middle East itself—in other words, providing local support to the US government's developing global strategy of winning the Cold War through modernization. AFME was effectively retiring from the domestic fray, surrendering American public opinion to the emergent "Israel Lobby."[20]

The battle was over; Kim Roosevelt's Arabist, anti-Zionist network had lost.

IN DECEMBER 1958, AFME DRAFTED a pamphlet, *Story of a Purpose*, which eloquently articulated the group's founding values: "sympathy toward Arab nationalism" and the "drive toward Arab unity," rejection of "the last vestiges of colonialism and imperialism," and a belief that "the Palestine Question is the very heart of the Middle Eastern problem," requiring a US policy "of friendly and sympathetic impartiality." Above all, *Story of a Purpose* portrayed AFME as a "people-to-people operation," an attempt to give organizational form to a tradition of personal interaction between Americans and Arabs based on tolerance, understanding, and "an enduring mutuality of interest" that was "apart from considerations of government." The pamphlet was quite firm on this point: "The foundations for such a policy were carefully laid by a century and a half of private American endeavor in this part of the world." Far from building on this tradition, US government intervention in the Arab world over the past decade had, if anything, eroded it: "Grants of money have not concealed our failure to act, person-to-person, by the American ideals of the past. . . . We have felt, indeed, that the great failure of the West in the Middle East in the last decade has stemmed from substitution of elements of power, such as pressures, pacts, aid programs and doctrines, for the simple element of human understanding."[21]

What *Story of a Purpose* failed to mention was another aspect of the US government's new involvement in the Arab world: government officers' growing use of the earlier tradition of private, personal interaction as an instrument of official policy. One example was the Eisenhower administration's interest in harnessing the power of religious faith to the US Cold War effort in the Middle East, especially after 1956, when Nasser lost his status as the United States' most favored Arab head of state to King Saud, Ike's personal candidate for the role of Muslim leader. In the spring of 1957, an Operations Coordinating Board working group that included the Iran expert and CIA part-timer Donald Wilber compiled an inventory of US government and private groups with links to Islamic organizations "as an aspect of overseas operations." The working group's report recommended increasing government support for private organizations "promoting Muslim-Christian cooperation" and "the community of ideas which Islam and Islamic countries share with the U.S." There were echoes here of the AFME circle's hopes for an interfaith alliance against godless communism, but the exercise was geared less to mutual theological exchange than political warfare, making it more reminiscent of much earlier, British efforts to mobilize Islamist groups against the secular Arab left.[22]

Another, even more blatant example of the Cold War weaponization of the US missionary tradition involved the American University of Beirut. In the fall of 1956, officials in Washington grew concerned that the presidency of AUB—"an important instrument for the advancement of American interests and influence in the Middle East"—had remained unfilled since the death of Stephen Penrose a few year earlier. Participating in discussions about possible successors to Penrose were his fellow OSS Arabist Harold Hoskins, both Dulles brothers, and the pro-Western Lebanese foreign minister Charles Malik. One suggestion given serious consideration as in "the interest of the free world" was that Malik be appointed to serve as a "front man in Lebanon and in the U.S." while an American vice president "handle the University administration." It is difficult to imagine this Machiavellian idea meeting with the approval of the AUB founder, the sternly moralistic New England missionary Daniel Bliss.[23]

The irony is that, with its concealed funding by the CIA, the American Friends of the Middle East itself served as yet another example of this colonization of the private sphere by the official. At first, "the dual nature and operation of the organization," as Garland Hopkins put it, operated successfully, AFME's government and nongovernment elements working together harmoniously, united by shared values and aims. Gradually, however, as Eisenhower administration policy diverged from the Arabist, anti-Zionist agenda of Kim Roosevelt's state-private network, the duality became problematic. It was other anti-Zionists and Arabists who first noticed that there were something odd about the organization, an artificiality about its actions and statements that suggested it must be operating under some hidden constraints. Eventually, in a development similar to events in several CIA front groups on the Non-Communist Left, AFME's covert patrons in government abandoned the pretense of consensus and asserted their control of the purse strings, dictating changes in the organization's policy and leadership. From being a state-private alliance, AFME became, in Hopkins's phrase, a vehicle primarily for the CIA's purposes.

Kim Roosevelt had thrown American Arabism a lifeline in the shape of secret CIA subsidies to AFME, but at the same time he had fatally corrupted it.

EIGHTEEN

Archie's Turn: Syria, 1956

REINING IN NASSER'S US SUPPORTERS in the American Friends of the Middle East was part of the Eisenhower administration's response to the nationalization of the Suez Canal, but a more pressing concern was what to do about the man himself. The answer came in the form of a top-secret planning document drafted after a series of emergency meetings between State Department, Pentagon, and CIA officials (the latter including Allen Dulles, Kim Roosevelt, and Miles Copeland) at John Foster Dulles's Georgetown home. Authored on August 4, 1956, by Dulles's special assistant Francis Russell (ironically, the chief US negotiator in the earlier ALPHA peace talks), "U.S. Policies Toward Nasser" proposed various policies "designed to reduce and, if possible, eliminate Nasser as a force in the Middle East and Africa." These included discussion with the United Kingdom of "covert steps which might result in Nasser's replacement by a regime disposed to cooperate with the West"; the use of "all suitable opportunities, overt and covert, to plant among other Arab countries suspicions and fears of the Egyptians," the aim being to produce an anti-Nasser alignment "between King Saud and the Hashemite Houses of Iraq and Jordan"; and, finally, preparation for "drastic steps to bring about a moderate government in Syria" (the Syrians now being perceived as Nasserite fellow-travelers). To sum up the new strategy presented in Russell's paper, the United States was effectively changing sides in the so-called Arab Cold War, from supporting the nationalist Young Effendis to backing the old, colonial-era governing classes.[1]

This program was at once reactionary and extraordinarily ambitious in scope, requiring all the covert expertise at the US government's disposal. To help carry it through, Washington called up one of the CIA's most experienced Arabists.

"AS YOU KNOW, ARCHIE, WE'RE much concerned about what's going on in Syria—especially the way the Communists and nationalists appear to be ganging up for some kind of action there," said Foster Dulles. The secretary of state had summoned the young CIA officer to his home and was seated behind the piles of paper that covered his desk, speaking in his customarily diffident manner. "I'd like you to fly out to Damascus right away, talk to our ambassador, and see . . . what can be done about it."[2]

In the years since his first Middle Eastern postings, Archie Roosevelt had strayed from the road to Samarkand—his quest for knowledge and understanding of the Arab and Muslim worlds. His spell with the Voice of America had been followed in 1951 by a posting as CIA station chief in Istanbul and then, when his tour of Turkey ended in 1953, a desk job back in Washington, serving as a branch chief and chief of operations in the Agency's Soviet division. His new life had its consolations, among them his young Lebanese American bride Selwa ("Lucky"), who had excelled in the role of CIA wife in Istanbul, performing the diplomatic duties required by Archie's State Department cover with great aplomb. Now, back in the United States, she was charming her initially skeptical Roosevelt in-laws while forging a promising career in her own right as a Washington journalist. Still, Archie missed the Middle East and what he regarded as the core mission of the CIA officer: intelligence gathering in the field. Unlike his high-flying cousin Kim, he was no great player of the Washington game.[3]

In early 1956, with the United States suffering one setback after another in his old stamping ground, Archie was gradually shifted back into

Middle East affairs. In April, after the collapse of ALPHA, he became deputy chief of the CIA's Near East Division, assisting first Roger Goiran, then Goiran's successor as division chief, the Yale-educated lawyer Norman S. Paul, in implementing the new OMEGA program. With conditions in Syria deteriorating especially fast—the Ba'ath-dominated government hosted a visit from the Soviet foreign minister in June and then recognized communist China—Archie acquired specific responsibility for WAKEFUL, the operation intended to bring about regime change in Damascus, becoming, as he put it later, the Agency's "point man on Syria." Then came the summons to Georgetown and the secretary of state's instructions to go to the Levant.[4]

Archie, or "FELS," to give him his CIA code name, arrived in Beirut on July 1, accompanied by "NEARMAN," the CIA's assistant deputy director and the Dulles brothers' "Mr. Middle East," Kim Roosevelt. The Lebanese capital was to be the cousins' staging post for a three-week tour of the surrounding region, during which they would assess the prospects for covert action in Syria and try to mobilize Arab opposition to Nasser. The twelve years that had elapsed since the Roosevelts first traveled the Middle East together had not diminished the familial resemblance between them. Both were now slightly thicker around the waist, but the small frames, high foreheads, and scholarly mien were the same, lending them the appearance of "bespectacled angle-worms," as Joe Alsop put it. That said, the Roosevelts had acquired different travel habits, as observed by Allen Dulles's troubleshooter Wilbur "Bill" Eveland, who greeted them shortly after they arrived in Beirut. "A late sleeper, Kim didn't come fully alive until after noon; then he was charged up to continue on way past midnight and after dinner was the best time to speak seriously with him," Eveland wrote later. "Archie followed the sunrise with breakfast and was at his best during the day; even formal dinners found him dozing and a nodding head often threatened to collide with his soup."[5]

With Eveland preceding them by a day so as not to arouse Syrian suspicion, the Roosevelts drove across the mountains to Damascus. After announcing themselves at the American embassy—happily, Archie knew Jimmy Moose from his days in Baghdad, and the ambassador, a long-time foe of Nasserism, proved highly receptive to the CIA men's proposals for covert action on his turf—Archie went to visit the Syrian army's chief of staff, Shawkat Shuqayr. The junior of the Roosevelt cousins had high hopes for this meeting: Shuqayr was a distant cousin of Lucky's and a prominent member of the nationalist officer class that was now playing such an important role in Syrian politics. In the flesh, however, Shuqayr proved disappointing: a grey bureaucrat who parroted the standard Nasserite line. He was, in any case, toppled from his command position a matter of days later.[6]

Far more promising was another contact arranged by Bill Eveland. Mikhail Ilyan, a wealthy Christian landowner from Aleppo and powerful conservative politician, had already spent a large amount of his own money plotting against the government of the Damascene Shukri al-Quwatli (earlier the victim of Husni Za'im's coup plot). As such, he seemed to fit well with the US strategy of encouraging the internal Syrian right to arrest the country's leftward drift, as opposed to the British and Iraqi strategy of external intervention. For his part, Ilyan was keen to meet the Roosevelts, perhaps partly because he was under the impression that they were sons of FDR. Eveland did not disabuse him of this notion. Instead, he suggested a meeting with Archie in Ilyan's suite at the New Omayad Hotel.[7]

As Ilyan sat spinning his worry beads, Archie got quickly to the point. What would Syrian conservatives need to prevent the communists and their sympathizers taking over the country? he asked in Arabic. Ilyan responded, so Eveland recalled later, "by ticking off names and places: the radio stations in Damascus and Aleppo; a few key senior officers; and enough money to buy newspapers now in Egyptian and Saudi hands." Eveland was agog—"Ilyan was talking about nothing short of a coup d'état"—but Archie appeared unfazed. "Could these things, he asked Ilyan, be done with U.S. money and assets alone, with no other Western or Near Eastern country involved?" "Without question," Ilyan answered. Apparently satisfied with what he heard, Archie departed soon afterward, leaving Eveland "with a Syrian who was smiling like the cat who'd just swallowed the canary."[8]

After further excursions to Jordan and Saudi Arabia to drum up opposition to Nasser, the Roosevelt cousins returned to Washington, where they reported their confidence in the ability of Syrian conservatives—with appropriate assistance from the United States—to prevent the satellization of their country. With the secretary of state indicating presidential approval, Kim directed Eveland to obtain from Ilyan a precise estimate of the amount of US assistance he would require and a time frame for the action he was proposing. The sum named was half a million Syrian pounds, and August 31 was set as the date on which right-wing elements would rally against the current government. Archie was back in the game.[9]

AT FIRST GLANCE, ARCHIE ROOSEVELT'S leading role in a coup operation against an Arab nationalist government appears even more puzzling that his cousin Kim's leadership of the plot to remove the Iranian Mohammed Mosaddeq in 1953. During World War II, Archie had championed the cause of Arab nationalism against European imperialism. Later, he came to share his cousin Kim's enthusiasm for Gamal Nasser. "Here was a man we could work with," he concluded after meeting the Egyptian in 1953. "This might be the leader who could unite the Arab world in seeking . . . solutions for the area's problems." Archie was therefore dubious about John Foster Dulles's march toward confrontation with the Egyptian and about the underlying assumption that pan-Arabism was dangerously susceptible to communism. The Soviets might have tried "to exploit the forces unleashed by Nasser," he believed, "but they never gained control of them." Writing his memoirs after his retirement, Archie even sounded skeptical about the perceived threat of communist takeover of Syria in 1956: yes, there was a leftist front of Arab nationalists and "a small contingent of true Marxists including the minuscule Communist party, abetted by the Soviets," but, in truth, "the aims of Communists and nationalists were diametrically opposed."[10]

Then there was Archie's basic conservatism as a spy, his preference for intelligence gathering over political machinations. Interviewed many years later, Lucky Roosevelt recalled how during his spell as station chief in Turkey, a role that involved oversight of covert operations in the Balkans, her husband became "profoundly upset" about infiltration missions the Agency was running behind the Iron Curtain. "He believed in diligent intelligence work, carefully prepared," she remembered. Instead, the CIA was dropping émigré operatives with almost no training into enemy territory, where they were rounded up and never heard from again. Archie complained vociferously to headquarters (he could not have known at the time that many of the operations had probably been compromised by the British double agent Kim Philby). Later,

Archie would also express objections to the Agency mounting "giant paramilitary operations in disputed parts of the Third World," such as the 1961 invasion of Cuba at the Bay of Pigs, echoing Kim Roosevelt's criticisms of the 1954 action in Guatemala. "Local forces essentially govern these nations' own political systems," he wrote, "and we can influence the course of events only when we give our support to a force strong enough to prevail." Although he went on to mention TP-AJAX as an example of an operation that successfully harnessed such forces, privately Archie voiced reservations about cousin Kim's Iranian adventure. "I don't think he said or did anything to embarrass or undermine Kermit at the time," recollected Lucky, "but he told me he thought it was a big mistake." Archie's memoirs even contain an implied dig at Kim and Miles's crypto-diplomatic efforts to resolve the Arab-Israeli dispute. "Intelligence officers have an obligation to provide an understanding of the constantly changing nature of the problem," Archie admonished. "The diplomats must take it from there."[11]

How, then, to explain Archie's command of the 1956 operation to topple the Syrian government, a plan that, in the words of British writer Tom Bower, "reeked of nineteenth-century manipulation"? Scattered clues suggest some possible answers. To begin with, despite his protests about amateurish agent drops in the Balkans, the young CIA officer did not object to covert operations per se. Indeed, he was an enthusiastic exponent of another effort to penetrate the Iron Curtain and roll back communism: appealing to the anti-Russian sentiment of Muslims and other minority groups on the southern flank of the Soviet Union, the communist "underbelly." According to Miles Copeland, while Archie was based in Lebanon during the late 1940s, he ran operations into Soviet Azerbaijan, Armenia, and Georgia, including a personal tour of the region on foot and horseback. This claim has some plausibility in light of Archie's subsequent assignments to the Voice of America, Turkey, and the CIA's Soviet division. There is also evidence that Archie worked with the American Committee for Liberation (AMCOMLIB), a CIA front organization with the mission of organizing Soviet-bloc émigrés, including Turkic Muslims, into a secret force capable of spearheading the liberation of their homelands. These various activities echoed the prediction that Archie had made when he was serving during World War II in North Africa that Islam would be a force to reckon with in the postwar world—except that now, in the midst of the Cold War, Archie was turning his sympathetic interest in Muslims to political warfare purposes. Much later, after the Cold War was over, CIA covert operations involving anti-Soviet Islamists would return to haunt the United States in Afghanistan and elsewhere, but Archie, a dedicated anticommunist since his youth, appears not to have foreseen such blowback.[12]

Not only was Archie a dedicated Cold Warrior, ready to resort to anticommunist measures that, in retrospect, seem ill-advised; he was also a loyal public servant, disinclined to question direct orders from the secretary of state. Writing in his memoirs, he explained the principles that guided him as an intelligence officer. A "natural curiosity to seek out the ways of the many tribes of mankind" and an "intimate understanding" of different cultures: these were fine qualities in themselves and also prerequisites for intelligence work, he explained. But the spy must also "believe in his own society, his country, and its form of government." If he did not, he risked the cynicism of characters in the novels of John Le Carré, "who find their side no less amoral than the other" and end by becoming traitors to their country. To avoid this trap, the intelligence officer "must not only know whose side he is on, but have a deep conviction that it is the right one"—even if that meant, as in the Arabist Archie's case, having to subordinate his sympathy for Arab nationalism to his patriotic duty to serve his government.[13]

The apparent contradiction between Archie's Arabism on the one hand and his actions in the summer of 1956 on the other could then be explained by his Cold War activism and his patriotism. To these might be added other motives evident earlier in his career—a tendency to defer to the British in their Middle Eastern "Covert Empire" and the Rooseveltian appetite for adventure in the spyscape of the Arab world—as well as, possibly, some personal, psychological considerations. After several years of watching cousin Kim carry all before him in Washington while he himself performed honorable but less spectacular service at the division level or in the field, Archie was enjoying being back at the center of things. In his memoirs, he wrote with obvious relish of frequent meetings in 1956 with his old family friend, CIA director Allen Dulles, and listening as "Allen" spoke on the telephone with "Foster" or the president. Kim largely owed his legendary reputation to his success in Iran; now, perhaps, Syria offered the other Roosevelt Arabist a similar shot at fame: the chance to be able to tell future generations the story of his own Middle Eastern coup.[14]

UNFORTUNATELY FOR ARCHIE, KIM HAD used up the cousins' share of luck in 1953. A combination of adverse factors—Arab resistance, British duplicity, and the contradictions inherent in the American strategy itself—would frustrate not only the CIA's plans for a coup in Syria but also the other objectives outlined in Francis Russell's crucial paper of August 4, 1956: the forging of an Arab front against revolutionary Egypt and the elimination of Nasser as a force in Middle Eastern politics.

At first, the prospects for one of these goals—aligning the Hashemite and Saudi monarchies against Nasser—seemed quite good. In Hashemite Jordan, the CIA had succeeded in establishing a channel to the twenty-one-year-old King Hussein through a young intelligence officer, John Dayton, in the tiny station in Amman. Hussein had something of a playboy reputation, and Dayton was, according to British journalist Richard Beeston, "a swinger" with "an extremely pretty young Southern wife who, envious cynics said, was chosen to catch the eye of the king." After years of dependence on the British, the Hashemite throne lacked an independent intelligence service, so Dayton arranged for a monthly payment of $5,000 Jordanian dinars (about $15,000) to enable Hussein to run a small spy ring out of his palace, the money arriving on the royal desk in a brown manila envelope. Awakened to the benefits of American patronage, Hussein asked to see Bill Eveland when the king visited Beirut to attend a sports car rally, and intimated that he would welcome the United States taking over responsibility from the United Kingdom as Jordan's main source of Western support. Although Kim Roosevelt headed off further contact between Eveland and Hussein, he did give his blessing to the monthly CIA subsidies, which acquired the code name NO-BEEF (NO was the country prefix for Jordan). Even allowing for retrospective exaggeration, it is clear that Archie was delighted with the young monarch ("NORMAN") when he first met him during his July 1956 tour of the region, writing later that Hussein impressed him as "the finest, most truly motivated leader of the Arab world." Here at last, it seemed, was a possible candidate besides Nasser for the role of pan-Arab "necessary leader."[15]

If the signs in Jordan were surprisingly encouraging, in Saudi Arabia, supposedly the lynchpin of the new US strategy in the Arab Cold War, the picture was less bright. As Archie explained in his memoirs, King Ibn Saud's successor, his son Saud, "had taken the easy road of collaboration with Nasser in his attacks on the West." Not only that,

compared to his virile warrior father, Saud was "weak—physically, men-
tally, and morally"—or so Archie decided after meeting him during his
July 1956 tour. In an effort to disrupt the burgeoning Egyptian-Saudi
collaboration (and smuggle some liquor to an old friend, US ambassador George Wadsworth), Archie made several return trips to Saudi
Arabia later in the year, culminating in another audience with Saud in
his gaudy, Western-style palace in Riyadh. (Archie, ever the romantic
Arabist, was dismayed by signs of the creeping Americanization of Arabian culture.) The audience was "an unpleasant affair." When Archie
handed Saud a list of American complaints about Saudi complicity in
Nasser's anti-Western propaganda campaign, the king "reacted with
some anger, reading a few of the items with a sarcastic comment." Having accomplished nothing "except arousing royal rage," Archie departed
empty-handed. It seems that cousin Kim also tried reasoning personally
with King Saud during a separate trip in late summer 1956, although the
outcome of his visits to Riyadh is less clear.[16]

Better documented is another secret US mission to Saudi Arabia
featuring two familiar faces: Bill Eveland and Robert Anderson, the
Texan leader of the unsuccessful GAMMA peace talks in Cairo. The aims
of this exercise, which seems to have first been suggested to President
Eisenhower by oil executive Howard Page, then operationalized by
Kim Roosevelt, were laid out in a recently declassified CIA cable sent
to Eveland in Rome on August 22, 1956. Anderson, representing his
friend the president, was to meet with King Saud and respectfully explain to him why Saudi interests were not served by his present policy of cooperation with Nasser. The Egyptian leader's recent actions
and rhetoric had revealed his "ambition to dominate the Muslim world
from Morocco to Indonesia"; his "growing capability to create dis-
order," currently targeted at the West, could just as easily be turned
against rival Arab governments; and it was "Nasser's picture, not
Saud's," that was being waved at anti-Western demonstrations around
the Arab world. If this appeal to Saud's ego did not work, Anderson
was to resort to an implied threat, telling the king that the regional
instability caused by Nasser's antics, especially his seizure of the Suez
Canal, was causing the Western powers to look to energy sources other
than Arab oil, including a "stepped-up American effort on [the] scale of
the Manhattan project" to increase the "industrial use of atomic energy."
This last assertion, which was untrue, echoed ongoing discussions in

the Eisenhower administration about possible methods of deliberately deceiving Middle Eastern oil producers as to the true extent of Western dependence on the area. It also lends some credence to the later claim by Miles Copeland that the Middle East Policy Planning Group considered launching an energy deception program, Operation Rainbow, involving the construction of a dummy experimental facility somewhere in the American West, "complete with klieg lights and guard dogs in the manner of one of those plants you see in James Bond movies." As often was the case with Copeland anecdotes, a substratum of truth lay underneath the fanciful detail.[17]

The ruse did not work. The Anderson mission arrived in Dhahran on August 23 and then moved to the neon-lit royal palace in Riyadh for a series of audiences with Saud and his brother, Prince Faisal. When it became obvious that the Saudis were not ready to risk antagonizing Arab opinion by coming out against Nasser, Anderson played the nuclear energy card. The Saudi response came early the following morning in a handwritten note from Saud, which Bill Eveland translated from the Arabic for the benefit of the rest of the party. "Prince Faisal, it appeared, had done considerable reading on the subject of nuclear energy and rejected as impossible Anderson's assertions that we could provide Western Europe an alternative to petroleum." Abruptly terminated, the mission left Riyadh the same morning with nothing to show for its efforts. As the plane climbed through the Arabian sky, Eveland reflected uncomfortably on how "these simple people of the desert had caught us bluffing."[18]

If the effort to rally the region's monarchs against Nasser was faltering in Saudi Arabia, so too were the plans for regime change in Syria. Part of the problem was offstage Iraqi and British plotting, which constantly threatened to undo the American plan for engineering a coup from within Syria. The Anglo-Iraqi candidate to take over from Quwatli was the exiled former military dictator Adib Shishakli, who announced his interest in a return to power by appearing in Beirut in July. American observers were unnerved by this development—in their view, Shishakli was a "political opportunist" and "heavy drinker" who had long outlived his usefulness—and were therefore relieved when he seemed to have second thoughts, returning to Europe with a share of the Iraqi funds intended to finance the coup. This left the field open to the United States' preferred candidate, Mikhail Ilyan, but the Americans' problems were not over yet. Ilyan was himself closely associated with Iraq's ruling Hashemite family and in Iraqi pay. Moreover, able and energetic though Ilyan was, his Christianity counted heavily against him in a majority Muslim society. This was all the more unfortunate because, much like the Soviet émigré population the CIA was trying to organize through AMCOMLIB, the exile Syrian community in Beirut was seething with internal divisions and feuds, making any sort of concerted planning there difficult if not impossible.[19]

Meanwhile, conditions in Syria itself were growing steadily less favorable to American covert action. The nationalization of the Suez Canal had produced a surge of pro-Nasser sentiment among ordinary Syrians, and nationalist, anti-Western elements were consolidating their control over the government. Particularly worrisome from an American point of view was the growing power of the chief of the Syrian security service, 'Abd al-Hamid Sarraj. A cool, reserved young man with a reputation as "something of a lone wolf," Sarraj had first been taken up as a junior army officer by his fellow Kurd Husni Za'im, who after the 1949 coup placed him in Syrian military intelligence. Having survived the many changes of government of the early 1950s, partly by dint of accepting an appointment as assistant military attaché in Paris, Sarraj was appointed head of the Deuxième Bureau in March 1955 by Lucky Roosevelt's cousin Shawkat Shuqayr. He had since distinguished himself as a skillful detector of Western plots and, in the words of the US embassy in Damascus, was the "foremost obstacle to efforts [to] diminish [the] influence of pro-Nasser and pro-Soviet groups in Syria."[20]

Sadly for Archie Roosevelt, US assets in Syria were no match for Sarraj. Lodged in a stuffy, windowless office in the embassy, the Damascus CIA station was understaffed—Bill Eveland counted only five officers, in contrast with the "empire" Kim Roosevelt had built up in Cairo behind Nasser—and low in morale. Not even the occasional visit by Miles Copeland—who attempted to revive his old contacts in the Syrian army and once, reportedly, smuggled a local informant out of the country in the trunk of a CIA car—could lift the gathering gloom. Making Archie's job in Syria all the more difficult was the laxness of security surrounding WAKEFUL's planning in Beirut. The Lebanese capital happened to be the informal headquarters of the Western press corps in the Levant, and the appearance there in July 1956 of both Roosevelt cousins—not one but two grandsons of TR—stirred so much excitement that reports of it made their way into the pages of the *New York Times*. The CIA Beirut station chief, the Lebanese American Ghosn Zogby, even threw a cocktail party for the Roosevelts attended by American reporters, exasperating Bill Eveland, who lived in fear of being exposed as a CIA contract employee. "When the day of your coup comes, are you going to sell tickets?" the Egyptian ambassador to Lebanon mischievously asked a passing Miles Copeland.[21]

With the planning talks beset by problems, the plotters moved back the date of the projected coup, from August 31 to October 25. In September, Eveland collected from the CIA station in Beirut the half million Syrian pounds he had promised Ilyan and set out for Damascus with the cash stuffed in a suitcase in the trunk of his car. Rendezvousing with the Syrian in the lobby of the New Omayad, Eveland was briefed about the latest coup plans. Conservative colonels in the Syrian army, Ilyan explained, were to seize control of Damascus and other major cities, while armored units sealed the borders with Jordan, Iraq, and Lebanon; once the country had been brought under complete control, the army would hand power to a civilian government headed by Ilyan himself. (This explanation omitted several key details of the plot that smelled of Anglo-Iraqi collusion, including coordinated tribal uprisings in southern and western Syria, and incursions by paramilitary forces of Iraqi-armed exiles, one of which would enter Damascus disguised in police uniforms and assassinate key left-wing officers and politicians.) After a nerve-wracking day's wait, Eveland met Ilyan again at a deserted French casino in the mountains above Damascus and handed over the money. Now there was nothing left for him to do but return to Beirut and cool his heels.[22]

This left a third challenge for Washington's covert Cold Warriors: what to do about Nasser? As usual, American attitudes toward the Egyptian president were fundamentally ambivalent. Desirous though Foster Dulles was of getting rid of Nasser, he was reluctant to support the extreme solutions being proposed by the British, which included ever more elaborate MI6 assassination plots, such as a scheme to inject poison into his chocolates. Dulles feared that such action would further discredit the Western powers in the Middle East and in other Third World theaters of the Cold War, and, in any case, President Eisenhower himself had indicated his disapproval.[23]

In an effort to head off the British, the secretary of state once again turned to the crypto-diplomats of the CIA. Arriving in London in late

August 1956 on the first leg of a world tour of CIA stations, Allen Dulles tried but failed to damp down British enthusiasm, reporting home that "'they' were more determined than ever to proceed along a certain line." The following month, Miles Copeland and James Eichelberger were enlisted in another initiative of the secretary's, the Suez Canal Users' Association (SCUA), a proposal to place control of the contested waterway in the hands of an international body representing the Western powers that made most use of it. Scornfully rejected by Nasser, who pointed out that, contrary to European predictions, Egyptian engineers were doing a perfectly good job of operating the canal on their own, SCUA nonetheless afforded Miles and Eich an amusing diversion and, as it would turn out later, a promising new career opportunity. More importantly, the CIA Arabists were, even at this late stage of the crisis in Egyptian relations with the West, keeping open their own channels to Nasser's circle, with Kim Roosevelt meeting 'Ali Sabri and Muhammad Haikal in New York to discuss the possibility of a negotiated settlement to the Suez dispute. Might Kim still work the magic he had performed securing the Anglo-Egyptian agreement of 1954?[24]

Even if Nasser had been amenable, too many factors were working against such an outcome, including constant lobbying for more drastic measures by the British. While Prime Minister Eden and Foreign Secretary Lloyd dripped anticommunist words into the ear of Foster Dulles, MI6 Middle East chief George Young harangued his CIA colleagues about their failure to support London's plans for "bashing the Gyppos," warning Chester Cooper at a Mayfair cocktail party, "Your friends at home had better come up with something constructive pretty soon." Such pressure could also take on more subtle forms. American correspondents in the Middle East often relied heavily on British sources, and there were hints that Whitehall was deliberately using these channels to shape the already pro-Israel US media's coverage of the Suez dispute. These included a growing American tendency to imitate the British practice of likening the Egyptian president to Adolf Hitler, despite the numerous differences between the two men noted in a State Department report on the subject, such as the fact that, whereas "Hitler was noted for ranting and raging at visitors, Nasser tends to a relaxed and rational attitude." With the American Friends of the Middle East ordered to stand down from their domestic anti-Zionist campaigning in the summer of 1956, the Israeli publicity or *hasbara* effort in the United States, now largely unopposed, kicked up a gear, swaying American public opinion further against Nasser. Even within the CIA itself, support was draining away from the Arabists. "James Angleton, who wanted to make use of Israel, was exerting more influence than Kermit Roosevelt," Charles "Chip" Bohlen, US ambassador to the Soviet Union, informed his Egyptian counterpart in Washington, Ambassador Hussein. An acquaintance of Miles Copeland gloatingly told him, "I think we've finally got you Nasser lovers on the run."[25]

Nowhere were these contradictions more obvious than in Operation MASK, a joint Anglo-American program "to bring about by peaceful methods President Nasser's removal as quickly as possible" (as State Department NEA chief William Rountree described it). Originally proposed on September 20, 1956, when Foster Dulles was dining in London with Eden, MASK was developed in early October during discussions in Washington between a British delegation that included George Young and an American team made up of State Department Middle East hands and two unidentified CIA representatives, one of whom was almost certainly Kim Roosevelt and the other most likely Miles Copeland. Miles wrote later of participating in Anglo-American talks about Nasser's removal shortly before the Anglo-French attack on Suez—and of his amused surprise when the British produced a supposedly top-secret diagram of the Egyptian intelligence service that he recognized as his own handiwork from his earlier assignment to Cairo as a Booz-Allen executive.[26]

The different perspectives represented in the US-UK Working Group on Egypt were evident from the first. While the British officials urged the adoption of aggressive economic, political, and psychological measures "to 'disembarrass' ourselves of Nasser," the Americans insisted on a more cautious approach, cavilling in particular at the suggestion that they agree to a date for the Egyptian leader's ouster. Although the Working Group did produce a joint report on October 3, Foster Dulles, who had just heard his president repeat his disapproval of operations targeting Nasser personally, was reluctant to sign off on it. Objecting especially to the first two paragraphs about Nasser, which baldly stated "the necessity for U.S.-U.K. collaboration to eliminate the threat he poses," Dulles recalled that it "was unusual to seek written agreement at the top political level to operations of this kind"; normally, "a general oral understanding" was sufficient. Clearly, the Americans were suspicious of British intentions; a later CIA report noted of this period that "estrangement" between the two sides "was becoming dangerously acute." The matter of the MASK report was still not resolved at the end of October, when, as William Rountree put it in a memorandum to Dulles, it was rendered "academic" by "current developments."[27]

Rountree was referring to the war in Egypt that had broken out on October 29, leading to the so-called Suez Crisis. Conceived in the weeks following Nasser's nationalization of the Suez Canal, the Tripartite Aggression, as it was known in the Arab world, involved an unlikely secret collusion between Britain, France, and Israel. The plan was for the Israelis to attack Egypt in the Sinai and march on the Canal Zone; the two European powers would then intervene on the pretext of restoring peace and reassert their control of the canal, in the process toppling Nasser. Militarily, the operation went as planned, with the Egyptian army and air force rapidly succumbing to vastly superior forces. Politically, however, the Tripartite Aggression was a disaster for the invaders, especially the French and British, who in the face of furious American condemnation were humiliatingly forced to accept a UN ceasefire on November 7. Rather than being knocked from his perch, Nasser skillfully exploited the opportunity to pose as the hero of the Arab world and consolidate his power base, both domestically and regionally.

There were several reasons why Washington objected so strongly to the Suez Crisis: its potentially calamitous consequences for the Western position in the Middle East and the rest of the Third World; the fact that it distracted international attention from the Soviets' brutal suppression of the Hungarian uprising, which was unfolding at exactly the same time; and its no less unfortunate timing on the eve of a US presidential election. Perhaps the most deeply felt American grievance, though, was the element of deception involved. The British had been secretly planning this operation for weeks while talking to their American cousins about other measures for dealing with Nasser. So much, then, for the Special Relationship.

In fact, individual British officials, apparently torn between the demands of loyalty to their government and personal friendship, had hinted to their American counterparts that a major operation was in the works. "I'm going to have to get in my uniform," MI6's John Bruce-Lockhart informed the CIA's Al Ulmer. "We can't let Suez go, you realise it's the lifeline of our Empire." During a tense family picnic, Patrick Dean, chair of the British working party on MASK, confided in Chester Cooper, "You and I are in for much trouble, and it won't be because of Hungary." Reporting to Foster Dulles during a meeting of the UN General Assembly in New York, Kim Roosevelt ran into an old Foreign Office friend. "Speaking with great feeling, he said . . . that the British and the French were about to do something extremely foolish," Kim wrote later. When the CIA officer repeated what he had just heard to the secretary of state in his suite at the Waldorf-Astoria, "adding that the Britisher's gloomy prognostication was amply supported by American intelligence reports," he was greeted with a surprising display of indifference. "Is that all?" Foster asked, looking out of the window. When Kim indicated it was, the secretary simply said, "Thank you."[28]

This anecdote, which Kim told to several interviewers, has a strongly self-exculpatory element to it, suggesting as it does that Foster Dulles received good intelligence from the CIA about British plans yet chose to ignore it. One of the interviewers noted that Kim appeared "mad" about Dulles's claim that Suez had taken him by complete surprise. Yet combined with the other evidence of British "chatter" prior to October 29, the story seems plausible enough and raises the question of why Dulles and other American officials put "the telescope to [their] blind eye," in Kim's words. One probable reason was that Washington calculated that Jordan was a more likely target of Israeli attack than Egypt, and evidence of Israeli mobilization was interpreted in that light. Another was that James Jesus Angleton, acting on assurances from the Israeli embassy in Washington, advised Allen Dulles that Israel's intentions were peaceful (prompting Deputy Director Robert Amory to utter the oft-quoted claim that Angleton was a "coopted Israeli agent"). A third possibility, which perhaps explains Kim's habit of heaping blame for all American setbacks in the region on Foster Dulles, was that the CIA's Middle East hands were by this point so preoccupied with covert action that they were neglecting their intelligence-gathering duties.[29]

This brings us, finally, to another, less-remarked reason for American anger about the Anglo-French-Israeli attack on Egypt: its effect on the situation in Syria. A few days earlier, on October 18, Bill Eveland had learned that the date of Mikhail Ilyan's coup was being moved back again, from October 25 to October 29, for reasons that were not entirely clear. Later, after it had turned out that this was the very same day as the Israeli invasion of Egypt, Eveland began to suspect that the British had "used the Iraqis to set this up," planning to exploit the confusion caused by the Suez Crisis to wrest control of Syria and "leaving the

United States and Ilyan as the scapegoats in the event the coup failed."
Whether or not this was the case—no such British operation material-
ized after the attack on Egypt—the consequences of the coincidence for
Archie Roosevelt's hopes of a second TP-AJAX were calamitous. Believing that he was being set up as a fall guy, Ilyan fled Syria and arrived
at Eveland's apartment in Beirut the following day, full of bitter recrimination. Meanwhile, the Syrian intelligence chief Sarraj, who had probably known of the plotting all along, began rounding up the conspirators
Ilyan had left behind. Watching from Washington as the operation un-
raveled, the Dulles brothers reluctantly decided to abandon Syria to its
fate, at least for the time being. Trying to make sense of the mess, Bill
Eveland could draw only one firm conclusion: "Archie Roosevelt knew
no more about staging coups than I did—nothing at all, that is to say."[30]

For the Anglophile and dedicated intelligence professional Archie,
it was a bitter pill to swallow; interviewed about Syria decades later, he
still had not forgiven the British for their perfidy. Still, the CIA Arabists were not done playing games yet, as events the following year
would prove.[31]

NINETEEN

Game On:
Jordan, Lebanon, Syria, 1957

ACCORDING TO OUTWARD APPEARANCES, THE Suez Crisis marked an abrupt end to British imperial pretensions in the Middle East. After a disgraced Anthony Eden departed from Downing Street in January 1957, his successor, Harold Macmillan, appeared to adopt a chastened approach to the region, enacting policies that more accurately reflected Britain's reduced circumstances in the post–World War II world. Meanwhile, the United States, whose refusal to support the Anglo-French-Israeli misadventure of the previous fall had earned considerable goodwill among Arabs, responded much as it had to Britain's withdrawal from Greece and Turkey ten years earlier, proclaiming in the same month as Eden's resignation the Eisenhower Doctrine, a new commitment to defending Middle Eastern states menaced by Soviet expansionism. The days of British empire and imperial-style adventurism were, it seemed, over at last.[1]

Or were they? Behind the scenes, American and British officials were behaving in ways that belied Suez's reputation as a watershed in Western relations with the Middle East, actually escalating their joint campaign against radical Arab nationalism, a force now grown more powerful thanks to the botched British attempt to dislodge Nasser. On the US side, Eisenhower quickly swallowed his personal anger with the British and even contemplated rebuilding their position in the region as part of a wider American strategy of supporting pro-Western, conservative Arab governments against nationalist revolutionaries. The Eisenhower Doctrine was, in this sense, a public declaration of the principles promulgated the previous year in the secret OMEGA project. The British, not surprisingly, played along with this policy, gently massaging US fears of communist subversion in the Middle East, a technique also employed by the conservative Arab regimes themselves. Harold Macmillan prided himself on his subtle handling of his trans-Atlantic cousins, discreetly nudging them away from their earlier, naïve anti-imperialism toward a more "realistic" understanding of their new responsibilities in the postcolonial era.[2]

Helping cement this quiet Anglo-American rapprochement were the secret services. In the immediate wake of Suez, hurt feelings on both sides had caused a temporary suspension of official contact between the CIA and MI6. The fiery George Young complained that, "When the moment came [the United States] was not prepared to lift a finger." "A.[llen Dulles] is suspicious of our cousins," a transcript of a conversation between the intelligence chief and his brother, the secretary of state, recorded. "If they want a thing, he thinks we should look at it hard." It was perhaps only to be expected, therefore, that the first attempt to reopen official channels—a goodwill mission by Kim Roosevelt to London very soon after the crisis—should have been unsuccessful, with Kim for once receiving a less than enthusiastic reception in Whitehall. When another CIA officer, the Grotonian quarterback Tracy Barnes, made the same trip in December 1956, however, the welcome was much warmer. Early in 1957, it was the British turn to try to thaw out relations, with the new chief of MI6, Dick White, traveling to Washington in order to meet his American counterpart. White, who shared Harold Macmillan's strong interest in cultivating the Americans, was delighted when Allen Dulles took him to his favorite Washington club, the Alibi. He was even more thrilled when Dulles played a practical joke on him, inviting him to sit in his plush office chair before flicking a hidden massage switch. Such pranks were, White felt sure, reserved only for family friends.[3]

The stage was set for a new surge of covert activism by the CIA Arabists. By now, the focus had shifted from Egypt, Kim Roosevelt having finally given up on his vision of promoting his friend Gamal Nasser as the leader of a modern, progressive, pro-American Middle East. Unlike the British, though, Kim appears not to have become obsessed with the idea of getting rid of Nasser. Admittedly, the evidence here is ambiguous: several sources, including the memoirs of Bill Eveland, attest to an intensification of the sort of anti-Nasser methods contemplated in the MASK talks of the previous fall, and it is clear that the British, despite Macmillan and Dick White supposedly curbing the more swashbuckling elements of MI6, in fact carried on plotting to assassinate the Egyptian leader. On balance, though, the evidence points toward CIA actions following a pattern similar to that of 1956; that is, the Agency Arabists played along with the extreme solutions proposed by the British but ultimately refused to pull the trigger. The denouement of Edward Sheehan's novel *Kingdom of Illusion* captures this fundamental ambivalence about as well as any existing historical account. Abetted by his Copeland-like henchman Cornelius MacFlicker, the Kim figure, Paul Pullmotor, does eventually attempt to mount a coup against his old friend, the prime minister of Al Khadra, Mustafa ibn Mabrouk. When Mabrouk foils the plot and taunts Pullmotor by sending an army band to play "Anything You Can Do, I Can Do Better" under his hotel window, the American is secretly pleased. Indeed, as he prepares to leave Al Khadra for the last time, and realizes he probably will never see Mabrouk again, the cynical Pullmotor suddenly experiences an emotion he has never felt before: regret.[4]

Rather than Egypt itself, the CIA would concentrate its efforts on containing the spread of Nasserism into other Arab states—a huge challenge, considering the massive popularity Nasser enjoyed throughout the Arab world as a result of Suez. Some countries were lower down the list of operational targets than others. Confronted by the surging tide of anti-Western, revolutionary pan-Arabism, the Saudi monarchy was thinking better of its flirtation with Cairo and starting to close ranks with the Hashemite kingdoms of Jordan and Iraq. A successful official visit to the United States by King Saud in January 1957, organized with the help of the CIA Arabists and Bill Eveland, expedited this development. As for Iraq, whose crown prince 'Abd al-Ilah was in Washington at the same time as Saud, its pro-British government likewise seemed securely within the Western camp, although here too the United States did not leave anything to chance, providing training and other forms of support for Iraq's internal security forces.[5]

With Iraq lined up behind the West, Saudi Arabia moving in the same direction, and Egypt beyond redemption, the CIA trained its sights instead on the three states in the most apparent danger of surrendering to revolutionary Arab nationalism and thereby, according to the Cold War logic of John Foster Dulles, communist influence: Jordan, Lebanon, and Syria. These unfortunate countries, each only just emerging from the shadow of European imperialism, would constitute the playing field for the most hectic phase of CIA game playing yet.

IN THE SPRING OF 1957, Jordan was still the "little, artificial, impoverished country" Kim Roosevelt had described nearly a decade earlier in *Arabs, Oil, and History*, an improbable creation of British imperialists forced to depend on regular cash injections for its very survival. Now, however, it was facing a set of even greater challenges. The British were withdrawing in the wake of Suez, taking their money with them. Despite urging from various sides, including young King Hussein, Whitehall, and even the US ambassador in Amman, Lester Mallory, Washington appeared reluctant to commit itself, at least publicly, to taking over the patronage of what was so obviously a client state—"pulling a British chestnut out of the fire," as several officials put it.[6]

Meanwhile, with encouragement from both Cairo and Damascus, nationalist opposition to the Hashemite monarchy was growing within Jordan, especially among the country's large population of displaced Palestinians. The king's clever if ineffectual prime minister Sulayman al-Nabulsi seemed content to cooperate with leftist, republican elements. Even more worrying from the palace's point of view, army officers such as 'Ali Abu Nuwar, Glubb Pasha's suave and opportunistic successor as commander of the Arab Legion, were beginning to question Hussein's personal authority. Many Western observers regretfully concluded that, like the Egyptian Farouk before him, the young king's days were numbered.

The contest between the palace and the opposition elements reached a climax in April. A face-off between Hussein and Prime Minister Nabulsi was accompanied by a series of ominous army maneuvers reputedly orchestrated by Abu Nuwar. On the evening of April 13, fighting broke out at the Zerqa military base north of Amman between junior Free Officers and bedouin soldiers loyal to the throne. Forcing Abu Nuwar to go with him, Hussein rushed to the scene and waded into the melee, rallying the loyalist troops, who mobbed and kissed him. Cowering in a staff car, Abu Nuwar begged his king's forgiveness and the following day was allowed to slink into exile in Syria. The only thing that had foiled the coup plot was young Hussein's bravery.[7]

Or such, anyway, was the official version of the events at Zerqa. Within days, an alternative interpretation had begun to circulate, one that portrayed the crisis as deliberately contrived by royal officials and the American embassy in order to discredit the nationalist leadership and provide a pretext for restoring palace rule—as, in other words, an Iran-like countercoup. Perhaps not surprisingly, Nabulsi, Abu Nuwar, and several other alleged plotters all insisted on the accuracy of this second version. Less to be expected, so too did several Western sources, including none other than *Time* magazine. In late April, it carried a report, "The Road to Zerqa" (touted as "a wild story that combined the dash of a Latin American army coup with the wile of an Arabian Nights adventure"), claiming that what from the outside appeared to be "a nationalist-inspired mutiny" had in fact been "carefully planned" by the king.[8]

The truth about Zerqa, a seminal moment in Jordanian history, remains hotly contested even today. Undoubtedly, the king's personal conduct in the darkness and confusion at the army base was impressive, and there certainly was a general air of mutinousness in the Jordanian army in the spring of 1957. However, the notion that there was a concerted plot to get rid of the king probably owed more to the royal imagination than to reality. The evidence subsequently used to convict the Free Officers accused of conspiring against Hussein was flimsy at best, and the lenient treatment received by Abu Nuwar and other supposed ringleaders in the conspiracy amounted to a tacit admission by the palace that the charges against them were only half-baked.[9]

What about the claim by Abu Nuwar and others that US officials helped Hussein manufacture the crisis? For once, Miles Copeland has very little to say about Zerqa, suggesting that he, at least, did not play any part. There are, however, other sources that shed some light on the question. British embassy reports to London indicate that, like Husni Za'im before his 1949 coup in Syria, Hussein signaled his intentions to the Western powers prior to making his move. According to one British official, "the Americans seem to have been more closely in touch with King Hussein over all this than we have been." As the Roosevelt cousins had observed during their visit to Jordan in 1956, the CIA station in Amman was in regular contact with the king, passing him money to fund a personal intelligence service and offering a means of secret communication with Washington. Evidently, the Agency's new regional headquarters in Lebanon provided a second back channel to Hussein's palace. In his memoirs about the comings and goings at the St. Georges Hotel bar, the international press corps' preferred watering hole in Beirut, journalist Saïd K. Aburish described a local CIA officer, James Barracks, consorting regularly with Jordan's military attaché in Lebanon, Colonel Radi 'Abdullah, in the run-up to Zerqa. In Aburish's account, his father, the well-regarded *Time* reporter Abu Saïd, followed Barracks and 'Abdullah to Amman and witnessed them staying together at the royal palace. This was the basis of the late-April *Time* story that portrayed Zerqa as the culmination of a royalist plot. Most intriguing of all, John Foster Dulles's papers contain a tantalizing hint that Kim Roosevelt was in Jordan just as the power struggle was reaching its climax. Speaking about Jordan with his brother Allen on April 21, "the Sec. asked if Kermit Roosevelt was still there." Was Kim in Amman fomenting a royalist countercoup against a nationalist prime minister, just as he had in Tehran in 1953? Miles Copeland's *Game of Nations* does offer one tidbit about Zerqa. Nasser, so Miles claimed, believed that Kim had passed "'disinformation'" to Nabulsi and Abu Nuwar "to delude them into thinking they could effect a coup against Hussein, thereby pushing them into Hussein's trap."[10]

Whatever the American contribution to Hussein's *coup de palais*, Zerqa marked a turning point in US relations with Jordan. The earlier hesitancy about rescuing a British chestnut was gone. When on April 24, 1957, Hussein, facing a leftist backlash against his Hashemite restoration, used CIA channels to notify Washington that he intended to suspend the Jordanian constitution and impose martial law, the White House issued a public statement of support, warned Israel not to intervene, and ordered the Sixth Fleet to the Lebanese coast. Significantly, the language American officials used to describe Hussein also underwent a transformation: the young king graduated from being a "playboy" or "sophomore" to "a man and a monarch on our side." On April 29, the United States granted Jordan $10 million of assistance, followed by another $10 million in May. In the same month, Eisenhower, on learning that Syrians were hatching plots against Hussein in Damascus, declared "that this was the time for CIA [to] worm its way in and attempt to . . . counter these moves." The Agency stepped up its security relationship with the Jordanian palace, the following year sending a young intelligence officer, Jack O'Connell, to foil a suspected Egyptian plot against Hussein; O'Connell subsequently became one of the king's closest advisers. By 1958, annual US financial support for Jordan amounted to about $40 million. America had effectively inherited Britain's tutelary role in the tiny Arab kingdom: the CIA was taking over from Glubb Pasha.[11]

Nor was this the only covert American intervention in the Arab Cold War during the spring of 1957. In Lebanon, the Francophile Maronite president Camille Chamoun was facing an incipient Arab nationalist insurgency. As in Jordan, Washington prevaricated before becoming involved on Chamoun's side; had not earlier generations of Americans in the Levant supported Arab nationalists *against* the pro-French Christian Maronites? However, a crucial round of elections in Lebanon was looming in June, and with both Egypt and Syria obviously interfering in the campaigning, the Eisenhower administration gradually succumbed to entreaties from Britain, France, and Chamoun himself, who, like other Middle Eastern leaders before him, adeptly played the communist card. Clandestine payments, including briefcases stuffed with Lebanese pounds personally delivered by Bill Eveland to the presidential palace, helped tip the elections in favor of Chamoun's pro-Western candidates. Indeed, as Allen Dulles himself admitted, the US intervention was perhaps *too* effective, as the "opposition to the current regime had been almost entirely eliminated, and the opposition did include some good men."[12]

In the early summer of 1957, with Lebanon saved from Nasserite takeover, albeit on terms that undermined the legitimacy of President Chamoun's government, Washington's Cold War planners could be forgiven for patting themselves on the back. The Arab world's conservative regimes were beginning to come together in opposition to the radical nationalists, as envisioned by the Eisenhower Doctrine. In terms of the personal contest between Kim Roosevelt and Gamal Nasser, the American seemed at last to be winning; the Egyptian was, so Allen Dulles crowed to his brother Foster, "fit to be tied *re* Jordan." Now, with one mission apparently accomplished, American attention turned to a job left over from the previous year: overthrowing the pro-Nasser, leftist government of Syria.[13]

THE COLLAPSE OF ARCHIE ROOSEVELT'S coup plot in the wake of Suez had all but destroyed the US position in Syria. Friends of America such as Mikhail Ilyan had been forced to flee the country, while 'Abd al-Hamid Sarraj, the leftist head of Syria's intelligence organization, the Deuxième Bureau, capitalized on his successful detection of the plot to confirm his position as the dominant force in Syrian politics. With Americans now perceived as imperial intriguers in the mold of the British and French, local communists gained in respectability, and Soviet advisers began surfacing in Damascus. The announcement of the Eisenhower Doctrine in these conditions elicited only suspicion and scorn.

Still, Washington had not given up on Syria altogether. The examples of Iran and Guatemala seemed to teach that it was possible to change regimes "without any military action whatsoever on the part of the United States," or so at least Foster Dulles concluded. In November 1956, Allen Dulles had reported to the State Department on CIA capabilities in Syria after the dissolution of the coup network. "We are concentrating on building up our intelligence assets," reads his recently declassified, and still partially redacted, report. "We are also intensively restudying the [redaction] with a view to reactivating it." Special responsibility for Syria appears to have remained in the hands of Archie Roosevelt, who in January 1957 took over as acting chief of the Agency's Near East division. Shortly afterward, Archie met with Mikhail Ilyan and agreed to fund another stab at unseating the Syrian government. In March, Syrian conservatives attempted to oust Sarraj from the Deuxième Bureau. On the afternoon of April 17, the Syrian national day, Allen Dulles told brother Foster, "they are keeping their fingers crossed *re* Syria for today."[14]

As before, nothing came of Archie and Ilyan's plotting. Sarraj not only survived the efforts to remove him but turned the tables on the Americans by using Syrian assets to destabilize the pro-Western governments in neighboring Jordan and Lebanon. Then, following resounding leftist victories in by-elections in May, the intelligence chief moved to create a Revolutionary Command Council, a Syrian version of the Egyptian Free Officers' RCC. State Department observers concluded that the US government no longer possessed "any significant leverage in Syria" and was therefore unable "to influence directly the course of events in that country." Allen Dulles, however, blamed the situation on a lack of conservative leadership—"no one there has guts or courage"— and insisted that "we have to start new planning. The situation is not hopeless."[15]

It was time for the other Roosevelt cousin, the hero of Tehran, to take over. Arriving in Beirut, Kim held a series of planning meetings with a senior MI6 officer, Frank Stallwood, and representatives of the Lebanese, Iraqi, and Jordanian governments (in the last case, Radi 'Abdullah, the military attaché suspected of helping plot King Hussein's counter-coup). By now, the Americans were desperate enough to consider a leadership role for Adib al-Shishakli, the disreputable former president. The talks still led nowhere. According to Bill Eveland, who filled in for Kim when he departed on a side trip to Saudi Arabia, Frank Stallwood's contribution was vitiated by his "fondness for Beirut's bars"; moreover, the choice of meeting place—the ill-concealed apartment of the CIA Beirut station chief, Ghosn Zogby—meant that the comings and goings of the various representatives were under constant surveillance. "So obvious were their 'covert' gyrations," Eveland claimed later, "that the Egyptian ambassador in Lebanon was reportedly taking bets on when and where the next U.S. coup would take place."[16]

At the same time that Kim Roosevelt was showing up in Beirut, a new CIA face appeared in Damascus. The son of an amateur boxer from Cincinnati, raised in poverty, and partially deaf, Howard E. "Rocky" Stone enjoyed none of the advantages of the Agency's Grotonian set. However, he had worked his way to the CIA, where he had served with distinction in Kim Roosevelt's TP-AJAX team, winning himself a reputation as a covert operations expert at the age of twenty-eight. Arriving in Damascus under official cover as embassy second secretary, the likable, no-nonsense Stone immediately set to work applying the lessons of Iran to Syria, trying to harness the forces of homegrown opposition—to "light a match," as he put it later. Accompanying him in this mission was his intrepid wife, Alice Marie "Ahme" Stone, who during the earlier Tehran operation had helped guard Ardeshir Zahedi, son of Mosaddeq's replacement, General Fazlollah Zahedi, hiding a pistol under her knitting.[17]

It was not long before Stone realized that there was no viable indigenous opposition in Syria. Undaunted, he began looking for potential conspirators among junior officers in the Syrian army, a search that led him to a charismatic young tank commander, Captain 'Abdullah Atiyyah. According to Atiyyah's later testimony, he and Stone met late one evening in early August at the apartment of a female US embassy official (possibly Elizabeth Sudmeir or Polly Curtis, both later identified as members of the Damascus CIA station by Bill Eveland). Stone, who was joined at the meeting by his deputy, Francis Jeton, spent several hours earnestly explaining the reasons why the young Syrian should oppose the communization of his country and then went on to outline the operational plan for the proposed coup, which involved tanks securing the city of Qatanah and occupying key positions in Damascus. In response, Atiyyah demanded a personal meeting with the coup's Syrian leaders before promising his cooperation. The talks ended at six the following morning with an agreement that an "ample" bundle of money would be left in the front compartment of an unlocked Ford parked on a nearby street for collection by a civilian accomplice of Atiyyah's.[18]

The task of arranging the meeting demanded by Atiyyah fell to another Damascus CIA officer, Arthur C. Close, a young Arabist of missionary stock who was on close terms with the ex-president Shishakli and his former intelligence chief, now military attaché in Rome, Colonel Ibrahim al-Husseini. According to Eveland, the plan was to smuggle Husseini ("a moose of a man") from Beirut into Damascus in the trunk of Close's car. Meanwhile, Atiyyah was to go to a coffee shop at a prearranged time and wait for a signal: Rocky's wife, Ahme, would pull up in a car with diplomatic tags, climb out, and write in a pad. The plan almost went awry when a small boy informed a nearby policeman that "this lady might be a spy trying to draw something." Ahme escaped apprehension, however, and the meeting between Atiyyah and Husseini, the latter adorned by a fake beard and mustache, went ahead in a shuttered room in another CIA safe house. Despite the disguise, the two men recognized each other— Atiyyah had once served under Husseini—and the young officer pledged his allegiance to the leadership of the projected coup. Having sworn an oath of secrecy on a copy of the Koran he kept in his pocket, Husseini then explained that he was only conspiring with the Americans, or "donkeys" as he referred to them, because doing so presented the possibility of restoring Syria to its former greatness. "We shall not care for them," he told Atiyyah, but "they are giving everything," and "we must . . . gain as much as we can from them." The conspirators "agreed to begin the move" and tied a knot in Atiyyah's string of worry beads, signifying a date later in August; Francis Jeton then entered the room, and the men synchronized their watches. Everything seemed set.[19]

The only problem was that Atiyyah was a government informer. When first contacted by the Americans, he had immediately told his commanding officer, who in turn dispatched him to alert a "responsible man" in Damascus, where he turned over the money he had received from Stone to Sarraj's Deuxième Bureau. Similar meetings with several other junior officers, in which payments of up to $3 million changed hands, were likewise reported to the authorities. Sarraj, it seems, had allowed the conspiring to carry on so that he could see where it would lead. Ironically, just at this moment, early August 1957, the announcement of a trade agreement with Moscow caused a rift in Syria's governing leftist coalition between communists and Ba'athists, the latter resenting the growing Soviet influence on Syrian politics. This genuine political division offered the Eisenhower administration a much more promising opportunity for halting Syria's leftward slide than any cooked-up military coup.[20]

In any case, Husseini's surreptitious visit to Damascus seems to have persuaded Sarraj that things had gone far enough. On August 12, the Syrian government announced that it had discovered an "American plot," arrested the leading Syrian conspirators (but not Husseini, who had returned to Rome), and surrounded the US embassy with thirty armed policemen. The following day, both Stone and Jeton were told to leave the country within twenty-four hours, along with the American military attaché, Robert W. Molloy, a blustery, rambunctious man who, although probably not involved in the coup planning, had a record of irritating the Syrian authorities. The US government responded in kind, declaring the Syrian ambassador in Washington persona non grata. While emphatically denying that there was any truth to Syrian charges, privately American officials acknowledged that the CIA had indeed been plotting a coup. Stone, depicted in newspaper reports as a bewildered embassy official with a hearing aid, was flown back to Washington. In one last, impotent gesture of defiance, Molloy deliberately ran the Syrian motorcyclist escorting him to Lebanon off the road just before reaching the border.[21]

Both Kim and Archie Roosevelt were fond of cautioning that regime change by covert means is impossible without the willing cooperation of substantial internal elements in the country concerned. Would that they had heeded their own advice in Syria.

THE FAILURE OF KIM'S COUP plan in 1957 added to the damage done by Archie's abortive operation of the previous year: more Syrian conservatives were purged, Sarraj's reputation benefited from the exposure of yet another Western plot, and Soviet influence spread still further, with the KGB sending a senior officer to reorganize the Deuxième Bureau. While the Soviets took advantage of the CIA's failures in Syria to score a minor victory in the Cold War, the undoubted victor in terms of inter-Arab politics, the Arab Cold War, was Gamal Nasser. The Egyptian exploited the exposure of the "American plot" to bring Damascus, long considered the strategic key to achieving regional supremacy, closer into Egypt's orbit and away from Hashemite Iraq. The conservative ascendancy of the early summer was fading, revealing the limits of the Eisenhower Doctrine. In the beleaguered US embassy in Damascus, a running joke captured the growing American sense of helplessness in the face of rampant Arab nationalism: "Que Serraj, Serraj; whatever will be, will be."[22]

Yet even now Washington could not resist the urge to meddle. Indeed, with internally produced regime change now ruled out, the Eisenhower administration began to consider more drastic solutions to the Syrian "crisis." Recycling the code name for the Anderson peace mission of early 1956, which by this point must have seemed a very long time ago, on August 21 Foster Dulles convened GAMMA, a top-secret task force with representatives from State, Defense, and the CIA (the last including Frank Wisner and Archie Roosevelt) charged with working "through the clock . . . to formulate a recommended program of further actions." GAMMA's main contribution was to agree to a proposal to send the eminent foreign service veteran Loy Henderson on a tour of the Middle East that seemed intended to incite military aggression against Syria by its Arab neighbors. Reporting back to Washington on September 7, Henderson told a meeting in the White House that he had discovered a deep sense of anxiety about Syria in the region, yet little concerted will to act; only Turkey, a NATO ally, showed much appetite for intervention, and encouraging the Turks risked alienating the other Arab countries, even possibly provoking the Soviet Union. Nonetheless, Foster Dulles was determined to press ahead. If the United States failed to prevent the satellization of Syria, he told the White House gathering, "the success would go to Khrushchev's head," and the West might find itself "with a series of incidents like the experience with Hitler."[23]

It was no coincidence that the secretary of state was employing an analogy previously used mainly by British observers of the Middle East; as Foster Dulles also informed the September 7 meeting, he and his staff had been in "close contact with the United Kingdom" throughout the previous weeks. It was Harold Macmillan who could claim the main share of credit for what Dulles described, rather fulsomely, as this "genuine, intimate, and effective cooperation." Shortly after the crisis had begun in August, the British prime minister had written "Foster," expressing his gratitude "for the frank confidence which so clearly exists between us," and his conviction that "unless something can be done to stop the Communist infiltration, the whole position may collapse." Macmillan's next step was to send his well-regarded private secretary, Frederick Bishop, to Washington to discuss the possible establishment of an ultrasecret US-UK committee to consider joint approaches to the problem. Bishop was assisted in his mission by the new British ambassador to the United States, Harold Caccia, who shared his prime minister's interest in luring the Americans deeper into the Middle East. ("I would suggest that our first aim should be to exploit the opening which [the] latest Communist moves in Syria have given us," he wrote the Foreign Office. "That could lead to the partnership in the Middle East which we have been seeking for years.") An Anglo-American Working Group on Syria was duly constituted in early September, with Kim Roosevelt representing the CIA, and reported on the eighteenth. Caccia was delighted. "As in the hot wars in 1916 and 1941, the Americans have only come in reluctantly and late," he wrote, perhaps betraying a lingering British bitterness about the American response to Suez. "But there is now a prospect in the Middle East which has never existed before."[24]

The working group's report was, in effect, a mishmash of earlier American and British proposals for covert action against Syria: stimulating internal resistance to the government, including the elimination of key figures such as Sarraj; provoking border incidents that would serve as a pretext for intervention by Iraq and, possibly, Jordan; and triggering tribal insurrections within Syria itself. Foster Dulles was not persuaded. There was, he complained during a meeting with British foreign secretary Selwyn Lloyd on September 21, a lack of "real evaluation of what could be done on a subversive basis in Syria." Furthermore, he was now convinced "that Iraq and Jordan alone could never carry out the operation." As Henderson's tour had shown, the only regional power with the will and ability to do anything about Syria was Turkey, and the secretary of state was coming around to the view that, whatever the risks of a Turkish intervention—antagonizing Arab opinion and provoking Soviet retaliation, to which the United States would in turn have to respond—

they were preferable to the alternative, allowing a Soviet satellite to appear in the heart of the Arab world. In other words, Foster Dulles was contemplating the possibility of an armed confrontation with the Soviet Union over the Middle East. Something of Dulles's emotional agitation at this time can be gauged from his instruction to those attending his meeting with Lloyd "that anyone having possession of the [top-secret] Report [of the Anglo-American Working Group] should protect it with his life if necessary."[25]

By now, the British were beginning to regret their strategy of deliberately fanning the flames of US anticommunism. The Americans were behaving recklessly, seemingly willing to gamble everything on the riskiest of ventures. Syria had the makings of a "Suez in reverse," wrote Macmillan privately. "If it were not serious . . . it would be rather comic." Ironically, whereas in earlier crises it had been London that advocated external intervention in one or another Arab country, while Washington argued instead for internal measures, now the positions were reversed, with Whitehall urging the merits of the working group's "Preferred Plan" over the "Turkish alternative."

Fortunately for the British—indeed, for all concerned—events in the Middle East itself eventually steered the United States toward a more moderate course of action. With Egyptian propaganda stoking the fires of nationalism across the Arab world, the region's more conservative regimes opted to tone down their calls for action against Syria and encouraged the Americans to do the same. Combined with discreet pressure from Macmillan and intimations from Moscow that a Turkish invasion of Syria would be met by a Soviet military response, these developments compelled a Dulles rethink. The secretary of state "was now firmly opposed to unilateral Turkish action and indeed has convinced himself this was always the case," Caccia informed London on October 16. There was "no need for us to 'rub it in,'" Macmillan responded. "Rather let us get Foster thinking about the next phase."[26]

The "next phase" arrived soon enough in early November, when Dulles and Lloyd instructed the Anglo-American Working Group on Syria to initiate combined planning for a joint military intervention in Jordan and Lebanon in the event that either country's government was again threatened by a coup (a plausible scenario, as events turned out the following year). Meanwhile, in an atmosphere of seriously dented American confidence caused by the Soviet launch of *Sputnik*, Washington drew yet closer to London, setting up a series of top-secret Anglo-American committees modeled on the Syria Working Group to coordinate planning in a variety of other Cold War areas, the first such formal mechanisms for US-UK dialogue created since World War II. At the end of the year, Macmillan delightedly noted that the spirit of discord created by Suez had finally been dispelled. The reconciliation between the "cousins" that had begun in the intelligence services had not been derailed by the failure in Syria. Indeed, if anything, the crisis atmosphere that arose after the detection of the "American plot" helped cement relations. The British tactic of using secret back channels to secure American material support for traditional imperial interests in the Middle East had worked. The players might have been different after Suez, but the rules of the game were the same.[27]

KIM ROOSEVELT AND HIS FELLOW Arabists had come to the Cold War Middle East hoping not only to prevent the Russians from taking it over but also to help the Arabs throw off the colonial domination of the French and British. The Suez crisis had seemed to mark a historic moment of opportunity for the Arabist vision, with the United States briefly emerging as the champion of Arab independence from European imperialism. It took less than a year, however, for that promise to be squandered. Thanks to a combination of Foster Dulles's rigid worldview and subtle pressure from both the British and conservative Arab leaders, the Eisenhower administration came down decisively on the side of the old imperial order—and, ironically, the CIA became the main instrument of the new antinationalist policy. The Arabists did not even have the consolation of pulling off some spectacular coup, as they had in 1953. Indeed, the main effect of repeated attempts at regime change in Syria was to drive that country further into the arms of the communists.

For the CIA Arabists, the appeal of the Arabist cause had always been as much personal as political. A childhood fascination with the Orient, a powerful sense of patriotic duty, the chance for personal adventure: these were what had drawn Kim and the others to the Arab world in the first place. And so it would prove in the end, as CIA Arabism entered its terminal crisis. The reasons that the Arabists would quit the game were not just political; they were personal as well.

TWENTY

Game Over

SEVERAL TIMES DURING THE MID-1950s, as winter descended on Washington, DC, Kim and Polly Roosevelt flew south to stay at the Florida residence of oil executive Charles B. Wrightsman. Decorated and furnished at vast expense by Wrightsman's art collector wife, Jane, the Palm Beach mansion boasted a huge swimming pool filled with heated seawater and tennis courts on which guests could play against professionals from a nearby club. After rising late, Polly would swim and Kim would play tennis before joining their hosts for a four-course dinner and, sometimes, dancing accompanied by musicians flown in from New York. In January 1955, the Roosevelts' fellow guests included, besides Allen Dulles, the shah and queen of Iran, who took them waterskiing and shopping for "costly trinkets" at Cartier and other stores on Palm Beach's Worth Avenue. On the final day of their visit, the two young couples drove to Miami in the Pahlavis' blue Rolls Royce, the shah behind the wheel discussing Iranian affairs with Kim, while the queen fussed over her lapdog. That evening the foursome dined at Maxim's and listened to Louis Armstrong at the Beachcomber nightclub.[1]

After these glamorous interludes, Polly found it hard returning to the "work-a-day world" of Washington. Even after several raises to

GS-18 on the Agency pay scale, Kim's government salary of $18,000 was not enough to cover the Harvard and Groton fees of sons Kermit and Jonathan, who had recently been joined by two new siblings, Mark and Anne, let alone the upkeep of a summer house on Nantucket. In July 1955, only a few months after Kim had received the National Security Medal at the White House, Polly found herself (as she confessed to mother-in-law Belle) having to borrow money from her children's nanny to pay the household bills. Roosevelts had never flaunted their status, but this was sailing too close to the wind.[2]

Relative impecunity was not the only challenge facing the families of intelligence officers. Polly, on her own at home for months at a time while Kim traveled overseas, fretted constantly about her husband's safety. "I hate, hate, hate, hate the prospect of this trip," she told her mother-in-law on the eve of one of Kim's expeditions. "The whole thing by air, the semi-war conditions in the countries he must go to, the fact that he is going round the world, the loneliness I anticipate and the pointlessness of my existence without him." Although Archie Roosevelt's wife, Lucky, enjoyed an independent career as a Washington newspaper columnist, she too suffered the emotional stresses and strains of marriage to an overseas operative. "Riots and revolutions seemed to follow him," she wrote in her memoirs; "he flew in dangerous airplanes held together by luck and by God." Then there was the additional burden of official secrecy, which meant concealing the reason for such trips from friends and relatives. "You know, it's getting a little embarrassing to tell people you're away all the time—people must think we've had a quarrel or something," Lucky once wrote her husband. It was also difficult not to feel a little envious when contemporaries who had chosen more conventional careers began to reap such public honors as ambassadorships and invitations to join boards of directors. "Here he was, this brilliant man who knew so many languages," remembered Lucky. "Why wasn't he an ambassador? That was very difficult for him too, because he didn't like looking like a failure."[3]

The Groton ethic of selfless public service was still a powerful influence on the outlook of the Roosevelt cousins, but it was coming under increasing strain. It did not help that the CIA Arabists were, by the second half of 1957, thoroughly disillusioned with the Eisenhower administration's handling of Middle East policy. According to his autobiography, Archie's misgivings about his political masters' approach to the Arab world—their conflation of nationalism and communism, their tendency to overestimate the American ability to influence local developments, and their failure to heed the advice of area experts—came to a head at a meeting of the GAMMA committee, the interdepartmental group convened in late August to consider the next step after the detection of the "American plot" in Syria. When discussion turned to Foster Dulles's proposal to send Loy Henderson on a tour to line up other Arab governments against the Syrian regime—a patently misconceived scheme likely to increase rather than reduce nationalist feelings throughout the region—Archie slipped a note to his CIA superior, Deputy Director Charles P. Cabell, stating, "I wish to voice my strong dissent from the opinions expressed here." Cabell, "a soldier who saluted when a commander gave him his orders," responded with another note saying, "It is not for us to give our views on matters of policy." Consequently, when Dulles canvassed the meeting's opinion, Archie kept his "eyes on the table and remained silent." The next morning, unable to contain his disquiet, Archie tried to track down Henderson, but the senior diplomat had already left on his ill-advised mission. Much later, Archie claimed, Henderson told him, "I heard you were trying to get hold of me, and I knew why. The decision was a mistaken one."[4]

These feelings were shared by the other Roosevelt cousin. In an interview with OSS historian R. Harris Smith, Kim claimed actually to have complained to Allen Dulles about the State Department and White House adopting "bad policy" and then, when it failed, asking the CIA, "Please overthrow this gov[ernmen]t for us." TP-AJAX only worked, Kim explained, because there was a domestic force, the Iranian army, that supported the shah over Mosaddeq. As such, the operation represented a "very special situation, one that could not be done repeatedly and at will." The Eisenhower administration's "adventurist policy" was "intolerable. . . . You can't go around overthrowing any gov[ernmen]t." Allen Dulles "sympathized," Kim recalled, "but said there was nothing he could do about it."[5]

There was a strong hint in these later comments of being wise after the event: both cousins were, after all, involved in covert efforts to overthrow various Middle Eastern governments, and they clearly enjoyed the opportunities for adventure offered by such operations, including the chance of temporary escape from the perhaps unhappy or workaday conditions of their domestic lives. Still, some contemporary evidence indicates that the Roosevelts did indeed try to rein in Foster Dulles. In September 1957, for example, when the secretary of state was excitedly contemplating American support for a Turkish invasion as a possible solution to the "Syrian crisis," Kim informed the secret Anglo-American Working Group on Syria that the Saudi foreign minister, Prince Faisal, had personally expressed to him "concern lest the United States should encourage the Turks to attack Syria." The following month, after a somewhat calmer Dulles accepted the working group's conclusion "that unilateral Turkish military intervention at this time would be undesirable," attention shifted to contingency planning for possible nationalist coups against the pro-Western Arab governments on Syria's borders. On November 9, the CIA stated its strong belief, presumably through its representative, Kim, "that the disadvantages of [military] intervention in the case of Jordan would be greater even than those of inaction. . . . Arab opinion would be solidly united against us; Hussein, if rescued only by such intervention would be regarded as a complete puppet; and his regime would collapse as soon as United Kingdom/United States forces were withdrawn." In other words, Kim had not yet abandoned the skepticism he had voiced years earlier in *Arabs, Oil, and History* about the viability of Jordan's client monarchy. There was little enthusiasm here for extracting Britain's chestnut from the fire.[6]

Nor, apparently, had Kim given up altogether on his other major Arabist ambition for the Middle East—besides replacing imperial-era regimes with nationalist ones—that is, securing an equitable resolution to the Palestine conflict. "The Governments of the United States of America and the United Kingdom agree that the unsolved Arab-Israel problem presents a grave obstacle to the peaceful and prosperous development of the peoples of the Middle East, and that tranquility will never come to the area without a just settlement of that problem," read a draft statement brought before the Anglo-American Working Group in October 1957. "Any settlement must make provision for the three basic elements of refugees, security, and boundaries," the text continued, with territorial agreements representing "some form of compromise between the present armistice lines and the boundaries proposed in the United Nations resolution of 1947." The CIA members of the working group were reportedly "very keen" that this statement be adopted, but State Department representatives blocked the move. In this respect, the debate echoed a dispute that had taken place the previous December, when the CIA representatives on an Operations Coordinating Board working group on Middle East policy failed to persuade its other members to include a statement in their report to the effect "that U.S. interests and solution of problems in the Near East depend upon an immediate settlement of the Arab-Israel dispute." Even now, Kim and his fellow Arabists were, it seems, not quite ready to surrender the dream of a "just" peace that had animated ALPHA a few years earlier.[7]

But these lingering hopes signified nothing. Much as the British swiftly worked their way back into American favor after Suez, so the Israelis too quickly rehabilitated their reputation, emerging as a pro-Western island in a sea of revolutionary Arab nationalism. Reviewing the recent setbacks in US Middle East policy, Allen Dulles asked Bill Eveland, "I guess that leaves Israel's intelligence service as the only one on which we can count, doesn't it?" Beginning in 1958, there was a considerable expansion of the "Connection," the informal alliance between the CIA and Mossad. The United States provided the money as the Israelis established collaborative programs with other non-Arab secret services in the region—in Turkey and Iran—and began branching out into sub-Saharan Africa, where they helped the Americans combat penetration by the KGB. The rivalry between the Near East and Israel divisions in the CIA, nearly as old as the Agency itself, was being decided in favor of the latter; James Jesus Angleton had bested Kim Roosevelt. It was another Arabist defeat to add to a list that already included the failure to control Nasser, the collapse of ALPHA, and the "loss" of Syria.[8]

The CIA Arabists were not alone in their discontent with John Foster Dulles's management of US foreign policy: a growing number of Middle East hands within the State Department itself were beginning to question the wisdom of the Eisenhower Doctrine. Ironically, though, this dissident mood, and the creeping sense of demoralization that accompanied it, tended to focus less on Dulles himself than on the CIA crypto-diplomats charged with carrying out his orders on the ground in the Middle East. In Syria, for example, where the US diplomatic corps had been greatly reduced as a result of the abortive coup attempt of August 1957—in addition to the expulsion of Rocky Stone's operatives, Ambassador Jimmy Moose, on leave at the time of the plot's discovery, was instructed not to return to Damascus—there was clearly a good deal of ill feeling toward the CIA. Arriving in Damascus in 1958, the new ambassador, Charles W. Yost, set about trying to rebuild American relations with Syrians by drawing a line under the events of the previous few years, when, as he put it later, "we were trying rather clumsily to get into some of their domestic affairs." There were echoes here of the earlier problems in Henry Byroade's Cairo embassy caused by the crypto-diplomacy of Kim Roosevelt and Miles Copeland, "this tendency to fall back on the spooky channel, so to speak, rather than doing it through the official diplomatic channel," as junior embassy official William Lakeland described it. "We were actively intervening—in very ham-handed ways in some cases—all over the landscape," recalled State Department Middle East hand Harrison M. Symmes. "Allen Dulles just unleashed people, many of whom were very good operatives. . . . But there were some people over there also who were utterly unprincipled."[9]

Criticism from foreign service colleagues was nothing new, but the CIA Arabists were also being targeted from other quarters. In the course of Senate Foreign Relations Committee hearings about the Eisenhower Doctrine in early 1957, senators referred indiscreetly to officials from "another Government agency" undermining George Allen's mission to Cairo and even conspiring with Nasser against Naguib. More surprisingly, a panel appointed by the Eisenhower White House in 1956 to look into American covert operations and made up of two stalwarts of the foreign policy establishment, David K. E. Bruce and Robert A. Lovett, returned with a startlingly negative report that condemned "the increased mingling in the internal affairs of other nations of bright, highly graded young men who must be doing something all the time to justify their reason for being." The report continued with a declaration that could easily have been interpreted as a personal attack on Kim Roosevelt: "Busy, moneyed and privileged, [the CIA] likes its 'King Making' responsibility (the intrigue is fascinating—considerable self-satisfaction, sometimes with applause, derives from 'successes'—no charge is made for 'failures'—and the whole business is very much simpler than collecting covert intelligence on the USSR through the usual CIA methods!)." No doubt the Arabists simply shrugged off some of the barbs coming their way. Still, for men who had been reared and educated to prize honor above material rewards, they must have stung a little.[10]

That said, the first CIA Arabist to abandon public service was no Grotonian. Miles Copeland shared the Roosevelt cousins' deep sense of frustration with the Eisenhower Doctrine. "All of us were quite prepared to believe that the plan might have made sense in some subtle and delicate domestic political context beyond the ken of us 'field' people, but in the light of extant intelligence on the Arab world, it made no sense at all," he wrote later. Not only that, Miles was starting to grow bored with his planning job in the increasingly cumbersome bureaucracy of CIA headquarters. There was growing pressure to package intelligence, which now was usually derived from impersonal, technological rather than living, human sources—"SIGINT" rather than "HUMINT"—to support predetermined policy decisions, as opposed to intelligence shaping policy. "The CIA itself became a budget-happy agency in which solutions came first," he lamented. Above all, Miles, the game player supreme, was fed up with always being on the losing side, not least as it meant being teased by Nasser, with whom he was still in frequent, friendly contact. "The genius of you Americans," Nasser taunted him, "is that you never made clear-cut stupid moves, only *complicated* stupid moves." It was "a turning point in my life," Miles wrote later. "I thereafter adjusted my own personal game."[11]

In May 1957, Miles resigned his government post and prepared to move to Beirut, where he and his old friend Jim Eichelberger were planning to establish a consultancy business, conducting research for American commercial interests throughout the region. Kim and Polly Roosevelt gave them "a grand farewell party," Lorraine Copeland recalled later. "We were much envied, [and] people tried to make friends who hadn't 'seen' us before!" Arriving in Beirut in July, the Copelands rented a large apartment overlooking the sea and arranged for their children to attend the American school. Lorraine was introduced to various archaeologists excavating in Lebanon and joined her first dig as "chief bottle washer," a humble launch of what would prove to be an illustrious academic career. Miles, meanwhile, rented a "Copeland & Eichelberger" office next door to TAPline's headquarters and opened for business. His first clients were oil executives he and Eich had met the previous year when researching Foster Dulles's ill-fated idea for a Suez Canal Users' Association. The Pittsburgh-based Gulf Oil Corporation wanted information about regional developments that might affect its drilling operations in Kuwait, and Copeland & Eichelberger were delighted to oblige, in part because doing so meant upstaging Gulf's previous advisers, British Petroleum (as the Anglo-Iranian Oil Company had been renamed in 1954). After landing two other major clients, one of them Pan Am, the former CIA officers were earning at least three times their government salaries. As during his spell working for Booz, Allen & Hamilton, Miles remained a CIA "loyal alumnus," staying in regular touch with, and performing frequent tasks for, his old boss, Allen Dulles. This time, however, there would be no return through the "revolving door" to government service. Miles's days as a full-time intelligence officer were over.[12]

Next, it was Kim Roosevelt's turn. Late in 1957, Kim was drawn, apparently unwillingly, into CIA planning to overthrow the Indonesian leader Sukharno, a prominent Third World "neutralist." The details are not clear, but Miles wrote later of Kim's "confidence [taking] another blow in a conversation with Allen [Dulles], Frank [Wisner] and the head of the FE Division [Desmond Fitzgerald] about a proposed operation in Indonesia." On September 12, around the height of the Syrian crisis, Polly told Belle Roosevelt that "Kim had a terrible flap at the office last night," adding that "he is very discouraged about the Middle East." Later in the same letter, Polly again brought up "the sordid question of money," noting that Groton fees had just gone up and that the family would have difficulty paying Harvard that month. To make matters worse, there was a strong possibility that Kim might have to drop everything and take off abroad on Agency business, leaving Polly holding her "breath through the day, . . . hoping that this evening's news will be better." With the autumn nights drawing in, a deep sense of gloom settled on the Roosevelt household.[13]

There was only one solution. Shortly before Christmas, 1957, Kim announced his intention of resigning from the Agency and taking up a position with a private employer. In January he attended a CIA stag dinner given in his honor by Allen Dulles—"Speeches, etc. will proclaim loudly that they are all sorry to see Kim leave government service," Polly predicted of the event to Belle, with heavy irony—and began commuting to the Pittsburgh headquarters of Gulf Oil to discuss terms. Soon afterward, he was installed in a plush Washington office as a Gulf vice president in charge of government relations, liaising between his new employer, the various relevant bureaucracies in Washington, and royal families and high officials in oil-producing Middle Eastern states—"a top-level advocate, door-opener, smoother of problems," as his old Groton and Harvard classmate, Benjamin Welles, now described him.[14]

Like Miles, Kim did not sever his ties to the CIA; indeed, he routinely passed on the reports that Copeland & Eichelberger compiled for

Gulf Oil to his old colleagues, and he even encouraged Miles to cultivate his friendship with Nasser, his unique "inside track" in Cairo, for
intelligence purposes. Kim, too, was a loyal alumnus, in other words.
Still, after two decades of government employment interrupted only by
spells of public advocacy for the Arab cause, "the lucrative corporate
embrace of big business" (as Welles put it) was a decisive shift. Would
the Rector have approved? Perhaps Kim, who had just turned forty,
had already done enough to satisfy the Groton ethic and the Roosevelt
expectation of wartime sacrifice to one's country: the citation for the
Distinguished Intelligence Medal he earned on the eve of his departure
from the CIA noted that, as "the principal architect of United States
political action operations in the Near East," he had performed work
"of greatest importance to the national security of the United States."
In any case, he could at least now afford the Groton fees—and a larger
house in Washington, where he and Polly moved shortly after he started
his new job.[15]

Of the CIA's original Arabist triumvirate, this left just Archie Roosevelt. Despite his unhappiness about Eisenhower administration policy,
there was never much question of Archie quitting the Agency: he was
too dedicated an intelligence officer for that. However, early in 1958,
he was moved out of the Arab world into a new post as station chief in
Madrid, leaving division chief Norman Paul in complete control of the
Near East. The causes of this move are not documented, but evidently
Archie was not happy about it. "Imagine sending me to one of the few
countries where I don't speak the language," he told Lucky. "I've spent
so much of my life studying the Middle East—what do I know about
Spain?" Was Archie being punished for the failure of successive coup
attempts in Syria, or had his discontent with the administration line become too obvious? It is not clear.[16]

What was clear was the sum effect of all these changes: as Bill Eveland described it later, a complete "changing of the CIA guard over the
Middle East," similar to the emptying out from government service of
the OSS Arabists after the partition of Palestine in 1947. Even Eveland
himself would shortly follow his Agency colleagues into the private sector, leaving his government post in 1959 for a job in the construction
industry.[17]

The Arabist moment that had begun ten years earlier, when Kim,
Archie, and Miles had stood together on the citadel battlements in
Aleppo, was over.

THERE WAS STILL ONE ACT left in the drama, however: the denouement of the antinationalist Eisenhower Doctrine.

The year 1958 was to feature upheaval throughout the Middle East, a first Arab Spring, so to speak, as the wave of Nasserite nationalism finally engulfed the conservative regimes left over from the days of the British and French Empires. On February 1, the Egyptian and Syrian governments merged to form the United Arab Republic (UAR), signifying Egypt's victory in the long regional contest for control of Syria (although the union would prove short-lived, Syria seceding in 1961). The Iraqi and Jordanian monarchies responded by creating the rival Arab Union, a futile gesture that served only to inflame nationalist feeling against them. Carrying on the inglorious tradition of the ill-fated Syrian coup plot STRAGGLE, an Arab Coordinating Committee made up of representatives of the conservative Arab governments sat in Beirut hatching various schemes against Nasser and the Syrian intelligence chief Sarraj, as the Western secret services looked on somewhat nervously. In March 1958, Sarraj "made a monkey" out of King Saud by exposing a particularly crude Saudi plot to bribe him personally into opposing the formation of the UAR. The resulting scandal effectively forced the abdication of Saud (lest it be forgotten, Eisenhower's candidate for Arab necessary leader), leaving the Saudi throne to Prince Faisal, a far less desirable occupant in American eyes. Everywhere one looked in the Arab world, nationalists were routing pro-Western conservatives.[18]

But the worst was still to come. In May, sectarian tensions in Lebanon, stirred by Nasser and Sarraj, boiled over into a full-scale uprising against President Camille Chamoun. Encouraged by leading Lebanese businessmen and an unnamed oil company, probably Gulf, Miles Copeland volunteered in June to use his inside channel to Cairo to try to work out a truce. Neither Chamoun nor Nasser proved amenable, though; indeed, Miles found his Egyptian friend in an unusually truculent mood, complaining that the United States "regard[ed] him as [a] problem child rather than [a] responsible official." Meanwhile, a defiant Chamoun retreated inside the presidential palace, where Bill Eveland, apparently an ardent supporter of the Lebanese president despite his later professions of sympathy for Arab nationalism, visited him regularly, braving rebel gunfire in his white and gold DeSoto and helping stash the Chamoun family jewels in the US embassy safe. The next flash point was Jordan, where in early July the "Brave Young King" Hussein claimed to have detected another army plot against him, this one also involving a threat to the Hashemite monarchy in Iraq. As the young CIA officer Jack O'Connell helped unravel a conspiracy involving twenty-two Jordanian officers, an Iraqi infantry brigade summoned to defend Hussein's throne happened to pass through Baghdad in the early morning of July 14. Apparently, no one in the Iraqi capital had heeded Jordan's warnings about a possible coup, because what happened next took the CIA and MI6 stations there by complete surprise.[19]

At six AM the troops fanned out and seized key positions, attacked Prime Minister Nuri's residence (the CIA station chief Carlton Swift, sleeping on the roof of his house because of the summer heat, was awakened by the sound of gunfire from across the Tigris) and then descended on the royal palace. There they confronted and shot to death King Faisal and Crown Prince 'Abd al-Ilah, Archie Roosevelt's old friend. The following day, a city mob dug up 'Abd al-Ilah's hastily buried body, mutilated it, and dragged it naked through the streets. Nuri, disguised as an old woman to elude capture by the army, was recognized by the crowd and murdered; his body suffered a similar fate. Several Europeans and Americans also died that day, among them a Californian, Eugene Burns, later identified, with terrible irony, as a relief worker for the American Friends of the Middle East. The carnage dismayed observers in London and Washington; they now feared the complete collapse of the old monarchical order across the whole region.[20]

Believing that Lebanon would be the next Arab state to succumb to nationalist revolution, Chamoun implored the United States to intervene militarily, invoking the Eisenhower Doctrine. This posed a major dilemma for the Eisenhower administration. Despite constant Lebanese and British assertions that the country's problems were due to communist and Nasserite interference, most American observers knew full well that in fact it was internal communal divisions that were the main threat to Chamoun's increasingly unpopular government. Yet Lebanon had become a crucial test of credibility for the United States: if Washington did not respond to Chamoun's entreaties, then other pro-Western governments in the region would surely conclude that they were better off accommodating themselves to the forces of Nasserite nationalism. Americans on the ground in Beirut offered conflicting advice. In a classic scene of crypto-diplomat versus regular diplomat, Bill Eveland urged support for Chamoun, while the US ambassador, Robert McClintock, advised listening to the opposition.[21]

Significantly, though, the loudest local voice cautioning against military action belonged to the old Arabist William Eddy, who had moved from Saudi Arabia to Lebanon several years earlier to help run ARAMCO's TAPline and was now living out his retirement in his country of birth. "Armed intervention by the Western Allies in the civil strife in Lebanon would be a catastrophe to American interests," he told McClintock. As a Maronite Christian, Chamoun was not representative of Lebanon's population, Eddy explained; for that matter, he was not even representative of the Maronite community, whose patriarch was trying to live in peace with the Muslim majority (this is an echo of Eddy's earlier interest in promoting Christian-Muslim dialogue). Military support for the president would, therefore, be tantamount to "an act of aggression against at least half of the population," invoke memories of earlier colonial depredations, and even invite comparison with the Soviet Union's treatment of the "captive nations." Moreover, Eddy continued, it would place Western troops in unnecessary danger, as the experience of the British in Palestine and the French in Algeria showed that occupying armies "are powerless to stem a spreading wave of violence and hate for the invaders." Similar sentiments were also articulated by the other surviving member of the first generation of OSS Arabists, Harold B. Hoskins, who warned the State Department that a US landing in Lebanon might serve to "align the U.S. with the colonial powers and against the Moslem majority in the area." "So long as the strife is so obviously domestic," Eddy concluded in another of several such communications, this one to the president of TAPline, "I trust not one American nor British nor French soldier will set foot in Lebanon, to revive the memories of [the] Allies in Egypt, or Russians in Hungary."[22]

Eddy's advice was disregarded. In a desperate effort to rescue American credibility, the administration ordered troop landings in Beirut on July 15 and reluctantly supported a similar British action in Jordan two days later. The simultaneous operations, whose planning dated back to discussions in the Anglo-American Working Group on Syria the previous fall, were the most dramatic indication yet of the extent to which American power in the Middle East, once associated with an effort to replace the old imperial order with something new, had now become identified with the failing British and French colonial regimes. The whole affair evoked memories of Victorian "gunboat diplomacy," or "the whiff of musketry" that Dean Acheson had detected in Egypt just before the 1952 Revolution. At the same time, there was a slightly surreal quality to the landing itself, which far from meeting with local opposition seemed to inspire indifference. Many accounts since have dwelled on the fact that disembarking marines waded ashore among bikini-clad sunbathers and street boys hawking sodas. Bill Eddy, dismayed by the whole spectacle, tried at least to take pleasure in the presence in Beirut of his beloved Leathernecks and of President Eisenhower's personal representative, his old friend Robert Murphy, who back in 1942 had paved the way diplomatically for the Operation TORCH landings in Morocco and Algeria.[23]

It was a final irony that Eddy, who sixteen years earlier had used his Arabist knowledge to prepare a World War II bridgehead for American forces to liberate North Africa, should now be watching aghast, as US troops returned to the Arab world to defend the old imperial order.

TWENTY-ONE

Epilogue

IRONICALLY, THE PROSPECTS FOR AMERICAN-ARAB relations brightened briefly after the CIA Arabists' departure from the scene. Shaken by the calamities of 1958, the Eisenhower administration called a truce in its confrontation with Nasserism. In a decision full of resonance for a later era, Ike and his advisors chose not to take military action against revolutionary Iraq, reasoning that doing so would lose the United States further support in the Arab world and create insuperable problems for any American occupation force. (They did, however, entertain various suggestions for covert action against the new Iraqi leader, 'Abd al-Karim Qasim, among them a scheme proposed by the CIA's Health Alteration Committee involving a poisoned handkerchief; it is also possible that the Agency was linked to a 1959 attempt on Qasim's life involving a young Ba'athist assassin by the name of Saddam Hussein.) The naturally pragmatic instincts of the president came further to the fore when, desperately ill with cancer, John Foster Dulles resigned as secretary of state in April 1959 and died the following month. The grudging accommodation with Arab nationalism that marked the final days of the Eisenhower presidency carried over into the administration of John F. Kennedy, who even tried to reach out personally to Nasser, his very near contemporary.[1]

It was not long, however, before JFK ran into the same problems as his predecessor: the intractability of the Palestine conflict and the cleavage within the Arab world between the forces of nationalism and conservatism, which in 1962 coalesced around a civil war in the tiny Arabian country of Yemen, with the Egyptians and Saudis backing republican and monarchist proxies respectively, and the United States inevitably falling in behind its long-standing Saudi allies. Then came November 1963 and the elevation to the White House of Vice President Lyndon Johnson, a veteran Texan politico who turned out to be the most pro-Zionist president since Harry Truman, perceiving Israel as a sort of Middle Eastern Alamo and Nasser a latter-day Santa Anna. In response, the Egyptian leader rallied his nationalist base with increasingly anti-American speeches, proclaiming that he was "not going to accept gangsterism by cowboys." Meanwhile, relations between Israel and its Arab neighbors worsened steadily, emboldening extremists on both sides and driving the region to the edge of all-out war.[2]

If the Arabist defeats of the Eisenhower era established the basic pattern of US relations with the Middle East in the years that followed, they also shaped the outcome of subsequent domestic debates about the Arab-Israeli dispute. In 1963, Senate Foreign Relations Committee hearings about "foreign agent" registration, chaired by William Fulbright (with some research assistance from Elmer Berger), revealed that Israeli-financed lobbying efforts in the United States, including "monitoring and combating of the efforts of 'hostile' groups," had grown massively since the early 1950s. At the same time that the influence of the Israel Lobby was increasing, the structures of social and political power that had once supported Kim Roosevelt's Arabist, anti-Zionist state-private network were breaking down. The previously undisputed ethnic dominance of East Coast Anglo-Americans was eroding; senior Protestant clergy such as Edward Elson, for example, no longer commanded the privileged access to national media they had enjoyed during the early 1950s. The botched 1961 invasion of Cuba at the Bay of Pigs (precisely the sort of military action Kim and the other Arabists had advised against) led to the forced resignation of Director of Central Intelligence Allen Dulles and tarnished the once-golden image of the CIA (Dulles died eight years later, in 1969). The first stirrings of domestic opposition to the Vietnam War were chipping away at the anticommunist consensus that had enabled the CIA to maintain its cover in front organizations such as the American Friends of the Middle East. Indeed, Zionist publications like Si Kenen's *Near East Report* had begun to hint heavily that AFME was receiving secret government funds. In 1966, fearing its exposure, Secretary of State Dean Rusk ordered a review of "continued U[nited] S[tates] G[overnment] support of AFME through CIA channels." "They were planning for ways to cut it loose," one of the organization's officers explained later.[3]

These efforts came too late. On February 17, 1967, three days after carrying an advertisement announcing *Ramparts* magazine's imminent exposé of CIA links with US student groups, the *New York Times* identified AFME as a recipient of grants from an Agency "pass-through," the J. Frederick Brown Foundation. Similar stories about other foundations that had funded the group appeared over the course of the following week. This very public confirmation of what they had long suspected delighted AFME's enemies. Rabbi Philip S. Bernstein, chair of the American Israel Public Affairs Committee (AIPAC), appealed to President Johnson to put an end to government funding for AFME, pointing out (according to one newspaper report) that the organization had "'disseminated anti-Israel and anti-Zionist views prejudicial to the state of Israel,' had slandered a large segment of the American people, and was a major supporter of the Organization of Arab Students, 'which abuses the hospitality of the United States.'" Several pro-Israel congressmen chimed in with similar statements. AFME's directors responded by insisting that they had not known about the true source of their funds and therefore that their program was unaffected by it (a common self-defense among "blown" Agency fronts) while scrambling to speed up the handover from the CIA to new, private sponsors. A meeting of the board to discuss these moves was scheduled for June 5, 1967. Hope was beginning to grow that AFME might yet survive what its new executive vice president, Orin D. Parker, later called "our 1967 War."[4]

It was at precisely the moment that the directors were gathering in AFME's Washington headquarters that word arrived of a surprise Israeli attack on Egypt. As Parker recalled later, the remainder of the day was spent "watching as the Six-Day War became hour by hour more devastating for the Arab states" (after destroying the Egyptian air force, the Israelis had turned their attention on Jordan and Syria). Before a week was out, Israel had drubbed the Egyptian, Jordanian, and Syrian armies, and had captured territories three times its original size, including the Sinai, Gaza Strip, West Bank, and Golan Heights. Meanwhile, with the United States now thoroughly identified in the Arab mind with Israel, violence against American targets escalated throughout the region. Even the pro-Arab AFME was compelled to close field stations in Jerusalem, Damascus, and Baghdad (the office in the Iraqi capital was sacked and burned by a mob of students, its chief intended beneficiaries) and to order the evacuation of representatives' families from Cairo, Tripoli, Beirut, and Amman. At home, pleas from the organization's leaders to President Johnson that the United States "stop Israeli aggression by any measures necessary" fell on deaf ears. Coming as it did so soon after the *Ramparts* revelations, the Six-Day War completed the rout of the American Friends of the Middle East.[5]

DRAMATIC THOUGH THE EVENTS OF 1967—the two wars, one foreign and one domestic—undoubtedly were, the truth was that Kim Roosevelt's Arabist, anti-Zionist citizen network had long been a spent force. The most poignant evidence of this was the unhappy personal fates of some of its best-known members: Dorothy Thompson, bitter until her death in 1961 about her treatment at the hands of the Zionists; Elmer Berger, increasingly isolated in the American Jewish community and eventually deposed from the leadership of the American Council for Judaism after the Six-Day War; and William Eddy, who died in Beirut in 1962, painfully conscious of the eclipse of American-Arab goodwill that the last years of his life had witnessed.

As for Kim Roosevelt himself, he never recaptured the élan and influence of his early life. His post-CIA business career was reasonably successful, especially after he resigned from Gulf Oil in 1964 and set up his own consultancy business, Kermit Roosevelt & Associates, using his contacts in Middle Eastern courts and cabinets to smooth the path in the region for such corporate clients as Raytheon and Northrop. A 1974 Northrop report estimated the value of contracts he had helped win for the company in Iran and Saudi Arabia at about a billion dollars. The following year, however, Kim was mired in scandal when a Senate Foreign Relations subcommittee uncovered evidence of payoffs by Northrop to two Saudi air force generals in a fighter plane deal, and pages of Kim's correspondence with the company were made public, revealing that he had consulted with his "friends in the CIA" about the moves of rival firms.[6]

Kim's once promising literary career also tailed off in middle age. The *Saturday Evening Post* rejected his essay about the Suez crisis, "The Ghost of Suez," and sales of his travelogue memoir about his trip to Africa retracing the footsteps of TR, *A Sentimental Safari*, proved disappointing. To rub salt in the wound, Miles Copeland's 1969 debut, *The Game of Nations*, whose revelatory contents caused Kim much "trouble and embarrassment," did relatively well. Most regrettably of all, what should have been the crowning glory of Kim's career, the publication in 1979 of the well-rehearsed story of the 1953 Iran coup, turned out to be anything but. Even before it was published, *Countercoup* ran into problems: First, the opposition of the shah, who, after seeing an early draft, reportedly objected to his depiction as a "waverer forced into various crucial decisions" (it is not clear whether this protest influenced the flattering portrayal of the king contained in the book's final version). Next, MI6 came forward demanding that all references to its involvement in the planning of TP-AJAX be removed. Rather than embarking on a complete rewrite, Kim hit on the ruse of simply substituting the name of the Anglo-Iranian Oil Company for that of the British secret service throughout the manuscript. When BP (as the AIOC now was) got wind of this development, it threatened libel action, causing Kim's publisher, McGraw-Hill, to pulp the first print run after copies had already gone out to reviewers. By now, the Iranian Revolution that overthrew the shah and installed the Ayatollah Khomeini as supreme leader had taken place, and what previously had looked to most people like a US victory in the Cold War had become instead a classic case of blowback. As one reviewer who had seen a copy of the pulped edition put it, the 1953 coup was "an event that changed dramatically the course of modern Iranian political history," yet here it was, represented as "an act of personal adventure entirely appropriate for the son of one of America's great families." Kim tried to acknowledge these developments in his foreword to the final version of *Countercoup*, which was eventually released in 1980, after one last delay caused by the US hostage crisis in Tehran. "What was a heroic story," he lamented, "has gone on to become a tragic story."[7]

Even if the 1979 Revolution had not taken place, it seems doubtful that Kim's Kipling-esque account of the 1953 coup would have fared much better, given that the tastes of the reading public had now shifted to more "realistic" espionage novels like John Le Carré's tales of double agents, betrayal, and cynicism—the world of Kim Philby rather than of *Kim*. Reviewing the course of Kim Roosevelt's final years, one senses a man being left behind by the march of history. If only he had lived earlier, at the same time as his grandfather or father, when a family like the Roosevelts could exercise its political will relatively unchallenged, when spying was the occupation of club-land amateurs rather than salaried civil servants, and when international travel was the preserve of a handful of intrepid explorers, not a crowd of jet-propelled tourists. Still, for all the disappointments and frustrations, Kim succeeded until the end in retaining the poise and self-assurance that had so eluded Kermit Sr. "I have had a satisfactory, often exciting life, of which I am appropriately proud," he declared in his Harvard sixtieth-reunion report, shortly before his death, at age eighty-four, in 2000. Predictably, perhaps, Kim's obituaries all dwelled on TP-AJAX and its unintended consequences; few remarked on his Arabism.[8]

What of the other, less famous Roosevelt cousin? After being assigned away from the Middle East in 1958, Archie served for another seventeen years in the CIA, in Madrid and in London, where he succeeded Frank Wisner as station chief in 1962 (Wisner struggled with mental illness and ultimately died by suicide in 1965), and finally in Washington as chief of the Africa and European divisions. It was a model career for an intelligence professional, and when he left the Agency in 1975 to build up a retirement nest egg working for David Rockefeller in Chase Manhattan Bank's international division, Archie was awarded the Distinguished Intelligence Medal and showered with heartfelt encomia. However, his memoirs, published in 1988, reveal that he had by this point become badly disillusioned with the Agency's leadership—Directors James Schlesinger and William Colby had both, in his view, betrayed their office by pandering to politicians—as well as with successive administrations' failures to heed the advice of area experts. The Agency, he felt, had lost its founding esprit de corps and was "no longer a happy place to work." As with cousin Kim, there was a palpable feeling of wistfulness about Archie's later life, an elegiac note of nostalgia for the past glories of the Roosevelt family and the childhood lure of the Golden Road to Samarkand. Still, the regret was tempered by Archie's capacity for wry, self-deprecatory humor—he was happy to tell, for instance, of how the barber in the shop next to the Chase Manhattan headquarters would address him as "Mr. Rockefeller," and how Lucky was sometimes greeted as "Happy," the name of Nelson Rockefeller's wife. He was also delighted when Lucky was appointed chief of protocol in the Reagan White House and thereby acquired the rank of ambassador. Archie was, in other words, still very much enjoying life when he unexpectedly died in his sleep at the age of seventy-two, in 1990.[9]

And what, finally, about the third member of the triumvirate, the original self-styled "Game Player"? Miles Copeland and his family stayed on in Beirut during the 1960s, occupying a splendid Arabesque villa overlooking the Mediterranean. The former CIA man still enjoyed his inside track in Cairo and, in the role of loyal alumnus, shuttled back and forth across the region trying to avert the Arab-Israeli crisis of the late 1960s. Conditions in Lebanon were deteriorating, however, and Miles's consultancy business ran into trouble when Jim Eichelberger eloped with the wife of a third partner, John Lufkin. By 1970, Nasser was dead of a heart attack, Miles was in bad odor with many of his former colleagues for having published *The Game of Nations* (CIA director Richard Helms was reportedly "furious" with him), and the Copelands had relocated to leafy St. John's Wood in London. The family's adventures were far from over, though. With the children acquiring fame and fortune in the music and entertainment industries, and Lorraine building her reputation as an archaeologist, Miles branched out into journalism, writing for the conservative American journal *National Review* (senior editor James Burnham had admired *The Game of Nations*) and appearing frequently on British radio and television as an indiscreet commentator on espionage and the Middle East. This new career did not prevent him from keeping his hand in as a high-level business consultant and occasional crypto-diplomat: shortly after the Iranian Revolution, at the suggestion of friends in the State Department, he teamed up again with Kim Roosevelt and his old Syria playmate Steve Meade to plan a rescue mission for the US embassy hostages. He even found time to help design a board game based on *The Game of Nations* for the British games manufacturer Waddington's, in which players representing "Superpowers" manipulated "Leaders" and "Secret Agents" to gain control of the imaginary region of Kark. ("Skill and nerve are the principal requirements in this amoral and cynical game," declared Miles on the box. "The first objective of any player is to keep himself in the game.")

Miles eventually began to slow down in the late 1980s, as injuries sustained in a serious car accident and arthritis took their toll, and he settled down to writing his autobiography, *The Game Player*, which appeared in 1989. He died of heart failure in 1991, age seventy-four, shortly after serving as a consultant on Scotland's investigation of the Lockerbie airline bombing.[10]

Miles had done very well in life, rising above his original station and passing the Roosevelt cousins as they moved in the other direction. Much the same was true of several other covert operatives from non–Ivy League backgrounds who had thrived in the heady excitement of World War II and the Cold War: Steve Meade, who after retiring from the military enjoyed a second career as a financial advisor, and Rocky Stone, an energetic campaigner for the deaf following his retirement from the Agency. The only individual of Miles's parvenu stock who did not fare so well was Wilbur Crane Eveland. During his spell in Beirut as Allen Dulles's personal agent, Eveland had developed a friendship with the British mole Kim Philby, then living and working in the Lebanese capital as a Middle East correspondent. Unwisely, the Arabist adventurer maintained contact with the double agent even after the latter's defection to the Soviet Union in 1963, exchanging jokey cards and letters with him in Moscow. Reports about Eveland's ongoing dealings with Philby found their way into CIA and FBI files on him already made thick by reports about his marital affairs and grievances filed by various officials whom he had crossed during his crypto-diplomatic peregrinations around the Middle East. Eveland lost his security clearance and suspected a hidden official hand when a business deal went bad and he wound up in jail in Singapore in 1976. He even claimed that a hit-and-run motor accident in which he was involved after the publication of his revelatory memoir *Ropes of Sand* in 1980 was an attempt on his life. Denied a government pension, Bill Eveland died in poverty in Boston in 1990.[11]

Game playing, it seems, did carry some risk of personal injury after all.

IT WOULD BE UNJUST NOT to recognize some of the CIA Arabists' positive accomplishments. Building on the tradition of personal interaction with the Arab world they inherited from their predecessors in the OSS, they rapidly acquired an impressive level of firsthand experience and knowledge of the Middle East that belied the United States' lack of prior official engagement with the region. They enjoyed a degree of access to and influence among Middle Eastern leaders—including the foremost Arab figure of his day, Gamal Nasser—that no generation of American officials has been able to reproduce since. They made a sincere and imaginative effort to solve the Arab-Israeli conflict that, although it ended in failure, anticipated key aspects of later, more successful peace initiatives. And they tried to rein in the worst antinationalist excesses of Secretary of State John Foster Dulles and their counterparts in MI6. Compared with some of the gross missteps that would come later in US policy toward the Middle East, the early CIA's emphasis on nonmilitary, covert operations to secure American goals in the region looks almost prudent in comparison.

In the end, though, the failures and unintended consequences of CIA Arabism seem more significant. Kim Roosevelt and the others might have wanted to build a new kind of Western relationship with the Arab world, a nonimperial, non-Orientalist one that reflected Americans' record of "disinterested benevolence" in the region. In fact, though, they ended up replicating much of the British imperial experience in the Middle East, shoring up client monarchies with covert interventions and secret subsidies, first in Iran and then in the Arab countries too. Even in those instances in which they did support progressive Arab nationalists— that is, in Syria (if Husni Za'im counts as such) and in Egypt—they also fueled a tendency toward military authoritarianism and the creation of the repressive, Bonapartist states that Arabs are still trying to cast off today. Britain's Covert Empire became America's Covert Empire; Britain's Great Game became America's Great Game.

The Arabists' efforts to garner sympathy and support for the Arab cause at home in the United States were similarly ill-fated. The arrangement of secret CIA funding for the American Friends of the Middle East, while briefly ensuring that a pro-Arab voice was at least heard in domestic debates about US policy toward the region, in the end did more harm than good. For all their love of storytelling, the Arabists failed to tell the story of the Arabs in ways that captured the imagination of their fellow Americans. Where was the Arabist equivalent of *Exodus*, the wildly successful novel about the founding of Israel by the Zionist Leon Uris?[12]

The Arabists themselves were not necessarily to blame for these failures. They were constantly obstructed and frustrated by factors beyond their control: the meddling of Secretary of State Dulles, the scheming of their British counterparts in MI6, and the resistance to their designs of the Arab world itself. That said, internal flaws in CIA Arabism arguably doomed it from the outset. These included lingering traces of the very imperialist and Orientalist modes of thought that it professed to reject, a strong personal inclination toward romantic adventurism, and an aristocratic impatience with the ordinary processes of democratic government that manifested itself in the Arabists' readiness to resort to crypto-diplomacy abroad and secret government funding for Kim Roosevelt's Arabist, anti-Zionist network at home. In this regard, the Arabists' experience was typical of the early drift of the CIA from its original intelligence-gathering mission toward a growing preoccupation with covert operations of dubious value; in the imagery of *Kim*, the Game had distracted them from the Quest.

More than half a century on, the echoes of the CIA Arabists' experience are manifold: in recent efforts by politicians to manipulate intelligence about Iraq so that it suited predetermined policy outcomes; in the continuing controversy about US policy concerning the Arab-Israeli dispute, including debates between Zionists and anti-Zionists within the American Jewish community about appropriate levels of support for Israel; in discussions about the CIA's potential role in bringing about regime change in Middle Eastern countries with repressive governments (some recent pronouncements about the Agency's lack of assets in Syria could easily have dated from the summer of 1957); and in the ongoing tension in US Middle East policy, brought into dramatic relief by the Arab Spring, between the strategic desire for regional stability and the impulse to support the democratic aspirations of ordinary Arabs— between, as Miles Copeland might have put it, Machiavellianism and idealism.

Evidently, the era of the CIA Arabists was foundational to the current American relationship with the Middle East. At a time of renewed and profound flux in the Arab world, it would serve all those concerned with US policy in that region to study the earlier moment carefully, to understand better the underlying historical forces, domestic as well as foreign, cultural and emotional as well as political, that have shaped the fraught American–Middle Eastern encounter ever since.

Notes

Abbreviations

ABRP	Archibald B. Roosevelt Jr. Papers
ACJP	American Council for Judaism Papers
AR	Archie Roosevelt
AWF	Ann Whitman File
DDEL	Dwight D. Eisenhower Library
DTP	Dorothy Thompson Papers
FAOHP	Foreign Affairs Oral History Project
FO	Foreign Office
FRUS	*Foreign Relations of the United States*
HSTL	Harry S. Truman Library
JFDP	John Foster Dulles Papers
JNP	John Nuveen Jr. Papers
KR	Kermit "Kim" Roosevelt
KRBRP	Kermit Roosevelt and Belle Roosevelt Papers
MC	Miles Copeland
NA	US National Archives, College Park, MD
PRO	UK Public Record Office, Kew, London
RG	Record Group
WAEP	William Alfred Eddy Papers
WCEP	Wilbur Crane Eveland Papers
WHCF	White House Central Files

Preface

1. Two such articles are particularly noteworthy: Douglas Little, "Mission Impossible: The CIA and the Cult of Covert Action in the Middle East," *Diplomatic History* 28, no. 5 (2004): 663–701; and W. Scott Lucas and Alistair Morey, "The Hidden Alliance: The CIA and MI6 Before and After Suez," *Intelligence and National Security* 15, no. 2 (2000): 95–120.

2. See, for example, the Special Forum in the September 2012 issue of *Diplomatic History*. Academic historians of American foreign relations will notice the influence of other recent scholarly concerns on the pages that follow, in particular gender, Orientalism, modernization theory, and nongovernment actors in state-private networks. Explicit discussions of these concepts can be found occasionally in the endnotes.

3. An excellent example of this approach in the field of intelligence history is Evan Thomas, *The Very Best Men: Four Who Dared: The Early Years of the CIA* (New York: Simon & Schuster, 1995).

One: Learning the Game

1. Kermit "Kim" Roosevelt Jr. (hereafter KR), "The Lure of the East," *The American Boy–Youth's Companion* 58 (May 1931): 58.

2. KR, *A Sentimental Safari* (New York: Knopf, 1963), xiii.

3. See Edward W. Said, introduction to *Kim*, by Rudyard Kipling (London: Penguin, 1989), 30–46.

4. Archie Roosevelt (hereafter AR), *For Lust of Knowing: Memoirs of an Intelligence Officer* (Boston: Little, Brown, 1988), 4; KR to Edith Roosevelt, December 18, 1944, Part II, box 12, folder 6, Kermit Roosevelt and Belle Roosevelt Papers (hereafter KRBRP), Library of Congress, Washington, DC; KR, *Sentimental Safari*, xx.

5. KR, *Sentimental Safari*, vii–viii.

6. Kermit Roosevelt quoted in Peter Collier, *The Roosevelts: An American Saga* (New York: Simon & Schuster, 1994), 198–199; Theodore Roosevelt quoted in Michael B. Oren, *Power, Faith, and Fantasy: America in the Middle East, 1776 to the Present* (New York: Norton, 2007), 319; Rudyard Kipling to Kermit Roosevelt, August 2, 1917, I, 61, Kipling, Rudyard, KRBRP.

7. Kermit Roosevelt [Sr.], *War in the Garden of Eden* (New York: Scribner's Sons, 1919), 14–15, 25. Later, Kim Roosevelt too would testify to a similar childhood fascination with the *Nights*, specifically citing the translation by the great British explorer Sir Richard Francis Burton. KR, *Arabs, Oil, and History: The Story of the Middle East* (Port Washington, NY: Kennikat, 1969), 21.

8. Kermit Roosevelt, *War in the Garden of Eden*, 165; Kipling to Kermit Roosevelt, September 3, 1918, I, 61, Kipling, Rudyard, KRBRP.

9. Kermit Roosevelt, *War in the Garden of Eden*, 201–204.

10. Priya Satia, *Spies in Arabia: The Great War and the Cultural Foundations of Britain's Covert Empire in the Middle East* (Oxford: Oxford University Press, 2008); T. E. Shaw [Lawrence] to Kermit Roosevelt, December 27, 1928, I, 89, Shaw, Thomas Edward, KRBRP.

11. Kermit Roosevelt III, interview by author, Washington, DC, April 12, 2010.

12. Lodge quoted in Robert D. Dean, *Imperial Brotherhood: Gender and the Making of Cold War Foreign Policy* (Amherst, MA: University of Massachusetts Press, 2001), 21; TR quoted in ibid., 19; Walter Isaacson and Evan Thomas, *The Wise Men: Six Friends and the World They Made: Acheson, Bohlen, Harriman, Kennan, Lovett, McCloy* (New York: Simon & Schuster, 1986), 48.

13. Peabody quoted in Isaacson and Thomas, *Wise Men*, 47; Peabody quoted in Thomas, *Very Best Men*, 82; Lodge quoted in Charles S. Maier, *Among Empires: American Ascendancy and Its Predecessors* (Cambridge, MA: Harvard University Press, 2006), 22.

14. KR to Belle Roosevelt, October 22, 1928, II, 12.3, KRBRP; Endicott Peabody, Monthly Report, December 14, 1928, II, 12.8, KRBRP; William E. Mott to Belle Roosevelt, February 19, 1929, II, 12.3, KRBRP; KR to Belle Roosevelt, February 1, 1929, II, 12.3, KRBRP.

15. KR to Belle Roosevelt, May 24, 1929, II, 12.3, KRBRP; KR, untitled poem, no date, I, 14, Roosevelt, Kermit Jr. (Kim), KRBRP.

16. Kermit Roosevelt to KR, July 24, 1934, I, 14, Roosevelt, Kermit Jr. (Kim), KRBRP; KR quoted in Thomas, *Very Best Men*, 108.

17. KR to Ethel Roosevelt, March 1, 1935, II, 12.4, KRBRP; KR to Belle Roosevelt, October 15, November 2, July 9, July 25, and July 30, 1935, II, 12.4, KRBRP.

18. KR to Belle Roosevelt, December 4, 1935, II, 12.4, KRBRP; KR to Belle Roosevelt, July 9, and October 19, 1936, II, 12.5, KRBRP; KR to Kermit Roosevelt, April 20, 1937, II, 12.5, KRBRP; Peabody to Kermit Roosevelt, February 26, 1938, I, 79, Peabody, Endicott, KRBRP.

19. KR to Belle Roosevelt, November 24, 1940, I, 142, Roosevelt, Kermit, KRBRP. For more about the Room, see Joseph E. Persico, *Roosevelt's Secret War: FDR and World War II Espionage* (New York: Random House, 2001), 10–13.

20. For more on Donovan, see Douglas Waller, *Wild Bill Donovan: The Spymaster Who Created the OSS and Modern American Espionage* (New York: Free Press, 2011). KR to Kermit Roosevelt, March 11, 1941, I, 14, Roosevelt, Kermit Jr. (Kim), KRBRP; KR to Belle Roosevelt, no date, I, 142, Roosevelt, Kermit (son), KRBRP; KR, *Countercoup: The Struggle for the Control of*

Iran (New York: McGraw-Hill, 1979), 23–24; "Theater Service Record," December 26, 1944, 658, Roosevelt, Kermit, Personnel Files, 1941–45, Records of the Office of Strategic Services, Record Group (hereafter RG) 226, National Archives (hereafter NA), College Park, MD.

21. Peabody to Belle Roosevelt, June 16, 1943, I, 142, Roosevelt, Kermit, KRBRP.

Two: Beginning the Quest

1. AR to Katherine Tweed, no date, 12.7, Archibald B. Roosevelt Jr. Papers (hereafter ABRP), Library of Congress, Washington, DC.

2. AR, *Lust of Knowing*, 11, 33, 19.

3. Ibid., 26.

4. Ibid., 14, 16.

5. Ibid., 24, 26.

6. Ibid., 23. The nonconformist trait in the Archibald Roosevelt family was even more pronounced in the case of Archie's sister Theodora, who moved to South America in the late 1930s to pursue a career in modern dance. Later, as Theodora Keogh, she published a series of novels noted for their daring form and subject matter.

7. AR to Grace Roosevelt, no date, 12.7, ABRP; John M. Potter to G. E. Buxton, June 3, 1942, 658, Roosevelt, Archibald Bulloch, Personnel Files, 1941–45, RG 226, NA.

8. TR quoted in Oren, *Power, Faith, and Fantasy*, 319; Jardine quoted in Peter L. Hahn, *Crisis and Crossfire: The United States and the Middle East Since 1945* (Washington, DC: Potomac Books, 2005), 2.

9. For an authoritative recent account of US-Arab relations emphasizing the missionary tradition, see Ussama Makdisi, *Faith Misplaced: The Broken Promise of U.S.-Arab Relations: 1820–2001* (New York: PublicAffairs, 2010).

10. Theologian Samuel Hopkins, quoted in Abbas Amanat and Magnus T. Bernhardsson, eds., *U.S.-Middle East Historical Encounters: A Critical Survey* (Gainesville: University Press of Florida, 2007), 2. See Rashid Khalidi, *Resurrecting Empire: Western Footprints and America's Perilous Path in the Middle East* (Boston: Beacon, 2004), 30–35.

11. Jack Philby's influence would later return to haunt both the Americans and the British in the shape of his son, the double agent Kim Philby.

12. See Thomas W. Lippman, *Arabian Knight: Colonel Bill Eddy USMC and the Rise of American Power in the Middle East* (Vista, CA: Selwa, 2008).

13. Carleton S. Coon, *A North Africa Story: The Anthropologist as OSS Agent, 1941–1943* (Ipswich, MA: Gambit, 1980), 15–16.

14. William Eddy, "The Moors Draw Their Knives in Tangier," 1957, 17.1, William Alfred Eddy Papers (hereafter WAEP), Seeley G. Mudd Manuscript Library, Princeton University, Princeton, NJ; Eddy quoted in R. Harris Smith, *OSS: The Secret History of America's First Central Intelligence Agency* (Berkeley: University of California Press, 1972), 51.

15. Patton quoted in Stewart Alsop and Thomas Braden, *Sub Rosa: The OSS and American Espionage* (New York: Harcourt, Brace & World, 1964), 87.

16. In an otherwise quite critical account of TORCH, historian Bradley F. Smith notes that "Eddy had performed his intelligence tasks brilliantly" (*The Shadow Warriors: O.S.S. and the Origins of the C.I.A.* [New York: Basic Books, 1983], 156).

17. AR, *Lust of Knowing*, 64, 50; AR, unpublished essay about Siblini, 3.5, ABRP; AR, *Lust of Knowing*, 68.

18. AR, *Lust of Knowing*, 70; see, for example, AR, "Anti-American Activities of French Among Arabs," January 23, 1943, II, 1.9, KRBRP.

19. AR, *Lust of Knowing*, 79; AR, "Anti-American Propaganda Conducted by the French Authorities Among the Arabs," March 23, 1943, II, 1.10, KRBRP.

20. AR to Jay Allen, February 15, 1943, II, 1.9, KRBRP; AR, "Conversation with the Sultan of Morocco," March 23, 1943, II, 1.10, KRBRP; AR to Robert Sherwood, "Annual Pilgrimage to Mecca," September 15, 1943, 3.6, ABRP.

21. Smith, *OSS*, 64.

22. AR, "A Few Facts about the Bey's Abdication," no date, 3.9, ABRP; AR, *Lust of Knowing*, 101, 108; AR, "Summary of the Arab Situation in Tunisia," no date [July 1943], 3.9, ABRP.

23. AR, "Report on My Activities," no date [July 1943], 3.10, ABRP; AR, *Lust of Knowing*, 114.

24. AR, *Lust of Knowing*, 110.

25. There is a strong similarity between Archie Roosevelt's kind of Arabism and the "post-Orientalist," Cold War US discourse about the Middle East described by cultural historian Melani McAlister in her groundbreaking book, *Epic Encounters*. According to McAlister, "American power worked very hard to fracture the old European logic and to install new frameworks," emphasizing the values of "affiliation, appropriation, and co-optation" instead of "distance, othering, and containment." McAlister detects expressions of this post-Orientalist impulse in American popular culture; I do so in CIA covert operations. See Melani McAlister, *Epic Encounters: Culture, Media, and U.S. Interests in the Middle East since 1945*, updated ed. with a post–9/11 chapter (Berkeley: University of California Press, 2005), 11, 2.

Three: OSS/Cairo

1. Collier, *The Roosevelts*, 303; KR to Kermit Roosevelt, February 23, 1932, II, 12.3, KRBRP; AR, *Lust of Knowing*, 350, 118.

2. KR, *Countercoup*, 23–24. One of Ted Roosevelt's sons, Quentin II, did in fact enter Chinese aviation, dying in a plane crash in 1949 while en route from Shanghai to Hong Kong on a mission for the CIA. Collier, *The Roosevelts*, 449.

3. Dean Acheson to Peter Karlow, June 27, 1946, I, 142, Roosevelt, Kermit (son), KRBRP; Belle Roosevelt, diary, June 10, 1942, I, 136, Diaries 1942–1945, KRBRP.

4. KR, *Countercoup*, 36. A son of missionaries and critic of European imperialism, Landis worked to dissolve British monopolies in Egypt and quietly encourage Egyptian nationalists. See Oren, *Power, Faith, and Fantasy*, 458–460.

5. KR, *Arabs, Oil, and History*, 4; Stephen Penrose to T. F. Bland, April 2, 1944, 658, Roosevelt, Kermit, Personnel Files, 1941–45, RG 226, NA; Prospectus for NE Project #27, SOPHIA, April 18, 1944, 55, "History of OSS Cairo," RG 226, NA.

6. AR, *Lust of Knowing*, 349–350.

7. KR, *Arabs, Oil, and History*, 3, 4; Bickham Sweet-Escott, *Baker Street Irregular* (London: Methuen, 1965), 73; Macmillan quoted in Matthew Jones, "'Kipling and All That': American Perceptions of SOE and British Imperial Intrigue in the Balkans, 1943–1945," in *The Politics and Strategy of Clandestine War: Special Operations Executive, 1940–1946*, ed. Neville Wylie (London: Routledge, 2007), 99.

8. Secretary of State Hull to Ambassador Winant, August 27, 1942, *Foreign Relations of the United States* [hereafter *FRUS*], *1942: Vol. 4: The Near East and Africa* (Washington, DC: Government Printing Office, 1942), 27, 28. See also Smith, *OSS*, 124–125.

9. Sweet-Escott, *Baker Street Irregular*, 136; "For Hoskins from Donovan," January 3, 1943, 3.9, Harold B. Hoskins Papers, Seeley G. Mudd Manuscript Library, Princeton University, Princeton, NJ.

10. Captain John Toulmin, "Recommendation for Award to Mr. Stephen B. L. Penrose," November 11, 1944, 5.12, Stephen B. L. Penrose Jr. Papers, Whitman College, Walla Walla, WA.

11. Jane Smiley Hart, interview by Frances Stickles, October 1, 1990, 3.9, Penrose Papers; Barry Rubin, *Istanbul Intrigues* (New York: McGraw-Hill, 1989), 134; Stephen Penrose to Gordon Loud, July 28, 1943, 5.4, Penrose Papers.

12. KR, *Arabs, Oil, and History*, 5; Hart interview.

13. Penrose to Mr. Howland, November 12, 1942, declassified OSS records, Penrose Papers.

14. KR, *Arabs, Oil, and History*, 7, 15, 39.

15. KR, *Countercoup*, 37.

16. Michael P. Zirinsky, "Render Therefore Unto Caesar the Things Which Are Caesar's: American Presbyterian Educators and Reza Shah," *Iranian Studies* 26, nos. 3–4 (1993): 354; Donald N. Wilber, *Adventures in the Middle East: Excursions and Incursions* (Princeton, NJ: Darwin, 1986), 135–137.

17. AR, *Lust of Knowing*, 121.

18. Ibid., 124; AR to Katherine Tweed, June 22, 1944, 1.3, ABRP.

19. AR, *Lust of Knowing*, 350–351, 313.

20. Jones, "'Kipling and All That,'" 104; "Theater Service Record" and Lewis G. Leary, "Assessment of Kermit Roosevelt," January 8, 1945, 658, Roosevelt, Kermit, Personnel Files, 1941–45, RG 226, NA.

21. Anthony Cave Brown, ed., *The Secret War Report of the OSS* (New York: Berkeley Publications, 1976), 179; Toulmin, "Recommendation for Award."

Four: Great Game Redux

1. AR, *Lust of Knowing*, 209–210.

2. Ibid., 128, 127; see AR to K. W. Roosevelt, February 12, 1945, 1.6, ABRP; AR, *Lust of Knowing*, 208.

3. AR, *Lust of Knowing*, 169.

4. AR, diary, April 3, 1944, 1.5, ABRP; AR, *Lust of Knowing*, 137.

5. AR, *Lust of Knowing*, 207, 206; AR, "Notes on the Tribal Populations of Iraq," December 1, 1945, 2.6, ABRP; AR, *Lust of Knowing*, 169.

6. AR, *Lust of Knowing*, 413.

7. Ibid., 36; AR, "A Study in Effrontery," *New York Herald Tribune*, February 15, 1940. See also AR, *Lust of Knowing*, 40–42.

8. AR, *Lust of Knowing*, 219.

9. Ibid., 201, 34.

10. Philip Hitti to AR, September 4, 1945, 1.6, ABRP; AR, *Lust of Knowing*, 212; AR, diary, December 27, 1945, 1.5, ABRP; AR, diary, January 5, 1946, 1.7, ABRP.

11. Churchill quoted in Stephen Kinzer, *All the Shah's Men: An American Coup and the Roots of Middle East Terror*, 2nd ed. (Hoboken, NJ: Wiley & Sons, 2008), 39.

12. For more on this promising early history, see Mansour Bonakdarian, "Great Expectations: U.S.-Iranian Relations, 1911–1951," in Amanat and Bernhardsson, eds., *U.S.-Middle East Historical Encounters*, 121–141.

13. Loy Henderson to Dean Acheson, "The Present Situation in the Near East—A Danger to World Peace," no date [December 1945], *FRUS 1946, Vol. 7*, 2. For a synthesis of recent historical scholarship about Soviet intentions toward Iran, see Odd Arne Westad, *The Global Cold War: Third World Interventions and the Making of Our Times* (Cambridge: Cambridge University Press, 2005), 60–64.

14. AR, *Lust of Knowing*, 228, 215, 230.

15. Ibid., 231.

16. Ibid., 204.

17. Ibid., 226, 237–238; AR, diary, June 20, 1946, 1.7, ABRP.

18. AR, *Lust of Knowing*, 240, 437.

19. Ibid., 438; AR to K. W. Roosevelt, January 20, 1945, 1.6, ABRP; AR, diary, June 19, 1946, 1.7, ABRP.

20. George V. Allen, unpublished memoir about service in Iran, 70–71, George V. Allen Papers, Harry S. Truman Library (hereafter HSTL), Independence, MO; AR, book manuscript, 2.8, ABRP.

Five: Zion

1. Quoted in Rhodri Jeffreys-Jones, *The CIA and American Democracy*, 3rd ed. (New Haven, CT: Yale University Press, 2003), 30.

2. Peter Grose, *Gentleman Spy: The Life of Allen Dulles* (Boston: Houghton Mifflin, 1994), 104; Allen Dulles, "Memorandum Respecting Section 202 (Central Intelligence Agency) of the Bill to Provide for a National Defense Establishment," April 25, 1947, 2, 224–234 (April 1947), General Records of the Department of State, RG 59, Supplementary Documents from the Foreign Relations Series Relating to the U.S. Intelligence Community, HSTL.

3. Celler quoted in H. W. Brands, *Inside the Cold War: Loy Henderson and the Rise of American Empire, 1918–1961* (New York: Oxford University Press, 1991), 189.

4. For differing views on the question of Henderson and anti-Semitism, see ibid., 190–191, and Elihu Bergman, "Unexpected Recognition: Some Observations on the Failure of a Last-Gasp Campaign in the U.S. State Department to Abort a Jewish State," *Modern Judaism* 19, no. 2 (May 1999): 165–166.

5. See, for example, Penrose to Fred F. Goodsell, December 9, 1942, OSS Records, Penrose Papers; Penrose to redacted, February 4, February 17, and March 11, 1943, 5.3, Penrose Papers.

6. See, for example, Penrose to L. Wendell Fifield, December 31, 1942, OSS Records, Penrose Papers. "I am anxious to prevent the execution of policies which long study has convinced me are dangerous not only to the Near East but in the long run to the proponents of the policies themselves," Penrose wrote.

7. Analyst quoted in Robert Vitalis, *America's Kingdom: Mythmaking on the Saudi Oil Frontier* (Stanford, CA: Stanford University Press, 2007), 64.

8. "Summary of Lieutenant Colonel Harold B. Hoskins' Report on the Near East," enclosed with Cordell Hull to Franklin Roosevelt, May 7, 1943, *FRUS 1943, Vol. 4*, 782; "Memorandum of Conversation, by Lieutenant Colonel Harold B. Hoskins," Washington, DC, September 27, 1943, *FRUS 1943, Vol. 4*, 812, 813.

9. For a detailed account of the meeting between FDR and Ibn Saud emphasizing Eddy's role, see Lippman, *Arabian Knight*, 133–144.

10. Truman quoted in Oren, *Power, Faith, and Fantasy*, 484.

11. See Lippman, *Arabian Knight*, 219–226, and Michael J. Cohen, "William A. Eddy, the Oil Lobby, and the Palestine Problem," *Middle Eastern Studies* 30, no. 1 (1994): 166–180; Truman quoted in Lippman, *Arabian Knight*, 218.

12. The story of the run-up to Palestine's partition and Harry Truman's recognition of Israel in May 1948 has been told in countless books and articles, most recently Allis Radosh and Ronald Radosh, *A Safe Haven: Harry S. Truman and the Founding of Israel* (New York: Harper, 2009).

13. "The Consequences of the Partition of Palestine," Office of Research Estimates 55, November 28, 1947, 214, President's Secretary's File: Intelligence File, 1946–53, HSTL. See Lippman, *Arabian Knight*, 232–234; see also Thomas W. Lippman, "The View from 1947: The CIA and the Partition of Palestine," *Middle East Journal* 61, no. 1 (2007): 17–28.

14. William Eddy, statement, October 10, 1947, 8.6, WAEP. See Lippman, *Arabian Knight*, 234–235.

15. For the change in the meaning of "Arabist," see Robert D. Kaplan, *The Arabists: The Romance of an American Elite* (New York: Free Press, 1993), 98; for the circulation of Orientalist imagery of Arabs in the postwar United States, see Douglas Little, *American Orientalism: The United States and the Middle East Since 1945* (Chapel Hill: University of North Carolina Press, 2002), 25–33; for the cultural resonance of Zionism in postwar America, see Michelle Mart, "Constructing a Universal Ideal: Anti-Semitism, American Jews, and the Founding of Israel," *Modern Judaism* 20, no. 2 (2000): 181–208; and for missionary attempts to educate Americans about the Arab world, see Ussama Makdisi, "'Anti-Americanism' in the Arab World: An Interpretation of a Brief History," *Journal of American History* 89, no. 2 (2002): 541–542.

16. AR, *Lust of Knowing*, 293, 295. Mike Mitchell was identified by pseudonyms in Archie Roosevelt's *Lust of Knowing* and Miles Copeland (hereafter MC), *The Game Player: The Confessions of the CIA's Original Political Operative* (London: Aurum, 1989): Luke Gabriel and Nick Michelson, respectively. His real name appears in OSS records and the transcript of KR, interview by R. Harris Smith, no date, 10, R. Harris Smith Collection, Hoover Institution, Stanford University, Stanford, CA. Archie Roosevelt did not name Dennett in his memoirs, but the deceased CIG officer is identified in Copeland's *Game Player*, 81. This identification is confirmed in Michael Mitchell to AEXP, "Archibald Roosevelt," March 28, 1947, 658, Roosevelt, Archibald Bulloch, Personnel Files, 1941–45, RG 226, NA.

17. AR, *Lust of Knowing*, 293.

Six: The Guest No One Invites Again

1. MC, *Game Player*, 2; John Keay, *Sowing the Wind: The Seeds of Conflict in the Middle East* (New York: Norton, 2003), 390. Copeland's books are: *Game Player*; *The Game of Nations: The Amorality of Power Politics* (London: Weidenfeld & Nicolson, 1969); *Without Cloak or Dagger: The Truth About the New Espionage* (New York: Simon & Schuster, 1974).

2. Confidential source; Philby quoted in Karl E. Meyer and Shareen Blair Brysac, *Kingmakers: The Invention of the Modern Middle East* (New York: Norton, 2008), 352.

3. Lorraine Copeland, e-mail to author, November 20, 2010; MC, *Game Player*, 4, 6; Miles A. Copeland III, interview by author, Hollywood, CA, February 22, 2010; Wilbur Crane Eveland, *Ropes of Sand: America's Failure in the Middle East* (New York: Norton, 1980), 96; Jenna Weber, W. S. Hoole Special Collections Library, University of Alabama, e-mails to author, November 23 and November 29, 2010.

4. MC, *Game Player*, 8–9; Dan Morgenstern, telephone interview by author, November 22, 2010; Patrick White, e-mail to author, November 18, 2010; MC, DD/Personnel Data Sheet, November 4, 1955, CO5650522, CIA Freedom of Information Act (hereafter FOIA) request by author.

5. MC, *Game Player*, 11–12; James L. Gilbert, John P. Finnegan, and Ann Bray, *In the Shadow of the Sphinx: A History of Army Counterintelligence* (Washington, DC: Government Printing Office, 2005), 32.

6. MC, *Game Player*, 28.

7. Lorraine Copeland e-mail, November 20, 2010; MC, Personal History Statement, no date [1945], CO5651590, CIA FOIA.

8. MC, *Game Player*, 54, 56; MC, Personal History Statement.

9. Lorraine Copeland e-mail, November 20, 2010; MC, *Game Player*, chap. 10; Kermit Roosevelt III interview.

10. MC, *Game Player*, 79, 80.

11. Ibid., 81; *Daily Telegraph*, June 2, 1990, 13.4, ABRP; Selwa "Lucky" Roosevelt, interview by author, Washington, DC, April 13, 2010.

12. MC, *Game of Nations*, 11; MC, *Game Player*, 112; AR, diary, September 20, 1947, 1.7, ABRP.

Seven: Game Plan

1. KR, *Countercoup*, 51. Kim's *Harper's* articles included: "The Arabs Live There Too," *Harper's Magazine* (October 1946): 289–294; "Egypt's Inferiority Complex," *Harper's Magazine* (October 1947): 357–364; "Triple Play for the Middle East," *Harper's Magazine* (April 1948): 359–369. Substantial chunks of these articles found their way verbatim into KR, *Arabs, Oil, and History*.

2. Polly to Belle Roosevelt, June 1, [1947], I, 142, Roosevelt, Kermit, KRBRP.

3. KR to Belle Roosevelt, June 14, 1947, I, 143, Roosevelt, Mary Gaddis (Polly), KRBRP.

4. KR, *Arabs, Oil, and History*, 87, 106, 103, 117, 103.

5. Ibid., 251, 250, 67.

6. Ibid., 7, 259.

7. Ibid., 98, 146, 43.

8. Ibid., 265, 11, 156.

9. Ibid., 84.

10. Ibid., 184–185, 178.

11. Jonathan Roosevelt, interview by author, Washington, DC, February 20, 2010.

12. Ibid.; KR, "Arabs Live There Too"; George Levison to Elmer Berger, April 7, 1948, 74.9, American Council for Judaism Papers (hereafter ACJP), Wisconsin Historical Society, Madison; State Department memo quoted in Hahn, *Crisis and Crossfire*, 23. Kim's articles and letters from this period include "The Middle East and the Prospect for World Government," *Annals of the American Academy of Political and Social Science* 264 (July 1949): 52–57; "Will the Arabs Fight?," *Saturday Evening Post*, December 27, 1947, 20–56; "The Puzzle of Jerusalem's Mufti," *Saturday Evening Post*, June 12, 1948, 26–166; letter, *New York Times*, June 8, 1948, 24.

13. This article, which appeared in the January 1948 issue of the *Middle East Journal*, was reprinted as KR, *Partition of Palestine: A Lesson in Pressure Politics* (New York: Institute of Arab American Affairs, 1948). The quotations are from pages 1, 2, and 14 of the pamphlet.

14. Arab Office quoted in Rory Miller, "More Sinned Against Than Sinning? The Case of the Arab Office, Washington, 1945–1948," *Diplomacy and Statecraft* 15, no. 2 (2004): 311, 318. For more on Totah, see Colin Rutherford, "The Education of Dr. Khalil Totah" (master's thesis, California State University, Long Beach, 2010).

15. The best previous effort to anatomize the emergent Arabist, anti-Zionist, state-private network is Matthew F. Jacobs, *Imagining the Middle East: The Building of an American Foreign Policy, 1918-1967* (Chapel Hill: University of North Carolina Press, 2011), chap. 5.

16. AR, diary, November 6, 1947, 1.7, ABRP; William Mulligan, biographical sketch of J. T. Duce, 1.17, William E. Mulligan Papers, Special Collections, Georgetown University Library, Washington, DC; KR, *Arabs, Oil, and History*, chap. 16. Historian Robert Vitalis has recently challenged the canonical version of ARAMCO history, documenting harsh treatment by the company of its Arabian employees in *America's Kingdom*.

17. Thomas A. Kolsky, *Jews Against Zionism: The American Council for Judaism, 1942–1948* (Philadelphia: Temple University Press, 1990); Elmer Berger, *Memoirs of an Anti-Zionist Jew* (Beirut: Institute for Palestine Studies, 1978); Jack Ross, *Rabbi Outcast: Elmer Berger and American Jewish Anti-Zionism* (Washington, DC: Potomac Books, 2011).

18. Berger to Levison, September 23, 1946, 74.7, ACJP. Other information about the ACJ's State Department links is from Kolsky, *Jews Against Zionism*.

19. Levison to Berger, June 16, 1947, 74.8, ACJP.

20. James M. Baumohl to Donald Bolles, November 25, 1947, 63.12, ACJP; Levison to James Baumohl, November 8, 1947, 74.8, ACJP; Berger to Dorothy Thompson, February 14, 1949, 122.2, ACJP.

21. Jonathan Roosevelt interview; Kermit Roosevelt III interview; Polly Roosevelt to Berger, no date, 4, Kermit Roosevelt Jr. 1954, Addition M67–130, ACJP; Levison to Lessing Rosenwald, March 20, 1953, 75.3, ACJP.

22. Virginia C. Gildersleeve, KR, and Garland Evans Hopkins to Allen Dulles, February 21, 1948, 49.10, Allen W. Dulles Papers, Seeley G. Mudd Manuscript Library, Princeton University, Princeton, NJ; Virginia Crocheron Gildersleeve, *Many a Good Crusade: Memoirs* (New York: Macmillan, 1954), 171ff. For women and associations, see Helen Laville, *Cold War Women: The International Activities of American Women's Organisations* (Manchester, UK: Manchester University Press, 2002).

23. "New Committee Opposes U.N.'s Palestine Plan," *Herald Tribune*, March 3, 1948, 45.3, ACJP; "A 20-Year Story," *Near East Report,* October 1964, B-13; Berger to Levison, April 16, 1948, 74.9, ACJP.

24. Gildersleeve, *Many a Good Crusade*, 409–410; Levison to Berger, no date [probably March 19 or 20, 1948], 74.9, ACJP.

25. Truman quoted in Oren, *Power, Faith, and Fantasy*, 495; KR, statement, April 12, 1948, 45.3, ACJP; KR to Rosenwald, April 15, 1948, 45.3, ACJP; KR to Berger, May 10, 1948, 45.3, ACJP.

26. Gildersleeve to Berger, November 26, 1948, 45.3, ACJP; KR to Berger, May 25, 1949, 106.1, ACJP; Berger to Levison, February 18, 1949, 74.10, ACJP; Berger to KR, March 3, 1949, 106.1, ACJP. On Gildersleeve and Jewish students, see Rosalind Rosenberg, "Living Legacies: Virginia Gildersleeve: Opening the Gates," *Columbia University Alumni Magazine*, Summer 2001, http:// www.columbia.edu/cu/alumni/Magazine/Summer2001/Gildersleeve.html.

Eight: The Right Kind of Leader? Syria, 1949

1. Lorraine Copeland, e-mail to author, November 23, 2010; AR, *Lust of Knowing*, 325–326.
2. AR, *Lust of Knowing*, 296–297.
3. MC, *Game Player*, 91–92; MC, *Without Cloak or Dagger*, 48n.
4. Mitchell cable quoted in AR, *Lust of Knowing*, 296; Ian Copeland, *Wild Thing: The Backstage, on the Road, in the Studio, off the Charts: Memoirs of Ian Copeland* (New York: Simon & Schuster, 1995), 34; Mitchell quoted in AR, *Lust of Knowing*, 296; AR, diary, October 14 and October 24, 1947, 1.7, ABRP.
5. MC, *Game of Nations*, 34–36; MC, *Game Player*, 86; MC, *Game of Nations*, 34.
6. Lorraine Copeland e-mail, November 23, 2010.
7. KR, *Arabs, Oil, and History*, chap. 15.
8. MC, *Game Player*, 89; "Policy Statement," January 5, 1949, 11, Policy Statement—Syria and Lebanon, Lot 54D403, Bureau of Near Eastern, South Asian, and African Affairs, Office of Near Eastern Affairs, Subject Files 1920–54, RG 59, NA.
9. KR, *Arabs, Oil, and History*, 268–270.
10. Miles Copeland III interview; Rebecca Goodman, "Cincinnati Native Fought in WWII, Worked for CIA," *Cincinnati Enquirer*, May 22, 2004; MC, *Game Player*, 93, 88, 89.
11. Deane R. Hinton quoted in Douglas Little, "Cold War and Covert Action: The United States and Syria, 1945–1958," *Middle East Journal* 44, no. 1 (1990): 55; Joseph Satterthwaite, "Background of Army Coup d'Etat in Syria," March 30, 1949, 11, folder January 1, 1949, Lot 54D403, RG 59, NA.
12. Syria Joint Weeka, December 3, 1948, 22, 350 Syria (Joint Weekas), Syria, Damascus Embassy, Classified General Records, 1943–63, Foreign Service Posts of the Department of State, RG 84, NA; Stephen J. Meade, "Syrian Army Commander's Plans to Seize Power," March 10, 1949, 20, 1 of 4, 1949 January–March, Syrian Politics, Syria Classified General Records, RG 84, NA.
13. MC, *Game of Nations*, 42; MC, *Game Player*, 93–94, 99.
14. MC, *Game Player*, 184, 94. For criticism of Miles's account, see, for example, Andrew Rathmell, "Copeland and Za'im: Re-evaluating the Evidence," *Intelligence and National Security* 11, no. 1 (1996): 89–105.
15. Little, "Cold War and Covert Action," 56n29; Hinton quoted in Andrew Rathmell, *Secret War in the Middle East: The Covert Struggle for Syria, 1949–1961* (London: Tauris Academic Studies, 1995), 182n153; Syrian foreign minister quoted in Little, "Cold War and Covert Action," 56n29.
16. MC, *Game Player*, 94–98.
17. "U.S. Attaché Fights Off Gunmen," *New York Times*, March 10, 1949, 6; Miles Copeland III interview; Syria Joint Weeka, March 18, 1949, 22, 350 Syria (Joint Weekas), Syria Classified General Records, RG 84, NA.

18. Syria Joint Weeka, March 18, 1949; Philip Broadmead to London, March 15, 1949, FO 371/75529, Public Record Office (hereafter PRO), Kew, London.

19. MC, *Game Player*, 100; Patrick Seale, *The Struggle for Syria: A Study of Post-War Arab Politics, 1945–1958* (New York: Oxford University Press, 1965), 44; MC, *Game Player*, 101.

20. James Keeley to Acheson, April 1 and April 5, 1949, 20, 2 of 4, 1949 January–March, Syrian Politics, Syria Classified General Records, RG 84, NA.

21. Keeley to Acheson, April 1, 1949, 20, 2 of 4, 1949 January–March, Syrian Politics, Syria Classified General Records, RG 84, NA; Meade quoted in Little, "Cold War and Covert Action," 55; memorandum of conversation between Za'im and Meade, April 20, 1949, 20, 2 of 4, 1949 January–March, Syrian Politics, Syria Classified General Records, RG 84, NA; Meade, "King Ibn Saud's Advance Knowledge of Syrian Coup d'État," May 26, 1949, 20, 2 of 4, 1949 January–March, Syrian Politics, Syria Classified General Records, RG 84, NA; MC, *Game of Nations*, 44.

22. "TAPline Convention in Syria; Possible Ratification by Military Government," April 6, 1949, 19, Syria and Lebanon, 1948-Memoranda, Lot 53D468, Records of Bureau of Near Eastern, South Asian, and African Affairs, Office Files of Assistant Secretary of State George C. McGhee, 1945–53, RG 59, NA; Keeley to Acheson, April 28, 1949, 20, 2 of 4, 1949 January–March, Syrian Politics, Syria Classified General Records, RG 84, NA; Meade, "Zaim Organizes Special Strongarm Squad," April 28, 1949, 20, 2 of 4, 1949 January–March, Syrian Politics, Syria Classified General Records, RG 84, NA; Syria Joint Weeka, April 15, 1949, 22, 350 Syria (Joint Weekas), Syria Classified General Records, RG 84, NA. Za'im's peace feeler to Israel later became the subject of heated dispute among Israeli historians after Avi Shlaim argued that it was a historic missed opportunity. See Avi Shlaim, "Husni Zaim and the Plan to Resettle Palestinian Refugees in Syria," *Journal of Palestine Studies* 15, no. 4 (1986): 68–80.

23. Seale, *The Struggle for Syria*, 58.

24. Keeley to Acheson, April 4 and June 4 1949, 20, 2 of 4, 1949 January–March, Syrian Politics, Syria Classified General Records, RG 84, NA; "Political Summary No. 6 for Month of July, 1949," FO 371/75528, PRO; "Zayim Decorates Americans," *New York Times*, July 24, 1949, 4.

25. Seale, *The Struggle for Syria*, 61n8; "Political Summary No. 7 for the Month of August, 1949," FO 371/75528, PRO. For more on the Sa'adah affair, see Rathmell, *Secret War*, 44–50; Seale, *The Struggle for Syria*, chap. 8.

26. R. Harrison to Acheson, August 11, 1949, 21, 3 of 4, 1949 January–March, Syrian Politics, Syria Classified General Records, RG 84, NA; Lorraine Copeland e-mail, November 23, 2010. Rathmell reviews the evidence concerning Za'im's execution in *Secret War*, 50–51.

27. MC, *Game Player*, 101–102; MC, *Game of Nations*, 45.

Nine: American Friends of the Middle East

1. NSC 10/2, June 18, 1948, *FRUS 1945–50: Emergence of the Intelligence Establishment*, 714.

2. Quoted in AR, *Lust of Knowing*, 299; Status and Efficiency Report, June 9, 1949, CO5640569, CIA FOIA.

3. Personnel Evaluation Report, October 1952–October 1953, CO5654072, CIA FOIA; KR, *Countercoup*, 110.

4. A former Near East division head in the State Department, Allen Dulles worked during the late 1940s as legal counsel to Overseas Consultants Inc., a private US venture advising the Iranian government on development issues, and toured the Middle East in his capacity as president of the Near East College Association.

5. AR, *Lust of Knowing*, 298, 299; Personnel Action Request, September 1950, CO5654133, CIA FOIA; MC, *Game of Nations*, 51.

6. Prior to his appointment as NEA division chief, Kim had worked as a part-time consultant for the OPC from April to June 1949, assisting with "the establishment of a major operational program." Personal Service Contract, April 1949, CO5654059, CIA FOIA.

7. KR to CJP members, June 21, 1948, 45.3, ACJP; "Liaison Body Formed for Near East Relief," *New York Times*, September 12, 1949, 8.

8. Peter Kurth, "Remembering Dorothy Thompson," October 26, 2004, www.ifamericansknew.org/media/dthompson.html. See also Peter Kurth, *American Cassandra: The Life of Dorothy Thompson* (Boston: Little, Brown, 1990); Marion K. Sanders, *Dorothy Thompson: A Legend in Her Time* (Boston: Houghton Mifflin, 1973).

9. See, for example, Berger to Thompson, January 27, 1949, 122.2, ACJP; Berger to KR, February 8, 1949, 106.1, ACJP; Eddy to Thompson, no date [probably July 1950], 10.9, WAEP.

10. See Hugh Wilford, *The Mighty Wurlitzer: How the CIA Played America* (Cambridge, MA: Harvard University Press, 2008). The CIA recently made available, in heavily redacted form, its own history of this operation: Michael Warner, *Hearts and Minds: Three Case Studies of the CIA's Covert Support of American Anti-Communist Groups in the Cold War, 1949–1967* (Langley, VA: Central Intelligence Agency, 1999). Some clues in the unredacted text, such as a reference on page xiv to an organization aimed at "educated Arab Muslims," suggest that Chapter 4 of this work, entitled "A Hidden Policy," is devoted to the American Friends of the Middle East. The chapter is, unfortunately, entirely redacted.

11. See, for example, Berger to KR, June 9, 1950, 106.1, ACJP; Berger to Levison, June 21, 1950, and December 8, 1950, 74.11, ACJP; Eddy to Cornelius Van Engert, December 28, 1950, uncatalogued box, Postwar Correspondence and MSS, folder 1950–51, Cornelius Van H. Engert Papers, Special Collections, Georgetown University Library, Washington, DC; Engert to Eddy, December 30, 1950, Engert Papers; Sanders, *Dorothy Thompson*, 335; Berger to Levison, January 23, 1951, 75.1, ACJP.

12. Berger to Thompson, March 16, 1951, 2.10, Dorothy Thompson Papers (hereafter DTP), Special Collections Research Center, Syracuse University Library, Syracuse, NY; Berger to Levison, March 31, 1951, 75.1, ACJP; "Interview with Miss Dorothy Thompson," April 5, 1951, 2.10, DTP; Thompson, April 5, 1951, 2.10, DTP; M. Snyder to Miss Sansom, May 11, 1951, 24.12, Allen Dulles Papers; *AFME Annual Report, 1951-52*, 59.1, John Nuveen Jr. Papers (hereafter JNP), University of Chicago Library, Special Collections Research Center.

13. Engert to Thompson, June 29, 1951, 2.15, DTP; Thompson to Guaranty Trust, July 1951, 38.5, DTP; Engert to Thompson, June 1, 1951, 2.15, DTP; Eddy to Hopkins, January 11, 1954, 3.1, DTP.

14. Patrice Gaudefroy-Demombynes (Eliot's stepson), telephone interview by author, July 7, 2009; Mather Greenleaf Eliot to Samuel and Elsa Eliot, July 10, 1950, 1.4, Papers of the Eliot Family, Archives Service Center, University of Pittsburgh; Eliot to parents, June 2, 1951, 1.5, Eliot Papers; Eliot to parents, November 18, 1951, 1.5, Eliot Papers.

15. Wilford, *The Mighty Wurlitzer*, 152; "American Friends of the Middle East: Second Meeting of the Charter Members," December 12, 1951, 2.13, DTP; "Heard in Washington," *Near East Report*, March 7, 1967, 19.

16. Berger to Levison, December 20, 1951, 75.1, ACJP.

17. *AFME Annual Report, 1951–52*; "Application for Consultative Membership to the Economic and Social Council of the United Nations," no date, 4.13, DTP; *AFME Annual Report, 1953–54*, 59.1, JNP.

18. Various AFME annual reports, 59.1, JNP.

19. *AFME Annual Report, 1954–55*, 59.1, JNP; Harold Lamb, "The Hope of One American," May 15, 1951, 19, Beg. of AFME, Harold Lamb Papers, Department of Special Collections, Young Research Library, University of California, Los Angeles; Eddy quoted in Lippman, *Arabian Knight*, 277; *AFME Annual Report, 1953–54*.

20. "American Friends of the Middle East," no date [1951], 4.13, DTP.

21. Engert to Hugh Bullock, April 19, 1952, uncatalogued box, folder 1952–53, Engert Papers; "Tentative Statement Regarding the Position of the American Friends of the Middle East on United States Policy in the Middle East," September 17, 1956, 59.2, JNP; "American Friends of the Middle East: Second Meeting of the Charter Members," December 12, 1951, 2.13, DTP; Eddy to Robert A. McClure, January 9, 1951, 2.14, DTP; Eddy to Thompson, June 7, 1951, 2.4, DTP.

22. "American Friends of the Middle East" and "Tentative Draft of Press Release," no date [1951], 4.13, DTP.

23. *AFME Annual Report, 1953–54*.

24. Hopkins to John Foster Dulles, June 19, 1953, 611.80/6-1953, RG 59, NA; J. M. Troutbeck (British Embassy, Baghdad) to Anthony Eden, May 28, 1952, FO 371/98247, PRO; "Draft, Story of a Purpose," September 19, 1958, 59.3, JNP.

25. See, for example, *AFME Annual Report, 1953–54*; Berger to Levison, October 29, 1951, 75.1, ACJP; Berger to Morris Lazaron, March 11, 1952, 73.7, ACJP; Berger to Levison, July 30, 1952, 75.2, ACJP.

26. Thompson to Gildersleeve, August 2, 1951, 38.6, DTP; Thompson to Berger, December 5, 1952, 122.2, ACJP; Thompson quoted in Kurth, *American Cassandra*, 428.

27. Eddy to Thompson, October 11, 1951, 2.14, DTP.

28. Eveland, *Ropes of Sand*, 125; confidential source; ibid.

29. Armin H. Meyer to G. Lewis Jones, "American Friends of the Middle East," September 24, 1959, quoted in *U.S. Propaganda in the Middle East—The Early Cold War Version*, ed. Joyce Battle, National Security Archive Electronic Briefing Book No. 78, December 13, 2002, http://www.gwu.edu/~nsarchiv/NSAEBB/NSAEBB78/essay.htm; Eddy, "U.S. Government Aid Through Private Institutions," February 14, 1959, 11.11, WAEP.

30. Burton Berry to State, "Special IIA Projects for Islamic Countries," October 1, 1952, 511.80/10-1952, RG 59, NA.

31. Eliot to parents, April 15 and May 31, 1953, 1.6, Eliot Papers; Gaudefroy-Demombynes interview.

32. See, for example, H. Ben Smith to Nuveen, September 15, 1958, 59.3, JNP; Lorraine Nye Norton, interview by author, Seattle, WA, August 15, 2009; Hopkins to Harold U. Stobart, May 11, 1954, 3.7, DTP; Kurth, *American Cassandra*, 422; Thompson to Hopkins, May 20, 1954, 5.11, DTP; Norton interview.

33. Eveland, *Ropes of Sand*, 125, 291; Andrew Tully, *CIA: The Inside Story* (New York: Morrow, 1962), 78–79; *AFME Annual Report, 1954–55*; *AFME Annual Report, 1951–52*.

34. Eliot to parents, December 29, 1953, 1.6, Eliot Papers. For a notable work about the relationship between the CIA and the Non-Communist Left, see Frances Stonor Saunders, *The Cultural Cold War: The CIA and the World of Arts and Letters* (New York: New Press, 2000).

35. MC, *Game Player*, 110; AR, *Lust of Knowing*, 300–301, 306.

36. AR, *Lust of Knowing*, chap. 23; Selwa "Lucky" Roosevelt, *Keeper of the Gate* (New York: Simon & Schuster, 1990), chap. 14; MC, *Game Player*, 111; "A. B. Roosevelt Jr., Miss Showker Wed," *New York Times*, September 2, 1950, 24.

Ten: In Search of a Hero: Egypt, 1952

1. Burton Hersh, *The Old Boys: The American Elite and the Origins of the CIA* (1992; rpt., St. Petersburg, FL: Tree Farm Books, 2002), 221; MC, *Game Player*, 123, 116, 121.

2. Thomas, *Very Best Men*, 65, 72; KR to Belle Roosevelt, July 17, 1952, I, 142, Roosevelt, Kermit (son), KRBRP; Dulles quoted in Grose, *Gentleman Spy*, 415; MC, *Game Player*, 127, 111.

3. Acheson quoted in W. Scott Lucas, *Divided We Stand: Britain, the US, and the Suez Crisis* (London: Hodder & Stoughton, 1991), 14; Acheson quoted in Little, *American Orientalism*, 164.

4. KR, *Arabs, Oil, and History*, chap. 11; KR, "Egypt's Inferiority Complex," 357–364; "Egypt Detains Kermit Roosevelt," *New York Times*, January 19, 1951, 10. According to the *Times*, Kim was traveling as an "unofficial Middle Eastern consultant to the State Department."

5. KR, *Arabs, Oil, and History*, 99; MC, *Game Player*, 131; KR to Belle Roosevelt, June 11, no year [1951], I, 142, Roosevelt, Kermit (son), KRBRP.

6. MC, *Game of Nations*, 51; KR interview by R. Harris Smith; MC, *Game Player*, 144–145; MC, *Game of Nations*, 51.

7. Polly to Belle Roosevelt, March 7, 1952, I, 143, Roosevelt, Mary Gaddis (Polly), undated, 1950–59, KRBRP; KR interview by R. Harris Smith.

8. MC, *Game of Nations*, 53; MC, *Game Player*, 148–156. In a recent book, intelligence historian Gordon Thomas directly quotes comments supposedly made by Nasser concerning these meetings, but there is no indication of his source. See Gordon Thomas, *Secret Wars: One Hundred Years of British Intelligence Inside MI5 and MI6* (New York: Thomas Dunne Books, 2009), 143–144.

9. NSC staff study, January 18, 1952, quoted in Lucas, *Divided We Stand*, 13; among the several works mentioning Evans's role are Joel Gordon, *Nasser's Blessed Movement: Egypt's Free Officers and the July Revolution* (New York: Oxford University Press, 1992), 164; Rami Ginat, "Nasser and the Soviets: A Reassessment," in *Rethinking Nasserism: Revolution and Historical Memory in Modern Egypt*, ed. Elie Podeh and Onn Winckler (Gainesville: University Press of Florida, 2004), 233; KR, *Arabs, Oil, and History*, 87, 96; William Lakeland, telephone interview by Michael Doran, April 4, 2010, Seeley G. Mudd Manuscript Library, Princeton University, Princeton, NJ; MC, *Game Player*, 148.

10. Lakeland interview (Lakeland goes on to acknowledge the possibility that Copeland and Roosevelt did meet with junior members of the Free Officer movement); Julian Amery to Eden, December 22, 1951, 680, 1/2 General Political, 1945–57, Julian Amery Papers, Churchill Archives Centre, Churchill College, Cambridge, UK; Gordon, *Nasser's Blessed Movement*, 162; Eveland, *Ropes of Sand*, 98n; KR, telephone interview by Kennett Love, May 5, 1970, 4, Kennett Love

Papers, Seeley G. Mudd Manuscript Library, Princeton University, Princeton, NJ; KR interview by R. Harris Smith; Belle to Polly Roosevelt, April 3, 1952, I, 143, Roosevelt, Mary Gaddis (Polly), undated, 1950–59, KRBRP.

11. Owen L. Sirrs, *A History of the Egyptian Intelligence Service: A History of the Mukhabarat, 1910–2009* (New York: Routledge, 2010), 26; Michael Doran, "Who's Bill?," *Princeton Alumni Weekly*, October 13, 2010, http://paw.princeton.edu/issues/2010/10/13/pages/8702/index.xml.

12. MC, *Game of Nations*, 63; "Draft Note to Dorothy Thompson," September 8, 1952, 2.17, DTP; MC, *Game of Nations*, 52.

13. "Draft Note to Dorothy Thompson"; "Dr. Edward L. R. Elson's Visit to the Middle East on Behalf of 'American Friends of the Middle East,'" uncatalogued box, Postwar Correspondence and MSS, folder 1952–53, Engert Papers; MC, *Game of Nations*, 62.

14. Lakeland interview; Doran, "Who's Bill?"; see Kelly McFarland, "All About the Wordplay: Gendered and Orientalist Language in U.S.-Egyptian Foreign Relations, 1952–1961" (Ph.D. diss., Kent State University, 2010), chap. 1; MC, *Game of Nations*, 62; Laura M. James, *Nasser at War: Arab Images of the Enemy* (New York: Palgrave Macmillan, 2006), 4.

15. Ralph Stevenson, "Egypt: Annual Review for 1953," January 25, 1954, PREM 11/629, PRO; A. Kirkbride, minute, July 3, 1953, FO 371/104258, PRO; Roger Makins to Eden, April 3, 1953, FO 371/102731, PRO; Robin Hankey to James Bowker, June 23, 1953, FO 371/102731, PRO; Kirkbride, minute.

16. James, *Nasser at War*, 3; Willie Morris to Alan Rothnie, December 10, 1958, FO 371/133799, PRO; Mohamed [Muhammad] H. Haikal, *Cutting the Lion's Tail: Suez Through Egyptian Eyes* (New York: Arbor House, 1987), 33; Muhammad al-Tawil, *La'bat al-umam wa 'abd al-nasir* (Cairo: Al-Maktab al-Misriyy al-Hadith, 1986), 50; Anthony Nutting, *Nasser* (New York: Dutton, 1972), 45, 58; Nasser quoted in David W. Lesch, "Abd al-Nasser and the United States," in Podeh and Winckler, eds., *Rethinking Nasserism*, 223.

17. Donald Neff, *Warriors at Suez: Eisenhower Takes America into the Middle East* (New York: Linden/Simon & Schuster, 1981), 87.

18. KR to MC, no date, reproduced in Tawil, *La'bat al-umam*, 390.

19. T. E. Lawrence, *Seven Pillars of Wisdom: A Triumph* (Garden City, NY: Doubleday, Doran, 1935), 8, 73, 67, 91.

20. Gamal Abdul Nasser, *Egypt's Liberation: The Philosophy of the Revolution* (Washington, DC: Public Affairs, 1955), 87–88.

21. MC, *Game Player*, 111.

22. Gildersleeve to John Foster Dulles, March 26, 1953; Lamb to John Foster Dulles, February 16, 1953, 9, Roa-Rus (2), Personnel Series, John Foster Dulles, Secretary of State: Papers 1951–59 (hereafter JFDP), Dwight D. Eisenhower Library (hereafter DDEL), Abilene, KS.

23. Levison to Rosenwald, March 20, 1953, 75.3, ACJP; Grose, *Gentleman Spy*, 386; Berger to Levison, March 2 and 10, 1953, 75.3, ACJP.

Eleven: Mad Men on the Nile

1. "Dulles Sees Need to Act in Mid-East," *New York Times*, May 10, 1953, 4.

2. Dulles quoted in Ray Takeyh, *The Origins of the Eisenhower Doctrine: The US, Britain, and Nasser's Egypt, 1953–57* (New York: St. Martin's, 2000), 9; "Memorandum of Conversation, Prepared in the Embassy in Cairo," May 12, 1953, *FRUS 1952–54, Vol. 9*, 19–25; Mohamed Hassanein Haikal, *The Cairo Documents: The Inside Story of Nasser and His Relationship with World Leaders, Rebels, and Statesmen* (Garden City, NY: Doubleday, 1973), 43.

3. Haikal, *The Cairo Documents*, 42; "United States Objectives and Policies with Respect to the Near East," NSC 155/1, July 14, 1953, 5, NSC 155/1-Near East (2), White House Office, Office of the Special Assistant for National Security Affairs, NSC Series, Policy Papers Subseries, DDEL.

4. Lorraine Copeland, e-mail to author, November 25, 2010; MC, *Game Player*, 116–120, 113; Personnel Evaluation Report, June 1953, CO5651569, CIA FOIA.

5. Eveland, *Ropes of Sand*, 103; MC, *Game Player*, 129. For more on the origins of psychological warfare, see Kenneth Osgood, *Total Cold War: Eisenhower's Secret Propaganda Battle at Home and Abroad* (Lawrence: University Press of Kansas, 2006), chap. 1.

6. MC, James Burnham obituary, *National Review*, September 11, 1987, 37; MC, *Game of Nations*, 260.

7. Barbara S. Heyl, "The Harvard 'Pareto Circle,'" *Journal of the History of the Behavioral Sciences* 4, no. 4 (1968): 316–334.

8. MC to James Burnham, April 15, 1970, 6.4, James Burnham Papers, Hoover Institution, Stanford University, Stanford, CA; MC, Burnham obituary, 37; Miles Copeland III interview.

9. MC, *Game Player*, 140–141.

10. Ibid., 141, 142; "History of Booz Allen," http://www.boozallen.com/about/history. For more on Lansdale, see Jonathan Nashel, *Edward Lansdale's Cold War* (Amherst: University of Massachusetts Press, 2005). For an excellent example of recent scholarship about US foreign policy and modernization, see Michael E. Latham, *The Right Kind of Revolution: Modernization, Development, and U.S. Foreign Policy from the Cold War to the Present* (Ithaca, NY: Cornell University Press, 2011). Most of the literature about modernization theory, the set of ideas that guided the United States' modernization program, has stressed the intellectual influence of Harvard's Talcott Parsons and detected a shift from, in the first years of the Cold War, an emphasis on liberal development strategies to, from the late 1950s on, a more coercive, authoritarian approach, as seen in the doctrine of "military modernization." The example of Kim Roosevelt and Miles Copeland suggests another, previously overlooked strand of modernization theory, originating in Harvard's Pareto Circle and more conservative from the outset, that found operational expression in CIA support for nationalist military governments in the Middle East several years before notions of military modernization began to catch on more widely.

11. MC, *Game Player*, 158–161.

12. Ibid., 161; Lorraine Copeland e-mail, November 25, 2010; Copeland, *Wild Thing*, 36.

13. MC, *Game Player*, 163, 161. For more on Kearns and his relationship with the CIA, see the excellent documentary *Frank Kearns: American Correspondent* (PBS, 2012).

14. MC, *Game of Nations*, 164, 239; Lorraine Copeland e-mail, November 25, 2010. On Miles's continuing friendship with Nasser, see, for example, Raymond Hare to John Foster Dulles, December 8, 1958, 7, 320 UAR/US Relations, Egypt Classified General Records, RG 84, NA: "Copeland visited Cairo again December 3–4 [1958] for [the] purpose [of] obtaining background. As usual he saw NASSER, who apparently was friendly and in talking mood."

15. Haikal, *Cutting the Lion's Tail*, 42; Wolfgang Lotz quoted in Thomas, *Secret Wars*, 141.

16. Copeland titled chapter 16 of *The Game Player* "The Nasserist Honeymoon"; Haikal refers to "this almost honeymoon period" in *Cutting the Lion's Tail*, 42. For Jackson's views on the Middle East, see C. D. Jackson, log, April 13, 1953, 68, Log-1953 (1), C. D. Jackson Papers, DDEL.

17. Lorraine Copeland, e-mail to author, November 29, 2010; Eichelberger quoted in MC, *Game of Nations*, 74, 241–256.

18. MC, *Game Player*, 165; MC, *Game of Nations*, 82; MC, *Game Player*, 166–167; MC, *Game of Nations*, 88; Sirrs, *History of the Egyptian Intelligence Service*, 34. The training in the writing of intelligence summaries was probably provided by Charles D. Cremeans, an officer in the CIA's Office of National Estimates and scholarly authority on Arab nationalism whom Miles Copeland referred to as performing "a special diplomatic assignment to Egypt during 1955" (MC, *Game of Nations*, 257). Cremeans's presence in Egypt in that year is confirmed in Eveland, *Ropes of Sand*, 145–146.

19. MC, *Game of Nations*, 86–88.

20. "Extract from a Letter," March 18, 1954, 679.3, 1/2 General Political, 1945–57, Amery Papers. The Afrika Korps was the German expeditionary force in North Africa decisively defeated by the Allies at El Alamein in 1942.

21. André Gerolymatos, *Castles Made of Sand: A Century of Anglo-American Espionage and Intervention in the Middle East* (New York: Thomas Dunne Books, 2010), 134–137; Timothy Naftali, "Reinhard Gehlen and the United States," in Richard Breitman et al., *U.S. Intelligence and the Nazis* (Cambridge: Cambridge University Press, 2005), 404–405, 417n166.

22. Naftali, "Reinhard Gehlen," 405; Sirrs, *History of the Egyptian Intelligence Service*, 33. It is probably just coincidence that by 1959 the CIA station chief in Madrid was Archie Roosevelt.

23. MC, *Game of Nations*, 84; Christopher Simpson, *Science of Coercion: Communication Research and Psychological Warfare, 1945–1960* (New York: Oxford University Press, 1994), 74; "Expenses of Lawrence W. Teed During Trip to Middle East," 5.12, Paul M. A. Linebarger Papers, Hoover Institution, Stanford University, Stanford, CA. Although Linebarger's papers contains little else relating to the work he performed for the CIA, his status as a consultant is confirmed in Harrison G. Reynolds to Paul Linebarger, June 13, 1956, 5.12, Linebarger Papers.

24. Eden and Churchill quoted in Michael T. Thornhill, *Road to Suez: The Battle of the Canal Zone* (Stroud: Sutton, 2006), 123.

25. MC, *Game Player*, 116–118; "Kermit Roosevelt Sees Naguib," *New York Times*, January 25, 1954, 5; Makins to Foreign Office (hereafter FO), March 9, 1954, FO 371/108415, PRO; Tawil, *La'bat al-umam*, 390–391; Hagerty quoted in Lucas, *Divided We Stand*, 16.

26. Nasser quoted in Saïd K. Aburish, *Nasser: The Last Arab* (New York: St. Martin's, 2004), 54. On the possibility of CIA involvement in a staged assassination attempt, see Gordon, *Nasser's Blessed Movement*, 179–180; James, *Nasser at War*, 7.

27. William L. Cleveland and Martin Bunton, *A History of the Modern Middle East*, 4th ed. (Boulder, CO: Westview, 2009), 307.

Twelve: Authoring a Coup: Iran, 1953

1. Two recent works to which this chapter is indebted are the highly readable narrative account by Kinzer, *All the Shah's Men*, 2nd ed. (Hoboken, NJ: Wiley, 2008), and a collection of essays by leading scholars in the field, Mark J. Gasiorowski and Malcolm Byrne, eds., *Mohammad Mosaddeq and the 1953 Coup in Iran* (Syracuse, NY: Syracuse University Press, 2004).

2. See Maziar Behrooz, "The 1953 Coup in Iran and the Legacy of the Tudeh," in Gasiorowski and Byrne, eds., *Mohammad Mosaddeq*, 102–125.

3. "Man of the Year," *Time*, January 7, 1952. For an influential discussion of Orientalist perceptions of Mosaddeq, see Mary Ann Heiss, *Empire and Nationhood: The United States, Great Britain, and Iranian Oil, 1950–1954* (New York: Columbia University Press, 1997), 229–233.

4. See Malcolm Byrne, "The Road to Intervention: Factors Influencing U.S. Policy Toward Iran, 1945–1953," in Gasioworksi and Byrne, eds., *Mohammad Mosaddeq*, 216–217, and Mark J. Gasiorowski, "The 1953 Coup d'Etat Against Mosaddeq," in ibid., 235–236; Ivan L. G. Pearson, *In the Name of Oil: Anglo-American Relations in the Middle East, 1950–1958* (Eastbourne: Sussex Academic, 2010), 21; for the text of NSC 136/1, and a revealing March 1953 progress report on its implementation, see the National Security Archive's Electronic Briefing Book, *Mohammad Mossadeq and the 1953 Coup in Iran*, June 22, 2004, http://www.gwu.edu/~nsarchiv/NSAEBB /NSAEBB126/index.htm.

5. Monty Woodhouse, "Iran, 1950–1953," August 16, 1976, Christopher Montague Woodhouse Papers, Liddle Hart Centre for Military Archives/King's College Archives, London. For more on Woodhouse's role and British planning generally, see C. M. Woodhouse, *Something Ventured* (London: Granada, 1982), chaps. 8–9; Stephen Dorril, *MI6: Fifty Years of Special Operations* (London: Fourth Estate, 2000), chap. 27; Wm. Roger Louis, "Britain and the Overthrow of the Mosaddeq Government," in Gasioworksi and Byrne, eds., *Mohammad Mosaddeq*, 126–177.

6. "Notes on the Life of Allen Dulles," 10, Smith Collection.

7. MC, *Game Player*, chap. 18; Gasiorowski, "1953 Coup," 331n12.

8. Goiran quoted in Dorril, *MI6*, 584. See Gasiorowski, "1953 Coup," 331n10.

9. Smith quoted in Makins to FO, August 17, 1953, PREM 11/514, PRO.

10. Gasiorowski, "1953 Coup," 250.

11. The shah quoted in William Shawcross, *The Shah's Last Ride: The Fate of an Ally* (New York: Simon & Schuster, 1988), 70; KR quoted in KR, *Countercoup*, 196–197; the shah quoted in ibid., 199.

12. Woodhouse, *Something Ventured*, 135; Wilber, *Adventures in the Middle East*, 9, 189; MC, *Game Player*, 190–191.

13. See Darioush Bayandor, *Iran and the CIA: The Fall of Mosaddeq Revisited* (New York: Palgrave Macmillan, 2010).

14. Donald N. Wilber, "Overthrow of Premier Mosaddeq of Iran, November 1952-August 1953," CIA Historical Paper No. 208, March 1954. For the full text of this document, and a useful discussion of the circumstances of its leaking, go to the excellent website of the National Security Archive, http://www.gwu.edu/~nsarchiv/NSAEBB/NSAEBB28. For a recent study focusing on Mosaddeq's role, see Christopher de Bellaigue, *Patriot of Persia: Muhammad Mosaddeg and a Tragic Anglo-American Coup* (New York: Harper, 2012), 242–244.

15. Amanat quoted in Meyer and Brysac, *Kingmakers*, 347.

16. KR, *Arabs, Oil, and History*, 271.

17. KR, *Countercoup*, 2.

18. Woodhouse, *Something Ventured*, 120; Wilber, "Overthrow," 6; KR, *Countercoup*, 115; Wilber, "Overthrow," 94.

19. KR, *Countercoup*, 2, 77, 85–86.

20. Woodhouse, "Iran, 1950–1953"; Wilber, "Overthrow," 36; KR, *Countercoup*, 59; FO minute, August 24, 1953, FO 371/104570, PRO; KR, "Memorandum of CIA Representative," attached to Walter Bedell Smith to Dwight Eisenhower, no date [late August/early September, 1953], 32, Iran, 1953 through 1959 (8), International Series, Dwight D. Eisenhower Papers as President of the United States, 1952–61 (Ann Whitman File) (hereafter AWF), DDEL.

21. KR, *Countercoup*, 138; McClure to Jackson, September 14, 1953, 73, McClure, Robert, Jackson Papers, DDEL.

22. KR, *Countercoup*, 140, 191, 172.

23. Ibid., 205, 204; Wilber, "Overthrow," 80; Lord Salisbury, Record of Conversation, August 26, 1953, PREM 11/514, PRO; Wilber, "Overthrow," 84.

24. KR, "Memorandum of CIA Representative"; KR, *Countercoup*, 207.

25. J. A. Ford to D. B. Pitblado, September 2, 1953, PREM 11/514, PRO, quoting a letter from KR to William Strang; see KR, "Memorandum of CIA Representative"; KR, *Countercoup*, 209; Dwight D. Eisenhower, *The White House Years*, vol. 1, *Mandate for Change, 1953–1956* (Garden City, NY: Doubleday, 1963), 164.

26. Richard and Gladys Harkness, "The Mysterious Doings of CIA," *Saturday Evening Post*, November 6, 1954, 66, 68; Jonathan Roosevelt interview; Thomas Powers, "A Book Held Hostage," *Nation*, April 12, 1980, 438, 437.

27. Albert Hourani, "The Myth of T. E. Lawrence," in *Adventures with Britannia: Personalities, Politics, and Culture in Britain*, ed. Wm. Roger Louis (Austin: University of Texas Press, 1996), 23–24.

28. Rudyard Kipling, *Kim: Authoritative Text, Backgrounds, Criticism*, ed. Zohreh T. Sullivan (New York: Norton, 2002), 176.

Thirteen: From ALPHA . . .

1. Citation, September 23, 1953, I, 143, Roosevelt, Mary Gaddis (Polly), 1950–59, KRBRP. See also 45, National Security Medal, Confidential File, White House Central Files (hereafter WHCF), DDEL.

2. "F.B.I. Chief Wins Medal for Work on Security," *New York Times*, May 28, 1955, 4.

3. See, for example, David W. Lesch, *The Arab-Israeli Conflict: A History* (New York: Oxford University Press, 2008), 178–179. There is a substantial literature on ALPHA. The most comprehensive single treatment is Neil Caplan, *Futile Diplomacy*, vol. 4, *Operation Alpha and the Failure of Anglo-American Coercive Diplomacy in the Arab-Israeli Conflict, 1954–1956* (London: Frank Cass, 1997). None of the existing works pay much attention to the domestic US ramifications of ALPHA, the subject of this chapter.

4. Eveland, *Ropes of Sand*, 182.

5. Levison, "Notes on a Meeting Held April 8, 1953," 75.3, ACJP; Dulles quoted in Kolsky, *Jews Against Zionism*, 192; *AFME Annual Report, 1953–54*. The new policy was encoded in NSC Directive 155/1, which sought a "reversal of the anti-American trends of Arab opinion" and an end to the "preferential treatment" of Israel (quoted in Little, *American Orientalism*, 89).

6. Berger, *Memoirs of an Anti-Zionist Jew*, 41; Berger, notes, June 23, 1953, 7, Government— Henry A. Byroade 1953, Addition M68–068, ACJP; Berger to Levison, July 14, 1952, 75.2, ACJP.

7. Berger to Levison, March 11, 1952, 75.2, ACJP; Berger to Levison, May 20, 1953, 75.3, ACJP; Berger to Polly Roosevelt, June 8, 1953, 106.1, ACJP; on possible CIA support for ACJ projects, see, for example, Berger to KR, May 18, 1954, 4, Kermit Roosevelt, Jr. 1954, Addition M67–130, ACJP; Byroade quoted in Henry Byroade, interview by Neil M. Johnson, September 19, 1988, Association for Diplomatic Studies and Training Foreign Affairs Oral History Project (hereafter FAOHP).

8. "Views of Three American Editors Regarding Middle East Problems," January 8, 1954, 611.80/1–854, RG 59, NA; "Arab-Israel Issue in Campaign Scored," *New York Times*, October 30, 1954, 9; "Edward L. R. Elson Dies at 86; Influential Cleric in Washington," *New York Times*, August 28, 1993, 26.

9. Leonard Ware to [Richard H.] Sanger, "Suggestions from Damascus Concerning the American Friends of the Middle East," December 1, 1952, 511.80/12–152, RG 59, NA; Edward Elson,

interview by Paul Hopper, Washington, DC, September 22, 1968, *Columbia Oral History*, 230, 14.3–4, Edward L. R. Elson Papers, Presbyterian Historical Society Archives, Philadelphia; Elson to Eisenhower, February 24, 1957, 1.3, Elson Papers; Elson to John Foster Dulles, January 3, 1958, 128, Elson, Edward L., 1958, JFDP, Seeley G. Mudd Manuscript Library, Princeton University, Princeton, NJ; Elson, "Observations and Comments Concerning Cairo," no date [1957], 59.1, JNP; Elson to Eisenhower, August 4, 1958, 1.3a, Elson Papers; on Elson at the Eisenhower family home, see Berger to Clarence L. Coleman Jr., November 29, 1955, 8, Berger, Dr. Elmer 1955, Addition M68–068, ACJP.

10. Kolsky, *Jews Against Zionism*, 192–194; Eliot to his parents, April 27, 1954, 1.7, Eliot Papers; Elson to Eisenhower, July 24, 1958, 1.3a, Elson Papers; Eisenhower to Elson, July 28, 1958, 1.3a, Elson Papers. On People-to-People diplomacy, see Osgood, *Total Cold War*, and Christina Klein, *Cold War Orientalism: Asia in the Middlebrow Imagination, 1945–1961* (Berkeley: University of California Press, 2003).

11. *AFME Annual Report, 1953–54*; Memorandum of a Conversation, Department of State, Washington, January 27, 1955, *FRUS 1955–57, Vol. 14*, 28; Evelyn Shuckburgh diary, January 27, 1955, MS191/1/2/4, Evelyn Shuckburgh Papers, Special Collections, Cadbury Research Library, University of Birmingham, UK. "American efforts to 'deflate the Jews' over the last two years will not be sustainable much longer, when elections draw near," Dulles told Shuckburgh.

12. References to KR, Byroade, and Elson in Jon B. Alterman, "American Aid to Egypt in the 1950s: From Hope to Hostility," *Middle East Journal* 52, no. 1 (1998): 58, 60; for Nasser on Kim and Hussein, see Nutting, *Nasser*, 119–120; "K" and Tuhami quoted in Tawil, *La'bat al-umam*, 399, 153.

13. Berger to Lazaron, December 20, 1954, 3, Dr. Morris S. Lazaron 1954, Addition M67–130, ACJP; Eveland, *Ropes of Sand*, 92; John Foster Dulles to Eisenhower, December 23, 1954, 2, Strictly Confidential-A-B (4), General Correspondence and Memoranda Series, JFDP, DDEL; Elson interview, 257–258; Thompson to Jenner, January 6, 1955, 39.19, DTP; Byroade to Thompson, January 17, 1955, 3.9, DTP.

14. Elmo Hutchison to Eddy, November 28, 1955; Eddy to Devin A. Garrity, September 21, 1955; Eddy to James T. Duce, December 4, 1955, 8.8, WAEP. Besides Devin-Adair, Henry Regnery stands out as a publisher who was friendly to the AFME-ACJ network. See Nuveen to Eddy, July 29, 1955, 8.8, WAEP.

15. Nasser, *Egypt's Liberation*, 5, 9.

16. See Berger, *Memoirs of an Anti-Zionist Jew*, 68–70.

17. "Egypt: The Revolutionary," *Time*, September 26, 1955, 25–28; William Zukerman, "U.S. Jews Hysterical Over the Middle East," *Time*, November 28, 1955, 28.

18. Mark Glickman, "One Voice Against Many: A Biographical Study of Elmer Berger, 1948–" (Ph.D. diss., Hebrew Union College-Jewish Institute of Religion, 1990), 112; Ruth Berger, "The Israelis Gave Us Reason to Criticize," 1955, 8.8, WAEP; Blake Cochran to State/USIA, "Visit of Elmer Berger to Jordan," June 13, 1955, 032 Berger, Elmer/6–1355, RG 59, NA; Elmer Berger, *Who Knows Better Must Say So!* (New York: American Council for Judaism, 1955). Berger was also the spark plug for an effort to create a "Citizens' Committee to Support an American Policy of Sympathetic Impartiality in the Middle East," drawing on much the same pool of individuals as the Committee for Justice and Peace in the Holy Land in the late 1940s, among them Virginia Gildersleeve. Despite support from Henry Byroade, the committee failed to take off, apparently the victim of dithering by the proposed chair, the now-retired ambassador Caffery. Hopkins to Berger, December 21, 1956; Berger to Hopkins, January 21, 1955; Byroade to Hopkins, February 5, 1955, 6, American Friends of the Middle East 1955, Addition M67–130, ACJP.

19. State to Tel Aviv, etc., "Dr. Berger's Visit to the Arab States and Israel," August 1, 1955, 032 Berger, Elmer (Dr.)/8–155, RG 59, NA; Berger, *Memoirs of an Anti-Zionist Jew*, 58. Edward Lansdale, who was now coaching South Vietnamese president Ngo Dinh Diem the way he had earlier coached the Filipino Magsaysay, was reputed to be in the background of the American Friends of Vietnam, much as Kim Roosevelt was behind the American Friends of the Middle East. For more on this organization, see Joseph G. Morgan, *The Vietnam Lobby: The American Friends of Vietnam, 1955–1975* (Chapel Hill: University of North Carolina Press, 1997).

20. Isaac Alteras, *Eisenhower and Israel: U.S.-Israeli Relations, 1953–1960* (Gainesville: University Press of Florida, 1993), 106; Thompson to Jacob Blaustein, February 23, 1954, 39.8, DTP; Elson to Jennie C. Loewenthal, July 1955, 14.7, Elson Papers; Lilliam Levy, "State Dept. Official in Brazen Attack on Jews, Orthodoxy," *National Jewish Post*, November 9, 1956, 1.18, Elson

Papers; "Propaganda Pressures," *Near East Report*, June 3, 1957, 24. How much influence Elson exercised personally on Eisenhower is unclear. While some sources suggest a close relationship between the two, the president's secretary, Ann C. Whitman, claimed that her boss regarded his pastor as a "phony" (quoted in Jeffrey Frank, *Ike and Dick: Portrait of a Strange Political Marriage* [New York: Simon & Schuster, 2013], 172).

21. Ben-Gurion quoted in Alteras, *Eisenhower and Israel*, 35; *hasbara* officials quoted in Peter L. Hahn, "The United States and Israel in the Eisenhower Era: The 'Special Relationship' Revisited," in *The Eisenhower Administration, the Third World, and the Globalization of the Cold War*, ed. Kathryn C. Statler and Andrew L. Johns (Lanham, MD: Rowman & Littlefield, 2006), 227.

22. Malcolm Kerr, *The Arab Cold War, 1958–1967: A Study of Ideology in Politics*, 2nd ed. (Oxford: Royal Institute of International Affairs / Oxford University Press, 1967).

Fourteen: Crypto-Diplomacy

1. 'Amer quoted in "Egypt: The Revolutionary," 28.

2. MC, *Game Player*, 196.

3. MC to KR, November 29, 1954, quoted in Tawil, *La'bat al-umam*, 398. See MC, *Game of Nations*, 123–126; Eveland, *Ropes of Sand*, 99–102; Patrick Tyler, *A World of Trouble: The White House and the Middle East—from the Cold War to the War on Terror* (New York: Farrar, Straus & Giroux, 2009), 42–44.

4. KR to MC, January 2, [1955], quoted in Tawil, *La'bat al-umam*, 392–393.

5. KR to MC, January 2, [1955], quoted in ibid., 394. See MC, *Game of Nations*, 150; Samir Rafaat, "The Cairo Tower," *Cairo Times*, October 16, 1997, http://www.egy.com/zamalek/97-10-16.php; Lorraine Copeland e-mail, November 29, 2010.

6. [MC to KR], November 29, 1954, quoted in Tawil, *La'bat al-umam*, 398; MC, *Game of Nations*, 179–180; Nasser quoted in Neff, *Warriors at Suez*, 67.

7. Byroade to John Foster Dulles, May 11, 1955, 1, 320 Egypt-USA 1955, Egypt, Cairo Embassy, Classified General Records, 1953–55, RG 84, NA.

8. Nasser quoted in Neff, *Warriors at Suez*, 76; MC, *Game of Nations*, 129.

9. For an excellent discussion of this issue based partly on Russian and Czech archives, see Guy Laron, "Cutting the Gordian Knot: The Post-World War II Egyptian Quest for Arms and the 1955 Czechoslovak Arms Deal," Cold War International History Project, Working Paper No. 55, Washington, DC, 2007.

10. MC, *Game Player*, 199; Alterman, "American Aid to Egypt," 60; Tawil, *La'bat al-umam*, 153–155, 420–423; Lucas and Morey, "Hidden Alliance," 100; Laron, "Cutting the Gordian Knot," 28–30; KR, "The Ghost of Suez," unpublished ms., 6, 5, Roosevelt, Kermit, Love Papers; Byroade to John Foster Dulles, September 21, 1955, *FRUS 1955–57, Vol. 14*, 492–493.

11. Telephone Call to Mr. Hoover in Washington, September 20, 1955, 4, Telephone Conv.– General September 1, 1955–December 30, 1955 (5), General Correspondence and Memoranda Series, JFDP, DDEL; KR, interview by Kennett Love, Washington, DC, February 24, 1964, 5, Roosevelt, Kermit, Love Papers.

12. MC, *Game of Nations*, 133; Haikal, *Cairo Documents*, 51–52; Haikal, *Cutting the Lion's Tail*, 77; *FRUS 1955–57, Vol. 14*, 520.

13. MC, *Game of Nations*, 135; Lucas, *Divided We Stand*, 340; Trevelyan quoted in ibid., 60.

14. James N. Cortada, interview by Charles Stuart Kennedy, September 1, 1992, FAOHP; MC, *Game of Nations*, 137; Byroade and Nasser quoted in Haikal, *Cairo Documents*, 53.

15. KR and Johnston quoted in Neff, *Warriors at Suez*, 92; Eveland, *Ropes of Sand*, 148; Byroade quoted in Neff, *Warriors at Suez*, 92; Haikal, *Cutting the Lion's Tail*, 77.

16. Evelyn Shuckburgh diary, September 26, 1955, MS191/1/2/4, Shuckburgh Papers; Macmillan quoted in Memorandum of a Conversation, New York, September 26, 1955, *FRUS 1955–57, Vol. 14*, 518; CIA cable in *FRUS 1955–57, Vol. 14*, 521; George Allen, interview by Kennett Love, Arlington, VA, July 6, 1966, 4, Allen, George, Love Papers.

17. Haikal, *Cairo Documents*, 54; Telephone Call from Allen Dulles, September 29, 1955, 4, Telephone Conv.–General September 1, 1955–December 30, 1955 (5), General Correspondence and Memoranda Series, JFDP, DDEL; Byroade quoted in Neff, *Warriors at Suez*, 95; Allen interview; Neff, *Warriors at Suez*, 95.

18. Allen and Roosevelt interviews by Love; MC, *Game of Nations*, 142.

19. Embassy in Egypt to Department of State, October 1, 1955, *FRUS 1955–57, Vol. 14*, 539; MC, *Game of Nations*, 143.

20. MC, *Game Player*, 197; MC, *Game of Nations*, 136.

21. MC, *Game of Nations*, 143. The practice of crypto-diplomacy did not die out with the Eisenhower administration. In February 2011, foreign service veteran Frank G. Wisner II, son of the first head of CIA covert operations, visited Cairo as a special envoy of the Obama administration to talk the aging Egyptian dictator Hosni Mubarak into giving up power. The mission backfired when Wisner declared publicly that Mubarak should stay in charge so that he could oversee an orderly transition to democracy, thereby contradicting the calls for more urgent action coming from the White House and Obama's ambassador in Cairo, Margaret Scobey.

Fifteen: Peacemakers

1. Edward R. F. Sheehan, *Kingdom of Illusion* (New York: Random House, 1964), 80, 57, 149, 145, 182, 153, 56, 221.

2. Leonard Mosley, *Dulles: A Biography of Eleanor, Allen, and John Foster Dulles and Their Family Network* (New York: Dial, 1978), 348. On the tensions over Buraimi, see Tore T. Petersen, "Anglo-American Rivalry in the Middle East: The Struggle for the Buraimi Oasis, 1953-1957," *International History Review* 14, no. 3 (1992): 71–91.

3. K. to Big Brother, December 23, 1954, quoted in Tawil, *La'bat al-umam*, 399. See Caplan, *Futile Diplomacy*, 4:48; Michael B. Oren, "Secret Egypt-Israel Peace Initiatives Prior to the Suez Campaign," *Middle Eastern Studies* 26, no. 3 (1990): 361; Shimon Shamir, "The Collapse of Project Alpha," in *Suez 1956: The Crisis and Its Consequences*, ed. Wm. Roger Louis and Roger Owen (New York: Oxford University Press, 1989), 79.

4. For differing explanations of the separation of the Arab desk and the Israeli account, see AR, *Lust of Knowing*, 298, and Michael Holzman, *James Jesus Angleton, the CIA, and the Craft of Counterintelligence* (Amherst: University of Massachusetts Press, 2008), 152–153.

5. Telephone Call from Allen Dulles, January 6, 1956, 5, Memoranda of Telcon. General January 3, 1956–April 30, 1956 (8), General Correspondence and Memoranda Series, JFDP, DDEL.

6. *AFME Annual Report, 1955–56*, 59.1, JNP.

7. "Cairo Backed on Arms," *New York Times*, October 11, 1955, 4; State to Damascus, "AFME Views on Arab-Israel Problem," January 11, 1956, 684A.86/1–1156, RG 59, NA.

8. Telephone Call from Allen Dulles, January 6, 1956, 5, Memoranda of Telcon. General January 3, 1956–April 30, 1956 (8), General Correspondence and Memoranda Series, JFDP, DDEL; Diary Entry by the President, January 11, 1956, *FRUS 1955–57, Vol. 15*, 23; Polly to Belle Roosevelt, January 9, 1956, I, 143, Roosevelt, Mary Gaddis (Polly), undated, 1950–59, KRBRP.

9. Robert Anderson to State, January 19, 1956, 34, Alpha–Anderson Talks w/BG and Nasser, Carbons of Incoming and Outgoing Tels., Folder 1 of 2, Lot 59D518, Documents on Projects Alpha, Mask, and Omega, 1945–1957, RG 59, NA; Message to Anderson, February 1, 1956, *FRUS 1955–57, Vol. 15*, 119–120.

10. KR quoted in Neff, *Warriors at Suez*, 135.

11. Haikal, *Cairo Documents*, 56.

12. Message to Washington No. 22, January 24, 1956, *FRUS 1955–57, Vol. 15*, 61, 63.

13. Memorandum of a Conversation with the Secretary of State, October 18, 1955, *FRUS 1955–57, Vol. 14*, 612–613; "Take the Middle East Out of Domestic Politics! An Open Letter to Every American Citizen," *New York Times*, January 25, 1956, 20; Thompson quoted in "Yemen Aide Says West Loses in Mideast Because of 'Minority Pressure Groups,'" *New York Times*, January 27, 1956, 4.

14. Under Secretary of State (Hoover) to Cairo, January 31, 1956, *FRUS 1955–57, Vol. 15*, 117; KR, "Ghost of Suez"; Message to Athens No. 70, February 2, 1956, *FRUS 1955–57, Vol. 15*, 129.

15. Message to Washington No. 78, February 7, 1956, *FRUS 1955–57, Vol. 15*, 148; Memorandum to Washington, February 8, 1956, *FRUS 1955–57, Vol. 15*, 154; Message to Washington No. 83, February 20, 1956, *FRUS 1955–57, Vol. 15*, 195.

16. Thompson quoted in "Zionists Assail Tanks for Arabs," *New York Times*, February 20, 1956, 2; Eliot to Thompson, February 27, 1956, 14, AFME, January–February 1956, DTP; Eliot, "Arab-Israeli Peace Still Is Possible," February 26, 1956, 14, AFME, January–February 1956, DTP.

17. Message to Central Intelligence Agency No. 88, February 22, 1956, *FRUS 1955–57, Vol. 15*, 204.

18. MC to Allen Dulles No. 93, February 22, 1956, 34, Alpha–Anderson talks w/BG and Nasser, Incoming Telegrams—Jan.–Mar. 1956, Part 1, Lot 59D518, RG 59, NA (this message also appears,

with the identity of the author redacted, in *FRUS 1955–57, Vol. 15*, 209); Byroade to John Foster Dulles, February 23, 1956, *FRUS 1955–57, Vol. 15*, 211, 212.

19. Lloyd C. Gardner, *Three Kings: The Rise of an American Empire in the Middle East After World War II* (New York: New Press, 2009), 162; Shuckburgh diary, March 3, 1956, 403, MS191/1/2/4, Shuckburgh Papers.

20. KR interview by Love; Eden quoted in Lucas, *Divided We Stand*, 88.

21. Anderson to John Foster Dulles, March 6, 1956, *FRUS 1955–57, Vol. 15*, 305.

22. Caplan, *Futile Diplomacy*, 4:252; Shuckburgh diary, March 8, 1956, 414, MS191/1/2/4, Shuckburgh Papers.

Sixteen: . . . to OMEGA

1. MC, *Game Player*, 194.

2. Ibid.

3. This and other biographical details are from the published version of Eveland's memoirs, *Ropes of Sand*, and "Outlines," a manuscript draft contained in the Wilbur Crane Eveland Papers (WCEP), Hoover Institution, Stanford University, Stanford, CA.

4. MC, *Game Player*, 215.

5. Eveland, *Ropes of Sand*, 114.

6. Ibid., 169.

7. Ibid., 170; Eveland to Allen Dulles and Norman Paul, April 1, 1956, 6, WCEP; MI6 officer quoted in Eveland, "Outlines," 481, 6; Eveland to Dulles and Paul.

8. Chester L. Cooper, *The Lion's Last Roar: Suez, 1956* (New York: Harper & Row, 1978), 69; Haikal, *Cutting the Lion's Tail*, 103; Peter Wright, *Spycatcher: The Candid Autobiography of a Senior Intelligence Officer* (New York: Viking, 1987), 160–161; MC, *Game Player*, 201.

9. John Foster Dulles to Eisenhower, March 28, 1956, 5, File Received from Mr. Hoover, Jr., Office (1), Subject Series, JFDP, DDEL; Ivone Kirkpatrick to Makins, March 19, 1956, FO 371/118869, PRO; FO Intel 29, "Anglo-American Policy in the Middle East," February 23, 1956, PREM 11/1937, PRO.

10. Allen Dulles quoted in NSC minutes, February 17, 1955, 6, NSC Series, AWF, DDEL; John Foster Dulles to Eisenhower, March 28, 1956, 5, File Received from Mr. Hoover, Jr., Office (1), Subject Series, JFDP, DDEL; Selwyn Lloyd to Eden, April 6, 1956, PREM 11/1937, PRO. On Ike's hopes for Saud as a Muslim leader, see Nathan J. Citino, *From Arab Nationalism to OPEC: Eisenhower, King Sa'ūd and the Making of U.S.-Saudi Relations* (Bloomington: Indiana University Press, 2002), 95.

11. Lloyd to Makins, March 16, 1956, PREM 11/1463, PRO; Makins to Lloyd, April 6, 1956, PREM 11/1937, PRO; Memorandum of Conversation, "Bilateral Talk with British in Paris (Near East)," May 3, 1956, 55, Omega Vol. 4, Lot 61D417, Executive Secretariat, Meeting Summaries and Project Files, 1951–59, RG 59, NA; Allen Dulles to John Foster Dulles, May 11, 1956, 55, Omega Vol. 4, Lot 61D417, RG 59, NA.

12. KR quoted in Hersh, *The Old Boys*, 313. See also KR, *Countercoup*, 210. Miles Copeland made much the same point in *The Game Player*, arguing that the CIA should not have taken part in what was basically a paramilitary operation and declaring PB-SUCCESS a "national outrage" (MC, *Game Player*, 192).

13. Amory quoted in Hersh, *The Old Boys*, 449n32; Haikal, *Cutting the Lion's Tail*, 104; MC, *Game Player*, 165–166.

14. F. H. Russell to William Rountree, March 29, 1956, 38, Omega—Developments—Miscl., 1956, Folder 2 of 2, Lot 59D518, RG 59, NA; Middle East Policy Planning Group, "Suggested Near East Development Institution," April 9, 1956, 36, Omega—Meetings of MEPPG 4/9/56 to 6/30/56, Folder 1 of 2, Lot 59D518, RG 59, NA.

15. Roger Goiran and KR to Russell, May 18, 1956, quoting message of May 17, 1956, from CIA Cairo station, 37, Omega Memos, etc., from April 24, 1956, to June 30, 1956, 2 of 3, Lot 59D518, RG 59, NA; Memorandum for Middle East Policy Planning Group, "Cairo Station Views Pertinent to OMEGA Planning," May 2, 1956, 55, Omega Vol. 4, Lot 61D417, RG 59, NA; Byroade to John Foster Dulles, April 19, 1956, *FRUS 1955–57, Vol. 15*, 556–560.

16. Young quoted in Dorril, *MI6*, 609; Eveland, *Ropes of Sand*, 197.

17. Hersh, *The Old Boys*, 449; Shuckburgh diary, January 12, 1956, MS191/1/2/4, Shuckburgh Papers.

18. MC, *Game Player*, 176, 181; Wilber, *Adventures in the Middle East*, 191–192.

19. MC, *Game of Nations*, 16; Allen Dulles quoted in ibid., 171.

20. MC, *Game Player*, 285. See Thomas B. Allen, *War Games: The Secret World of the Creators, Players, and Policy Makers Rehearsing World War III Today* (New York: McGraw-Hill, 1987), 5; Sharon Ghamari-Tabrizi, "Simulating the Unthinkable: Gaming Future War in the 1950s and 1960s," *Social Studies of Science* 30, no. 2 (2000): 163–223.

21. Haikal, *Cairo Documents*, 58; John Foster Dulles quoted in Takeyh, *The Origins of the Eisenhower Doctrine*, 120.

22. Rountree to John Foster Dulles, May 23, 1956, 55, Omega Vol. 5, Lot 61D417, RG 59, NA; Hare quoted in Eveland, *Ropes of Sand*, 181.

23. Eveland, *Ropes of Sand*, 208.

24. Eveland, "Outlines," 586.

Seventeen: Increasingly a Vehicle for Your Purposes

1. Lucas, *Divided We Stand*, 120; Nasser quoted in Haikal, *Cairo Documents*, 68.

2. MC quoted in Eveland, *Ropes of Sand*, 193; Berger to Levison, August 6, 1956, 8, Dr. Elmer Berger 1956, Addition M68–068, ACJP.

3. Dulles quoted in Keith Kyle, *Suez: Britain's End of Empire in the Middle East* (1991; rept., London: Tauris, 2003), 130; "The Dramatic Gambit," *Time*, July 30, 1956, 9.

4. Nasser quoted in Lucas, *Divided We Stand*, 139; Allen interview; "How CIA Aide Upset Diplomacy in Egypt," *Washington Post*, September 24, 1956, 5; KR interview by Love. Noting that Kim Roosevelt "was almost as enraged as Nasser" by the loan cancellation, Allen Dulles invited him, Miles Copeland, and Frank Wisner to a joint CIA–State Department meeting to predict the Egyptian leader's reaction. According to Copeland's memoirs, Wisner did raise the possibility of Nasser nationalizing the Suez Canal, but the area specialists "pooh-poohed him into silence" (MC, *Game Player*, 200; see also ibid., 170–171).

5. There is a vast literature on the Suez Crisis. See, in particular, Kyle, *Suez*; Lucas, *Divided We Stand*; Neff, *Warriors at Suez*; and Thornhill, *Road to Suez*.

6. Freedman quoted in Thompson to Freedman, September 19, 1955, 6.2, DTP; James H. Sheldon, "American Friends of Israel's Foes," *American Zionist* (April 1953): 10–13.

7. Ross, *Rabbi Outcast*, 74; Alfred Lilienthal, "A Report on Operations of the AFME from a Member to Other Members," January 25, 1955, 3.9, DTP; Alfred Lilienthal, "Memorandum to Members of the National Council of the American Friends of the Middle East," June 11, 1955, 69.22, Alfred A. Lilienthal Papers, Hoover Institution, Stanford University, Stanford, CA.

8. George Camp Keiser to Alice B. Whelen, April 30, 1953, 24.6, ACJP; Walter Van Kirk to [Roswell P.] Barnes, January 25, 1954, and Martha A. Roy to Van Kirk, February 5, 1954, 16.2, RG 6, National Council of the Churches Records, Presbyterian Historical Society, Philadelphia.

9. Richard H. Sanger to [Parker T.] Hart, February 2, 1953, 511.80/2–253, RG 59, NA; G. H. Damon to Sanger, April 2, 1953, 4, Lot 68D99, Bureau of Near Eastern and South Asian Affairs, Office of the Public Affairs Adviser, Subject Files 1963–66, RG 59, NA; Sanger and Stephen P. Dorsey to Byroade, February 4, 1954, 511.80/2–454, RG 59, NA.

10. Eddy to Hopkins, January 11, 1954, 3.1, DTP; Eddy to Thompson, February 16, 1954, 3.4, DTP.

11. Kay Sisto to Thompson, March 9, 1954, 3.8, DTP; Lilienthal, "Report on Operations of AFME"; Sanger to Allen, January 21, 1955, 4, Lot 68D99, RG 59, NA.

12. "A Special Survey," *Near East Report*, October 1964, B-16; *AFME Annual Report, 1954–55*, 59.1, JNP; "Heard in Washington," *Near East Report*, March 7, 1967, 19.

13. Engert to Thompson, July 10, 1956, 3.16, DTP.

14. Hopkins to Stobart, no date [September 1956], 3.16, DTP; *AFME Annual Report, 1956–57*, 59.2, JNP. Hopkins's correspondence with Stobart makes clear that the latter controlled a large budget and had a long personal acquaintance with Hopkins.

15. Thompson to Charles Hulac, January 8, 1957, 6.17, DTP; Thompson to John N. Wheeler, December 23, 1956, 6.16, DTP; Thompson quoted in Kurth, 536.

16. *AFME Annual Report, 1956–57*; Hopkins to Stobart, no date [September 1956], 3.16, DTP; *AFME Annual Report, 1957–58*, 59.3, JNP.

17. Theodore R. Frye to Mr. Kretzmann, April 1, 1957, 4, Lot 68D99, RG 59, NA; Memorandum of Conversation, "United States Relations with the Middle East," May 8, 1958, 4, Lot 68D99, RG 59, NA.

18. *AFME Annual Report, 1958–59*, 59.4, JNP; H. Ben Smith to Nuveen, September 15, 1958,

59.3, JNP; William T. Dodson to [redacted], July 10, 1958, 59.3, JNP; *AFME Annual Report, 1958–59*; *AFME Annual Report* for 1962–63, 1963–64, and 1964–65, 60.1, JNP; Orin D. Parker, interview by author, Oceanside, CA, July 10, 2009.

19. Hutchison to Eddy, September 28, 1955, 9.7, WAEP; Berger, *Memoirs of an Anti-Zionist Jew*, 103; Hutchison quoted in "Special Survey," *Near East Report*, B-19; see "Propaganda Pressures," *Near East Report*, October 15, 1958, 138; Telephone Call to Dr. Edward Elson, February 22, 1957, 6, Memoranda Tel. Conv.–Gen. Jan 1957–February 28, 1957 (1), General Correspondence and Memoranda Series, JFDP, DDEL; Berger, *Memoirs of an Anti-Zionist Jew*, 92.

20. "Special Survey," *Near East Report*, B-19. For more on the growing influence of modernization theory on US policy toward the Middle East after the late 1950s, see Jacobs, *Imagining the Middle East*, 164–186.

21. "Draft, Story of a Purpose," December 19, 1958, 59.3, JNP.

22. "Inventory of U.S. Government and Private Organization Activity regarding Islamic Organizations as an Aspect of Overseas Operations," May 3, 1957, 39, Ad Hoc Working Group on Islam, Lot 62D430, OCB Executive Secretariat, Regional and Country Operations Files, 1953–1961, RG 59, NA. See Robert Dreyfuss, *Devil's Game: How the United States Helped Islamic Fundamentalism* (New York: Metropolitan Books, 2005).

23. Minutes, Meeting of October 17, 1956, October 19, 1956, 2, Minutes IV, Lot 62D430, RG 59, NA; Edward P. Lilly to Elmer B. Staats, June 19, 1956, 78, 091.4 Near East (File 3) (6), OCB Central Files Series, White House Office, National Security Council Staff: Papers, 1948–61, DDEL.

Eighteen: Archie's Turn: Syria, 1956

1. Francis Russell, "U.S. Policies Toward Nasser," August 4, 1956, 38, Omega—Developments—Miscl., 1956, Folder 2 of 2, Lot 59D518, RG 59, NA.

2. Quoted in AR, *Lust of Knowing*, 445.

3. See Roosevelt, *Keeper of the Gate*.

4. AR, Biographical Material, 12.1, ABRP; AR, *Lust of Knowing*, 445.

5. Code names in Eveland, "Outlines," 539; Alsop quoted in ibid., 256; ibid., 545.

6. AR, *Lust of Knowing*, 445–446.

7. Seale, *The Struggle for Syria*, 275.

8. Eveland, *Ropes of Sand*, 189–190.

9. Ibid., 203.

10. AR, *Lust of Knowing*, 433, 443–444.

11. Selwa S. "Lucky" Roosevelt, interview by Charles Stuart Kennedy, November 24, 2003, FAOHP; Selwa Roosevelt interview by author; Dorril, *MI6*, chap. 19; AR, *Lust of Knowing*, 460, 447; Selwa Roosevelt interview by author; AR, *Lust of Knowing*, 366.

12. Tom Bower, *The Perfect English Spy: Sir Dick White and the Secret War, 1935–90* (New York: St. Martin's, 1995), 190; MC, obituary of AR. Archie interviewed Turkic Muslims for possible assignments with the Voice of America and other unspecified political warfare operations at the Munich headquarters of AMCOMLIB's radio station, Radio Liberation (Rusi Nasar, interview by Ian Johnson, May 10, 2006). On AMCOMLIB and the blowback from its operations, see the excellent book by Ian Johnson, *A Mosque in Munich: Nazis, the CIA, and the Rise of the Muslim Brotherhood in the West* (Boston: Houghton Mifflin Harcourt, 2010).

13. AR, *Lust of Knowing*, 429–432.

14. Ibid., 451–452. According to Bill Eveland, "Archie had a subconscious desire to oversee a coup in Syria and match his cousin's reputation in Iran" (Eveland, "Outlines," 544–545).

15. Richard Beeston, *Looking for Trouble: The Life and Times of a Foreign Correspondent* (London: Brassey's, 1997), 16; Nigel Ashton, *King Hussein of Jordan: A Political Life* (New Haven, CT: Yale University Press, 2008), 62–63; Eveland, *Ropes of Sand*, 188, 191n; Jack O'Connell with Vernon Loeb, *King's Counsel: A Memoir of War, Espionage, and Diplomacy in the Middle East* (New York: Norton, 2011), 5; AR, *Lust of Knowing*, 366.

16. AR, *Lust of Knowing*, 373–376; Eveland, *Ropes of Sand*, 199.

17. CIA guidance telegram, August 22, 1956, 38, Report of Special Mission to Saudi Arabia, August 20–27, 1956, Lot 59D518, RG 59, NA; see, for example, Telephone Call from Allen Dulles, Wednesday, April 4, 1956, 4, Memoranda of Telcon. General January 3, 1956–April 30, 1956 (3), General Correspondence and Memoranda Series, JFDP, DDEL; MC, *Without Cloak or Dagger*, 192–193. For a detailed discussion of Copeland's claims, which concludes that they are credible,

see Barrett J. Riordan, "The Plowshare Program and Copeland's Suez Energy Deception," *International Journal of Intelligence and Counterintelligence* 17, no. 1 (2004): 124–143.

18. Eveland, *Ropes of Sand*, 212–213. For a typically satirical secondhand account of the mission, see MC, *Game Player*, 207–208.

19. Allen to John Foster Dulles, "Adib Shishakli and the Possibility of a Coup in Syria," June 27, 1956, *FRUS 1955–57, Vol. 13*, 581; Seale, *The Struggle for Syria*, chap. 20.

20. Seale, *The Struggle for Syria*, 245; "Notes on Syrian Personalities," May 1, 1957, FO371/121857, PRO; R. C. Strong to Secretary of State, October 4, 1956, 30, Syria 350 Syria 1, 1956, Syria Classified General Records, 1943–1963, RG 84, NA.

21. Eveland, *Ropes of Sand*, 125; Parker T. Hart, interview by William R. Crawford, January 27, 1989, FAOHP; *New York Times*, July 16, 1956, 6; Eveland, *Ropes of Sand*, 190; ambassador quoted in MC, *Game of Nations*, 188.

22. Eveland, *Ropes of Sand*, 221; Seale, *The Struggle for Syria*, 276; Anthony Gorst and W. Scott Lucas, "The Other Collusion: Operation Straggle and Anglo-American Intervention in Syria, 1955–56," *Intelligence and National Security* 4, no. 3 (1989): 590; Rathmell, *Secret War*, 121.

23. Dorril, *MI6*, 633; Kyle, *Suez*, 275.

24. Allen Dulles quoted by John Foster Dulles in Richard J. Aldrich, *The Hidden Hand: Britain, America and Cold War Secret Intelligence* (London: John Murray, 2001), 483; MC, *Game Player*, 207–210; "Report of Conversation on Suez with Certain Egyptians, New York, 4 October," October 9, 1956, 11, Egypt, Lot 58D776, Subject Files of the Bureau of Intelligence and Research, 1945–60, RG 59, NA.

25. Young quoted in Bower, *The Perfect English Spy*, 193; OIR Special Paper No. 2, "Hitler-Nasser," August 14, 1956, 11, Egypt, Lot 58D776, RG 59, NA; Haikal, *Cutting the Lion's Tail*, 106; MC, *Game of Nations*, 178.

26. Rountree to John Foster Dulles, "Conversation with President Regarding Operation MASK," October 19, 1956, 36, Mask—U.S.-U.K. Bilateral, Lot 59D518, RG 59, NA; MC, *Game Player*, 201.

27. Memorandum of Conversation, "U.S.-U.K. Bilateral," October 1, 1956, 36, Omega Syria, Lot 59D518, RG 59, NA; "MASK," no date, 36, U.S.-U.K. Bilateral, Lot 59D518, RG 59, NA; Memorandum of Conversation, "Operation Mask," October 18, 1956, 36, Mask—U.S.-U.K. Bilateral, Lot 59D518, RG 59, NA; CIA report quoted in Kyle, *Suez*, 275; Rountree to John Foster Dulles, October 30, 1956, 36, Omega––Syria, Miscl.—Straggle, 1956, Folder 1 of 2, Lot 59D518, RG 59, NA.

28. Bruce-Lockhart quoted in Dorril, *MI6*, 641; Dean quoted in Cooper, *The Lion's Last Roar*, 159; KR, "Ghost of Suez."

29. KR interview by R. Harris Smith; KR, "Ghost of Suez"; Amory quoted in Hersh, *The Old Boys*, 368.

30. Eveland, *Ropes of Sand*, 227.

31. I am very grateful to Scott Lucas for sharing this information with me.

Nineteen: Game On: Jordan, Lebanon, Syria, 1957

1. For an authoritative account of the Eisenhower Doctrine, see Salim Yaqub, *Containing Arab Nationalism: The Eisenhower Doctrine and the Middle East* (Chapel Hill: University of North Carolina Press, 2004).

2. A number of recent books have favored a revisionist interpretation of post-Suez Anglo-American relations in the Middle East, the latest example being Simon C. Smith, *Ending Empire in the Middle East: Britain, the United States, and Post-War Decolonization, 1945–1973* (New York: Routledge, 2012), chap. 3.

3. Young quoted in Dorril, *MI6*, 648; Telephone Call to Allen Dulles, October 30, 1956, 5, Memoranda of Telcon. General Oct.1, 1956–Dec. 29, 1956 (3), General Correspondence and Memoranda Series, JFDP, DDEL; Dorril, *MI6*, 648–649; Bower, *The Perfect English Spy*, 215–216.

4. Sheehan, *Kingdom of Illusion*, 239, 277. Bill Eveland claimed secondhand knowledge of a plan, code name SIPONY, to carry out a "palace revolution" in Cairo, but he did not provide any more detailed information (see Eveland, *Ropes of Sand*, 244, 248). In contrast to Eveland, Miles Copeland wrote in his memoirs of "various desultory attempts to play along with the anti-Nasser mood of the moment," including "the tightening of a channel to Nasser by which to ensure that whatever came of our anti-Nasser measures a pro-Nasser rescue operation would be on hand to

replace them if they failed" (*Game Player*, 208). More recent studies by historians likewise differ concerning the extent of US involvement in direct action against Nasser. Two works playing down American activism are Matthew F. Holland, *America and Egypt: From Roosevelt to Eisenhower* (Westport, CT: Praeger, 1996), 136–137; and Lucas and Morey, "The Hidden Alliance," 112. A differing interpretation is offered in Little, "Mission Impossible," 681–682.

5. Eveland, *Ropes of Sand*, 242–243; Memorandum for the OCB Working Group on the Near East (NSC 5428), "Internal Security Program for Iraq," June 4, 1957, 44, 091.Iraq (3), OCB Central Files Series, White House Office, NSC Staff: Papers, 1948–61, DDEL. The US success with Saud might also have owed something to the efforts of Ronald Irwin Metz, ARAMCO's liaison with the Saudi king. Like Bill Eddy, Metz was an OSS veteran with close ties to the CIA. See Kai Bird's memoir of his Middle Eastern childhood, *Crossing Mandelbaum Gate: Coming of Age Between the Arabs and Israelis, 1956–1978* (New York: Scribner, 2010), chap. 3.

6. KR, *Arabs, Oil, and History*, 117; officials quoted in Pearson, *In the Name of Oil*, 113.

7. See Lawrence Tal, *Politics, the Military, and National Security in Jordan, 1955–1967* (New York: Palgrave Macmillan, 2002), 44–45; Avi Shlaim, *Lion of Jordan: The Life of King Hussein in War and Peace* (New York: Knopf, 2008), 135–140; Ashton, *King Hussein of Jordan*, 63–64.

8. Tal, *Politics, the Military, and National Security in Jordan*, 45–46; "The Road to Zerqa," *Time*, April 29, 1957, 27.

9. See, especially, Tal, *Politics, the Military, and National Security in Jordan*, 47–49.

10. British official quoted in ibid., 48; Saïd K. Aburish, *Beirut Spy: The St. George Hotel Bar* (London: Bloomsbury, 1989), chap. 5; John Foster Dulles quoted in Douglas Little, "A Puppet in Search of a Puppeteer? The United States, King Hussein, and Jordan, 1953–1970," *International History Review* 17, no. 3 (1995): 524n3; MC, *Game of Nations*, 209.

11. C. D. Jackson quoted in Yaqub, *Containing Arab Nationalism*, 138; NSC minutes, May 16, 1957, 7, NSC Series, AWF, DDEL; Little, "Puppet," 525.

12. Allen Dulles quoted in Yaqub, *Containing Arab Nationalism*, 143. See Pearson, *In the Name of Oil*, 145; Zachary Karabell, *Architects of Intervention: The United States, the Third World, and the Cold War, 1946–1962* (Baton Rouge: Louisiana State University Press, 1999), 159; Eveland, *Ropes of Sand*, 252.

13. Telephone Call to Allen Dulles, April 17, 1957, 6, Memoranda Tel. Conv.—General March 1957–April 30, 1957 (2), General Correspondence and Memoranda Series, JFDP, DDEL.

14. Conversation with Harold Caccia, December 24, 1956, 1, Memos of Conversation—General—A Through D (3), General Correspondence and Memoranda Series, JFDP, DDEL; Allen Dulles to Hoover et al., November 10, 1956, 7, CIA Vol. 1 (4), Subject Series, Alphabetical Subseries, White House Office, Office of the Staff Secretary, DDEL; Rathmell, *Secret War*, 127; Telephone Call to Allen Dulles, April 17, 1957, 6, Memoranda Tel. Conv.—General March 1957–April 30, 1957 (2), General Correspondence and Memoranda Series, JFDP, DDEL.

15. Edward L. Waggoner to Fraser Wilkins, May 13, 1957, 1, United States–Syrian Relations, Bureau of Near Eastern and South Asian Affairs, Office of Near Eastern Affairs, Records of the United Arab Republic Affairs Desk, 1956–62, RG 59, NA; Telephone Call to Allen Dulles, April 17, 1957, 6, Memoranda Tel. Conv.—General March 1957–April 30, 1957 (2); Telephone Call to Allen Dulles, May 28, 1957, 6, Memoranda Tel. Conv.—General May 7 1957–June 27, 1957 (4), General Correspondence and Memoranda Series, JFDP, DDEL.

16. Eveland, "Outlines," 714; Eveland, *Ropes of Sand*, 246.

17. "In from the Cold: A Former Master Spy Spins Intriguing Yarns of His Past Intrigues," *Wall Street Journal*, October 19, 1979, 1, 41; see also "Hearing-Impaired Activist and Spy Rocky Stone Dies," *Washington Post*, August 24, 2004, B6.

18. Eveland, "Outlines," 275, 306; "Statement by Captain Abdullah ash-Shaykh Atiyyah of the Armored Battalion on the American Conspiracy in Syria," 14.11, ABRP.

19. Eveland, *Ropes of Sand*, 254; "Statement by Captain Atiyyah."

20. See Rathmell, *Secret War*, 139; Yaqub, *Containing Arab Nationalism*, 154–155; David W. Lesch, *Syria and the United States: Eisenhower's Cold War in the Middle East* (Boulder, CO: Westview, 1992), 119.

21. See "In from Cold," 41; Eveland, *Ropes of Sand*, 254; Amman to London, August 26, 1957, FO 371/128245, PRO; Tim Weiner, *Legacy of Ashes: The History of the CIA* (New York: Doubleday, 2007), 139.

22. Quoted in Yaqub, *Containing Arab Nationalism*, 169.

23. John S. D. Eisenhower, Memorandum of Conference with the President, August 21, 1957, 48, Syria (3), International Series, AWF, DDEL; Minutes of Meeting in Room 5100, August 21, 1957, 1, Lot 66D123, Executive Secretariat, Records Relating to Project GAMMA, 1957–58, RG 59, NA; Memorandum of a Conversation with the President, September 7, 1957, *FRUS 1955–57, Vol. 13*, 687–688.

24. Harold Macmillan to John Foster Dulles, no date [late August/early September, 1957], 48, Syria (2), International Series, AWF, DDEL; Caccia to FO, September 14, 1957, PREM 11/2329, PRO.

25. Memorandum of Conversation, Joint U.S.-U.K. Working Group Report on Syria, September 21, 1957, 11, S/Miss Bernau, Subject Series, JFDP, DDEL. For further detail on the Working Group report, see Matthew Jones, "The 'Preferred Plan': The Anglo-American Working Group Report on Covert Action in Syria, 1957," *Intelligence and National Security* 19, no. 3 (2004): 401–415.

26. Caccia and Macmillan quoted in Pearson, *In the Name of Oil*, 136.

27. Stephen Blackwell, *British Military Intervention and the Struggle for Jordan: King Hussein, Nasser, and the Middle East Crisis, 1955–1958* (New York: Routledge, 2009), 86. For more on subsequent Anglo-American working groups, see Matthew Jones, "Anglo-American Relations after Suez, the Rise and Decline of the Working Group Experiment, and the French Challenge to NATO, 1957–59," *Diplomacy and Statecraft* 14, no. 1 (2003): 49–79.

Twenty: Game Over

1. Polly Roosevelt to family members, January 28, 1955, 143, Roosevelt, Mary Gaddis (Polly), undated, 1950–59, KRBRP.

2. Ibid.; Notification of Personnel Action, August 20, 1956, CO5654040, CIA FOIA; Polly to Belle Roosevelt, July 4, 1955, 143, Roosevelt, Mary Gaddis (Polly), undated, 1950–59, KRBRP.

3. Polly to Belle Roosevelt, January 3, 1950, 143, Roosevelt, Mary Gaddis (Polly), undated, 1950–59, KRBRP; Roosevelt, *Keeper of the Gate*, 162; Selwa Roosevelt interview by Kennedy.

4. AR, *Lust of Knowing*, 434.

5. KR interview by R. Harris Smith.

6. Caccia to FO, September 25, 1957, PREM 11/2521, PRO; Lloyd to Macmillan, October 15, 1957, PREM 11/2521, PRO; Caccia to FO, November 9, 1957, PREM 11/2521, PRO.

7. Caccia to FO, October 21, 1957, PREM 11/2521, PRO; Memorandum for Executive Officer, "Background on Draft Near East Progress Report (NSC 5428) dated December 14, 1956," December 18, 1956, 78, 091.4 Near East (File #4) (4), OCB Central Files Series, White House Office, NSC Staff: Papers, 1948–61, DDEL.

8. Dulles quoted in Eveland, *Ropes of Sand*, 309. On the "Connection," see especially Andrew Cockburn and Leslie Cockburn, *Dangerous Liaison: The Inside Story of the U.S.-Israeli Covert Relationship* (New York: HarperCollins, 1991), chap. 5.

9. Yaqub, *Containing Arab Nationalism*, 178; Charles W. Yost, interview by Thomas Soapes, September 13, 1978, 26, Oral History Project, DDEL; Lakeland interview; Harrison Symmes, interview by Charles Stuart Kennedy, February 25, 1989, FAOHP.

10. Senator Richard B. Russell quoted in *The President's Proposal on the Middle East: Hearings, Eighty-Fifth Congress, First Session* (Washington, DC: Government Printing Office, 1957), 709, 706; Bruce-Lovett Report quoted in Arthur M. Schlesinger Jr., *Robert Kennedy and His Times*, Vol. 1 (Boston: Houghton Mifflin, 1978), 475.

11. MC, *Game of Nations*, 182; MC, *Game Player*, 195; Nasser quoted in MC, *Game of Nations*, 183; MC, *Game Player*, 205.

12. Lorraine Copeland e-mail, November 29, 2010; MC, *Game Player*, 209–211.

13. MC, *Game Player*, 209; Polly to Belle Roosevelt, September 12, 1957, 143, Roosevelt, Mary Gaddis (Polly), undated, 1950–59, KRBRP. Copeland was probably referring to the disastrous Project Haik. See John Prados, *Safe for Democracy: The Secret Wars of the CIA* (Chicago: Ivan R. Dee, 2006), 166–180.

14. Polly to Belle Roosevelt, January 10, no year [1958], 143, Roosevelt, Mary Gaddis (Polly), undated, 1950–59, KRBRP; Benjamin Welles, "Serving Oil, Arabs, and the CIA," *New Republic*, July 26, 1975, 11.

15. MC to Anderson, September 5, 1964, 282, Con-Cop (4), Robert B. Anderson Papers, DDEL; Welles, "Serving Oil, Arabs, and the CIA," 11; Report of Awards Board, December 19, 1957, CO5654063, CIA FOIA.

16. Quoted in Roosevelt, *Keeper of the Gate*, 164.

17. Eveland, "Outlines," 762.

18. Eveland to John Foster Dulles, "Recent Developments with Respect to the Syrian Situation," January 28, 1958, declassified CIA document, WCEP; C. Tracy Barnes to Patrick Dean, March 21, 1958, FO 371/133799, PRO. See Eveland, *Ropes of Sand*, 273.

19. Nasser quoted in Raymond Hare to John Foster Dulles, June 18, 1958, 7, 320 UAR/US Relations, Egypt Classified General Records, RG 84, NA; Eveland, *Ropes of Sand*, 280; O'Connell, *King's Counsel*, chap. 1. For more on Miles's peace mission to Cairo, see MC, *Game of Nations*, 199–201. This is another case of Copeland's later claims being borne out by contemporary documentation.

20. Baghdad Embassy to State, "July 14 Coup, and Staff Conduct," August 2, 1958, 49, 350 Iraqi Coup, July 1958, U.S. Embassy and Legation, Baghdad, Classified General Records, 1936–61, RG 84, NA; Tully, *CIA*, 78–79; Eveland, *Ropes of Sand*, 291.

21. See Pearson, *In the Name of Oil*, chap. 6; Eveland, *Ropes of Sand*, 282–283.

22. Eddy to Robert McClintock, June 25, 1958, 1, Lebanon Crisis, May 1958, Lot 59D600, Records of the Bureau of Intelligence and Research, Lebanon Crisis Files, 1958, RG 59, NA; "For Under Secretary and Secretary through Henderson from Harold Hoskins," July 17, 1958, 5.38, Hoskins Papers; Eddy to John Noble, June 30, 1958, 1, Lebanon Crisis, May 1958, Lot 59D600, RG 59, NA.

23. Eddy to Children, July 20, 1958, 6.7, WAEP.

Twenty-One: Epilogue

1. See Roland Popp, "Accommodating to a Working Relationship: Arab Nationalism and US Cold War Policies in the Middle East, 1958–60," *Cold War History* 10, no. 3 (2010): 397–427. On Iraq, see Kenneth Osgood, "Eisenhower and Regime Change in Iraq: The United States and the Iraqi Revolution of 1958," in *America and Iraq: Policy-Making, Intervention and Regional Politics*, ed. David Ryan and Patrick Kiely (New York: Routledge, 2009), 4–35.

2. Nasser quoted in Oren, *Power, Faith, and Fantasy*, 523.

3. Berger, *Memoirs of an Anti-Zionist Jew*, 92; AFME/Headquarters to AFME/Board of Directors, August 12, 1963, 59.5, JNP; "Heard on the Propaganda Front," *Near East Report*, September 8, 1964, 76; Rodger P. Davies to Mr. Twinam, January 27, 1972, 3, Persian Gulf, 1972, Bureau of Near Eastern and South Asian Affairs, Office of the Deputy Assistant Secretary, Subject Files of Rodger P. Davies, 1967–74, RG 59, NA (my thanks to Roland Popp for drawing my attention to this document); Parker interview. For more on the Fulbright hearings, see Randall Bennett Woods, *Fulbright: A Biography* (Cambridge: Cambridge University Press, 1995), 309–311.

4. "5 New Groups Tied to CIA Conduits," *New York Times*, February 17, 1967, 1; "Whitney Trust Got Aid," *New York Times*, February 25, 1967, 10; "Halt Asked for CIA Millions for Friends of Middle East," *National Jewish Post and Opinion*, March 31, 1967; Parker interview.

5. Orin. D. Parker, "Interesting Times . . . and Places . . . and People: Comments on My Life Experiences," unpublished memoir, 238; Director of Programs to Board of Directors, June 26, 1967, 60.2, JNP; "News about AFME," Special Issue No. 1, 1967, 60.2, JNP. AFME was later reconstituted as AMIDEAST, a genuine nongovernment organization specializing mainly in student exchanges between the United States and the Middle East.

6. Thomas V. Jones to Raymond Crim, August 23, 1974, 4, Iran/Roosevelt/Northrop, Jonathan Kwitny Collection, National Security Archive, George Washington University, Washington, DC; Welles, "Serving Oil, Arabs, and the CIA," 10.

7. KR interview by Love; "Roosevelt / on Copeland," May 5, 1970, 5, Roosevelt, Kermit, Love Papers; Court Minister Asadollah Alam quoted in Bayandor, *Iran and the CIA*, 178n14; Powers, "A Book Held Hostage"; Herbert Mitgang, "Publisher 'Correcting' Book on CIA Involvement in Iran," *New York Times*, November 10, 1979, 13; Richard W. Cottam, review of *Countercoup: The Struggle for the Control of Iran*, by Kermit Roosevelt, *Iranian Studies* 14, nos. 3/4 (1981): 269; KR, *Countercoup*, ix.

8. KR quoted in Gwen Kinkead, "Kermit Roosevelt: Brief Life of a Harvard Conspirator, 1916–2000," *Harvard Magazine*, Jan.–Feb. 2011, http://harvardmagazine.com/2011/01/kermit-roosevelt?page=0,1.

9. AR, *Lust of Knowing*, 474; Collier, *The Roosevelts*, 474.

10. Lorraine Copeland, e-mail to author, December 7, 2010; Helms quoted by confidential source; "Miles Copeland, RIP," *National Review*, February 11, 1991, 18; MC, *Game Player*, chap.

23. Miles Copeland III remembers the family receiving frequent calls from friends seeking clarification of the Game of Nations' extremely complicated rules (Miles Copeland III interview).

11. See, for example, Kim Philby to Bill Eveland, received July 13, 1978 (mailed June 27), 5, FBI FOIA, WCEP ("Come the English Revolution, I wouldn't mind a *dacha* in the Cotswolds," Philby told Eveland); 3, CIA FOIA, and 5, FBI FOIA, WCEP; Mary Barrett, "A Respectful Dissenter: CIA's Wilbur Crane Eveland," *Washington Report on Middle East Affairs* (March 1990): 28.

12. Efforts by Kim Roosevelt's fellow quiet American Edward Lansdale to interest the US public in the Cold War fate of the Far East, especially Vietnam, were much more successful. Kim seems to have lacked Lansdale's exceptional talent for manipulating the US media. See Wilford, *The Mighty Wurlitzer*, chap. 8.

Index

'Abdullah I (king of Jordan), 80, 208, 213, 214
'Abdullah, Radi, 267, 270
Abu Nuwar, 'Ali, 265–266, 267
Aburish, Abu Saïd, 267
Aburish, Saïd K., 267
Acheson, Dean, 32, 33, 87, 93, 114, 115, 135, 136, 137, 144, 288
Adie, Elizabeth Lorraine, 70–71, 94–95, 97, 101, 102, 107, 151, 152, 153, 154, 283, 296
Advertising industry, influence of, 148
Afghanistan, 48, 241, 251
African Game Trails (Theodore Roosevelt), 171
AJAX operation, 164–165, 166, 169–174, 175, 203, 224–225, 227, 250, 270, 279, 294, 295
Al Sa'ud, 'Abd al-'Aziz. *See* Ibn Saud
Alexandria Quartet (Durrell), 151
Algeria, 28, 288, 289
Allen, George V., 53, 198–199, 200, 234, 282
ALPHA project, 176–177, 181–182, 183, 184–188, 192, 193, 195, 196, 203–204, 205, 211, 213, 214, 218–219, 222, 225, 227, 231, 281
    See also GAMMA operation
Alsop, Joe, 15, 247
'Amer, 'Abdel Hakim, 189, 197
American Camp, 61
American Committee for Liberation (AMCOMLIB), 250, 255
American Council for Judaism (ACJ), 87–89, 90, 91, 92, 93, 117, 125, 177–179, 180, 182, 183, 184, 185, 186–187, 293
American Friends of the Middle East (AFME), 287
    accused of being a front organization, 235, 292
    and allegations of anti-Semitism, 125–126
    and ARAMCO, 119, 183, 236–237, 238
    criticisms of, among previous supporters, 234–238
    defeat of, 293
    duality of, 185, 239, 243–244

and efforts to improve the image of post-revolutionary Egypt, 139, 140
and the Eisenhower administration, 177, 179–180, 181, 243–244
formation of, 118–119, 125, 217
funding of, 118–119, 120, 121, 244, 298
Kim's level of involvement in, 121, 125, 129, 130, 185
location of field offices, 121, 240
major leadership changes in, 238–240
on military assistance for Saudi Arabia, 211
mission and purpose of, 123–124, 180–181, 242
"New Look" taken by, 207–208
and Project ALPHA, 181, 182, 183, 184–185, 187
rallying to support promotion of Kim, 144–145
reining in, 245, 257
relationship between the CIA and, 130–131
relocation of headquarters, 240
repercussions of the Six-Day War on, 293
shift in program of, 240–241
statement on Israel, 178
support for Nasser, 183, 184, 238, 239, 240, 241
supportive role during Operation GAMMA, 206–208, 210
use of, for tactical purposes by the CIA, 127–130
values and beliefs of, 122–123, 125, 130
wide-ranging program of, 121–122
Zionist counteroffensive against, 186–187
    See also American Council for Judaism (ACJ)
American Friends of Vietnam, 185
American Israel Public Affairs Committee (AIPAC), 187, 292
American University in Cairo, 22, 80
American University of Beirut (AUB), 21, 22, 35, 36, 59, 63, 64, 80, 85, 124, 131, 145, 243